Additional titles by Kevin J. Clancy:

The Marketing Revolution: A Radical Manifesto for Dominating the Marketplace
Kevin J. Clancy and Robert S. Shulman (HarperCollins, 1991)

Marketing Myths That Are Killing Business: A Cure for Death Wish Marketing
Kevin J. Clancy and Robert S. Shulman (McGraw Hill, 1993)

Simulated Test Marketing: Technology for Launching Successful New Products
Kevin J. Clancy, Robert S. Shulman, and Marianne Wolf (Lexington Books, 1995)

Uncover the Hidden Power of Television Programming ... And Get the Most from Your Advertising Budget
Kevin J. Clancy and David W. Lloyd (Sage Publishing, 1999)

Counterintuitive Marketing

ACHIEVE GREAT RESULTS
USING UNCOMMON SENSE

Kevin J. Clancy and Peter C. Krieg

Founders, Copernicus Marketing Consulting and Research

THE FREE PRESS
New York   London   Toronto   Sydney   Singapore

THE FREE PRESS
A Division of Simon & Schuster, Inc.
1230 Avenue of the Americas
New York, NY 10020

Designed by Stratford Publishing Services, Inc.

Manufactured in the United States of America

3   5   7   9   10   8   6   4   2

Library of Congress Cataloging-in-Publication Data
Clancy, Kevin J.
Counterintuitive marketing : achieve great results using uncommon sense /
Kevin J. Clancy and Peter C. Krieg.
p.   cm.
Includes bibliographical references and index.
1. Marketing. I. Krieg, Peter C., 1951– II. Title.
HF5415.C5277   2000
658.8—dc21   00-055109
ISBN 0-684-85555-0

For Kathleen and Deborah, our loving, forgiving, and accomplished wives, who have contributed mightily to our personal happiness and professional success.

Contents

Preface   ix

SECTION I

Revolutionaries, Pioneers, and Cowboys:
How Testosterone Drives American Business

1   Strategic Plan Your Way to Nowhere   3
2   Driving Growth: The Little Engine That Could   16
3   Testosterone Decision-making: The Manly Way to Screw Up   30
4   Warning: Commonsensical Research Can Be Dangerous
        to Your Career   45

SECTION II

Counterintuitive Thinking Behind
Great Marketing Strategies

5   Stunted Brands: Too Much Juice, Too Little Equity   61
6   Marketing Visionaries: Seeing What Is Not There   74
7   Guess Again: Intuitively Appealing Targets Are Rarely the
        Most Profitable   87
8   Positioning: . . . And That Would Mean What?   108
9   Sleeper and Subliminal Effects Don't Increase Sales   130
10 Direct Marketers Need More Than Just Better Lists   152
11 Three Scoops for a Quarter Is Two Too Many   172
12 Give All Your Customers a New Car   190

13 *Raise* Your Prices: Uncommon Approaches That Make Sense   205

14 E-commerce Rules Are the Same as T-commerce Rules   223

SECTION III
Implementing Counterintuitive
Marketing Programs

15 Prayers and Divine Intervention: No Marketing Miracles to Date   243

16 Testing in Cyberspace Is Better Than Testing in the World   258

17 Good Implementation May Be More Important Than a
Great Strategy   279

18 You Can't Measure Success Without a Score Card   294

19 Always Time to Do It Over; Never Time to Do It Right   313

Appendix   323

Acknowledgments   331

Index   335

About the Authors and Their Company   349

Preface

We are continually troubled by what we see as a decline in the performance of American companies and their marketing programs. We say this at a time when Asian economies are imploding, European economies face the uncertainty of a single currency, and the American economy—that is, American companies—has, by many measures, never been better.

We'll discuss the problems we see in American companies in more detail in Chapter 1; for now let's just say that a pervasive (and pernicious) pattern that is the cause of so much distress is what we label "over and over again marketing."

This is marketing characterized by flawed strategic decision-making based largely on management intuition followed by flawed implementation. The predictable, indeed inevitable, result: marketing programs that fail to achieve their objectives, advertising that shows little or no return on investment, direct response programs that are less and less effective, and new products and services that live about as long as chipmunks.

Over and over again marketing is the practice of running the same kinds of inadequate marketing programs year in and year out. The company develops the program . . . introduces it . . . watches it fail . . . develops a new program . . . launches it . . . watches it fail . . . develops a new program . . . launches it . . . watches it fail . . . over and over and over again.

Marketing does not have to be this way. It is possible—difficult, but possible—to do it right the first time and watch the company and its brands grow and thrive.

This book defines the problem. We set out the facts that explain the over and over again marketing phenomenon and give new insights into how counterintuitive thinking and research can be employed to develop and implement successful marketing programs.

Section I sketches some of the current problems with American business.

Too many companies since the late 1990s have shown little or no organic growth, masking their problems with mergers and acquisitions, downsizing, and reengineering. Marketing is the engine that drives growth, but it's thrown a rod. And a major problem we see is testosterone decision-making—usually male chief marketing officers, advertising directors, and brand managers choosing among alternatives quickly, decisively, and without real information. It's the manly way to screw up.

They tell us that their decisions are intuitively appealing. To us this means that it is the same decision everyone else would make. It's the commonsensical decision. Yet our research and experience suggest that decisions made on intuition alone rarely lead to successful outcomes. That, in fact, counterintuitive thinking grounded in rigorous analysis of unimpeachable data is the key to success in marketing.

Section II shows how technology can make a critical difference in targeting and positioning, advertising, new product development, and pricing—all the key elements that make up successful marketing. A chapter on vision points out the value of seeing not what is but what can be. A chapter on direct marketing suggests the alternative to renting one more list, and a chapter on customer satisfaction relates it to customer retention. The section concludes by communicating the electricity in electronic commerce.

Section III provides insights into how to implement a well-designed marketing plan. As anyone who has watched a great strategy crumble into little bits knows, implementation is as important as strategy and planning. In it we describe the difference between marketing plans based on convention and those based on science, the difference between how managers traditionally develop marketing programs and how they ought to be developing them using new technology. A chapter shows how the company can test the water without getting soaked. We note that you can't measure success without a scorecard, and it seems there is always time to do it over, never time to do it right—which is just the attitude this book hopes to stamp out.

Finally, at the very back you'll find a marketing questionnaire every CEO needs to keep the marketing department on track.

This is our fifth book. The previous books have been relatively technical (*Simulated Test Marketing: Technology for Launching Successful New Products* and *Uncover the Hidden Power of Television Programming . . . and Get the Most from Your Advertising Budget*) or came at the subject from very different directions (*The Marketing Revolution: A Radical Manifesto for Dominating the Marketplace* and *Marketing Myths That Are Killing Business: The Cure for Death Wish Marketing*).

This book necessarily builds on our previous books, but covers many ideas, experiences, and research that did not exist when we wrote them. Just as the world of business does not stand still, we have continued to grow and change. We are out of patience with marketing decisions based on intuition alone. We know how to do it right. And we want to help you do it right in your business.

SECTION I

Revolutionaries, Pioneers, and Cowboys: How Testosterone Drives American Business

1

Strategic Plan Your Way to Nowhere

Considered from one perspective, the 1990s were the best of times. A period of robust economic growth with thousands of new businesses creating hundreds of thousands—millions—of new jobs. A time of low interest rates, virtually nonexistent inflation, and a booming stock market and at the close of the decade rising corporate profits.

The phenomenal success of Internet companies has clouded our thinking about business. Tens of thousands of companies have been started. Billions of dollars invested. Market capitalizations greater than corporations with factories, tangible assets, and histories.

Considered from another perspective, the 1990s represented the worst of times. A time of corporate downsizing, Asian economies wracked by instability, workers on the brink of despair, and many great names suffering during a booming economy.

Coca-Cola's decline is a particularly sad story, although one that we believe might have been predicted based on observations we've made throughout this book. Coke announced in early February 2000 that it was cutting its work force by 20 percent—around 6,000 jobs, including nearly half of those at Coke headquarters, Atlanta—and shifting more power to executives abroad to try to boost sales around the world. The changes were the most dramatic in Coke's 114-year history.

We're New Englanders and are particularly unhappy to see local companies like Digital Equipment, Gillette, Lotus Development, Ocean Spray, Polaroid, Prime Computer, and Wang merged or hurting.

For many of America's largest corporations, the 1990s were a period of negative organic growth. Entire industries suffered—airlines, food services, property and casualty insurance, industrial and farm equipment, beverages, forest and paper products, railroads, health care, pipelines, building materials, glass, metals, petroleum refining, and entertainment. Even in 1998, when profits for the entire Fortune 500 were up over 23 percent, some industries were still showing profit declines: building materials and glass, forest and paper products, metals, publishing and printing, savings institutions, engineering and construction, electronics and electrical equipment, and motor vehicles.

Perhaps the most notable example of something amiss is the collapse of the Internet economy, which we began to see in the first quarter of 2000. Plagued by rising costs, stagnant sales, and modest to nonexistent profits, 70 percent (if not more) of the widely promoted Internet startups of the late 1990s are expected to be out of business within the next few years.

And how do businesses traditionally respond to sluggish growth and declining profits? By blaming the economy, downsizing the workforce, and making acquisitions.

The optimist will point to the growing companies; the pessimist will point to business failures.

Our point: *It doesn't make any difference.*

For the most part, both the companies that did not grow in the 1990s and many that did share a common failing: they do not know how to market their goods and services profitably. There is a yawning gap between promise and performance, one that we suspect will only widen if executives do not change.

No Matter What *Business Week* Says, P/E Ratios Are Too High

During the two years we have been working on this book, we have been predicting at every opportunity—professional presentations, meetings with clients, cocktail parties—that the stock market is on the verge of a significant correction or even collapse. We say this because we see little *real* growth. Businesses we have observed closely are, with a few exceptions, improving performance through mergers and acquisitions and through downsizing, not through successful marketing programs for established products and services or by introducing flourishing new products.

Then there are the Internet companies, which, despite poor or nonexistent profits, have watched their stock prices climb into the stratosphere: Amazon.com, AtHome, eBay, E*Trade Group, Excite, Infoseek, Lycos, and Yahoo!.

When price/earning ratios reached record heights, a *Business Week* magazine headline claimed, "They're not as loony as they look." Although the p/e ratio of Standard & Poor's 500-stock index stood at 26.7, almost 4 points higher than the historic 23 the index reached in the early 1990s, "Those p/e's didn't climb to Himalayan heights on mindless speculation," wrote the reporter, who said they are high for good reason: "Over the past three years, reported earnings have grown by more than 50 percent; long-term interest rates have fallen from 8 percent to less than 6 percent, even as gross domestic product expanded; and inflation has dropped from 3.3 percent to 1.4 percent."

Buttressing this argument, the magazine quoted a number of analysts. Edward M. Kerschner, PaineWebber Inc.'s chief investment strategist, argued that just because the long-term average price/earnings ratio was 15 (the actual number as we've calculated it is closer to 17), it is foolish to believe that p/e's must return to that average. "My average age is 23, but I'm never going to be 23 again," he said. "That 'reversion to the mean' thinking is a naive assumption. That was what investors did when they didn't have any better way to analyze the market, so you'd assume the average. With the computers and information we have today, you don't need to do that."

Despite the fact that Mr. Kerschner says "reversion" when he means "regression" (a statistical phenomenon studied for over a century) and that his comment on age is a non sequitur (it has nothing to do with his argument), he does raise an interesting question: Just because p/e ratios have held at around 17 to 1 for decades, does it mean they will be 17 to 1 forever?

In *Dow 36,000,* James Glassman and Kevin Hassett argue a resounding 'No!' They say that an appropriate p/e for stocks today is 100 to 1.

To Kerschner, Glassman, Hassett, and other stock market cheerleaders, we say "Whoa, hold on there." If there were underlying positive forces in the economy—population increases, productivity increases, significantly improved trade deficits, rising corporate profits, real growth projected well into the future—investors would be well advised to pay more for companies today than in the past. It would be rational to do so.

But when the future does not look significantly different from the recent past and the present, and when some economic factors are not what an investor would like to see, one has to wonder whether stock prices are simply irrational. Joseph Kennedy, Sr., is said to have remarked that when cab drivers and shoe shine boys are giving stock tips, it's time to get out of the market, which is how he avoided the crash of 1929.

We don't have to hearken back to 1929. We lived through the burgeoning stock and housing market of the 1970s and 1980s. People began buying because they expected significant appreciation. We watched the housing prices zoom at rates significantly higher than the stock market, only to collapse in 1988. It was recently reported that the Boston area's housing prices, for example, have just caught up to 1988's average.

Whatever the merits of our economic argument, it is hard to believe that a p/e ratio of 783, such as the one Yahoo! Inc. showed on June 15, 1999, or the Glassman-Hassett recommendation of 100 for the market generally, reflects anything more than the "greater fool theory." As you know, the theory holds that no matter what price an investor pays, someone with less sense will come along willing to pay an even higher price. Speculators use the greater fool theory to justify their gambling. A stock may be "fully valued" based on its balance sheet, but speculators believe new fools will drive the price up anyway. Unfortunately, while the world does have many fools, the supply is not infinite.

What happens to profitability when the company has no research and development and therefore no new products, no staff to introduce the new products even if there were some, and no more fat to cut?

MASKING WEAKNESS WITH MORE MERGERS

The intuitive answer to stagnant growth from a typical CEO-CFO duo, supported by their strategic planning department, is to acquire another company. We have seen phenomenal merger and acquisition activity in the past few years. In 1999, AOL merged with Time Warner and announced plans to acquire EMI Music; Exxon merged with Mobil; Ford bought Volvo; Newell bought Rubbermaid; America Online bought Netscape; Clorox bought First Brands; Federated Department Stores bought Fingerhut; DuPont bought Hoechst; Viacom acquired CBS.

Major corporations dropped off the 1998 Fortune 500 list, gobbled up by their rivals. They included Conrail (acquired by CSX and Norfolk Southern), Eckerd (acquired by J. C. Penney), McDonnell Douglas (acquired by Boeing), Morgan Stanley Group (acquired by Dean Witter Discover), Nynex (acquired by Bell Atlantic), Pacific Telesis Group (acquired by SBC Communications), Revco Drug Stores (acquired by CVS), and Vons (acquired by Safeway).

Companies that dropped off the 1999 list include Amoco (acquired by BP), BankAmerica Corp. (acquired by NationsBank), Beneficial (acquired by Household International), Chrysler (acquired by Daimler-Benz), Citicorp (acquired by Travelers Group), Digital Equipment (acquired by Compaq), Dresser Industries (acquired by Halburton), First Chicago NBD Corp.

(acquired by Banc One, now part of Bank One), General Re (acquired by Berkshire Hathaway), ITT (acquired by Starwood Hotels & Resorts), Long Island Lighting (acquired by MarketSpan), MCI Communications (acquired by WorldCom), Mercantile Stores (acquired by Dillard's), USF&G (acquired by St. Paul Cos.), Waste Management (acquired by USA Waste), and Western Atlas (acquired by Baker Hughes).

Were the last couple of years unusual for their merger activity? We looked at all of the largest 500 companies in the *Fortune* magazine listings between 1981 and 1999—those with annual sales greater than $1.3 billion or with assets greater than $3.6 billion. We had to look at both sales and asset measures because in 1981, *Fortune* was providing only asset information for companies like commercial banks, life insurance companies, and diversified financial companies such as securities firms.

Only 195 of those major corporations were still around in 1999; 305—or 61 percent—had been merged, bought, or taken over.

Clearly, when you add the sales and profits of another corporation to your own, you report the consolidated numbers and show growth. As we will see, however, the increases may be more deceptive than real. We suspect that hidden within many companies' quarterly financial reports is the shameful secret that they've been able to report growth *only* because they've acquired other companies. Strip away the mergers and the acquisitions, and you find a core business that has been limping along because it has ignored the basic purpose of a business: to find and keep customers. It has not put marketing at the center of its business universe.

Shrink Your Company to Greatness

The other intuitive answer to shrinking profits has been to tighten the corporate belt, which usually means reduce staff.

Two years ago we began working on a major strategy project for a corporate giant, one of America's ten largest companies. It involved 18 people from various groups throughout the corporation. Midway though the project we went to a lunch to celebrate a milestone. Half of the original group was gone.

The remaining managers said that every time there is a round of downsizing, the people who are left pick up the work. Said one of these managers, "They call it reengineering, but it's not; it's simply downsizing. There's no change in the processes."

Said another, "We're at our desks at 7:30 in the morning until 7:30 at night. We work on Saturdays, and we even put in a couple hours on Sunday. We hardly see our spouses and our kids don't recognize us." A number of managers believed that, in the next round of downsizing, they would be let go. Many did not seem to care; they were exhausted, saw no end in sight, and felt it might be better to start over at another company.

By the time we finished the study, not one of the original 18 still worked for the corporation. We presented the study to a new marketing vice president who had nothing to do with commissioning it, directing it, or following it. Moreover, this vice president was not a trained marketing professional. Like many people heading marketing departments, he was on rotation. He had been in finance for the last five years, in product development for four years before that. Like many executives, he was on his way to more general management positions. He was bright, aggressive, ambitious, and, as we discovered, a testosterone-driven decision-maker. We will talk about him and his ilk in detail a couple of chapters ahead.

This is a sad story. This once-great company had been declining in real growth because it lacked both vision and a strong captain at the helm. Though the view from the bridge seemed to be that shrinking would be followed by efficiencies that would produce the capital to grow the business, we've seen no indication that this is happening.

Gordon Bethune, president of Continental Airlines, talks about the effects of mindless efficiencies in his book *From Worst to First* (John Wiley & Sons, 1998). He found that when he landed at Continental in 1994, "We had cut costs so much that we simply had nothing to offer anymore. Our service was lousy, and nobody knew when a plane might land. We were unpredictable and unreliable, and when you're an airline, where does that leave you? It leaves you with a lot of empty planes. We had a lousy product, and nobody particularly wanted to buy it." Makes a lot of sense, but not everyone understands.

Indeed, consider the Sunbeam experience, which is a study for anyone interesting in marketing.

CHAINSAW AL TEARS THROUGH SUNBEAM

In October 1997, Albert J. ("Chainsaw Al") Dunlap, CEO of Sunbeam Corp., announced that he was putting the company up for sale: "Having successfully completed the turnaround of Sunbeam and being well on our way to dramatically growing the business, we feel that the timing is right."

Dunlap had gone through Sunbeam like a white tornado. Two days after arriving in July 1996, he was on a conference call to stock analysts: "I just bought $3 million worth of stock, and I love every dollar like a brother. I can tell you, had I been a shareholder and had I read all of the [previous management's] nonsense where there was an excuse for everything . . . I don't believe in excuses. I saw so many excuses, it's an amazement to me anything got done."

Within weeks Dunlap had announced that he would cut 6,000 jobs, half of Sunbeam's workforce; drop 87 percent of its product line, including clocks, thermometers, scales, furniture, and electric blankets; and cut its manufacturing and other facilities from 53 to 14. In 1996, Sunbeam took a $338 million charge to pay for the one-time costs associated with Dunlap's plan, including nearly $100 million of Sunbeam inventory.

Dunlap is the executive who spent 18 months at Scott Paper, fired 11,000 employees (including 70 percent of Scott's upper management), and contributed mightily to the decline of a once great brand name; he then sold the company to Kimberly-Clark, walking away with $100 million for himself. He wrote a book with Bob Andelman to explain his principles: *Mean Business: How I Save Bad Companies and Make Good Companies Great* (Times Business, 1996).

He presents himself as the shareholder's champion. Joseph Nocera wrote in *Fortune,* "A major theme of *Mean Business* is that in the corporate scheme of things, the shareholder is supreme—that creating shareholder value should be the only thing that matters to a shareholder. Much of his contempt for other CEOs stems from his belief that they are not as interested in creating shareholder wealth as he is."

Clearly, Dunlap has created wealth for some shareholders. Just days after Sunbeam announced that he was coming on board, the stock, which had been trading around $13 per share, rose 41 percent. By the end of 1997, the stock was over $50 a share. It did not hurt Sunbeam's stock that Dunlap announced record 1997 results: sales up 22 percent and earnings per share of $1.41—an impressive reversal from the 1996 per share loss of $2.37.

Potential Sunbeam suitors in 1997, however, were not impressed enough to buy the company. At the end of the year, no one was interested, so Dunlap himself went shopping. He overpaid for Coleman, the outdoor equipment manufacturer, which was losing money, buying it for $2.2 billion, or two times sales. He bought Signature Brands (Mr. Coffee) and First Alert (smoke detectors) for $425 million. Neither seller, *Forbes* points out, was all that interested in Sunbeam stock. Ronald Perelman took less than half Coleman's price in stock, and Thomas Lee at First Alert took cash. The acquisitions did make Sunbeam a $2.6 billion (sales) company, fulfilling Dunlap's 1997 promise to make Sunbeam a $2 billion company by 1999.

THE PROBLEMS WITH SUNBEAM'S REVENUE FIGURES

However, all was not well. According to Sunbeam's 10K, the company sold $60 million in accounts receivable to raise cash in December 1997. Sunbeam also instituted an "early buy" program for gas grills in the fourth quarter. Retailers such as Kmart and Wal-Mart could buy their summer's grills in November and December of 1997 but not pay for them until June 1998. Also, because retailers do not have a lot of space for off-season items like grills, Sunbeam started a "bill and hold" program that allowed customers to use its warehouses to store the goods they had bought but not necessarily paid for.

These two programs accounted for most of Sunbeam's 1997 revenue gains. They, in fact, did nothing for the company except shift sales from 1998 to 1997. Sunbeam reported a first quarter 1998 loss before taxes of $43.4 million, and when the word got out, the stock dropped 58 percent.

The *New York Times* reported that Dunlap met with analysts to explain the bad news. "I take full responsibility," said Dunlap, before making clear that it was everyone's fault but his. He blamed the weather. He blamed a retail chain for messing up grills that had to be recalled. Because he was busy working on the acquisitions, he "left a marketing guy in charge of operations. Mistake."

He denied that selling gas grills in November and December was an effort to "artificially pump up" 1997's profits. It was, he said, "a well-intentioned market-driven strategy that simply didn't work." It is not clear what that strategy might have been, other than an effort to make the company's finances look good to a not-terribly-inquisitive buyer.

Dunlap promised the analysts that he would be making big savings at Coleman, First Alert, and Signature Brands through plant closings and staff reductions—5,100 more workers to fire. That would make those divisions smaller, but would it make them grow? Sure it would.

In announcing first-quarter results, the company said, "Sunbeam expects the integration of its three recent acquisitions and planned new products to generate at least $265 million in incremental annual revenues. These new revenues are expected to come from leveraging complementary international distribution strengths, domestic sales synergies, and accelerated new product development." We love these euphemisms that CEOs come up with when they're driving their companies into the dumpster.

We'll never know whether Dunlap could have actually grown Sunbeam because the board of directors, mostly Dunlap's friends, fired him in mid-June 1998. The new chief executive, Jerry Levin, warned that Sunbeam's sales would suffer for the rest of the year as retailers worked off high inventories of Sunbeam products. Instead of shrinking Sunbeam to greatness, he had shrunk it to insignificance.

RUNNING THE BUSINESS AS IF PLANNING TO SELL

What Chainsaw Al did to Sunbeam (and to Scott Paper) is a notorious example of a situation that is not uncommon. As an executive whom business press reporters loved to hate, Dunlap received considerable coverage of his pronouncements and activities. He is not alone, however, in boosting sales through early bookings, low prices, and promotions. Many executives seem to be running their businesses like homeowners repairing the front steps and slapping a new coat of paint on a house they plan to sell.

They're selling in two ways. They're selling to the public, pushing up the stock price so that they can cash out when they exercise their options. And they're selling out to other companies that are happy to take them over, sometimes (if the seller is a private company) on an earn-out basis in which the buying company takes the selling company's stock and pays shareholders a multiple of earnings. But the buyer does not fork over the full price at the closing. Rather, the buyer puts up, say, 25 percent at the closing, then 25 percent at the end of the next three years. By the end of four years, the sellers have all their money. Meanwhile, the company must show consistent growth, say, 15 percent a year, to achieve the target sale price.

When owners sell on an earn-out basis, many do everything in their power to control earnings over the four-year period. The business may need a new information technology system or 170 new salespeople or three new product launches in the fourth year, but the former owners do not make the investment. They spend as little as possible on marketing, R&D, and human resources. They don't take a penny of profit to spend on a frill like the firm's future health. They take their money and run.

Even if the executives are not involved in a buy-out, those who want to cash out do everything they can to make the business show a profit. They put in a hiring freeze. They offer early retirement. They fire 10 percent of the employees across the board. They cut back advertising, research and development, MIS. They squeeze as much profit as they possibly can out of the business so that the P&L and balance sheet look terrific—and hope for the best. After all, how many stockholders, who can dump their holdings tomorrow, want to see management reduce earnings by investing in R&D, in new products, or increased advertising and promotion? The owners argue that this is not greed; it is common sense guiding self-interest.

These executives have, in short, no vision for the business (other than "For

Sale"). With such a mind-set, the customers are a distraction, with their endless whining for service and repairs, new products and features, and prompt delivery.

It seems that everywhere we go these days, business executives talk about cutbacks. In May 1998 we attended the American Marketing Association's Edison Awards Ceremony in New York City, at which major corporations—Colgate-Palmolive, Rubbermaid, Quaker State, and Dannon International, among 35 others—were being heralded as models for new product performance. We were struck by the number of speakers who talked about the cutbacks taking place in their companies and the growing difficulty to innovate and market new products.

We wonder, doesn't anybody see the problems ahead? Aren't the CEOs, CFOs, and strategic planning departments looking five years out? Aren't they working on anything but mergers, acquisitions, and downsizing problems? Where *is* the strategic planning department? What are they doing to build the business?

Who Knows What Lurks in Strategic Planning?

Only the Shadow knows. Consider this disturbing experience. We recently developed a marketing strategy for a multinational corporation, a plan that involves a $3 billion investment in the United States and another $3 billion investment in Asia. These expenditures will have an impact on the company for the next ten years. Because of the project's size, most meetings involved at least 10 people, and some had 20 or more. They included, of course, senior marketing executives, representatives from corporate headquarters, from the American division, from the Asian unit, from the firm's advertising agencies, and from the corporation's marketing group. But we never met—let alone worked with—a representative from this corporation's strategic planning department.

(While this has been generally true in our consulting assignments, perhaps it may be changing. We recently worked with three vice presidents of strategic planning on consulting engagements, but these are rare exceptions in two long careers.)

The corporation has a strategic planning department. The strategic planning division occupies a floor in a building separate from marketing. We don't know how big it is because we've only heard about it; we've never talked to the people or walked through their offices.

We found it odd that we were helping the corporation plan multibillion dollar investments and yet we never discussed the issues with the firm's strategic planners. They were not engaged. Periodically someone from the marketing department, which was leading the project, would say with a grin on his face at a meeting, "Strategic planning has a question."

These questions came out of the blue and were presented without a context. For example, "Strategic planning wants to know the price sensitivity in the marketplace; that is, what would happen if we decreased prices?" Or "When we introduce the new line extension, how much cannibalization will occur?"

These are good questions, but they have to be asked in a context of strategic marketing issues, such as "What target group are you talking about?" If the company is an on-line bookseller, it makes all the difference in the world whether strategic planning wants to know about the price sensitivity of upscale book buyers primarily concerned with convenience and service or the sensitivity of price-conscious consumers shopping for the best deal on the Web.

We answered the strategic planning department's questions, but it was clear even to an outsider that the marketing people and the strategic planners were not cooperating. They were not working together toward a common goal, and this is not uncommon. The strategic planners did not know anything (or seem to care much) about marketing, and the marketing people found the strategic planners a diversion.

STRATEGIC PLANNING ISSUES ARE ESSENTIALLY MARKETING PROBLEMS

If strategic planners determine that acquisitions, mergers, and downsizing, with all their sound and fury, can somehow lead to greater growth, that is fine. But the strategic planning department is often disassociated from reality. They're not involved in actually growing the company—they are a staff, not a line function—and even when they *are* involved, they don't really know what will happen as a result of the steps they recommend. They base decisions on judgment and intuition, which are often wrong.

What to do about the strategic planning situation is easy to state, not so easy to execute (it is a little like taking your own advice). The first issue is how to integrate strategic planning with marketing, since marketing is the most reliable way to grow a business. The problem is that, while the strategic planning department develops the plan to guide the corporation, marketing is often not integrated into strategic planning. (Or as we just saw, marketing develops its plans without consulting strategic planning.) Strategic planners chart the course, but in an appalling number of companies, the strategic planners do not even know the marketing people.

Consider a typical strategic question: A relatively small division within a corporation provides parts to another division that, in turn, provides parts to the end customer. What should this division's function be in the year 2005? Continue to provide parts internally? Provide parts to external customers as well? Should it continue to exist, or should its function be dispersed through the company? Should the company buy the parts from an outside supplier? Should the company invest in the division or try to sell it?

Another example: An international brewer is thinking about introducing its beer into the U.S. market. Expanding globally is part of its strategic vision. Should it make the investment?

More examples: The company has not seen any change in its p/e ratio in seven years, and its p/e ratio is low relative to competitors'. Earnings and profitability have been stalled. The company has cut costs and people, but downsizing has produced only a weaker and demoralized organization. What should it do?

Consider this problem: The company's flagship brand is declining, and to goad sales, management has cut prices and run trade and consumer promotions. Nothing good is happening. What should they do next?

And more: The company has not introduced a successful new product in five years. Now it has developed what it believes is a breakthrough concept, and the CEO wants to know whether to build the plant to produce the product. The plant will cost a minimum of $200 million.

These are the kinds of questions strategic planners tussle with every day. Yet they are, in fact, largely marketing questions. What is the market for the division's parts? How will the market change by 2005? (The only reasonable answer: It needs to be studied.) What do its customers need? How are those customers' needs changing? What—if anything—can the division do to influence those changing needs?

The brewer's questions include: How does marketing beer in the U.S. compare to marketing beer at home? What is the best target market for this new import? What positioning and advertising strategy will have the greatest impact on that target? What is the right pricing and distribution strategy? What will all this cost, and what return can the brewer reasonably expect? Marketing questions, all.

Indeed, we believe *most strategic planning issues are fundamentally marketing decisions*. Which means that marketing is not just important; it is central to the business solar system. Theodore Levitt in his classic *The Marketing Imagination* wrote, "The purpose of a business is to create and keep a customer." We argue that the purpose of marketing and the purpose of a business are fundamentally the same, since the purpose of marketing is to find and keep customers for the business.

Only through effective marketing does the core business grow. To thrive, a company has to find new customers, has to continue selling to existing customers, and has to sell more products or services to both new and existing customers. That's marketing's job. Yet, throughout the '90s, that appeared to be a counterintuitive notion.

But if marketing is the engine that drives business growth, at too many companies it has thrown a rod.

Driving Growth:
The Little Engine That Could

Marketing is the *only* way to grow a business. If we buy another company—for the sake of illustration, let's call it Coleman and also say it is a well-known marketer of camping gear—and we add the acquisition's sales and profits to our total, have we actually grown?

Sometimes. Sometimes the new corporation is able to build on the complementary strengths of the two partners, meet customer needs more effectively than either could alone, reduce costs by eliminating duplicate efforts, and actually grow more than either could alone.

But sometimes the acquired company, though large, is not growing. Sometimes the new partners have no complementary strengths and do not meet customer needs as well as they did alone. Sometimes the sales of one or both partners continue to decline. This would be the case if Coleman's former CEO took the name down-market with a proliferation of backpacks, coolers, lanterns, and tents it sold through mass-market retailers, eroding margins.

Assume further that Uncle Dan's, a Chicago-area camping retailer, represents Coleman dealers generally, and that Michael Fowler, Uncle Dan's vice president of operations, says, "They seem to have gone completely for the white-trash market," adding that Coleman's quality has slipped so badly that Uncle Dan's now limits its purchases to stoves, lanterns, and cheap accessories. Say that Coleman has problems overseas, that to reduce inventory it did not ship anything new to Japan during the second quarter of 1997, usually its strongest period. (By the way, *Business Week* did say these things in

March 1998.) This is the company that Chainsaw Al bought, but these are not issues that layoffs and factory closings will solve.

Firing workers and closing plants may cut overhead but will not grow the company. Consider, as an example, Procter & Gamble. In 1993, to compete with cheaper, private-label competitors, P&G cut 13,000 jobs (12 percent of the workforce), closed 30 factories, and took a $1.5 billion charge against earnings to pay for the restructuring. That clearly was not the answer to its problems because in July 1999, P&G announced that it was cutting 15,000 more jobs (13 percent of the workforce), closing 10 factories, and taking a $1.9 billion charge against earnings. More cutbacks and reorganization have followed, but the company is still struggling.

Take, as another illustration, the once mighty Kellogg Corp. of Battle Creek, Michigan. At the end of 1998, Kellogg was still thrashing about after taking four major "one-time" write-offs in as many years. It wasn't enough because in August 1999, Kellogg announced that it was closing part of its Battle Creek cereal plant, eliminating 550 jobs, and saving $35 million to $45 million a year. Slashing overhead and becoming more efficient may be necessary but does not attract new customers, nor by itself does it retain existing customers. Without effective marketing—attracting and retaining customers—a company will not grow.

THE PURPOSE OF A BUSINESS IS TO CREATE CUSTOMERS

That is not, we know, an original thought. Peter Drucker has written, "Because its purpose is to find and keep customers, the business enterprise has two—and only two—basic functions: marketing and innovation. Marketing and innovation produce results; all the rest are 'costs.'"

The purpose of a business is to create customers, not to reward stockholders, not to make a quarterly dividend. Dividends happen when the business creates and serves customers at a profit. No customers, no revenue. No revenue, no positive number at the bottom of the profit and loss statement, no dividends, and eventually no company.

The purpose of a business is not to do something you like to do nor to be your own boss, although those may be fringe benefits. Indeed, the more you love what you're doing, the more likely you are to satisfy customers. Without customers and the money they give you, there is nothing to pay the rent, the help, or yourself.

How do you find and keep customers? Only through marketing and innovation. Do not confuse marketing with sales. In Ted Levitt's words, "The difference between selling and marketing is that selling is getting rid of what you have, while marketing is having what people want." Marketing is not advertising, and it's certainly not aggressive price discounting. "Marketing," says Procter & Gamble's corporate lore, "is the discipline concerned with solving people's problems with products and services for a profit." Marketing involves sales, advertising, and pricing. But it also involves product development, buyer and trade promotion, channel management, public relations, and much more.

To thrive, a firm has to produce and deliver goods and services that people value at prices that are appealing relative to the products and services other businesses offer. This is the responsibility of those charged with marketing. No company today operates in an information vacuum. Customers have choices, so what you offer must be more attractive (in design, safety, features, taste, convenience, price, access, utility, functionality, fashion, packaging, service, reliability, whatever) than what someone else offers.

Levitt points out that no enterprise, no matter how small, can manage "by mere instinct or accident. It has to clarify its purposes, strategies, and plans, and the larger the enterprise, the greater the necessity that these be clearly written down, clearly communicated, and frequently reviewed by the senior members of the enterprise." Marketing, as we have said in the past and will be saying again and again, is the center of the business universe because it is businesses' link to the customer.

Yet many CEOs see their marketing departments as "ill-focused and overindulged," according to a Coopers & Lybrand survey of 100 companies (cited in Philip Kotler's *Kotler On Marketing,* the source for this paragraph). The McKinsey Company released a report saying that many CEOs saw their marketing departments as "unimaginative, generating few new ideas, no longer delivering." And Booz, Allen & Hamilton has issued a warning that CEOs thought "brand managers were failing to get to grips with commercial realities."

Procter & Gamble spent more than ten years integrating acquisitions and moving into emerging markets and lost its sales lead in toothpaste (Crest), diapers (Pampers, Luvs), and soap (Ivory). Durk Jager, who lasted 17 months as CEO, told a *Fortune* reporter, "The core business is innovation. If we innovate well, we will ultimately win. If we innovate poorly, we won't win. To innovate, you have to go away from the norm. You have to be rebellious or nonconventional. You have to do things differently." One of his favorite expressions is "If it ain't broke, break it."

While we agree with Jager that P&G, like most companies, needs to accelerate on the innovation curve, we wish that he had also said that P&G was rededicating itself to improving its marketing of new and established products. Procter & Gamble is no longer the symbol of marketing brainpower and muscle it once was. Worse, there are hints that it seems to be moving away from the fact-based, research-grounded marketing that we love.

IF MARKETING IS AT BUSINESS'S CENTER, BRANDS ARE AT MARKETING'S CORE

We can sympathize with the CEOs because we find at many companies that marketing is not at the center of the business, nor is it being done very well from the fringe. Many chief executives, given their backgrounds and interests, put finance at the center of the business. Some entrepreneurs put manufacturing or operations at the center. A few companies even put strategic planning or information technology at the center.

These are all important functions, but it is marketing that finds, attracts, and keeps customers. Only through innovation and marketing can a business grow. Customers do not care whether you hit your quarterly sales forecasts, whether the factory is efficient, or whether the employees have a generous dental plan. Customers—the selfish brutes—care only about *their* wants, *their* needs, *their* problems.

When we say marketing is the way to grow a business, we do not mean the stuff that many companies call "marketing" or "brand building" or "increasing brand equity." We find that many executives today mouth the words while simultaneously killing the brands under their care. Brand homicide is as common as brand creation. In many companies MBA stands for "Murderer of Brand Assets."

Marketing managers are cutting prices to make this quarter's numbers (turning brands into commodities), trimming quality to reduce costs, or making strategic marketing decisions based on hope, intuition, dotty thinking (such as brand juice), and dotty research (such as focus groups). As a result, few marketing programs work as well as they could, or should. Marketing should be the engine that drives growth, but at too many companies it has thrown a rod.

It should be obvious to even the most casual reader of the business press that, despite hope and hype, most marketing programs fail. Throughout this book we'll provide many examples of a bias favoring large companies. After all, if large companies with their clever strategists, large research departments, and mega-million-dollar budgets don't make smart marketing decisions, why should we expect smaller companies to? Let us focus for a minute on two recent mistakes made by marketing giants McDonald's and Burger King.

The McDonald's Arch Deluxe sandwich was promoted as "The hamburger with the grown-up taste." After market tests in Chicago and Baton Rouge, McDonald's spent $75 million to roll out the Arch Deluxe nationally. Rather than persuade adults they should try the sandwich, the advertising showed children who didn't like it. McDonald's put a brave face on the fiasco as the Arch Deluxe vanished into the sunset.

French fries are one of the main reasons why hungry people choose one fast food restaurant over another, and historically Burger King's fries have suffered in comparison to McDonald's. To solve this weakness Burger King spent many years and many millions of dollars to develop a new and improved fry.

In the fall of 1997 they thought they had one. Jim Watkins, senior vice president of marketing at Burger King, North America, stated, "We know, based upon nationwide independent consumer taste tests conducted in over 18 cities, that consumers prefer the taste of the new hotter, crispier Burger King French fry. In fact, by a landslide margin, 57 percent to 35 percent, they love this new fry." (The other 8 percent had no preference.) In a rare marketing coup, a company was able to leapfrog a competitor and claim superiority for a key motivating characteristic.

To make sure the word got out, Burger King spent $70 million on advertising and marketing efforts, including "Free FryDay" on Friday, January 2, 1998, when everyone visiting a Burger King in the U.S. received a small order of the new fries free—the largest one-day sampling event in the history of fast food. Free FryDay set record levels for trial in Burger Kings around the country. People lined up ten deep to see if the new product really had "The taste that beat McDonald's fries."

Unfortunately, the new fry was not much better than Burger King's old fry and certainly no better than the McDonald's fry. McDonald's knew this coming out of the starting gate. Ronald McD's product testing found results opposite to Burger King's: people still preferred McDonald's fries three to two. The Burger King fry, as a result, was an embarrassing product and a marketing and financial disaster. (And may have given CEOs everywhere one more reason to distrust their research departments.)

How about beverages to go with your burger and fries? Haven't we been told for years that Coca-Cola represents a school for training the marketing geniuses of tomorrow? But how long has it been since Coca-Cola had a major marketing success? Yes, Coke is successful because it's a colossal, powerful company that can afford to buy distribution, which is, as we'll discuss later, an increasingly important driver of sales in the soft drink category. Yet when was the last time Coke launched a very successful new product or blockbuster ad campaign? Coke's latest entry, Surge, is stumbling along with about a 1 percent share of the category, enough to be annoying to competitors but hardly a resounding success. And its advertising hasn't rung the bell on the cash registers since the kids on the hilltop were singing "I'd like to give the world a Coke" while many of our readers were still in high school.

BEST PRACTICE SCORES FOR AMERICAN COMPANIES

For the last ten years or so, we have been gathering information on the best practices in marketing to help companies understand what goes into exceptional marketing decisions. What characterizes the best marketing climate analysis? The best targeting decision? The best distribution/channel management?

Working with Gary Morris, now of Sibson & Company, we broke all marketing decision areas into 22 specific marketing management functions, everything from objectives and strategies to e-commerce implementation. We further split these 22 marketing management functions into 80 benchmark areas. For example, under new product development, we included new product planning and development process, new product idea generation and screening, new product development and evaluation, and new product testing and commercialization.

In total, we dissected approximately 700 marketing activities, analyses, and decision processes, and developed a method to score each. For example, under market targets: How many potential targets did the company evaluate using criteria related to profitability? One? 2 to 5? 6 to 10? 11 to 20? 30 or more? Best practice companies evaluate 30 or more potential targets.

Another example: How different is the company's target from the competitor's? Don't know/haven't researched? Very similar to competitor's? More similar than different? More different than similar? Very different in attitude, behavior, demographics? It does not take a Ph.D. in marketing to realize that it is better to have a target very different from the competition's.

Answers to these 700 questions show us where a company's marketing is relatively strong and where it is relatively weak. On a scale of 0 to 100 percent, the average marketing "Best Practices Score" for North American companies is 49. This is like buying a new car with a promised top speed of 120 mph, only to discover that you can't break 60 on the highway.

While we have found companies that are strong in one or more of the 22 marketing management functions, we have yet to analyze a company with an overall grade better than a "B" (80 on our scale). With such poor marketing practices common in even forward-looking companies (management has to

Table 2-1   Classification of Marketing Management Functions

1. Marketing objectives and strategies
2. Marketing climate analysis
3. Segmentation and targeting
4. Differentiation and positioning
5. Pricing
6. Product/service management
7. Advertising
8. Public relations
9. Promotions management
10. Direct-response marketing
11. Event/relational marketing management
12. Customer service excellence
13. Integrated marketing communications
14. Distribution/channel management
15. Trade customer marketing
16. New product development
17. Marketing intelligence systems
18. Brand equity
19. Sales management
20. E-commerce strategy and implementation
21. Marketing performance
22. Marketing organization

be somewhat forward-looking to submit to a best practices analysis in the first place), is it any surprise that we see so many disappointing marketing programs?

WHAT THE MARKETING PERFORMANCE BELL CURVE™ SHOWS

Most marketing programs do not work, and by "work," of course, we mean not how much the company sells but how much it sells at a profit. The evidence shows that—when management can even measure the return—most marketing programs do not provide an acceptable return on investment. Some executives believe that even when marketing programs do not generate a clear ROI, they produce a significant positive effect on sales. But even that is debatable. Most marketing programs do not achieve their sales goals. Most marketing programs do not obtain margins great enough to justify their existence.

We have been collecting data on the performance of marketing programs for consumer *and* business-to-business products *and* services for over a decade. The results are surprising. Like many things—intelligence quotients, people's

Figure 2-1   The Marketing Performance Bell Curve™

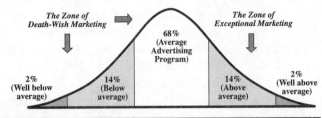

Marketing Performance	Embarrassing	Troubling	Disappointing	Pleasing	Amazing
Market Share Growth	Precipitous Decline	Significant Decline	Modest Decline	Significant Increase	Dramatic Increase
Successful Turnarounds	0%	3%	5%	15%	25%
New Product Success Rate	0%	5%	10%	25%	40%
Advertising Penetration per 1,000 GRPs	0%	3%	8%	13%	20%
Advertising ROI	Negative	0%	1–4%	5–10%	20%
Consumer and Trade Promotions	Disaster	Very Unprofitable	Marginally Unprofitable	Profitable	Very Profitable
Cutomer Satisfaction	0–59%	60–69%	70–79%	80–89%	90–95%
Customer Retention/Loyalty	0–44%	45–59%	60–74%	75–89%	90–94%
Cutomer Aquisition Programs	Disturbing Losses	Significant Losses	Marginal Losses	Break Even	Profitable
Brand Equity	Dramatic Decline	Significant Decline	Modest Decline	Stable to Improving	Dramatic Improvement

heights, SAT scores—marketing program performance can be illustrated on a curve such as the Marketing Performance Bell Curve™ in Figure 2-1.

Statisticians calculate a statistic called the standard deviation, which captures a figure plus or minus a certain amount. One deviation around the average represents axiomatically plus or minus 34 percent, or 68 percent of all the cases. Two standard deviations capture 95 percent of the cases. And plus or minus three standard deviations represent 99 percent of the cases. Both ends of the Bell Curve™, "Well below average" on the left and "Well above average" on the right, represent relatively few marketing programs. The majority (68 percent), of course, are in the middle; they are the average.

Below the Bell Curve™ we show different indicators of marketing performance. The first question we asked is "How is the average product or service doing?" To answer the question we turned to data collected by Nielsen and IRI for packaged goods and other sources for other product categories. What we've learned is that the average brand or product is losing about a third of a share point per year. It's moving ever so slowly, but inexorably, toward oblivion. That's no indication of great success.

Every three to four years top management looks at figures like this and, shocked at the brand's decline, calls the chief marketing officer into his office and bellows, "We've got to turn this brand around! Bring the advertising agency in here! We need a new campaign! How about R&D? Anything coming out of R&D? What about packaging? What about promotion?" Since CEOs under these circumstances tend to get what they want, the marketing and advertising people slap together a "turnaround" campaign. Three to six months from start to finish is about the norm.

Usually the company does not test the campaign's advertising using quantitative research methods—sometimes the campaign is not even shown to focus groups—and rarely does the company do any simulated test marketing (which we'll talk about in Chapter 16) to assess the marketing program's performance *before* introducing it into the world. The company launches the campaign, which, in 95 cases out of 100, fails to reverse the share decline. The brand continues to slip away.

Some people say that all the new product introductions cause share declines for established products and services. This, in fact, is true. New products do erode the performance of established products. But as we noted earlier, this is not to say that a great many new products or services are succeeding. Most new products fail, and they hurt the marketer's reputation as they crash and burn. And this failure rate is not restricted to consumer products. We've seen a comparable failure rate for new consumer services (admittedly most of our data is on financial services) and for business-to-business products and services.

Take, as a recent example, Procter & Gamble's February 2000 decision to abruptly suspend advertising for the new Noxzema skin care line, which they had been working on for years. Launched in the summer of '99, with a first-year budget of $55 million, the line's performance was underwhelming. Its collapse can't help but tarnish P&G's rep as a savvy marketer and at the same time confirm our view of how difficult new product marketing has become.

Robert McMath's New Products Showcase & Learning Center in Ithaca, New York, is filled with new product blunders, like Singles, a line of meals Gerber tried to market to seniors. Or PepsiCo's Crystal Pepsi and Miller Brewing's Clear Beer, both which might have been advertised as "All of the taste with none of the color." Tea Whiz, Nestea's yellowish carbonated beverage, apparently had the opposite problem.

Then there's the Apple Newton, which was supposed to inaugurate the "personal digital assistant" market, Kodak's PhotoCD, which was supposed to inaugurate the digital photographic market, and WebTV, a $249 box that transformed a television set into a Web-surfing e-mail machine. After Sony and Philips Electronics spent $50 million to introduce the new machine, they had sold only about 50,000 of them, since apparently couch potatoes do not seem that interested in an interactive medium.

These are not isolated examples. Most new products fail. According to Marketing Intelligence Ltd., in 1998 some 25,181 new consumer products made their way onto store shelves—90 percent of them to fail within three years. One reason, perhaps, is that a scant 5.9 percent of 1998's new products were truly innovative. And while no one tracks new business-to-business products and consumer service the same way, in our experience the record is much the same.

As the Bell Curve™ shows, the average new product and service success rate is 10 percent. Again, this is no indication of great market success. And this may be generous. Our experience with packaged goods, the arena with some of the biggest brains in marketing, suggests a success rate under 5 percent in the late '90s.

And what about advertising? Are most campaigns successful? We do know that ad programs—for reasons we'll discuss in depth later on—fail to penetrate buyer consciousness. It's far more likely that people remember nothing about a campaign. For example, after a media buy of $15 million (1,000 GRPs) in prime-time television, proven recall of the advertising averages under 10 percent. This is terrible.

What about ROI? On average, the return on investment of advertising is 1 to 4 percent. By our measures, this suggests that most companies would be better off taking their ad dollars and putting them into certificates of deposit.

This is not to suggest that more advertising programs could not be very profitable. The problem is not advertising per se, but rather the problematic way companies develop most advertising campaigns today.

Some people argue that if you want to see real advertising efficiencies, you need to look at direct-response programs through the mail, on the phone, and on the Net. Yet the average direct-response effort draws an 0.8 to 1.2 percent return and is declining. This represents a drop from a 1.5 percent average in the recent past and from approximately 3 percent 20 years ago. Decelerating performance is even faster on the Web. Surfers were clicking on Web ads 2.5 percent of the time in early 1997, 1 percent in early 1998, and less than 0.3 percent of the time today.

If advertising is so dismal, perhaps the answer is promotion: coupons, contests, events, rebates, and other short-term efforts. Today only one out of three marketing dollars goes into advertising; the rest goes to promotion. Twenty-five years ago the figures were reversed. Promotion has done so well because many marketers have been unable to demonstrate a convincing connection between advertising and sales, while promotion is clearly tied to sales. (That is slowly changing as research technology improves. Companies are now recording both the television commercials to which consumers are exposed *and* the products they buy at supermarkets and drugstores to discover a relationship between exposure and purchase.)

But how effective is promotion? Magrid M. Abraham, president of product development and marketing at Information Resources, Inc., and Leonard M. Lodish, professor of marketing at the Wharton School, found that only 16 percent of the 65 trade promotion events they studied were profitable, based on incremental sales of brands distributed through retailer warehouses. They found, in fact, that in many promotions it cost more than a dollar to obtain a dollar in incremental sales.

Our own experience is that consumer trade promotion programs are marginally unprofitable. Today companies spend more money on promotion than they spend on advertising, and yet careful analyses of promotion performance suggest that, more often than not, the campaigns cost more than they return. We occasionally find executives who proudly report the total sales from a promotion, but they have not stripped out the sales they would have obtained without the promotion. Such simple answers also fail to take into account the deleterious effects of promotion on brand equity, a topic we'll take up later. Promotion is not the answer to marketing success.

On average, customer satisfaction, based on worldwide studies, is in the disappointing 70 to 79 percent range. Customer retention is in the 65 to 79 percent range. We find these numbers almost comical in light of all the talk about delighting customers. After all, "100 percent customer satisfaction" and "100 percent customer retention" have been the banners management consultants have carried around the planet for the past decade.

As we have discussed in earlier books—and the situation has not changed—new customer acquisition programs are exciting for marketing people. These are programs in which you try to find new prospects, new buyers, and new customers, and many companies spend more on such efforts than on current customers. Yet, on average, the programs show losses.

A final indicator of marketing performance is brand equity. Simply put, brand equity is a measure of the "good will" that a product or a service enjoys, often reflected in buyer perceptions of product distinction and superiority. Brand equity numbers are declining for brands in a broad range of categories. One need not look any further than American automobile companies, airline companies, beverage companies, personal computer makers, and packaged goods companies for brands with equity scores that have been declining over time. Some show brand equity declines despite sales gains;

this occurs because of gains in distribution or enhanced marketing spending, the benefits of economies of scale, which often impact sales but not equity. Consider, for example, Coca-Cola. Its marketing muscle has helped to move the sales needle at the very same time its brand equity is in decline.

We have shown the Marketing Performance Bell Curve™ to marketing people at more than 50 of the Fortune 200 companies in the past three years and asked, "Do your marketing programs perform on average any differently from what we've observed in our practice?" No one has contradicted the findings. On the other hand, no one really wants to talk about it either. It's embarrassing.

Too many marketing programs fall into the Zone of Death-Wish Marketing, a concept we'll describe in detail in the next chapter. For now let's just say—doubtless confirming the experience of many readers—that most marketing programs fail to build loyalty, consideration, preference, or long-term volume.

COMMODITIES INTO BRANDS OR BRANDS INTO COMMODITIES?

At one time—and not very long ago, at that—many more products were commodities than are today: coffee, bath towels, pickles, salt, chicken, pineapples, and even water. Maxwell House, Ralph Lauren, Vlasic, Morton, Perdue, Dole, and Perrier changed that. They turned the commodities into brands.

Usually consumers distinguish a brand by attributes other than its price. The exceptions are those unusual brands built on price appeal, such as Motel 6, Marcal tissues, and Ameritrade, a Web-based securities broker. In theory, there are no commodity products or services. Everything can be branded because every product, every service can offer something more than price (and the basic elements required to compete in the category at all; to survive, even Motel 6 must offer clean rooms with comfortable beds). Morton salt is special because "When it rains, it pours." Perdue chickens are special because "It takes a tough man to make a tender chicken." Maxwell House coffee is still "Good to the last drop" almost five decades after *I Remember Mama*.

Today there is much talk in the trade press about commodities being turned into brands, and we agree that happens. We've seen our own client Mobil do this with automotive and industrial lubricants; Novartis do it with vegetable seeds; Green Mountain Energy do it with kilowatt hours; and International Beef and Pork and Excel Corp. do it with beef and pork.

At the same time, we see far more brands being transformed into commodities than the other way around. When an existing product loses its distinctive positioning, it turns into a commodity, a product (or service—say, trash pickup) that cannot be distinguished from its competitors except by price. What happens when the company has a short-term focus? Or has no clear target? Or emphasizes low price? Or engages in heavy promotion? Or allows product differences to disappear? Or never develops a compelling positioning? Or diffuses its original positioning? Commodity status is the result.

One frightening indication of brands being turned into commodities comes from our studies of the role of marketing-mix factors in driving market share across a broad range of product categories. What factors are becoming more important over time? Share of distribution and share of shelf facings!

Take the distribution levels and shelf facings of all the competitors in a category, add them up, and divide by the number of brands, and you have the share. Share of distribution and share of shelf facings today are increasingly correlated with share of market. This means that buyers are increasingly buying as if they were blindfolded. As brand equities diminish, consumers are less likely to "see" brand differences. More and more, what matters most is distribution.

These are all examples of marketing having thrown a rod. The brand slides toward commodity status. Nothing but price distinguishes it in the buyer's mind from competitive brands. And when that happens, the company has dissipated its brand equity, which is just the opposite of what you would like to do.

THERE IS HOPE: SOME COMPANIES ARE GETTING IT RIGHT

True, certain companies do market effectively and have grown because they do: British Airways, Dell, ExxonMobil, Harley-Davidson, Microsoft, Pepsi, and others. Other companies have grown because they capitalized on a product or service innovation: Nucor, MCI, Rubbermaid, and 3M, to name just four.

Nevertheless, while a company can go a long, long way on innovation, it must inevitably learn to market its products. Nucor, for example, began its extraordinarily successful steel business by building a mini-mill and using scrap as a raw material. As one result it was able to compete on price not only with integrated U.S. steel makers—Bethlehem, Inland, U.S. Steel—but with Japanese companies. However, as other companies built mini-mills and began using scrap, Nucor's innovation (and price advantage) became less significant, and marketing became more important.

Because marketing is a relatively new discipline, and because the environment has been changing so radically, it is not a surprise that most businesses do not do it well.

For years—certainly well into the 1950s—the challenge at most companies was simply to sell what the factory made. Only then did the marketing concept spread—the idea that organizations can satisfy their own long-term objectives, such as profitability, by coordinating and focusing all their activities on identifying and satisfying customer needs and wants. Today that idea is widespread, although not universal; a manufacturing manager at a chemical company recently said to us, "I'll tell you what's best for the customer. It's what runs best in my plant." He meant it, because he added, "That's what I can produce most efficiently, to the highest quality level, with minimum problems, and deliver on time. So what the customer really needs is what we can produce best."

Ken Olsen, founder and ex-CEO of Digital Equipment Corporation, is alleged to have said, "Marketing is what you do when your products aren't very good."

But even among executives who embrace the marketing concept, we find too many marketing programs doomed to failure because of mediocre decision-making based heavily on intuition and experience. And we've come to realize that these poor marketing decisions often result from too much testosterone.

3

Testosterone Decision-making: The Manly Way to Screw Up

Our first exposure to testosterone-driven decision-making goes back more than 20 years. We were young, life was slower, and we were a lot more naive about marketing. It is 1976 and small cars are about to revolutionize the American automobile market. We've had a gas crisis. The National Highway Traffic and Safety Commission is publishing guidelines on fleet gas consumption averages, so the government is regulating toward small cars. The Japanese car makers are starting to figure out what sells. We, like many other young Americans, are driving Volkswagen Beetles. And Yankelovich research (Clancy was a consultant to Yankelovich, Skelly & White at the time, Krieg a marketing researcher) shows that Americans are starting to think small, starting to think that a big car is a gas guzzler and not such a good thing anymore.

We are working with the late Florence Skelly, one of the intellectual giants in marketing research, and General Motors is a client. The executives are all middle-aged men, all living in Detroit, and all employed by General Motors for a long time. They drink Manhattans at lunch while they eat big steaks with potatoes. It might still have been the 1950s.

After one long, heavy lunch, we go up to the office in the GM Building, temple to the automobile, and Florence says, "Small cars. You gotta get ready." GM is paying us to be visionaries, so we predict, "Small cars are coming."

The senior marketing executive climbs out of his chair, looks out the window, and says, "I don't know what you're talking about. I don't see any small cars."

We say, "You don't see any small cars because we're in the General Motors Building in Detroit, Michigan, in the Midwest. People out here are all driving big iron."

He gives us a scornful look. "I don't believe it. I don't see any small cars." End of discussion. End of GM's total domination of the market.

In the last two chapters we made the case that companies are in trouble. They are beleaguered because their marketing is not at the center of the business, where it should be, and because even when marketing *is* at the center, most marketing programs are not very good. But why not? The tools for exceptional marketing—as we'll be showing through the bulk of this book—exist. Collectively, we have enough experience to know what works and what doesn't. Why don't executives employ the tools available? Why don't marketing programs perform the way they should? We've concluded that the cause is widespread testosterone-driven decision-making.

HOW TO TELL A TESTOSTERONE-DRIVEN DECISION-MAKER

We know from our experience and observation that testosterone-driven decision-making tends to be what guys do. Testosterone-driven decision-makers are the guys who assemble complex toys on Christmas Eve without reading the directions, cook without a recipe, make business decisions without research. This is the stuff of popular culture worldwide. It is the subject of Professor Deborah Tannen's books. Her bestseller *"They Just Don't Understand"* is must reading for all managers. There are T-shirts that say "Real Men Don't Use Road Maps." Women talk about the problem, and comics joke about it: Why does it take a million sperm to fertilize a single egg? Because they won't ask directions.

Testosterone-driven decision-makers feel that asking for help is tantamount to admitting weakness, and what real man admits weakness? Some of these decision-makers are admittedly candidates for Prozac therapy. One testosterone-driven CMO we once worked with had a sign on his door that read, "I'd rather be feared than loved." While he is not an evil man in his personal life—we find him to be a gracious and charming host—in his professional life he derived satisfaction from making people afraid of him. He accomplished that by yelling at people and by having what we saw as faux fits from time to time. Ultimately he reached the point where nobody wanted to go into his office and he could make his decisions in splendid isolation.

We know another testosterone-driven CMO who, if he has a drink at lunch, says, "Let's go back to the office and make the girls cry." We have objected to this behavior on more than one occasion, but he brushes us off. The "girls" are sensitive women and men, and this executive finds twisted satisfaction in calling someone into his office and blasting her to see if she will literally break down and cry. Sometimes she does. And usually, in time, she quits.

We know a testosterone-driven senior marketing executive who keeps a container of rusty railroad spikes on his desk. When one of his people does a piece of work he dislikes, he calls the miscreant into his office and roars, "You're dumb! Totally dumb! Here's this nail! This nail is one more nail in your coffin, and I'm going to be on your back until you straighten this out. You go back to your office and put that nail on the corner of your desk. It's going to stay there and everyone is going to know you've got a nail until this gets resolved." At that corporation, when you walk into someone's office who has a big spike on his—or her—desk, you know he's in hot water.

These men are, of course, exceptions. But the testosterone decision-making characterizing many marketing decisions today is not; it is normative.

We've Measured the Testosterone Rush

But to be true to our principle that intuition is not adequate to make a judgment, we could not be satisfied with our experience and our reading to identify testosterone-driven decision-making. We needed research. In preparation for last year's annual marketing meeting of the Conference Board, we designed and commissioned a study of 293 senior marketing managers (144 men, 149 women) representing a cross section of Fortune 1000 companies. The survey investigated perceptions of male versus female CMOs by the marketing managers who report to them in terms of 34 different aspects of decision-making and management styles. The complete results of the survey can be found on our Web site at copernicusmarketing.com.

Just as we had believed, we found that most marketing decisions are rushed, rely on little research, and focus on short-term results. We also found that these decision-making patterns are significantly more characteristic of male senior marketing executives than of female senior marketing executives.

Overall, the study revealed that senior marketing executives are perceived to make decisions quickly (89 percent), to make decisions based on focus group research (79 percent) and intuition (79 percent), to be focused on short-term versus long-term results (73 percent), and always to be in a rush (65 percent). More than half (59 percent) are viewed as paying too much attention to what their competitors are doing. Also, senior marketing executives are seen to overwhelmingly prefer to make the important decisions and delegate the implementation to others (96 percent), and to find it easy to make major decisions (88 percent). These respondents characterized both female and male

Figure 3-1   Percentage Who Say Statement Describes Decision-making Styles of Senior Marketing Executives

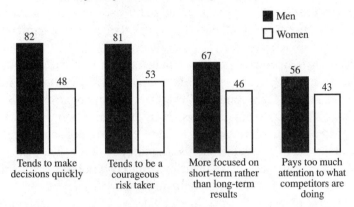

marketing executives as having aggressive personalities, yet they viewed both genders as enjoyable to work with.

As Figure 3-1 indicates, our respondents said that male CMOs make decisions quickly and are risk oriented. They tend to be more externally focused, paying "too much attention to what competitors are doing," and are short-term oriented.

Female senior marketing executives, on the other hand, were perceived to be more effective in building consensus when making decisions (84 percent applies to women, 60 percent to men) and more thoughtful in their decision-making processes (90 percent applies to women, 71 percent to men), carefully examining many options before acting.

Both men and women, MBAs and non-MBAs, highly experienced managers and less experienced shared these same views of the differences between male and female CMOs. Stated differently, wherever we looked, men were perceived by everyone, including themselves, to be hormonally driven decision-makers.

In short, these are the attributes of testosterone-driven decision-makers. They:

- Make decisions quickly.
- Rely on intuition.
- Are uncomfortable with ambiguity.
- Tend to force their views on their subordinates.
- Favor qualitative over quantitative research—they believe that focus groups are quicker and cheaper than surveys and are easier to understand.

Testosterone-driven decision-makers formulate key marketing decisions on judgment alone or on circuitous reasoning: "This is the way we made the decision last year." They defend their judgment calls by citing personal experience ("I don't see any small cars"). But if judgment and experience are so good, why are so many marketing programs so bad?

While testosterone-driven decision-makers do not often brag about their intuition as such, they *do* say things like "It's intuitively obvious to me," or "I like that decision. It feels good," or "I can feel it in my bones," or "Go with it. It smells good." Hardly anyone says, "I'm using intuition on this one," but since Webster's defines intuition as "the direct knowing of something without the conscious use of reasoning" that's what they're doing. They like intuition because it means they can make decisions quickly without a lot of expensive, time-consuming, and sometimes confusing research. They probably love the firm that ran a full-page ad in the Sunday *New York Times* in September 1999.

The firm offered to generate new product ideas, position a prototype or capability, or solve other branding needs in ten working days for no more than $25,000. The process "does not use focus groups or quantitative studies to create ideas, but relies solely on creative intuition and marketplace experience. The output is not ponderous evaluations, analyses, or reports of any kind. The output is ideas."

But not just any output. "The ideas are not prepared in consumer unfriendly research modes such as white cards, concept boards or product statements, but in the form of true-to-life introductory advertisements." And you get them quickly because "deliberation is the enemy of success . . . speed allows great brand building ideas to happen before overthinking and bureaucracy have a chance to gum up the works." The people who would hire this firm, says the ad, "trust their own judgment and strategic instincts."

No doubt they do, and no doubt they have faith in creative intuition, judgment, and strategic instincts. And no doubt they are mystified when their marketing strategies, ad campaigns, or new product ideas, unencumbered by overthinking and serious research, sink without a ripple.

FEEL THE ENERGY IN THE ENVELOPE

Perhaps because so many executives today are basing decisions on their intuition, book publishers—always alert to the trends—recently put out three titles that promise to improve intuitive decision-making: *Practical Intuition for Success* by Laura Day (HarperCollins, 1997), *The Executive Mystic* by Barrie Dolnick (HarperBusiness, 1998), and *The Hidden Intelligence* by Sandra Weintraub (Butterworth-Heinmann, 1998). This is not the advice you heard in business school. "To succeed in business is not a matter of 'beating the competition,'" Day writes. "It's simply a matter of being who you are."

What practical tips do these authors have for managers? Suppose product development has come up with three new options, and the company has the resources to exploit only one. Sandra Weintraub's advice: Put the name of each product into an envelope and seal it. Pick up each envelope and feel its energy. Bet the company on the envelope that sends the strongest sense of positive energy. Suppose you have only two options and you're short of envelopes. Laura Day suggests that you picture an apple. Now picture a second apple. If the second apple is larger than the first, the second option is the better one.

We are not making this up, although we doubt that these ideas are widely followed. We believe most marketing executives would find it a tad awkward to tell the executive committee, "We're going with our Internet project because that was the envelope with the strongest energy."

At the same time, and almost as absurd, they *do* say to their bosses, "We're going with the Internet project because our four focus groups were really hot for it." Since most bosses do not know much about marketing (if they did, would they have someone as benighted as this marketing executive working for them?), four focus groups makes sense to them. Of course, most of the time it would be cheaper and just as reliable to use the envelope method.

One related reason why executives make bad decisions is the "institutional imperative" that Warren Buffett discussed in a letter to Berkshire Hathaway shareholders. "In business school," he wrote, "I was given no hint of the imperative's existence and I did not intuitively understand it when I entered the business world. I thought then that decent, intelligent, and experienced managers would automatically make rational business decisions. But I learned over time that isn't so. Instead, rationality frequently wilts when the institutional imperative comes into play."

Examples of the institutional imperative at play: "Any business craving of the leader, however foolish, will be quickly supported by detailed rate-of-return and strategic studies prepared by his troops," wrote Buffett, "and the behavior of peer companies, whether they are expanding, acquiring, setting executive compensation, or whatever will be mindlessly imitated."

The mindless imitation of peer companies is one symptom of practices we described in earlier books as "death-wish marketing." Managers who are experiencing a testosterone rush practice death-wish marketing, our name for those efforts that managers, unconsciously or unknowingly, engage in to kill a product, a brand, or occasionally an entire company or their own careers.

Table 3-1 Death-Wish Marketing (a.k.a. Testosterone Marketing)

• Decisions are made quickly because there is no time to do it right.

• Top management demands short-term results.

• Competitors guide decisions.

• Real consumer needs and problems are unknown or ignored.

• Too few alternatives for each decision are evaluated.

• The profitability of marketing alternatives and actions is unknown.

• Marketing managers are often promoted prematurely.

HOW TO IDENTIFY DEATH-WISH MARKETING

The symptoms of death-wish marketing, driven by testosterone, include:

- *Decisions are made quickly because there is no time to do it right.*
- *Top management demands short-term results.*

These two points are related and are worthy of comment. Good marketing takes time. Nevertheless, we know that managers are pressed to make every decision quickly. We know that top management wants prompt results. Managers feel they must make decisions immediately. Yet the development, planning, and implementation of a serious marketing plan takes eight months to a year or more. Everyone wants to do it in three months, which is generally not possible. In Chapter 17 we'll discuss the typical steps and the time each requires to develop a transformational marketing program.

Sometimes, of course, the competitive situation means you don't have time for carefully evaluating alternatives, but if you are properly prepared you can react quickly. The firefighter who takes the time to lay out the needed clothing, boots, and gear before going to sleep can be ready to move quickly when the alarm sounds.

- *Competitors guide decisions.*

The company, as Buffett pointed out, uses peer companies to guide opportunities, strategies, direction. Ignore the fact that the competition may itself be making a terrible mistake or that its strategic situation may be very different. Watching the competition for guidance is testosterone marketing.

During the past 24 months we have watched Internet companies racing to be the dominant music store, personal computer store, drugstore, software

store, travel agency, professional employment service—you fill in the blank—
looking over their shoulders and, we suspect, racing over the cliff together.

- *Real customer needs and problems are unknown or ignored.*

Virtually every marketing manager we meet knows enough to say that his
or her company is sensitive to and geared to meet customer needs. But we
have found over and over that when you really investigate what the company
is doing versus what it is saying, customer needs and problems have a relatively low priority.

Last January, a major business-to-business manufacturer—one of the top
20 corporations in the Fortune 500—invited us to visit. The chief executive
officer, a newly hired chief marketing officer, and a senior vice president of
sales began with a presentation they had developed for the troops. They
talked about the corporate vision: focus on the problems of the customers.
They had a slide showing the firm moving from a manufacturing-centered to
a marketing-centered organization. They had another slide with the customer
in the middle. It was great to see this seemingly successful company adopting
everything we've talked about for years.

At the presentation's end the CEO says, "Well, what do you think we ought
to do next?"

We say, "We'd like to understand your business. Let's begin by talking
about what market targets you're going after and their problems."

The CEO says, "That's no problem. We've got it nailed."

Then the CMO says, "What do you mean we've got it nailed? We have a
segmentation, but where did it come from?" After a ten-minute discussion
they agree they have a segmentation based on judgment.

We ask, "Who is your most profitable market target within the segmentation?"

The CEO says, "I'm not sure we've figured that out yet."

"As an aside," we say, "we're curious. How big is your marketing research
department? What's the budget?" Embarrassed looks. The corporation has a
marketing research department in name only. The company has not conducted an original piece of research in years. "What kind of data do you have
about your customer? How do you know what their problems are?"

The VP of sales says, "We know what they buy."

The CMO says, "As near as I can tell, we haven't done any marketing
research, as such."

The CEO says, "I know what you're going to say next: how can we be a
marketing-centered organization with a focus on the customer if we don't
know anything about the customer?"

Then the marketing guy says, "I don't understand this either. At my last firm we had all kinds of data about the customer. But here I ask a question and we don't have the answer. It's discouraging." Then they all agreed that they were going to have to learn more about their customers. They recognized that insights into customer problems based on judgment and sales force anecdotes are inadequate.

- *Too few alternatives for each decision are evaluated.*

One of our principles is that there are many alternatives for every marketing decision, whether targeting, positioning, pricing, service configuration, or something else. There are tens, hundreds, thousands, and in some cases millions of possibilities that the company can evaluate, and today there are research tools that permit you to evaluate these options based on criteria related to profitability.

This said, a strange thing happens at corporate headquarters every day. The decision process gets narrowed down to sometimes three, often two, and usually just one option very quickly. As we show throughout this book, optimal marketing decisions require alternatives, usually the more the better.

In the chapters ahead, we'll discuss how companies make targeting decisions in a New York minute, typically selecting a target based on judgment alone rather than on research that weighs the differential profitability of many alternative targets. We'll talk about the way advertising agencies generally bring a client one or two campaigns to review. (If they've stayed up all night, maybe three or four.) We'll argue that the laws of probability dictate an unsuccessful campaign if a firm develops and tests only a few of the thousands possible. This is true not just for targeting and advertising but for all marketing decisions. The more ideas developed and tested, the more likely we are to find a blockbuster.

- *The profitability of marketing alternatives and actions is unknown.*

Because many marketing directors do not know (some don't even care about) manufacturing and distribution costs, they often cannot calculate profitability, and cannot therefore assess a marketing program's return on investment.

This spring a food products firm that had unsuccessfully launched a line of 100 percent natural products engaged us to develop a marketing plan. We told them we needed to know the margins on each item in the 35-product line and the costs for their various channels of distribution.

They asked why we needed to know. We said we wanted to give them a very profitable plan and to do so we needed to weigh the marketing costs against the projected sales and profits. They said they did not have time for all that, and in any case they wanted us to focus only on developing a marketing plan that would meet the CEO's sales objectives. Many marketing managers do not have access to cost and profit information, and our client may have been telling us that without using those exact words.

We developed a marketing plan and presented it to the client. Within days the client called to say it wasn't a good plan. It wasn't workable. Why not? The CFO had determined that it would not be profitable. To which we could only respond, "If you had shared cost information at the start, you would have gotten a workable plan."

For readers who think this is some kind of aberration, consider this: many companies today are using sophisticated trade-off and choice modeling tools to help identify financially optimal product and service configurations for consumer and business-to-business products and services. Yet, as we'll discuss in Chapter 10, clients rarely provide cost information on different product features and benefits. As a result, the research often yields the wrong answer: the least profitable product or service.

- *Marketing managers are promoted prematurely.*

Companies tend to promote marketing managers before they've had to live with the brands or programs they've launched. More than once we've seen an executive who can talk a superb marketing plan, but it's a mess when it reaches the market. Somebody else has to clean up because the instigator is long gone by the time the final results are in. Death-wish marketing is promoting managers before they've had to live with their brands and had to demonstrate a return on investment.

A variant of this problem is moving people into serious marketing positions who lack the experience. If your spouse had a metastasized melanoma, would you want the oncological surgery performed by an intern on rotation from psychiatry? Would you even want it performed by the best trauma surgeon in the land if she happened to be on call when your spouse needed the surgery? Of course not.

Yet there is some sense in many companies today that you don't need the best marketing people to get a superb marketing job done. Find smart people in planning or operations or IT, move them into marketing as part of a normal rotational program, and they'll get the job done.

Sometimes, of course, they do get the job done. We've seen nonmarketing professionals perform ably in marketing roles at ExxonMobil, but they were supported by a staff of trained marketing pros. In our experience, in most companies the nonmarketing professional knows no more about how to launch and manage a powerful marketing program than a dermatologist knows about how to do neurosurgery. And no two-week executive training program at Stanford or Harvard is going to make any difference.

Death-wish marketing is common because it is difficult to build a great program. A manager has so many decisions to make and so little time to make them. But when these decisions are based on intuition, a flawed basis for any kind of investment, the result is usually disaster. This has led us to spend a great deal of time thinking about what makes great marketing programs.

PRIZE-WINNING MARKETING: RIGHT PLACE, RIGHT TIME

A while ago, we wondered if intuition and testosterone were the keys to great marketing decision-making among winners of highly publicized national awards for demonstrated marketing effectiveness. The American Marketing Association's Effie Awards recognize the most effective marketing campaigns of the year. The Advertising Research Foundation's David Ogilvy Awards are for campaigns with proven advertising effectiveness.

In both cases, to win the competition, marketers and their advertising agencies must provide the judges with data on the development of the campaign and the proof that it worked. Entrants must convince the judges that the campaign did not arise out of thin air but was based on sound thinking buttressed by sound research. The evidence of effectiveness needs to be based on sales or tracking research (preferably both) that clearly shows the causal relationship between the campaign and its market performance.

BBDO advertising, as an illustration, talked about its four-point process for many years in its submissions for marketing and advertising awards. The points were:

1. Know your prime prospect (a.k.a. the best market target).
2. Know your prospect's problems (i.e., their unsatisfied desires and needs).
3. Know your product and how it can solve your prospect's problems (a.k.a. the positioning and product strategy).
4. And break the boredom barrier (i.e., create advertising that effectively, efficiently communicates the positioning strategy and imprints it in the buyer's mind).

The briefs the agency prepared in support of campaigns talked about this process in some detail, leaving readers with the unmistakable conclusion—in most cases a correct one—that it was the process that led to the great campaign. Take for example the Burger King "Have It Your Way" campaign, which won more awards and produced better sales results than any fast food campaign ever. This was a campaign that began with a serious research study designed to identify the prime prospects and their problems.

The target was the frequent fast food diner who wanted a customized burger. Burger King could address this problem, and the advertising ("Hold the pickle, hold the lettuce, special orders don't upset us") broke the barrier in terms of creativity based around memorable lyrics and orchestral score.

BBDO did well for its client in no small part because it had a strategy that not only drove a record number of customers to Burger King, but also was a result of a process that made it all seem logical and sensible to judges in advertising competitions.

But that's only one agency. Do most people who win Effie and Ogilvy awards have a system that enables them to win repeatedly in the marketplace? Is there some science underlying the campaign? Is there an approach, a methodology, some logic that will persuade a skeptical judge that the campaign was not a fluke? Or is success largely a function of intuition or, worse, lady luck?

Admittedly, every submission needs to be supported by research; it's a requirement. But a judge needs to ask whether the research and strategy the submission describes actually determined the outcome or whether they were introduced later on to support decisions already made. Stated differently, did the research precede or follow the development of the campaign? And how good was the research?

To answer this question, we tried to locate winners from 1985 through 1995 to see if they were able to repeat their successes. (By winners, we mean individual managers, the key person in the marketer's organization who received credit for the marketing or advertising award.) If they did, that would be evidence of a sound process, great intuition, or both. If they did not repeat their success, they would be like the singer who has one hit record, evidence perhaps of being in the right place at the right time.

The big surprise for us was that most of the winners could not be found. Despite our best efforts to locate them, they had moved on to places unknown. Perhaps they joined the shadows in strategic planning. Of those we did talk to, a few won a second (different) award for the *same* product or campaign a year or two later. None of the located winners, however, won again for *another* product or campaign. And—with one exception, which we'll discuss—all of the marketplace successes appeared to be based on good judgment and luck rather than the kind of "scientific" process endorsed by BBDO.

The exception was Anthony J. Pingitore, Jr., who was the new product director on Hershey's Chocolate Milk when it won a 1985 Effie; when we spoke to him, he had been promoted to general manager, special markets, at Hershey Chocolate USA. Pingitore's comments suggest that Hershey did (and does) have a marketing process: "I think the key to our success in new products is having a lot of concepts in what we call the funnel. Our goal is to have many new products in development—in research, in concept development, and in prototype development—at the same time so we can pick the one or two best ones and then take them further along the research chain. Of course, a big part of the product for us is capital. In many cases we have to spend huge amounts of capital to bring a new product into the system. So we have an ongoing process in which thousands of ideas turn into hundreds of concepts that turn into 50 ideas that are brought to prototypes and maybe one or two or three make the marketplace."

Pingitore contrasts this to the typical approach many companies took years ago (and some still take today): "Wake up!" says top management. "We need a new product to boost sales. Let's get one. Let's do some research, hope it wins in research, and we'll introduce it."

THE SUNDANCE NATURAL JUICE SPARKLER STORY

As a contrast to Hershey's process, consider Stroh Food's Sundance Natural Juice Sparklers, which won an Effie in 1988. Scott Rozek, now of the Unisearch Partners, was the brand manager when it won. He recalls that the idea for the product came from a California flavor house that had noticed consumers mixing juice and water together in the mid-1980s and thought, "We could to do that for them." After some experimentation, they found what seemed to be several ideal formulations.

"We looked for a name we thought was a little more upscale, a little more adult. When we were doing the package design, we tried to make it look very adult. We put it in four-packs of 10-ounce, very sleek bottles that definitely looked adult. We charged a premium price. All this made a huge difference in the way it was perceived. Instead of Sundance being just another kid's soft drink, it had very adult imagery, and the price made it fairly upscale."

Rozek feels that the timing was important: "One of the things that happens in the new-age beverage category is that every three to five years, something new comes up. It's as if consumers are looking for better products or just looking for something different from soft drinks. Certainly a certain segment of the population is doing that. Sundance happened to hit right into an opportunity to fill in one of those niches."

He says Sundance was successful because it was different. "Among our competitive set at the time, natural sodas were only a competitor in that they had this better-for-you feel to them. Sparkling waters were better for you, but they didn't have any flavor. Flavored seltzer was doing well for a while, but it had a major flaw in approach. Because it was a clear product, a clear bottle, and said 'no sucrose,' a lot of consumers thought it didn't have any calories. When consumers found out that wasn't true, the flavored seltzer business went south in a big way."

What happened to Sundance? Everything. The category attracted new competitors and began to change: "I think consumers in the new-age beverage category are experimenters anyway and are looking for different things." Not everyone in his organization was persuaded that Sundance was ever a good idea; they wanted to know why the company was putting resources against something outside their main business.

We would argue that Stroh stumbled into the natural juice sparkler business and essentially stumbled back out. Sundance Natural Juice Sparklers may have won a prize for the most effective marketing campaign of the year 1988, but like many such winners—Fab 1 Shot, Today Sponge contraceptive, Almost Home Soft Cookies, Oskar Food Processor, Snuggle Liquid, Fresh Chef Refrigerated Italian Sauces, and Teddy Ruxpin, just to name winners that no longer exist—it was in the right place at the right time.

We believe that is true of many marketplace successes: they right product was in the right place at the right time. Intuition and creativity and "catching a wave" were probably far more important than a logical process or sound research in carrying the day. Lightning struck, but because the people involved did not truly understand the marketing process, they could not call it down a second time.

AT THE SAME TIME, MANAGERS CAN'T CONTROL EVERYTHING

While we argue that a lot of marketing's problems can be traced to testosterone-driven marketing decision-making—and we will be showing that a company can improve its marketing successes dramatically—we know there are conditions beyond the manager's control.

A marketing manager cannot control a competitor's actions. A competitor can do something truly foolish and there is not much you can do but hunker down and wait for events to catch up with him. The people at Weber must have been taken aback when Sunbeam announced its "early buy" and "buy and hold" programs on gas grills in November 1997. Short of following Sunbeam over the cliff, there were only so many things Weber could do in response.

A marketing manager cannot control the giants in the category or the entry of serious Internet companies. Consolidation among one's customers shifts the balance of power. The arrival of a category killer down the street—a Wal-Mart, Best Buy, Home Depot, Staples, Toys"R"Us, Barnes & Noble, or an Amazon.com, Pets.com, or drugstore.com—limits a small store's options.

A marketing manager cannot control media proliferation. At one time—and not so very long ago, at that—there were three broadcast television networks, a relative handful of magazines, a few FM radio stations, and two or three daily newspapers in every major market. That has changed. Companies spend more money to promote themselves than ever before. Breaking through the clutter with a clear, compelling message is much more difficult than ever.

A marketing manager cannot control consumer motivations. The company cannot shove a product down the throats of the American people. Consumers have more product choices, more service options, more media alternatives, and access to more and more information than ever. When asked, most people will tell you that they don't *need* another option when they buy automobiles, books, CDs, clothing, detergents, food, PCs, pizza, shoes, telephone services, or whatever. Buyers are already inundated with choices. So we're *not* saying that a company's problem is only dopey decision-making. We are saying that because marketing is so much more difficult than in the past, the marketing decision-making process cannot rely solely on executive intuition and creative judgment. Rather, it must rest on counterintuitive thinking grounded in rigorous analysis of unimpeachable research. Unfortunately, much research in the late '90s was impeachable. And dangerous!

CHAPTER

4

Warning: Commonsensical Research Can Be Dangerous to Your Career

Last summer, a vice president of marketing at a packaged goods giant called us, a smart manager we'd worked for in the past. She told us that sales were declining for one of the company's flagship brands. Because the brand was not doing well, top management had cut the marketing budget faster than the brand's sales drop (like reducing a hungry man's rations). What could they do to reverse the situation?

Given the brand's size and national distribution, we believe that in such a situation the corporation needs a marketing audit, followed by a large-scale segmentation and positioning study to guide the development and testing of new repositioning concepts. Interestingly, this company's marketing research department traditionally focused on tactical, rather than strategic, issues. They were very comfortable testing four product formulations, three price levels, or two ads, but their day-to-day frame of reference did not include a major strategy study.

The marketing VP requested a proposal. We prepared one. She requested a presentation. We gave one to her and the brand's advertising agency. At the end the people in the room looked stupefied—deer in the headlights. Recognizing trouble, we asked, "Is there anything you didn't understand?"

She said, "There's a lot I didn't understand. I don't even know what I didn't understand." Because she is smart, we were puzzled.

We deconstructed the presentation: "Did you understand this? Did you understand that?" By the end she seemed to understand our approach and the reasons behind our recommendation.

But when the meeting broke up, she said, "You know, I'm really thinking we ought to just do some qualitative research"—that is, focus groups— "because it's less expensive, and it can be done quickly, and we can control it better. We're right in there watching the groups through a one-way mirror."

A month later she called to thank us for our time and presentation, but the company had decided to use focus groups. Why? "I don't have the money to do anything really solid, so we're going to make a judgment call on this one."

We kidded that focus groups are to serious research what bumper stickers are to philosophy and added that "the probability of that being a success is not terrifically high."

She said, "Don't talk to me about it. I know that. Maybe I won't even be around here to see what happens. I just have to live with the reality, and the reality is I don't have the time and I don't have the budget to do it right."

A year later she was gone, and the brand was still sliding toward hell. This company is not unusual. The majority of companies don't do good research, so top management is skeptical of all research.

Attendees at the annual Advertising Research Foundation conference in March 1999 heard that management was not satisfied with current research. A study reported that CEOs were insisting on more accountability but put less faith in marketing research than in most of their other sources of information. Management speakers from Sony, GM, AT&T, and Y&R said that research had been most disappointing in predicting new product success and in measuring advertising's true effectiveness.

DANGER: MARKETING RESEARCH AT WORK

As we said in the last chapter, many (mostly male) marketing executives make their decisions today using intuition. They buttress them with death-wish research, a subcategory of the death-wish marketing we've just talked about. Table 4-1 lists a variety of death-wish research techniques in common usage. All of them could be labeled with a warning: "Beware: Potentially Dangerous to Your Business and Career."

Focus groups are the best example of this school of marketing decision-making. Indeed, as we begin the new millennium, focus groups are the most popular tool for supporting practically every marketing decision.

A year ago, a packaged goods client decided to make a colossal packaging change, one that employed a radically new form of packaging that they hoped

Table 4-1   Examples of Death-Wish Research

1. Overreliance on fuzzy focus groups.

The results are unstable and do not represent any segment of the population; by their nature, focus group findings cannot be projected.

2. Asking people to tell you what's important.

People tell you what is obvious, often the price of entry in the category: four wheels in a car, taste in a food, cleaning power in a detergent.

3. Getting lost on a perceptual map.

This technique assumes that different people have the same perceptions of brands and products — that their individual maps are about the same. But there is no reason to believe this is true. Nor does a map indicate how to move your brand or product from one area to another.

4. Measuring consumer problems with gap analysis.

This analysis tries to discover gaps between what people want and their satisfaction with what they currently use. It is usually done on the aggregate level, which yields wildly misleading results.

5. Using correlation/regression analysis tools to infer causation.

If a soft drink's good taste ratings are highly correlated with preference, we assume that good taste causes people to prefer the brand. The opposite may be the case: people who buy the brand and prefer it tend to impute good taste to it. With this tool you can't tell the difference.

6. Concept testing by telephone.

Because researchers read a description of the concept to people over the telephone, they must distill it to a phrase or a couple of phrases. There is no clear analog to this in the real world, except perhaps a 10-second radio spot.

7. Satisfaction studies by mail.

People who respond to mail satisfaction surveys tend to say that everything is fine. Those who tend to be very pleased or very unhappy do not bother to respond.

8. Recognition measures to indicate advertising effectiveness.

Simply being able to recognize (or say they do) a slogan, visual element, or message after prompting is not the same as really remembering something (i.e., true recall). People often claim to recognize an ad that has never run.

9. Measuring concept interest in a competitive vacuum.

New products and services need to be tested in a competitive context. The more realistic this context, the more valid the scores.

10. Predicting new product success without accounting for costs.

Without cost information covering both manufacturing and marketing, it is impossible to project financial returns. A movie that sells $100 million worth of tickets but cost $120 million to make and market is very different from one that sells $100 million and cost $50 million.

11. Any decision in which you consider relatively few options.

Because reality and marketing are so complex, the more targeting, positioning, advertising, pricing, and other options you consider, the greater the odds of success.

would "turn the industry inside out and upside down." Instead of doing a more traditional in-home use study, the company held 18 focus group sessions. Consumers thought the new package looked wonderful. An in-home use project might have told them that the new package leaked. Because of the design flaw, which the groups did not (possibly could not) identify, the package was a costly blunder.

Companies do groups to understand the problems of their target, to explore alternative positionings, to get reactions to advertising campaigns and new product concepts, even to chart alternative pricing strategies. They do groups among physicians, retail store category managers, corporate purchasing agents, college professors, technology geeks—the complete directory of occupational specialties, hobbies, and product consumption habits. The practice has even spread to animals.

Business Week reported in June 1999 that to test a 30-second Whiskas Homestyle Favorites commercial, Britain's Waltham Center for Pet Nutrition ran focus groups for 200 cats. "In a 15-second teaser spot, pet owners are urged to fetch Fluffy for a viewing. The ad itself shows images of fish, yarn balls, and cat food. About 6 percent of the cats looked up, twitched their ears, or approached the TV, says a proud spokesman for Kal Kan," Whiskas' maker.

Today more than 5,000 research companies and individual practitioners sell their professional time to do focus groups. The New York chapter of the American Marketing Association publishes a 346-page directory of focus group companies and services. More than 1,000 locations in the U.S. alone offer meeting facilities for focus group moderators and their clients. There are even people who specialize in developing great menus for the agency and client managers sitting behind the one-way mirror observing the groups. Food specialists meet a real need, because any experienced focus group promoter quickly learns that good food is essential to a good group. If you want the people watching through the mirror to be happy—happy enough to come back for more groups—serve them the wonderful assortment platter from the local French-Thai-Chinese gourmet takeout.

Although, to the best of our knowledge, one cannot get a Ph.D. in focus group research, there are people and companies that specialize in training individuals to moderate and analyze focus groups. It does not make us feel comfortable to know that it requires a minimum of three years of graduate school education, an extended internship, two to five years working on a dissertation, and a licensing examination to become a professional clinical psychologist, while it takes a five-day $995 training program at the (imaginary) Focus Group Institute of America to become a (not imaginary) Certified Focus Group Director. But that is beside the point; it is the state of the profession.

There is nothing wrong with focus groups. In their place. They can and do provide a marketer with insights into how people feel about a new product, what a print ad communicated, or what language consumers would use to describe a new service. Focus groups can be a helpful first step in a serious research process, and we do a lot of them.

FOCUS GROUPS REFLECT FUZZY THINKING

But when this first step is the only step—the situation at too many companies—marketing is in trouble. Because researchers do not—cannot, in fact—select participants scientifically to represent the target market, corporations are basing multimillion-dollar marketing decisions on the offhand opinions of small groups of people who are willing to give up a couple hours for $50 or so and free sandwiches. Yet if the focus group company recruits participants on a different afternoon or in different malls, the results will be completely different—unless, of course, the moderator leads the group into a foregone conclusion, which is another danger.

Once the researchers assemble a group, dozens of irrational dynamics skew what the participants say. One man likes the sound of his voice and pontificates. A woman wonders whether she's giving the "right" answer. Another is uncomfortable confessing her true feelings—if only about laundry detergent—or lack of knowledge—say, about software—in front of strangers. Still another has no opinion about credit cards but feels obligated to contribute something. These factors mean that the information the group leader draws from the participants may have little real value. There are no facts in focus groups, only verbatims.

It is usually a good thing for the research to have a clear point of view on a particular topic so that the conversation does not wander off into irrelevancies. But sometimes the moderator and the analysis tend to emphasize that point of view, no matter what the product category. In one year, for example, we participated in ten focus groups for a telecommunications company and in six groups for a clothing company, all conducted for our clients by the same research firm. We saw an amazing coincidence: the group design, order and type of questioning, and analysis resulted in findings about the attitudes and values of Americans today that were dumbfoundingly similar. For example, respondents tended to talk about the stress in their lives caused by the shortage of discretionary time.

If one had not participated in both research studies, one would not have known that the moderator was shaping the questions and the discussion and that the group would have a similar perspective every time, no matter what the subject, the people in the group, or the client funding the project. The two clients who participated in these groups, ignorant of the consistency, were, of course, delighted with the findings.

JOIN THE FLAT EARTH SOCIETY

A recent development is the tendency to make the groups run longer. It used to be that a focus group ran about an hour or so. The industry then pushed the envelope to make it an hour and a half and then two hours. Today there are three-hour, four-hour, and even all-day groups taking place. The thinking is that if you want four hours' worth of data, it's more efficient to talk to 10 people for four hours than to talk to 30 people for an hour and 15 minutes apiece.

But there's also the sense that a mystical epiphany may occur in the group the longer the session runs. The longer the group, it is assumed, the more likely you are to draw out some very, very deep insights. Indeed, one hears the expression "drilling deep" today to characterize this phenomenon. We can assure our readers that the only magical thing that goes on in a four-hour group is that the respondents lapse into a coma.

In our experience sitting behind the window, when the group reaches the hour-and-a-half mark—certainly the two-hour mark—people are tired, bored, and want to go home, and the quality of the information reflects it. The only way you can reverse that situation is by making the groups gimmicky at the two-hour mark. The solutions here are to have participants cut pictures out of magazines, role-play, close their eyes and express their dreams, or maybe do age regression therapy.

Some researchers are actually enthused about the prospect of putting respondents to sleep. It's called "hypnotizing the respondent," something an Irvine, California, "pioneer in the field of hypnotic focus groups" is now doing.

Some clients and agencies claim they have held so many focus groups that the results must be quantitative—that it is possible to project the findings. There is, of course, no way to turn qualitative (exploratory) research into quantitative findings that can be projected onto the target market as a whole.

Coke Europe asked us for a proposal for a serious marketing strategy study and ultimately decided to make the decision after doing 40-plus focus groups. Yes, 40, not 4. We mailed them a humorous award for membership in the "Flat Earth Society" and wished them luck.

Which is the attraction? Executives think they understand focus group results. They have heard real opinions from real people. Even though executives may know little about marketing—or little about marketing research—they feel they can sit behind a one-way mirror and draw conclusions. They do not need to know about statistics . . . about sampling . . . about models. They are willing to bet the brand (or the company) on the half-baked opinions of eight people who have, in most cases, not thought for 10 minutes about the subject under discussion.

HOW TO MISUSE ONE-ON-ONE INTERVIEWS

This spring, a client called to ask if we would come to Chicago to spend an afternoon and an evening observing one-on-ones, typically an hour interview with an individual person. The company had arranged 11 one-on-ones. Ordinarily they would have taken 11 hours, but the firm was interested only in getting a superficial reaction from people to some ideas and to some ads. Because they were not going to probe any subject in depth, they felt they could shrink an interview to about half an hour. So we were to sit through 11 half-hour interviews—or almost 6 hours. Interestingly, there were something like 15 client and agency people sitting behind the one-way mirror watching the professional moderator interview people one at a time.

Our client wanted some guidance as to what the name of their new financial product should be, as well as what the respondents thought of different advertising approaches. After six interviews in which five people said one thing and one said another, the executives decided they had the answer to that issue and the moderator did not have to bring it up anymore.

This meant the first interviews ran about 30 minutes, but by the time we got to interviews number 7, 8, 9, 10, and 11, the moderator was able to whip right through them. There was less to discuss because various options were dropped.

Given the kinds of people the client wanted to interview, the company had to pay them $200 apiece—that's $2,200. The moderator for the day, the preparation, and the report were another $6,000. Six hours of the 15 people behind the mirror could easily have been another $40,000, plus the cost of the fusion food, the facility, the recruiting effort, and travel and lodging.

All to hear the opinions of 11 people—and not even all their opinions. For the same money the company could have personally interviewed several hundred people. But they could not have done it in a 24-hour period.

SEVEN-MINUTE STUDIES NOURISH PONZI SCHEMES

Qualitative research, of course, is not the only form of research that leads marketing management astray. One tool we see emerging is something we call a "seven-minute segmentation study."

A seven-minute segmentation study begins when a company's top management recognizes that they do not understand the market. They suspect that the total market has different segments. They could segment it by geography, by SIC code, by size of business, or by a constellation of variables (which we will talk about in the targeting chapter). Management does not know which segmentation is best or, more to the point, what target group is best. They do know they need to know something or they are wasting precious company resources on unprofitable targets.

So they contact several marketing research firms that tell them that, given the size of the category, the size of the corporation's business, and the importance of the targeting decision, it is critically important they do the segmentation right.

To do a segmentation correctly requires a large-scale study—we like 1,000 or more personal interviews, 45 minutes to an hour and a half long. It requires measuring psychographics, demographics, and lifestyles. It requires a variety of statistical or neural network algorithms to analyze the data. It requires three to five months from start to finish and costs $200,000 to $1.2 million, depending on the consulting firm and the scope of the project.

Testosterone decision-makers balk at the time and the price. They needed to make the decision yesterday. They can wait until next week, but they certainly can't wait six months, and they had not planned to spend half a mill on research. If there's a spare half mill in the budget, they'll spend it to take the management team to the Super Bowl to see the company's brand promotion. The company is not going to spend it on marketing research. The only real question is, what can you do in a short time for $25,000 or $50,000? Enter the seven-minute study.

The seven-minute study consists of hypothesizing which three or four variables out of the thousands possible might be best to segment the market and interviewing 300 buyers in the category, almost always by telephone or over the Internet. Firms do it this way because it's cheaper to interview by telephone and on the Web than to interview in person and because, theoretically, from a single location they can find a nationally representative sample. The analysis is simple—primarily cross tabulations—to say something as basic as "15 percent of the buyers in this category account for 85 percent of the volume." The odds that these segments actually reflect the company's best opportunities are virtually zero.

One hot arena for research today is Internet marketing. Firms launching Internet companies know that it is a useful thing for the prospectus to include a statement (an imprimatur, if you will) from a prestigious marketing research company attesting to the market's size, the economic value of the prospects, and the new dot-com's gargantuan potential. They ask the research company to design, field, and execute a Web-based project in record time. Worse, for a project that should cost upwards of $250,000 for a reliable, valid project (also known as serious, professional study), the Internet folks propose a $30,000 budget.

In one recent case we asked a well-funded Internet company founder whether his objective was to gain some significant insights into the market and the potential for his new service or to be able to make some research-based claims that would motivate prospective investors to invest. He told us it was the latter. His interest was not in knowledge but in hyping the stock. These kinds of studies should be clearly marked "Caveat emptor." They are reflective of rapidly emerging Ponzi schemes posing as Internet start-ups and IPOs.

GET THE WRONG ANSWER OVER THE TELEPHONE

New product testing by telephone is another popular form of dangerous research, although it's simple and it's cheap.

Ordinarily in concept testing, we show respondents the written concept. This is a one- or two-paragraph description of the concept idea that typically contains the product promise, e.g., "Tastes better," and the reason why, e.g., "Made with all fresh, natural ingredients." Sometimes the concept is executed in the form of an advertisement—a television commercial people can see and hear or a print ad they can see and read.

Following the presentation of the concept in whatever form, the researchers ask people a series of questions that predict buyer behavior. These questions include 5-point, 7-point, and sometimes 10-point rating scales; the researcher gives a respondent the rating scale and a written label or description of each point on a card to read before they answer.

In death-wish concept testing, researchers read a description of the concept to people over the telephone. Because they're reading and because respondents forget the first sentence by the time they hear the second, researchers must shorten the concept, distill it down to its bare bones. The bare bones sometimes can be as short as a sentence or a couple of phrases. They do that even though there is no clear analog to this telephone reading in the real world—except perhaps a 10-second radio spot. This is then coupled with rating scales with typically few points (i.e., less discrimination) than would be employed in a personal interview or Web-based survey.

In the real world the customer watches television or reads a print ad or looks at the package and digests the words, sounds, shapes, colors, whatever. Somebody hearing the concept over the telephone loses almost everything. In a personal interview the respondent can actually look at the ratings scale. She can contemplate, think about it, and decide where she wants to be. On the phone she has to remember the rating scale and give this stranger a number.

In the entertainment industry, as an illustration, the most popular way to test new movie ideas is to read a two-sentence concept to people over the telephone and then ask whether they would be likely to see the movie. This method is far removed from deciding to see a movie based on watching a trailer, reading a review, or seeing an ad. That's why it can't possibly work. Is it any wonder that for many movie studios the decision to green-light a new movie is akin to a night in Las Vegas? With the outcome the same: nine out of ten films don't make any money.

MARKETING RESEARCHERS AT THE TOWER OF BABEL

Because marketing researchers have often been their own worst enemies, many marketing executives do not respect research—the rock on which any successful marketing program is built.

Marketing researchers cause their own problems when they speak jargon and think the numbers they produce are the only things that count in the world. See Figure 4.1 for a new game you can play to pass the time at your

Figure 4-1   Research Jargon Bingo

Do you keep falling asleep in research meetings and seminars? What about those long and boring conference calls? Here is a way to change all of that!

How to Play: Check off each block when you hear these words during a meeting, seminar, or phone call. When you get five blocks horizontally, vertically, or diagonally, stand up and shout "Lunacy!!!"

R-squared	Logit Regression	Gap Analysis	Lisrel	ROI
Revisit the Numbers	Not Statistically Significant	Interaction	Brand Juice	Drilling Deep
Value Proposition	Brand Equity	Pareto Curve	Think Outside the Box	Pattern Recognition
Marketing Metrics	Best Practice	Knowledge Based	Optimal	Data Mining
Neural Network	Customer Relationship Management	Leverage	Ethno-graphic	Heavy Users

Testimonials from satisfied players:

"I had only been in the meeting for five minutes when I won." Henry G., Westport, CT

"My attention span at meetings has improved dramatically." Steve T., Boston, MA

"What a gas. Meetings will never be the same for me after my first win." Luisa F., Miami, FL

"The atmosphere was tense in the room as seven of us waited for the fifth box." John B., New York, NY

"The speaker was stunned as eight of us screamed 'Lunacy' for the third time in an hour." Kathleen O., Plattsburgh, NY

next research meeting. It's derivative of a business jargon game flying around the Internet and reflective of research meetings that take place in companies every day. Frankly, in many cases marketing management doesn't know what research people are talking about. Our mumbo-jumbo vocabulary masks real understanding of the work. Too many researchers seem to have the attitude "Isn't this a sophisticated presentation? Aren't you blown away?! Am I going to get an 'A' on my paper?" Too many are frustrated academicians.

As one result, CEOs and marketing executives have found that all too often research studies are not even marginally helpful; they don't help at all. Or, worse, they might cause mischief or lead you astray big time. After all, Coca-Cola researched Surge in the 1990s and New Coke in the 1980s before introducing them. Burger King researched their new French fries extensively before introducing them. Why do executives commission research at all?

Sometimes they do it because it's the company's policy . . . or because they want support for an intuitive decision they've already made . . . or because, occasionally, the research is actually helpful. If the company has a marketing plan and a budget for market research, the research department is supposed to spend the money. The boss will say, "Did you do the research? We can't move ahead without the research."

In November 1996, Jesse Kalisher, who writes a research column in *Brandweek* magazine, told the story of a brand manager he knew who recommended that the company introduce her product in a large size. The recommendation detailed the category's growth, the competitive volume in larger sizes, a strong endorsement from the sales department, and all the relevant financial figures. "The recommendation floated easily through her division, only to be held up by corporate. The brand group was then instructed to take two different large sizes that were mere ounces apart to focus groups before a new size would be approved." This is research for the sake of policy—as opposed to research for the sake of knowledge—and rotten research, at that.

But even if the researchers do something more serious, they may end up with data that has little actionable value. Recently a client showed us a study her corporation had commissioned from a well-known and reputable research firm and asked whether we could use it to help develop and implement a new marketing strategy.

The researchers surveyed a convenience sample of 300 women by telephone and asked 15 minutes of questions that left us scratching our heads. The client thought the study was useful, but it was hard for us to see what they could do with it. Even the research company prudently warned that the results might not represent women generally and might not even represent women who spent a significant amount on clothing. The study asked questions on which it would be hard to base marketing decisions, such as "How do you feel about life? How do you feel about fashion? How do you feel about the following brand names?"

Nonetheless, our client was delighted. She showed us the study, enthusing, "Isn't this great?" That always happens. People are happy with the research the day it comes in. Two months later they think, "What?" A year later they think, "Gee, I got nothing from that one." It takes time for the reality to sink in. At that point the fat report has become a doorstop.

THE DEVIL REALLY *Is* IN THE DETAILS

As we have been suggesting, management should not be surprised when commonsensical research leads to disappointing results. Good research usually takes time and money, and if management is impatient and parsimonious, it will continue to be disappointed with the results. But the issue is not "research" as such; it is poor research done poorly. Good research done well can help a company market its products and services effectively.

Dudley Ruch, one of the pioneers in our industry, once made the argument that the research department should report to the CEO, not the CMO. Its mission, he argued, was to be objective, and it's hard to be objective if your boss is the chief marketing officer.

Too much research is designed to confirm a decision management wants to make. If a given research study does not have the potential to tell you what you do not want to hear or to expand the possibilities you should consider, it's not very good research. You want a study that can say clearly, "Don't move ahead with this product." Or "Redesign the product." Or "This approach to the advertising campaign is weak." If the research does not carry the potential to contradict common sense, it should be automatically suspect.

Not long ago we did a study for a company that was planning to introduce a new product based on patented technology. Let's call it the Quark Razor. To introduce the razor, however, the company would have to build a new factory, and the plant and equipment would cost many millions of dollars.

The study went on for a long time. It was very complicated, and at every step the marketing execs told us how important it was to come up with solid numbers because an important decision hung in the balance. They seemed to be saying two contradictory things: "Don't come up with a positive number because if you do, we'll have to build a factory" *and* "Make sure you do everything you can to tease out more sales so we can go ahead and build the factory." Companies don't hire consultants to lie, but they often want them to support their judgments.

At the end of the project we met with the marketing research director and presented the preliminary forecast, which said, in effect, don't build the factory. He became furious: "I can't present this to my management! These numbers are impossible! They're insufficient!" And much, much more. Two days later, at nine in the morning, the marketing research director walked into our office unannounced. He wanted to talk about the product, the research, the methodology. He said he wanted to "revisit the numbers." That's a code phrase for "change the numbers, make them more favorable." He stayed until noon, debating the project, showing us data, going over old research reports. We scrupulously reviewed our work, but we could not make the forecast any better.

Two weeks later we made the big presentation to the division CEO. We usually start with the forecast and then get into the nitty-gritty detail supporting it. Five minutes into our talk, the marketing people took issue with the findings, and we took issue with them. After we had clashed for a few minutes, the CEO said to his research director, "I don't know why you're arguing this point. All the results we've gotten at every other stage have been mediocre. We know the product has a lot of problems, so don't take it personally." At that point the research director began to argue with his boss.

When the dust settled, the research director still had his job, but the company decided to abandon the product. This experience is not unusual. We routinely see managers become emotionally involved with their products, which is a good thing, but not when it clouds their judgment. What would have happened if the company had built a hundred-million-dollar plant and *then* discovered the product was a dud?

It's interesting to note that labels such as "segmentation," "market target," "positioning," "concept testing," "advertising research," "statistical analysis," and "survey research" are all used in almost every company as if there were a general consensus on their meaning and application. There isn't. Some applications of these terms, and the research they're connected to, are excellent; others are patently ridiculous. The trick is in knowing how to separate the good stuff from the bad. The devil *is* in the details.

Marketing research, we believe, poses many dangers and many opportunities. Bad research can, and often does, lead companies in the wrong direction. Good research, on the other hand, is the sine qua non of a counterintuitive approach to great marketing.

But before the company begins to do any research on anything, management should have a commitment to build brand equity not brand juice.

Counterintuitive Thinking Behind Great Marketing Strategies

5

Stunted Brands: Too Much Juice, Too Little Equity

In November 1999 we gave a presentation at the Conference Board's annual marketing conference on brand building. A week later we received a call from the head of a top Internet agency, an agency that specializes in helping launch dot-com businesses. They do everything from building innovative Web sites to creating Clio Award–winning television advertising.

He asked if we could develop a proprietary consulting and research technology to create more "brand juice" for his clients' new businesses. (We've created a few dozen proprietary technologies, so the request was not unusual, though what he went on to ask for was.) He called the research a "juice blender," saying that "the right research should provide insights into brand attitude, brand emotions, brand essence, brand personality, brand sociography, brand values, brand voice—the 'brand juice' every great brand needs." One more use of the prefix "brand," and we were going to laugh.

He was persuasive, however, and we decided to invest a little time to learn more. We didn't learn much more except a new vocabulary—new media mumbo jumbo. It reminds us, in retrospect, of a recent Dilbert cartoon. Dilbert gives a faux presentation to his troops (it's really a test to see if they can separate nonsense from common sense) and says, "I'd like to start with a diagram. It's a bunch of shapes connected by lines." He then puts up on the screen a typical strategic planning diagram. Then he adds, "Now I will say some impressive words. Synchronized Incremental Digital Integrated

Dynamic E-Commerce Space." After one nitwit asks for a copy of the presentation, Dilbert complains, "The results of my experiment are disturbing."

Don't get us wrong. Brand this and brand that can be good stuff, even important stuff, and will be touched upon in our chapter on positioning. But much brandspeak today masks a fundamental problem. In many cases the brand (or dot-com company) has no reason for being. It solves no buyer's problem. It is, and perhaps should remain, an uncapitalized thought.

Worse, many brands today have no clear strategy—no vision, no target, no positioning, no powerful advertising, no preemptive product or pricing, and so on. Our Internet CEO was interested in substituting fluff for facts, image for substance, words for ideas, brand juice for real equity.

We asked him for an example of a brand with lots of brand juice. He said Coke and told us why. We responded that Coke is in decline and that, given a choice between a Coke and a Pepsi, more Americans would choose a Pepsi. Our argument was that Coke's success has more to do with the Coca-Cola Company's power to distribute, promote, and price than with branding.

He then went on to talk about Nike and its swish. We said that "Just do it" was a very creative execution of an ambiguous strategy and that Nike, too, is in decline.

He then responded that he had a better example—and he had—Marlboro cigarettes.

Marlboro, once a woman's cigarette, is today (and has been for the past three-plus decades) a cigarette for people who want a full-flavored cigarette, one with rich taste; people who wish to be perceived as more masculine, tough, outdoorsy, maybe even as cowboys riding the range under big western skies.

But Marlboro is a rare case indeed; that is why it's been studied by academicians and practitioners forever. It's why every time you ask a brand juicer for a great example of what they're talking about, they're eventually likely to point to Marlboro.

They forget that Marlboro has a target and has successfully solved that target's psychological and taste problems since before many of our readers were born.

Listening to incoherent brandspeak, one might think that all you need to do is take a brand, product, service, or an entire dot-com company and dip it in brand juice. And voilà, something magical happens! You've transformed a nothing, through brand dip alone, into a powerful presence.

This is ridiculous and almost never happens. Do you want to build a powerful brand? Figure out who the target is and everything about them. Uncover their motivations, their problems, and their pains. And then configure your product or service or company, and price it appropriately, so that it addresses the target's motivations, solves their problems, alleviates their pain. Finally, unleash the power of communications to tell people with words and pictures why and how you do this better than anyone else in the industry.

When you're done, you've got a brand. You have something remarkable that people are willing to pay a premium for and go out of their way to find. You have something that stands out from the crowd and represents real value.

We told this to the Internet agency, and indirectly to their dot-com clients, and begged them to stop talking gibberish and get back to fundamentals: target, motivations, product solutions, positioning, pricing, communications, and so on. Attitudes and essence, values and personality are "nice-to-haves," but they're not essential to brand success. They're the sprinkles on the icing and certainly not the cake.

And today, when more brands are being transformed into commodities than commodities into brands, mastering the fundamentals has become an imperative.

WHAT'S THE MEANING OF A BRAND?

We fervently believe, as we've said before, that marketing is at the center of the business solar system (not finance, manufacturing, or IT) and brands are at the core of what marketing is all about. The word brand was used in the 19th century to indicate an owner's mark on cattle, and the process of branding—say, burning a big "CR" on a cow's rump—told potential rustlers that this was the property of the Copernicus Ranch.

Today we don't use branding irons on consumer and business-to-business products and services, but we do use names, labels, signs, symbols, designs, and colors to identify the goods or services of one seller and to differentiate them from those of a competitor. Disney's familiar script, Coke's red-and-white can and delivery trucks, McDonald's golden arches, IBM's bold block letters are elements of these popular brands' "brand architecture" that gives them a distinct identity.

Branding products and service began in earnest in the mid-19th century, and over the course of the next century, hundreds of thousands of new brands were created. Perhaps no two periods were more important for brand building than the 1950s—when television came of age—and the present time, when the Internet economy is booming.

Brands evolve from two different sources: commodities and new product categories. Consider all the traditional commodities that have spawned brands—fruits (Dole, Sunkist); fuel oil (ExxonMobil, Shell); kilowatt hours

(Green Mountain, ENRON); long-distance carriers (AT&T, MCI); poultry and beef (Perdue, Omaha); salt (Diamond, Morton's); and water (Aqua Fina, Perrier). And consider all the new product categories that have emerged in just the past three decades that were developed by brands: CD players (Mitsubishi, Panasonic); DVD players (Sony, Yamaha); garbage disposals, (Kitchen Aid, Insinkerator); Internet providers (AOL, Mindspring); microwave ovens (GE, Sharp); personal computers (Apple, IBM); portals (Yahoo!, Excite); printers, (Hewlett-Packard, Dell); and software (Microsoft, Netscape).

How Is a Brand Different from a Commodity?

According to Professor Kevin Lane Keller of the Tuck School at Dartmouth, "What distinguishes a brand from its unbranded commodity counterparts is the consumer's perceptions and feelings about the product's attributes and how they perform. Ultimately a brand resides in the minds of consumers."

Different companies have different approaches to brands. Some focus on building a single brand (e.g., American Express or Amazon.com); others divide their efforts between the parent company brand and individual products (e.g. Anheuser-Busch and PepsiCo); while still others emphasize their separate brands but not the parent company. How many consumers know, for example, that Hidden Valley Ranch, a popular salad dressing, is owned by Clorox or that the famous Claridge Hotel in London is a property of the Savoy Group?

Our own experience is that the "company domination" strategy is far more efficient than the "brand domination" strategy, except in cases in which the aim is to offer multiple competing entries in the same product category. Procter & Gamble, as an illustration, offers more brands of detergent in a typical U.S. supermarket than most companies have brands.

The Evolving Concept of Brand Equity

The first time we heard the expression "brand equity," we weren't sure what it meant. It was 1991. We were having a board meeting of our former firm, Yankelovich Clancy Shulman, and one of our academic advisers gave a presentation on the topic. He defined it as the "financial value of a brand." If, for example, Gillette wanted to buy Colgate's line of shaving creams, in order to build market share for Gillette's Foamy, what would the Colgate line be worth? What would be a fair price to pay for it?

Over time we learned that there are almost as many definitions of equity as there are practitioners talking about it. "The search for brand equity sometimes feels like whacking a piñata. It is blind; it is hit or miss. When you do

Table 5-1   Alternative Branding Models

Company Dominates Brands	Company Is Equal to Brands	Brands Dominate the Company
American Express (Credit Cards)	Anheuser-Busch = Budweiser	Alka-Seltzer (Bayer)
Colgate (Total Toothpaste)	Lipton = Cup-A-Soup	Hidden Valley Ranch (Clorox)
Disney (Theme Parks)	Estée Lauder = Clinique	Healthy Choice (Con-Agra)
General Electric (Appliances)	Kraft = Maxwell House	MCA Records (Universal Studios)
IBM (PCs)	PepsiCo = Frito-Lay	Kleenex (Kimberly-Clark)
L'Oréal (Cosmetics)	Time Warner = Warner Bros.	Marlboro (Phillip Morris)
Sony (Electronics)	3M = Scotch Tape	Crest (Procter & Gamble)
Holiday Inn (Crowne Plaza)	Marriott = Courtyard	Claridge (Savoy)

hit, you don't know if you want what showers down," say Michael Amoroso and Arthur Kover in a *Marketing News* article. And as we said in an earlier book, "No one is sure how to measure it. Brand equity is a nice idea until you have to use it or act on it. Unless it acquires some consistent and useful meaning soon, it will pass quietly out of a marketer's working vocabulary."

Among the definitions or indicators of equity in use by the mid-1990s were:

Awareness
Brand Bonding
Brand Personality
Customer Loyalty
Perceived Quality
Price Value
Product Differentiation
Repeat Purchase
Strength of Feelings
User Imagery

Some consulting firms define it as the incremental dollar value of the brand name as measured in a choice modeling or conjoint study, something we'll discuss in Chapter 11. Take, as an illustration, two Internet booksellers: Amazon.com and Barnes & Noble. Do a research study and hold relevant factors

Figure 5-1   Only Three Financial Services Brands Rank in the Top 100

Interbrand Ranking of the 100 Most Powerful* U.S. Brands

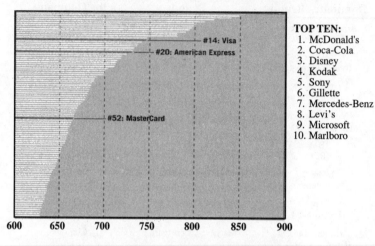

TOP TEN:
1. McDonald's
2. Coca-Cola
3. Disney
4. Kodak
5. Sony
6. Gillette
7. Mercedes-Benz
8. Levi's
9. Microsoft
10. Marlboro

*Brand power score is based on: **brand weight** — the influence or dominance that the brand has over its category or market; **brand length** — the stretch or extension that the brand has achieved or could achieve; **brand breadth** — the breadth of franchise in terms of age, spread, consumer types, and international appeal; and **brand depth** — the degree of commitment the brand has achieved.

Source: Interbrand

constant—such as types of books sold, ease of navigation, price discount, speed and cost of delivery, help in selecting books, book reviews, and so on. Then ask how interested shoppers are in buying from Amazon versus B&N. The answer in one recent example was that Amazon had 80 percent of the value of B&N, not bad for a company that's been around for only about five years, yet surprising because its market cap overwhelms that of its bricks-and-mortar competitor.

Interbrand measures equity—or what they label brand power—in terms of four dimensions: brand weight, brand length, brand breadth, and brand depth. Figure 5-1 comes from a published study in which the top 100 most powerful U.S. brands are ranked.

One multinational we work with measures brand equity for more than 300 brands worldwide. At this company "brand equity" means brand perceptions on approximately 30 different product attributes and benefits for each brand in every category. Assume that one of the categories is soft drinks. Table 5-2 shows most of the brands and half of the attributes and benefits that would be evaluated globally.

Table 5-2   Which Brand or Brands in this Category Do You Associate With?

	Coca-Cola	Pepsi Cola	Mountain Dew	Diet Coke	Dr. Pepper	Sprite	Diet Pepsi	7UP
Great Taste								
Thirst Quenching								
The Authentic, Original Cola								
For People Under 30								
Fun, Good Times								
Sweet Taste								
The Right Amount of Carbonation								
The Late 19th Century								
Refreshment								
Christmas								
Americana								
Lightness								
Citrus Flavor								
NASCAR Racing								
Snowboarding								

Note the fundamental differences between the Interbrand approach and that of the global marketer: they are measuring totally different things. The former, moreover, measures four dimensions but eventually constructs a single number—we're calling it equity here. The global marketer, on the other hand, measures 30 different things—all of which are tapping into different aspects of brand equity—and makes no attempt to create a single number called equity.

By the late '90s boardrooms were buzzing with talk about brand equity, while academics and practitioners were beginning to accept the notion that it is a sophisticated, multidimensional construct. David Aaker, a distinguished marketing professor, has written in a leading textbook on the topic that the major asset categories of equity are brand name awareness, loyalty, perceived quality, and brand associations. Only the last, we might add, is studied by the global marketer we've just discussed, and none of them are reflected in Interbrand's indicators of "brand power."

Beginning in 1995, we began to engage in research and development studies designed to better understand and measure the construct "brand equity."

Table 5-3   Illustration of Factors/Items Tested

Examples of 3 Factors	Internal Consistency Score	Scale Sensitivity Score	Construct Validity Score	Internal Validity Score	External Validity Score	Total Validity Score
Factor 1: Brand Permeation						
Is a well-known brand	91	83	81	85	83	84
Is a brand that is available everywhere	90	80	72	81	88	84
Is a brand everyone is familiar with	88	72	87	79	81	84
Factor 2: Brand Distinctiveness						
Clearly superior to competitors	86	93	92	90	97	94
Unique in its category	87	90	88	88	89	89
Offers qualities I can't find elsewhere	89	90	86	88	83	86
Factor 3: Brand Quality						
Is a brand I completely trust	88	77	78	81	78	80
A very high-quality product	86	82	82	83	89	86
Has an excellent reputation	85	95	85	89	89	89

We were particularly interested in being able to express "brand equity" as a single number for each brand in a category. We began by reviewing the brand equity literature, which resulted in a long list of hypothesized factors and items. We then studied the factors structure of these items based on a study of more than 20 brands and 500 respondents. We moved on to assess the internal consistency of each factor, test scale sensitivities, establish construct validity, and measure external validity by correlating each item and factor with market share. An illustration of this analysis is shown in Table 5-3.

Eight factors emerged from this analysis. They include:

Brand permeation: A weighted combination of brand and advertising awareness and availability.

Brand distinctiveness: A weighted combination of measures indicative of brand differentiation/uniqueness and superiority.

Brand quality: An assessment of the brand as a whole and its line extensions in terms of its overall reputation for quality of product or service.

Brand value: A weighted combination of measures that reflect the extent to which the brand delivers what buyers pay for—often known as "price value"

Brand personality: The extent to which the brand's image is congruent with who the buyer is or wants to be.

Brand potential: The extent to which consumers will pay more for, go out of their way for, or are willing to try this brand's not yet introduced new products or line extensions.

Competitive inoculation: The extent to which the consumer would stick with the brand in times of adversity or competitive pressure.

Brand behavior: The extent to which buyers prefer, buy, use, or have bought this brand and its line extensions.

We recommend that each of these factors be measured by three to five questions embedded in an Internet, face-to-face, or mailed questionnaire—in which respondents can see and rate brand logos. Since one of the factors—brand behavior—is redundant with market share (the variable we are trying to predict and explain), it is not included in our final brand equity equation but is used to help weight the importance of each factor in the overall model.

Each item and factor is weighted by its contribution to the overall brand behavior and preference vector to produce one overall assessment of brand equity for every brand studied. Each brand, as a result, can be characterized by a single brand equity number. These numbers, in theory ranging from zero to infinity, are standardized from 0 to 100 within a category to express "share of equity."

Think of this as having in your pocket seven different kinds of currencies (French francs, Canadian dollars, Brazilian reals and others), all of which can be totaled and expressed in their U.S. dollar value—a single number. If you are interested in brand equity across product categories (e.g., What's Amazon's equity in books, CDs, and movies?), this can be measured by weighting equity scores in each category a brand competes by the dollar size of the category.

THINGS WE HAVE LEARNED ABOUT BRAND EQUITY

Brand equity drives market share and profitability. Everything we have seen, every research study we have done suggests this. One primitive measure of brand equity is the reputation that a brand or company enjoys. Over the past fifteen years we have examined data on the relationship between reputation and marketing performance for more than 500 companies and brands. The relationship is not only linear; in category after category approximately 50 percent of the variance in market share can be explained by brand equity alone. For our readers who are not statisticians, this is extraordinary!

Fortune reaches a similar conclusion with very different data. Year after year they study the reputations of approximately 400 companies and relate the findings to financial performance. Year 2000 winners speak for themselves. They are:

1. General Electric
2. Microsoft
3. Dell Computer
4. Cisco Systems
5. Wal-Mart
6. Southwest Airlines
7. Berkshire Hathaway
8. Intel
9. Home Depot
10. Lucent Technologies

What's the implication here? Want a powerful brand? Leave the "juice blender" at home and build your brand's equity.

Another key learning from brand equity work is this: No matter how equity is measured, simple measures or more complex ones, some brands have more equity than market share; others have more share than equity. Table 5-4 illustrates this for a number of product categories.

If you plot the relationship between marketing investment and marketing performance in a category, you see a familiar exponential curve. Some brands are above the line, getting more performance per dollar; others below the line, achieving less performance per dollar. Brands with strong equity, not surprisingly, are the ones above the line; they appear to be able to more easily convert marketing investments into enhanced marketing performance. They are often in the "acceleration" range of their respective market response curves.

Green Mountain Energy, for example, built very strong "green" equity in the first two states in the U.S. to deregulate electric power. The company quickly converted this equity into market share, becoming the number-one deregulated brand in California and Pennsylvania, spending at a rate considerably lower than that of bigger companies with less equity.

Brands with strong equity also appear to have much more potential for growth than brands with weak equity. This suggests the value of measuring

Table 5-4   Brand Equity and Brand Share Are Not The Same

Higher Equity Than Brand Share	Lower Equity Than Brand Share
BMW	Lexus
Coors	Budweiser
Green Mountain	ENRON
IBM	Compaq
Marriott	Holiday Inn
Michelin	Goodyear
Mobil 1	Castrol
Pepsi	Coke
Pizza Hut	Domino's
Wendy's	McDonald's

equity for investment purposes. The brand depicted in Figure 5-2 on the next page shows the potential to more than double its market share.

This can also be seen when we compare brands with strong equity to those with less equity. Everywhere you look there are differences.

	Brands with Strong Equity	*Brands with Weak Equity*
Percent of all customers who are vulnerable	30% or less	50% or more
Percent of all customers who are loyal	60% or more	40% or less
Ratio of incremental business to current business	+30% to +200% or more	Under 20%

An example of the practical value of this insight comes from a recent case of a beer company acquisition. The seller asked for $3.2 billion; the buyer's financial analysis suggested $1.1 billion; a brand equity and market potential analysis suggested a value of $0.9 billion. There was little potential for growth!

Another key finding is that "brand distinctiveness" (read, superiority) and "perceived quality" are often, albeit not always, the strongest determinants of

Figure 5-2   Market Potential Analysis for a Brand with Strong Equity

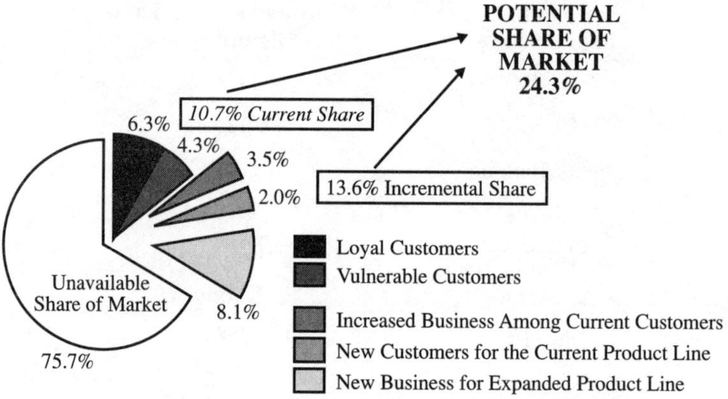

POTENTIAL
SHARE OF
MARKET
24.3%

6.3%   10.7% Current Share
4.3%
3.5%
2.0%   13.6% Incremental Share

■ Loyal Customers
■ Vulnerable Customers

Unavailable
Share of Market   8.1%
                          ▨ Increased Business Among Current Customers
75.7%   ▨ New Customers for the Current Product Line
                          ▨ New Business for Expanded Product Line

overall brand equity. Stated differently, they are usually the two most important factors. Note that they have little to do with "brand juice" and a great deal
to do with "brand substance"—solving people's problems with a great product or service. Brand equity scores, moreover, are strongly impacted by brand
perceptions. And brand perceptions are driven in large part by marketing
communications and the product/service strategy. See Figure 5-3 for a hypothetical example for the service station business.

WHAT DOES BRAND EQUITY REALLY MEAN?

Brand equity, like IQ, SAT score, or p/e ratio, is a number. It's an overall
assessment of the "good will" associated with a brand, which is reflective of
past marketing performance and predictive of future sales and profit potential. It is, we believe, as Professor Keller says, "in the minds of consumers"
and therefore, needs to be studied through surveys, not sales analyses. When
combined with a financial assessment of brand profitability, it provides a
complete accounting of the "value" of a brand to the corporation or the
"value" of potential acquisitions.

Brand equity, moreover, like IQs, SAT scores, and p/e ratios, has different
components. Each of the components of brand equity can be studied separately in order to diagnose its contribution to changing overall equity and
market share over time. Knowing a brand's equity—relative to competitors—
and what drives it, enables a manager to develop and implement stronger
marketing programs. This enables a brand to fly higher.

How do we develop a brand, a product, a service, or a dot-com company

Figure 5-3　A Model of the Determinants of Brand Equity

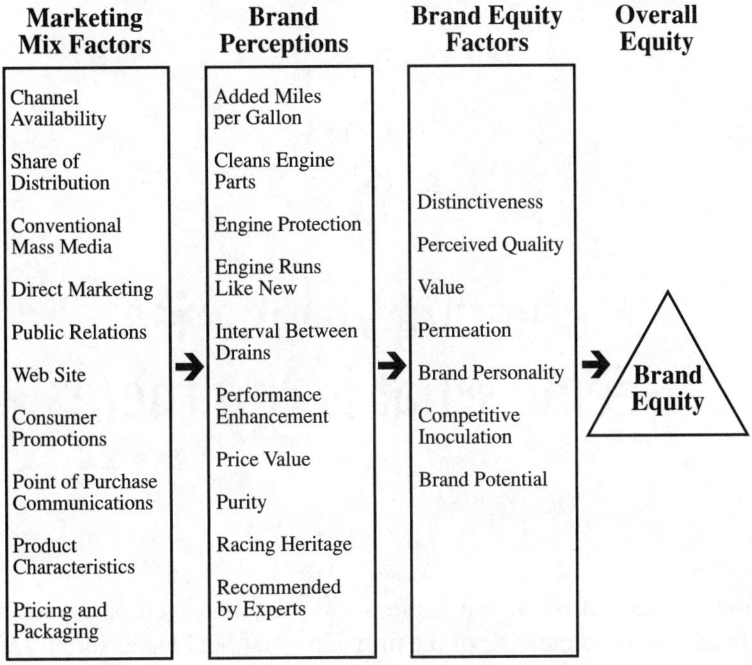

Marketing Mix Factors	Brand Perceptions	Brand Equity Factors	Overall Equity
Channel Availability	Added Miles per Gallon		
Share of Distribution	Cleans Engine Parts		
Conventional Mass Media	Engine Protection	Distinctiveness	
Direct Marketing	Engine Runs Like New	Perceived Quality	
Public Relations	Interval Between Drains	Value	
Web Site	Performance Enhancement	Permeation	
Consumer Promotions	Price Value	Brand Personality	Brand Equity
Point of Purchase Communications	Purity	Competitive Inoculation	
Product Characteristics	Racing Heritage	Brand Potential	
Pricing and Packaging	Recommended by Experts		

with strong equity? This takes us back to the beginning of this chapter. The answer is not "brand juice." It's the fundamentals. It's a great strategy!

Have a vision; pick a financially optimal market target and understand everything about them, particularly their motivations, their problems, and their pains. Offer a product or a service that addresses these motivations, solves the problems, and alleviates the pain, and price it appropriately. Now find a way to talk about your solution in a compelling, powerful way—that's positioning—and express your positioning as clearly and creatively as you can in everything you do. That's integrated marketing communications!

Do this and you'll have a brand with real value. How do you do all this? The next eight chapters provide some answers. Let's begin by talking about seeing in the dark, seeing what's not there.

CHAPTER

6

Marketing Visionaries: Seeing What Is Not There

Not long ago executives at one of the world's ten largest corporations invited us to participate in a meeting of the firm's international leadership team. One of the company's brands not only is number one worldwide in terms of sales, but is clearly the premier product in its category in terms of performance. The room held key people from all over the globe—South America to Europe, South Africa to Japan, the Middle East to Southeast Asia—all in town to discuss their brand's future.

The meeting started at eight in the morning; around three in the afternoon a manager from Italy complained to the CMO, "You keep saying we're the number-one brand, but we don't act like a market leader. We're not investment spending. We don't have an ad campaign that says—doesn't even imply—we're number one. We don't have salespeople out pushing as if we dominate the industry. And we don't behave toward our dealers as if we own the best product in the category. We act like we're number two or number three, even though you keep telling us we're number one."

We asked the group, "Do you guys have some vision? What's the vision for the brand or for the business?"

They said, in effect, "Huh?"

A few people around the table began to discuss the brand's sales objectives—which were set "top down" by the CEO—but they had nothing to do with what we would call a vision. Others talked about the brand's positioning strategy. But it was not even much of a positioning. Eventually a manager from England asked, "What do you mean by 'vision'?"

Our notion of a vision, we responded, is based heavily on the work of James Collins, a management consultant, and Jerry Porras, a professor of organizational behavior and change at Stanford University. Drawing upon a six-year research project at Stanford Graduate School of Business, they argue in their book *Built to Last: Successful Habits of Visionary Companies* that a "big, hairy, audacious objective" is critical to achieving corporate success today.

A VISION PROVIDES PURPOSE AND A SENSE OF MISSION

A vision, at its most basic, dictionary level, is, among other things, an ability to see something not visible. It is a force or power of imagination, something supernaturally revealed, as to a prophet. A vision provides a company with a purpose and a sense of mission. Visions define a few outstanding goals around which companies can organize their resources; they help to inspire the workforce to pursue common aims.

Most companies state their objective, but a challenging objective, though a key component of a vision, is not the same as a vision. A vision is a hope, a goal, a dream; it incorporates the values of the company (or entrepreneur), and it implies benefit for customers. A powerful vision looks outward—or the company is in trouble. A vision statement expresses *the end*. It expresses what the company wants to be in the future.

The vision must be exciting, even inspirational, to all the company's stake-holders: investors, the general financial community, employees, suppliers, prospective customers—everyone. The vision must be so big, so bold, and so ambitious that expressing it—never mind executing it—has a transformational effect. The company starts to become what it wants to be. The dream and the reality fuse.

Shakespeare captured the vision of Henry V, outnumbered ten to one, before the Battle of Agincourt in 1415: "Pray for not one man more. Those who are abed in London tonight will rue that they are not with us on this day."

A vision is John F. Kennedy in 1963: "I believe that this nation should dedicate itself to achieving the goal, before this decade is out, of landing a man on the moon and returning him safely to earth."

A vision is St. Jude's Hospital: "No child should die in the dawn of life."

A vision is the difference between a company designing a personal computer to be 15 percent cheaper than a comparable IBM model and a company—in the form of Apple's Steve Jobs and Steve Wozniak—dreaming of creating a PC "for every man, woman, and child in America."

Motorola has the vision of a world in which everyone is assigned a single telephone number for life—and can be reached by phone from any spot on earth. Microsoft's dream of "owning the desktop" helped it to dominate, first, operating systems, then applications software.

A vision is not "We're going to acquire until we own it all, or downsize until there's nobody left."

WHERE THERE IS NO VISION, THE COMPANY WILL PERISH

Many companies and most brands do not have a vision, and among those that do, it tends to be rather pedestrian. We know because we've studied the Fortune 500 companies. We've combed through 400 annual reports, studied more Web sites than we ever planned to, borrowed from the Stanford study reported by Collins and Porras, and interviewed CEOs, CMOs, brand managers, and communication executives as part of ongoing marketing engagements.

The most basic finding from our work is that most companies do not have much of a vision. At least it is not stated as such in the annual report or on the Internet, and senior officers of the company cannot articulate it. So we searched and listened and accepted as a vision anything that resembled one. Sometimes it was called an objective, sometimes a mission, but mostly it was just a rough idea buried in an avalanche of text.

Equally interesting, we discovered when we dug out these statements from reports, or ferreted them out of our interviews, that most of them sounded the same. It is as if the writers and crafters of corporate and brand visions all attended the same seminar—and not a very original one at that.

From our content analyses of annual reports and conversations with senior executives, we created a vision statement for more than 500 companies and brands and rated each on 10 criteria. These criteria include the following dimensions . . .

inspirational, uplifting; it moves you.
exciting; it gets your blood pumping.
aspirational; it is barely attainable.
readable; it is clearly communicated.
unique/special/different.
very specific, not general.
connotes superiority or domination.

bold and brash; it oozes confidence.

causes you to want to invest in/work for the company or buy the company's products.

transformational, revolutionary, not evolutionary.

For each of the 10 dimensions, we rated each vision statement on an 11-point scale, from "10-describes completely" to "0—does not describe at all." We averaged across the 10 dimensions to produce school grades that ranged from 0 to 100.

A transformational vision, represented by an "A+," is a score of 95 or better; a strong vision is an "A" or "B" with a score of 80 to 95; a weak vision is a pass with anything from 65 to 79; and no vision is a number less than 65. Most of the latter cases represent companies that literally have no vision; at least we couldn't find one.

Our estimate is that approximately two-thirds of the Fortune 500 companies have some kind of a vision. But only about 22 percent of these companies enjoy a strong or transformational vision. Table 6.1 shows the results of our work.

Try as we might, we couldn't find very many specific brands, products, or services (as opposed to companies) that have any vision at all. Even though almost every brand has an annual marketing plan, what we've discovered—to no one's surprise—is that these plans do not include any vision. Thus, the meeting we described at the beginning of this chapter is the norm. Their premier brand had no vision. Two-thirds of the brands we've studied have no vision.

These results are somewhat surprising because the executives we talk with often say the company has a big vision. Although, when we asked one CEO (who clearly did not like consultants) about vision, he stared out his window for a few minutes and then said testily, "If I tell you my vision, you—as marketing management consultants—will be back here in three months playing it back to me as your recommendation. I'm not telling you."

Our response, trying to bring a little levity into the interview, was "No, no,

Table 6-1　　*Vision in Fortune 500 Companies*

	Companies	**Brands**
No Vision	35%	67%
Weak Vision	44	25
Strong Vision	20	8
Transformational Vision	1	0

no—we'll wait about six months. By then you may have forgotten that you gave it to us."

When we try to pin executives down, however, the vision becomes so vague as to be useless. Proverbs 29:18 says, "Where there is no vision, the people perish." Although we do not believe a company and a brand *must* have a vision—it is not a sine qua non for success—we do believe it is very important and therefore highly desirable to have one. And not just any old vision, but a truly transformational one.

VISION STATEMENTS RATED AND GRADED

The following are a number of vision statements that we, playing professors, will score using the same 10 dimensions and 11-point scale described earlier. An exceptional, absolutely transformational vision statement earns a 95 or better; one that only its CEO/author could like will earn a 64 or worse.

"We enhance stockholder value through strategic business initiatives by empowered employees working in new team paradigms." That, by the pointy-haired boss in Dilbert's (unnamed) company, gets a 19.

An aerospace company: "Like many companies, we have a vision statement: It reads: People Working Together as One Global Company For Aerospace Leadership." It earned a 35.

An entertainment company: "We are home to the world's premier journalistic and creative artists. We distribute the products of their minds and imaginations to the broadest audience across the globe." This vision could put people to sleep and could be adopted by every entertainment company in the world. It does not say where they want to go, and we graded it a 54.

An airline: "We have taken major strides toward revitalizing this airline and returning it to a position of industry leadership. At the same time, we recognize what very much remains to be accomplished. We look forward to continued progress in 1998. As always, we are grateful for the support and commitment of our shareholders, and we pledge to you our best efforts to move forward into a prosperous future." We gave it a 63.

A steel company: "Our objective is to maximize stockholder value by achieving and sustaining superior rates of return on the capital we have invested in each of our businesses, and by effectively serving our customers, having partnerships among our employees, and by being a good corporate citizen. Our strategy for achieving this Vision is to: concentrate on steel, with a focus on being a low-cost, high-quality producer, rebuild our financial strength, and improve continuously in everything that we do." Wordy, perhaps, but worth a 69.

A fast food brand: McDonald's has been underperforming in recent years. Though still the market leader, its performance in terms of year-against-year, same-store sales has been sagging. Recent work suggests that Burger King and Wendy's have surpassed McDonald's as the fast food restaurant of choice when someone wants a burger. While we would not hang all of McDonald's troubles on its vision, the statement is not helping. It is a statement without much vision, and we graded it a 74. Here it is: "McDonald's vision is to dominate the global food service industry. Global dominance means setting the performance standard for customer satisfaction, and increasing market share and profitability through successfully implementing our convenience, value, and execution strategies."

A technology leader: "We will continue to drive new technology, serve global markets, increase consumer preference for the Intel brand and work to deliver excellent financial results to our stockholders. This strategy will serve as our road map into the next decade." That's not bad. It earned 79.

A soft-drink company: "This year, even as we serve 1 billion servings of our products daily, the world will still consume 47 billion servings of other beverages every day. We're just getting started. This is a business in its infancy, a true growth company with true, incomparable growth opportunities all over this world." That gets an 85. With such a solid vision, it's sad that this company is underperforming.

A pharmaceutical company: "We at Pfizer dedicate ourselves to helping humanity and delivering exceptional financial performance by discovering, developing, and providing innovative health care products that lead to healthier and more productive lives." We like this a lot, and scored it an 86.

A beer brand: "To be the #2 beer in North America by the end of the year 2000." We like this because it is simple and aspirational, although not terribly inspirational. But aspiration alone could help lift this brand from its current position. We thought it was pretty strong; we gave it the same grade, an 86.

A tire company: Ranked by all measures as the best tire and rubber company, we will be the industry's undisputed world leader by the end of the year 2000." This earned an 89.

Porras and Collins asked what Sam Walton's vision was for Wal-Mart in 1977, when sales were around $500 million. "To become a $1 billion company by 1980, offering a broad range of consumer household products at a reasonable price." We gave this a 90.

Green Mountain Energy: "GME will become the dominant green brand in the rapidly deregulating energy industry and beyond—one of the most admired brands in America." We liked this a lot, perhaps because we helped write it, and because it's a small company with big ambitions. We gave it a

96. It's as inspirational to the Green Mountain troops as was Henry V's exhortation at Agincourt or USMC Colonel "Chesty" Puller's words before the battle of Chosin Reservoir during the Korean War. Completely surrounded and outnumbered 20 to 1, Puller told his guys, "Now we've got them where we want them. We can fire in all directions." He went on to pull off one of the greatest victories in the annals of military history.

Given the companies that Green Mountain must compete against, this vision gives the brand plenty of room to grow. It gives everyone at Green Mountain a standard against which to measure what they do all day. It forces top executives and managers to ask whether any activity they engage in is going to help them become a dominant green brand in the energy business. If so, how? If not, why do it?

That's one of the functions of a vision: it is a goal to which people can aspire. A friend tells us that, when he was editor of an advertising industry trade publication, he routinely interviewed the editors and publishers of new magazines. "If they didn't have a clear vision of where the magazine was trying to go, we knew they were not going to make it. They did not know whether an article was appropriate for the magazine or not. When Gruner+Jahr, the German publishers of *Geo*, introduced an American edition, the editor could not tell us what it was going to be like. He could only say what it was *not* going to be like: 'It's not going to be like *National Geographic*. It's not going to be like *Smithsonian*. It's not going to be like the German *Geo*.'" As it turned out, readers apparently did not know what the magazine was supposed to be either, and after a year or so and several million dollars or so, Gruner+Jahr closed the books on the American edition.

WE ALSO NEED AN INSPIRATIONAL MISSION

Military forces need a mission to know what to do, where to go, whom to attack, and with what weapons. The mission statement expresses *the means* to the vision's end. It expresses what the company should do to achieve the vision.

The company's mission, like the vision, must be inspirational, but unlike the vision, it is operationally oriented. The vision may be to stand at the summit of Mount Everest; the mission lays out what has to be done to get there. It is a blueprint for directing management and employees in their everyday work. The mission is a prescription for how the company should be managed during a specified time period, over the next five years. Here are some examples.

Porras and Collins provide us with a great example in Winston Churchill's mission in 1940: "Our whole people and empire have avowed themselves to the single task of cleansing Europe of the Nazi pestilence and saving the world from the new dark ages. We seek to beat the life and soul out of Hitler and Hitlerism. That alone. That all the time. That to the end." Strong stuff that cannot be improved upon.

Here is another pharmaceutical company: "Our mission is to provide society with superior products and services—innovations and solutions that improve the quality of life and satisfy customer needs—to provide employees with meaningful work and advancement opportunities, and investors with a superior rate of return." Continuing with our grading exercise, we gave this a 71.

Another technology company says it has two fundamental missions: "We strive to lead in the creation, development, and manufacture of the most advanced information technologies." And "We translate advanced technologies into value for our customers as the world's largest information services company. Our professionals worldwide provide expertise within specific industries, consulting services, systems integration, and solution development and technical support." A little boring, perhaps, but a solid 80.

What about Pfizer, selected by *Forbes* magazine as its 1999 Company of the Year? "Over the next five years, we will achieve and sustain our place as the world's premiere research-based health care company. Our continuing success as a business will benefit patients and our customers, our shareholders, our families, and the communities in which we operate around the world." We graded this a 92.

A mission statement for Green Mountain Energy: "Over the next seven years, GME will become the dominant green brand in the rapidly deregulating energy industry. Towards this end, we will implement a disciplined strategy to build shareholder value, becoming the preferred source of green power for environmentally concerned homeowners throughout the nation. We will be recognized everywhere we compete by our extraordinary products and high value services which are based on power provided by the raging rivers of North America, the prevailing winds, and the sun. In so doing, we will leave a legacy of total commitment to exceeding the needs of our customers, and our planet." We thought this was terrific and gave it a 95.

THE FINANCIAL BENEFITS OF A STRONG VISION

A strong—or better yet, transformational—corporate or brand vision and mission is clearly helpful in setting overarching goals for an organization and motivating everyone in the organization, from top management to assembly-line and clerical workers. There is a sense of esprit de corps when everyone knows that they are on high ground, engaged in a common enterprise in which they are attempting to achieve the near impossible.

But there are benefits to a strong vision and mission that have an impact on the bottom line. Our own work with a subset of companies found among *Fortune* magazine's corporate reputation studies of 1997 and 1998 reveals a statistical correlation of .42 between our vision score and the extent to which these companies are admired (i.e., their reputation). Since we also know that corporate reputation is linked to financial performance, both in terms of price/earnings ratios and corporate profitability, it was no surprise to discover a modest but significant correlation of .23 between vision scores and several measures of financial return (e.g., total return to investors, 1987–99, and profits as a percentage of revenues in 1997). This is all the more surprising because so many companies have a weak vision or none at all, a statistical fact that mitigates the potential strength of a correlation coefficient.

Collins and Porras tell us that visionary companies (one characteristic of which is a strong or, in our words, transformational vision) attain extraordinary long-term performance. "Suppose you made equal $1 investments in a general market stock fund, a comparison company stock fund, and a visionary company stock fund on January 1, 1926," they write.

"If you reinvested all dividends and made appropriate adjustments for when the companies became available on the Stock Exchange (we held companies at general market rates until they appeared on the market), your $1 in the general market fund would have grown to $415 on December 31, 1990— not bad. Your $1 invested in the group of comparison companies would have grown to $955—more than twice the general market. But your $1 in the visionary companies stock fund would have grown to $6,356—over six times the comparison fund and over fifteen times the general market."

THE SOURCE OF TRANSFORMATIONAL VISION STATEMENTS

Where do vision statements come from? Much of this book suggests that managers need to balance intuition, judgment, and experience with rigorous analysis of unimpeachable data. We argue that too many executives make too many marketing decisions based on judgment and experience that are inadequate, flawed, or both.

This chapter is the exception to that general rule, insofar as we believe the formation of an inspirational vision and a propelling mission needs to be based heavily on intuition and judgment. This is not to say that after a vision and mission statement is written it cannot be tested using the criteria listed above, but that the vision itself stems from a creative process. There is no data that supplies a vision. Vision is a form of faith, a belief in the unknown and often unknowable.

As a consequence, many visions begin and end in the office of the chief executive officer. In some cases a vision statement might start with the folks responsible for corporate communications or human resources, or even an outside consultant, and filter up from there. The danger with this suggestion is that a CEO (like Dilbert's pointy-haired boss) may write a memo to the troops: "I want a vision statement on my desk by Monday morning." He deserves whatever he receives.

In October 1998 we gave a presentation on the importance of developing vision and mission statements at the Conference Board's annual marketing conference. Following the meeting, a global company called to ask if we would give the same presentation to their corporate staff. They were intrigued by the prospect of developing a vision for the corporation and for its major brands.

We pulled together a new presentation, which incorporated much of the same material this chapter covers, and to excite our prospective client, we provided some hypothetical examples. We wrote hypothetical vision and mission statements for them, and while they were not bad—without input from the client—they certainly didn't represent our best work.

We gave the presentation, which was well received. They said they wanted to go ahead and scheduled a meeting two weeks later to kick off the process and a consulting engagement. A week later our contact called to say the purpose of the meeting had changed. "We are now going to discuss vision/mission implementation rather than development."

We asked why.

He said, "Thanks to you, we now have our vision and our mission."

We said, "How is that possible?"

He said, "You gave it to us. We took your examples, and we played around with what you gave us a little bit, and now we've got it, and we're very, very happy with it. It's quite inspirational."

Inspirational, perhaps, but still generic. Rather than tinker with the words in someone else's vision and mission statement, we recommend that a company undertake a more widespread search, beginning with brainstorming sessions. The project manager (who will become the "vision editorial director") should bring groups of six to ten people together in the room for three-hour discussions. The groups should include top executives, including the CEO and CFO, and middle managers. In each a senior executive from corporate communications/public relations should help draft the presentation and questioning materials and help with group facilitation. These folks are usually the best writers in a company, and a great vision and mission is all about words.

The project manager describes what a vision is, provides good and bad examples (much as we've done), and begins to throw out ideas for what might be an extraordinary vision for the company. A powerful vision statement is exciting, inspirational, powerful, and bold. It should be designed to manifest itself in the company's actions. It must be believable, understandable, and put into terms to which all employees can relate. And it should be simple enough so that all employees can explain it to their mothers-in-law. The key questions to ask in developing a corporate and brand include:

1. Who are we as a company? What do we stand for and represent in the market to our potential customers?
2. What do we need to make our mark? What part of the market will we participate in or dominate?
3. How high do we want to shoot? What is the upper limit of our vision or our stretch goal/vision?
4. What do we believe in? What are the principles we believe will make our vision a reality?
5. Can we live our vision? Do we have the right people, resources, work ethic, and beliefs to realize our vision?

Out of this process the vision editorial director is responsible for taking all the ideas tossed out—the good, the bad, and the ugly—and distilling them down to three to ten alternative vision statements. There will be some redundancy between them and some capable of being researched on a more formal basis. Nevertheless, a transformational vision has at least four dimensions:

- It is *inspirational*. It moves stakeholders, prospective customers, your family. It sometimes makes people cry. We went to a meeting at which there was not a dry eye in an audience of 200 people as a hot new Internet brand vision was presented.
- It is *almost unattainable*. It makes everyone stretch. It makes sober, conservative competitors snort, "That's ridiculous!" when they hear it.
- It is *realistic*. There is a fit with company performance and current products and services. We are not going to climb an imaginary mountain.
- It offers a *competitive advantage*. This distinguishes the company or brand from every other in the industry. It connotes superiority and distinctiveness.

Each statement can be evaluated among a cross-sectional sample of key stakeholder groups. (The samples need not be large; the firm is not looking for methodological purism. The samples should represent critical targets—senior and middle management, employees, buyers, analysts, retailers.) The groups evaluate each vision on the 10 criteria, using the five questions given above, to come up with a total score.

QUESTIONS FOR DEVELOPING A MISSION STATEMENT

Once you have a vision statement, the next step is to develop a powerful mission statement. Like a brand vision, the mission is inspirational to employees and other stockholders. Unlike a vision, however, the mission is operationally oriented. Questions to help develop a mission statement include:

1. What business are we in with this brand? The specific definition of which product or service or associated value does the company provide for what served market?
2. Who are our customers? Which target group is the focus of our marketing efforts as a company?
3. What will the brand's business be in the future? As a result of the company's action defined in the mission, what kind of business will the company be in the future?
4. What is the value of the brand to the customers? What is the brand worth—what needs does it satisfy or value does it provide to our target customers?
5. How will we get it done? What internal or external resources can we use to achieve the mission?
6. What can be achieved in what time frame? We don't want to promise too much and we don't want to settle for too little.
7. What are all the good things that will accrue to our company and our stakeholders if we achieve our mission, and what's likely to happen if we fail?

A VISION SHOULD LIVE ON AND ON . . . AND ON

The working assumption in this whole process has to be that the vision will survive over a long period of time. Missions change; company or brand objectives change. Sales or profit objectives could even change from one quarter to the next, but what we're talking about here is institutionalizing the vision. It should become part of the culture of the company, of the lore.

That does not mean that a vision cannot change, but it will change only when circumstances change radically. One of those circumstances could be achieving the vision. At that point the company needs another vision. Most companies never quite succeed in their vision: having one continues to propel them onward and upward.

By the nature of many brand management systems—a relatively young executive becomes a brand manager, is in the job for two years, and moves on—it is difficult to inculcate a vision. Difficult but not impossible. One can have a multigeneration brand vision, one passed down from one brand manager to another.

Often we are asked, "What is the connection between the vision and mission and the rest of marketing strategy?" Take Green Mountain: "GME will become the dominant green brand in the rapidly deregulating energy industry and beyond—one of the most admired brands in America." Implicit in the vision and explicit in the mission statement are the elements of targeting and positioning that we will talk about in the next two chapters. A strong vision and a strong mission statement mirror aspects of the targeting and positioning strategy for the company or brand, because they should be a constant reminder of whom the firm is trying to impact and what it is trying to say about itself to differentiate itself from competitors. Implicit in the vision and mission is a sense of who should be your customers—a counterintuitive idea.

In other words, the vision, and certainly the mission, should not be developed in a vacuum. Management should have some idea of who the target is for the company or brand and how the company will be differentiated from competitors—its positioning.

To do this requires the kind of counterintuitive thinking and research we will discuss in the next two chapters. Sometimes the targeting and positioning work precedes the articulation of a vision and mission; sometimes it follows; sometimes they happen at the same time.

In either case, every company and every brand needs a mission and a vision. And to do this the marketing visionary needs to see what is not there.

So let's move on and talk about targeting.

7

Guess Again: Intuitively Appealing Targets Are Rarely the Most Profitable

When we began working for a large firm we'll call the Crispy Crunchy Corporation, we discovered that the firm's chief executive loved heavy buyers of ready-to-eat-cereal as a target market. "You've got to fish where the fish are biting," he advised us at an early meeting. "We want the twenty percent of the market that accounts for eighty percent of the sales. Let everyone else go after the small fry."

The marketing vice president added his two cents: "We don't see Crispy Crunchy as a niche player. We're going after the frequent buyers."

This makes a lot of sense to many marketers. If Crispy Crunchy knows the characteristics of heavy cereal buyers, they can go after Kellogg's, Post's, and General Mills' heavy users—a logic so many companies embrace that this is today the world's most popular, intuitively selected market target.

The problem with this logic is that heavy buyers are often price conscious (as they should be; they're buying so much), deal prone, and as a result, disloyal to any brand. Many heavy buyers are psychologically "locked" into a competitive brand and cannot be shaken loose by advertising, salesmanship, free samples, or bribes (i.e., rebates).

Heavy buyers, moreover, are usually far more heterogeneous than homogeneous. They all buy a lot of cereal (or gasoline or soft drinks or PCs or

Table 7-1   Target Group Profitability Analysis

| | (in Millions) | | |
| | $ Sales | $ Profit | ROI |
Target Type	Potential	Potential	Index
Women Managers	50	35	70
Generation Xers	72	42	79
Moderate Users	85	36	116
Macho Personality Types	107	45	88
Young Professionals	114	55	212
"Prestige" Conscious	125	72	158
$50,000+ Income	211	104	133
College Graduates	228	29	75
Frequent Travelers	260	26	60
Heavy Users	330	18	40

insurance—fill in your own category), but other than that, they are very diverse. Some have big families, so they buy a lot of cereal. Others love cereal. Others have no time to cook, so they eat cereal. When one looks at their motivations to determine what Crispy Crunchy might say to prospective buyers, and when one looks at demographics because that is how you buy media, heavy users are all over the place.

Unfortunately, our client stuck with the heavy user target, and their flagship brands, as a result, are in decline.

The following is an illustration of this phenomenon from an analysis done for a major financial services company. The client loved heavy credit card users, so we examined this group versus more than a thousand alternative target groups in terms of three criteria:

1. Sales potential (which reflects card usage patterns and average charges)
2. Profit potential (which takes into account the costs of winning and keeping each customer)
3. Return on investment (which indexes the ratio of profit potential to the expected mass media and direct response costs to achieve that potential)

Table 7-1 shows only ten of the thousand targets. Note that heavy users account for the lion's share of the sales potential ($330 million), yet only a small share of the profit potential ($18 million). The index, based on all thousand-plus targets, reveals that heavy user profitability is projected to be only 40 percent of the average target. Why?

The heavy users in this situation are simply too difficult to dislodge; they are happy with a competitor's card, largely because it is accepted everywhere they would want to use a card and because they are locked into the competitor's loyalty program. They are too sensitive to price promotion and too expensive to reach with media.

Does this mean that heavy users of a credit card—or heavy buyers in general—are automatically poor targets? Of course not. We can think of times in our consulting careers when heavy buyers turned out to be an excellent target. *There is, on the other hand, no reason to believe automatically, a priori, and without research that heavy users—or any other group, for that matter—are a great target.* Only hard thinking and thoughtful analysis can tell you whether they are or not. In contemporary marketing this would appear to be a very counterintuitive idea.

TARGETING IS ESSENTIAL TO A BRAND STRATEGY

Targeting is perhaps the single most important element in a marketing plan. It is essential to a "brand" or "brand positioning" strategy—you can't even write a positioning statement without knowing whom it is for. And all other plan elements—pricing, product features, and so on—depend on the brand (targeting and positioning) strategy. As Phil Kotler continues to remind us, "To get it right the first time, the most important steps are targeting and positioning. If you nail these two components of strategy, everything else follows."

Yet we find that targeting—and "market segmentation" generally—is one of the least well-developed skills in marketing today. Some marketers don't even seem to realize they need to specify a "market target." We've seen numerous marketing plans and attended numerous strategy meetings in which the question "Who is the target?" is not asked until we bring it up.

This is particularly true with many of the new Internet companies and Web site developers who obsess over maximizing the number of "eyeballs" at their site. When we suggest that not all eyeballs are created equal and that a firm should make efforts to assess which eyeballs would be most profitable to attract, people look at us as if we were three-eyed fish.

If traditional or cyberspace marketers discuss targeting strategy, it is often a throwaway part of the plan. One client manufactures a consumer product at the high end of its category. It is priced at a 250 percent premium over "average" category products and, not unreasonably, the brand has only a 2 percent market share in units sold. In dreaming of increased sales, the business's strategy was to make "category users—all users—aware and desirous of the benefits of this brand." We suggested that, while significant share and penetration increases were possible, this brand would never be for all users. It was simply too expensive and offered benefits not everyone wanted. Management's reaction? They were certainly not convinced and maybe just a little annoyed.

Other marketers do have a "targeting strategy," but it, too, is characterized by certain dreamlike qualities, more middle-of-the-night "vision" than anything fact based. One target that struck us as positively nutty when we first described it in our last book is the "non-buyers, non-users" of the product category. We told the story of a $300 room air cleaner that the management decided to promote to people who had never used or bought an air cleaner because they represent a huge percent of the population.

At one point in our careers, we regarded this target as unusual, but like a virus, its appeal has turned into an epidemic. On multiple occasions in the past two years, we have been advised by very smart people at very successful companies that this is whom they plan to go after. The CEO of a giant theme park company informed us that her new marketing target was ABRs—people who don't like theme parks and therefore don't go to them (i.e., *a*ttitudinal and *b*ehavioral *r*ejectors). Why? Because there are so many of them. "They can be converted," she argued, "because our park is so different." When we protested, she brushed off our warnings about the inefficiency of such an attempt. Her testosterone-to-marketing IQ ratio was simply too high for her to listen to reason.

An American brewer, concerned about declining beer sales for their flagship brand, has prepared new marketing plans that point to light buyers, non-preferrers as the key target for future activities. At a recent planning meeting, the vice president of marketing stepped up to a white board and constructed a 2×2 table. The columns were heavy and light drinkers; the rows, people who preferred his brand and those who preferred a competitor's. Taking a red pen, he slashed an X in the light drinker, non-preferrer box and said, "This is our future!" Heavy discussion followed, but he could not be dissuaded.

Here are more examples of intuitively appealing targets.

"Female heads of households who are time-pressured and yet, at the same time, want to meet their families' expectations of them as a wife, mother, keeper of the home." Doesn't this describe virtually all female heads of households?

"Consumers who appreciate the benefits of our superior product." This from a company whose product awareness is under 10 percent and positioning penetration less than 5 percent.

"15- to 22-year-olds who are just starting to form brand preferences . . . preferences they will keep for life!" This is a target that makes a lot of sense if you're in the fashion business or soft drink business and the customer has tremendous lifetime value. But this came from an automobile company that needs to figure out what to do with its middle-aged customers now!

"People who look just like our best customers." This from the CMO of a regional cellular telephone company that has achieved near-saturation levels among its upscale target audience and is unlikely to attract people from an audience it has not attracted in more than ten years of marketing communications.

One more example. We recently attended some focus groups conducted by an ad agency for one of our clients. They conducted three groups in one city in one night. The next day they appeared with a segmentation scheme, including nine segments. A vision must have appeared to them during the night. Moreover, they had intuited that one of the groups was much more appealing than the others and recommended it as the target to go after.

Fortunately, many marketers do conduct major research projects designed to develop, with serious quantitative data, a segmentation of the marketplace with the aim of finding one or more highly profitable targets to pursue. These projects are not inexpensive—they often cost $200,000 to $500,000 (or more). They take three to six months (sometimes longer). And they usually call for some significant commitment of time from the client and the consulting organization. And this does not mean the project will necessarily be successful.

SEGMENTATION CAN MOVE EVEN MORIBUND MARKETS

Targeting is knowing where to concentrate your forces. "To win a war you need to know where to attack," Dwight Eisenhower might have said to an audience of business managers. "We wouldn't have brought the Nazis to their knees if we had landed the Allied forces at Calais instead of the beaches of Normandy."

For two decades the major gasoline brands were in a state of *pax gasolina*—they went comfortably about doing their business, market shares changing only slightly from one year to the next. True, there were periodic price wars and promotions characterized by giving away NFL glasses and selling discounted Coca-Cola, but nothing so substantial as to wake the industry up from a deep complacency.

By the mid-1990s, however, new low-price brands began showing up everywhere, and the major brands started to work hard to differentiate themselves, with an aim toward gaining more margin from the business. In that context Mobil Corporation (now ExxonMobil), one of the most innovative marketers on the planet, commissioned a large-scale study to better understand its customers and prospects. The study results, reported in the *Wall*

Street Journal, form the basis for one of the most exciting marketing strategies ever launched—the Mobil Friendly Serve campaign.

The study found five distinct consumer groups, all roughly the same size numerically. We've changed the labels and the numbers for the sake of confidentiality.

Car Buffs are generally higher-income, middle-aged men who drive 25,000 to 50,000 miles a year . . . buy premium gasoline with a credit card . . . purchase sandwiches and drinks from the convenience store . . . will sometimes wash their cars at the car wash.

Loyalists are men and women with moderate to high incomes who are loyal to a brand and sometimes to a particular station . . . frequently buy premium gasoline and pay in cash.

Speedsters are upwardly mobile generation Xers . . . constantly on the go . . . live in their cars and snack heavily from the convenience store.

Soccer Moms are usually housewives who shuttle their children around during the day and use whatever gasoline station is based in town or along their route of travel.

Price Shoppers generally are not loyal either to a brand or to a particular station and rarely buy the premium line . . . frequently on tight budgets . . . and efforts to woo them have been the basis of marketing strategies for years.

But if Car Buffs and Loyalists represent only 38 percent of the population, as Figure 7-1 shows, they account for 77 percent of the potential profitability. Once Mobil knew the target, it knew whom to talk to and where to find them, how to communicate with them, in which media, about which products and services, at what price. As the *Journal* reported, "These targets want classier snacks from the convenience store; human contact; quality products; top-notch, quick service; privileges for loyal users; attendants who recognize them; and a nationally available brand. They also want a reasonably competitive price, but that's not the most important consideration."

Mobil addressed the needs of these two groups with Friendly Serve—sparkling clean restrooms, cappuccino in the convenience store, and a concierge to assist customers.

Just six weeks into the campaign, which Mobil supported with television, spot radio during drive time, newspapers, point-of-purchase, and billboards, the company found statistically significant gains in brand and advertising awareness versus the pre-wave of tracking. Respondents were playing back much stronger perceptions of Mobil as having attendants who go out of their

Figure 7-1   *Car Buffs Represent 20% of the Population—*
and Account for 45% of Potential Profitability

	Share of U.S. Households	Share of Station Spending	Share of Potential Profitability	ROI Index
Car Buffs	20%			
		34%	45%	275
Loyalists	18%			
Speedsters	21%	29%		
			32%	177
Soccer Moms	21%	16%		
		12%	9%	43
Price Shoppers	20%		8%	38
		9%	6%	30

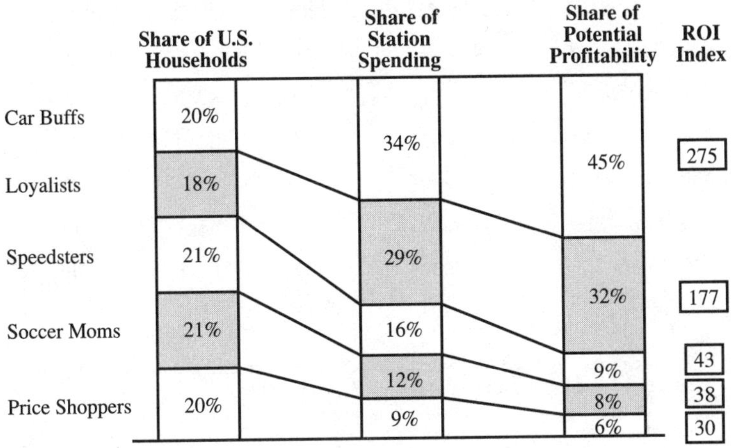

way to help, caring more about its customers, and having clean stations and restrooms. By the end of the test-marketing phase, Mobil year-to-day sales were up substantially—this in an industry in which a 1 percent share gain calls for a fiesta. Mobil rolled Friendly Serve into the rest of the country, communicating the idea of friendly, fast service in clean stations. Consumer perceptions of Mobil as the friendly, fast, clean service station rose markedly over a two-year period along with sales, until Mobil passed Shell as the number-one gas station in consumer preference. Sales and preference did not rise for Mobil for any other reason, and in fact, Mobil is the only major gasoline retailer to enjoy double-digit sales gains for three years running.

Meanwhile, Mobil was awash with letters, faxes, telephone calls, and e-mail from customers (mostly women) all over the country, thanking them for their great service and especially clean bathrooms. Writer after writer said that she would never again go to a competitive station. Among stations that fully implemented the program—keep in mind that most Mobil dealers operate independently—the results were nothing short of breathtaking, and for a time management, dealers, and customers alike were very happy.

In every product category—even those as unchanging as retail fuel—it is possible to segment customers and reveal very profitable target groups. In Table 7-2 we show the marketing costs per acquired customer in a range of product categories, from automobile dealerships looking for new buyers to utility companies looking for customers in the newly deregulated environments of California and Pennsylvania. (In these states you can choose among

Table 7-2   Marketing Costs Per Customer*

	Undifferentiated Market	All Prospects	A Good Target	An Optimal Target
Private Banking	$50,000+	$12,100	$6,300	$3,500
Software Services	1,000+	644	357	216
Automobile Dealerships	1,000+	325	150	99
Utility Companies	800+	417	132	75
Personal Computers	500+	366	155	83
Credit Cards	300+	182	88	49
Packaged Goods	80+	63	39	18

* These figures are based on a small number of cases in each product category and hence are meant to be illustrative rather than definitive.

as many as 40 different companies bringing electric power to your home or business; within five years almost all readers of this book in the United States will have the same opportunity. Electric power is going the way of the telephone.)

The table reveals the marketing costs per customer under four conditions. Since the figures are based on a small number of marketers in each product category, they should be read with caution—think of them as illustrative rather than definitive.

The first column represents the cost per customer in an "undifferentiated" market situation in which, for example, the marketer is going after all households or all small businesses.

The second column represents cases in which the marketer has narrowed the focus to all known prospects in the product category; for example, all people who plan on buying an automobile in the next three years, all people owning or considering owning a credit card, all people who would consider a private banking service, and so on.

The third column represents buyers who would be considered a good target. Not exceptional or optimal, but good. These might be people who buy new cars and whose current car is more than three years old. It might be people who carry only one major credit card and are unhappy with the current vendor. It might be people with a family income over $100,000 a year.

The final column represents the acquisition costs per customer among people who are considered to be an optimal market target—the best target that state-of-the-art research and counterintuitive thinking could find.

As you move from left to right, note that marketing costs drop rapidly and the optimal market target everywhere is approximately half as expensive to reach as a good target and a fraction of an undifferentiated, let's go-after-all-the-eyeballs-we-can-find marketing effort.

The objective of a great segmentation and great targeting is to find more optimal targets.

SEGMENTATION STUDIES — WHO NEEDS THEM?

The ExxonMobil experience and our marketing acquisition costs discussion notwithstanding, not all companies reap benefits from their segmentation efforts. More than once we have seen a segmentation study end badly for all concerned. The marketing managers pronounce the study "useless"; the research director at the client is embarrassed; the research supplier goes from the "approved vendor" list to the "never-use-again" list.

Why? First, there are usually numerous different "end users" at the client for a segmentation project, and nobody ever bothers to define all their different needs. Senior management wants to prioritize and focus everybody's efforts. Advertising management (and the agency) wants communications guidance. Product management wants help designing/enhancing the product. Sales management wants to prioritize the channels it pursues. The client list is extensive and often somewhat contradictory.

And each constituency's needs, and expectations are not modest. These projects are usually featured as the everything-you-always-wanted-to-know studies. The company expects the study to resolve all pent-up questions, needs, and visions. A prospective client once questioned us on what he could expect from a segmentation study. "Will it tell me how I reach the best consumers? How I talk to them? What products I should make for them? How I reach them in the store? What colors I should offer?" After 30 minutes of this, one of his associates finally asked, "Ira, do you want them to drive you home, too?"

But if it's not clear how the study will be used, the project is doomed. Or if it's not clear what "targeting" means to the company, how it can and should guide its efforts, it is also doomed. For example:

- The most common "application," of course, is for communications/advertising strategy. The study must produce segments with different, "exploitable" needs. This leads to a unique preemptible positioning strategy. It also must produce segments that are differentially reachable with media, which means different demographics or, better yet, different media exposure patterns.

- In business-to-business marketing, in which direct selling is still a way of life, the segmentation must be usable by the sales force—even as they're sitting in their cars. It must help salespeople classify prospects into "A," "B," or "C" categories and provide a powerful "selling script" so they know where and how to best spend their time.
- In direct marketing, sending mailings is still a way of life. The segmentation here must be applicable to databases so that these mailings (and other programs) can be segmented. Companies often accomplish this by appending to each respondent in the segmentation study information from the client's own databases and external databases, such as financial data, block-level census demographics, Prizm clusters, Polk data on automobile registrations, and so forth. The market researcher uses the appended data to develop an equation to predict membership in the optimal segment. Armed with this information, the marketer can begin to build lists of hot prospects.

But sometimes that doesn't happen. In the business-to-business cases, we know of many instances in which companies developed overly complex segmentation schemes, schemes understood mainly by the consultants and researchers who developed them. The sales force could not or would not use them. This is often the case when the result is a 10-, 12-, or sometimes an 18-segment solution. No one can remember the names, never mind the action plans, for that many segments.

In the direct-response situation, we are aware of several multimillion-dollar segmentation projects that failed to produce a scheme that could be applied to company databases. The company develops an elaborate segmentation of consumers using data from a large-scale consumer survey, but only after the fact someone asks, "By the way, how can we classify our customers or our lists into these segments?" They cannot, and by then it's too late. The point in all this is to make sure you understand the needs and expectations of all potential users of the segmentation study.

Some advertising agencies—BBDO, Fallon-McElligott, and Leo Burnett, for example—make sure that they are intimately involved with segmentation work, including their creative, media, account, and even design (logo/packaging) groups.

Some marketers, such as AT&T and Microsoft, recognize that their sales force will use a segmentation scheme only if it takes advantage of existing databases (e.g. Dun & Bradstreet) and goes beyond them only in a very straightforward way (five additional variables, three of which can be ascertained without even entering a prospect's office and two by talking by phone to the receptionist).

Some direct marketers, especially retailers, are connecting their list segmentations with their surveys/studies. Saks Fifth Avenue made sure that its segmentation is based on customer "needs" (as measured in a survey), account data (as appended to the survey data), and block-level census data (which can be purchased easily and cheaply). Saks can classify customers into segments—segments that differ in terms of "needs" and demographics, as well as account history—using account data only.

Segmentation Approaches — What You Use Dictates What You'll Get

Not looking ahead to end-user needs and how the segmentation will be applied is one problem. Another is that the specific methodology (also known as model, algorithm, or procedure) that researchers employ to divide up the world often leads to suboptimal solutions. Table 7-3 shows the most common segmentation approaches taken by practitioners today. It also shows the pros and cons of each. Since the cons often outweigh the pros, it's troubling.

One of the most intriguing aspects to all this is that the segmentation approach is often determined intuitively, a priori, before the data is even collected. Indeed, the data collected is driven by the a priori segmentation and the belief systems of the firm commissioned to do the research.

Until a few years ago, if you retained McKinsey management consultants or BBDO to do the work, you almost automatically got a "heavy buyer" segmentation. This remains the most popular approach to segmentation. Other companies segment in terms of gender, age, or income. Consider the packaged-goods world's traditional fascination with 18- to 49- (now 25- to 54-) year-old women, which has persisted for more than over four decades. Financial services companies, on the other hand, are fixated on income, $100,000 in family income, to be more specific. (With every financial services company chasing this small segment, is it any wonder that most are relatively unsuccessful?)

A current favorite popping up all over is "brand loyalty groups," in which the world is divided into the degree of attachment that a customer or prospect has with your product or service. Other consultants might try to solve your problems with syndicated research and standardized "lifestyle" segments. And if you call any number of "custom research" firms and ask for a segmentation study, they almost always assume you want a "needs-based" cluster analysis. Because of its widespread use, we should say more.

The genesis of needs-based segmentation can be traced back to the 1960s, when it was popular to employ statistical analysis to group people into differ-

Table 7-3   *Pros and Cons of Different Modes of Segmentation*

Common Approaches	Pros	Cons
Need/Benefit Segmentation Example: Five types of PC buyers: the performance oriented, the brand conscious, the price shoppers, the word processors, the Internet surfers	• A so-called "natural" segmentation because buyer needs seem so simple, so basic • Intellectually interesting • People love to name the groups • Good for new product ideas	• Needs should not be mistaken for problems Different techniques for measuring needs yield different outcomes • Common approaches understate the true importance of intangible attributes and benefits • Generally, the groups have similar brand preferences, consumption patterns, demographics, and media exposure patterns
Behavioral Segmentation Example: 32% of decision-makers in small to medium-size businesses account for 74% of all the purchases in this segment of the market	• Ability to pinpoint a small group who account for much of category volume • Simple and capable of being understood by everyone in the organization • Because it's based on only 1 or 2 questions, the segmentation can be easily found in other databases	• Heavy buyers are often price conscious or psychologically locked into competitive brands • Product usage is often generally only modestly related to other variables of interest • Generally, the groups have similar brand preferences, consumption patterns, demographics, and media exposure patterns • Little understanding of the differential needs of the target compared to other targets – they are more heterogeneous than homogeneous
Demographic Segmentation Example: 25- to 54-year-old women	• Simple and easily understood by everyone in the organization • People you're familiar with: your wife, daughter, next-door neighbor • Media services and agencies find it easy to work with • Groups are differentially reachable in media	• Groups not very different in any other way, including brand preferences • Not being different, they are an inefficient media buy because of the problem of heterogeneity • Little understanding of different needs
Competitive Attack Segmentation Example: We're going after Budweiser drinkers	• Ability to pinpoint a small group who account for much of category volume • Simple and capable of being understood by everyone in the organization • Because it's based on only 1 or 2 questions, the segmentation can be easily found in other databases • Appeals to the testosterone rush	• Going after "enemy brand users" is like targeting the enemies' strongest defensive positions • Generally, the groups have similar brand preferences, consumption patterns, demographics, and media exposure patterns • Little understanding of different needs

ent categories based on their personalities. Researchers would interview a large cross section of consumers and administer a half-hour-long battery of personality items. The researchers used a now-defunct statistical model called Inverse Factor Analysis to put respondents into groups with names such as "The Anxious," "The Depressed," "The Irritables," "The Aggressives," and "The Cheerfuls." The results were almost always fascinating. Sometimes companies called in credentialed psychologists to help interpret these groups and detect their hidden meanings for managers. We once brought in the world-famous Dr. Ernest Dichter.

Sadly, as intellectually stimulating as these groups proved to be, they rarely differentiated consumers in terms of buyer behavior. In their buying patterns, "The Irritables" were very similar to "The Cheerfuls" and to everyone else in terms of everything but personality. This disappointing finding prompted the need for a different approach to segmentation, which was solved by Dr. Russell Haley, at that time research director of Grey Advertising and later a professor of marketing at the University of New Hampshire. By the early '70s Haley had demonstrated that segmenting markets in terms of consumer needs was superior to segmenting them in terms of psychographic characteristics. He laid the foundation for what has come to be known as 'benefit segmentation."

Haley's procedure was to ask a large cross section of buyers to rate 50 to 100 different benefits (e.g., stops tooth decay) and attributes (e.g., contains fluoride) of a toothpaste in terms of importance (extremely important to not at all important). He then employed statistical analyses to group people into "benefit segments" (i.e., segments looking for different things in a product). The beauty of his procedure was that it was so logical—find out what different segments want—and could be applied to every type of business: consumer and industrial, product and service.

In retrospect, it is no surprise that this methodology has reigned supreme as the preferred segmentation methodology for three decades. Benefit segments have been researched and revealed in product categories as diverse as airline travel, alcoholic beverages, credit cards, computer software, frozen microwave entrees, heavy industrial equipment, lawn mowers, office equipment, small sailboats, soft drinks, telecommunications, and tractors.

Segmentation studies turn out to be a good example of the need for counterintuitive thinking, since each of these approaches makes a lot of sense on the surface. Six months later it may be a different story. In fact, we have been called in several times by companies that conducted a large-scale segmentation study and, though initially happy with it, were thoroughly disappointed a year later and wanted advice.

A typical example was an association of beef producers. They sought to stay "in touch" with consumers' changing food attitudes and behaviors. They commissioned a large survey of American adults, and the research vendor (with some encouragement by the client, to be sure) proceeded to sort the respondents into five segments based on their answers to 40 "agree/disagree" statements, such as "I worry more and more about eating properly," "I always read nutrition labels," "Fat calories are really bad for you," and the like.

The groups that were formed seemed to make intuitive sense: there were three groups that, to varying degrees, said they were health conscious and two groups that generally didn't care. Made perfect sense to everyone. The researcher gave cute names to each group and everyone was happy. One year later, according to industry sales data, beef consumption had stayed fairly strong. The association conducted another survey just to update their consumer data. This data suggested that the health-conscious segments had increased significantly. That's odd, they thought—beef consumption should be down.

Another year goes by. Beef sales not only remain strong but increase slightly. The association conducts another "tracking" survey. The health-conscious segments have increased in size again. We get a call from the director of the association. He's perplexed and his members are disgruntled: they're not unhappy that sales are up, but they want to know what's going on.

The association sent us the raw data from the surveys, including the algorithms that were used to create the original five-group solution. As we've seen in many other cases, the researchers (and client) assumed that certain consumer attitudes toward beef were fundamental to the situation, and without considering other characteristics (such as age or family size), they used those attitudes to create the "clusters."

A counterintuitive approach was to test to see which of the "agree/disagree" attitude statements were, in fact, related to beef consumption. What we found startled the client: of the 40 statements, only half were correlated with beef consumption at all. That is, on 20 of the items there was no difference in beef consumption between the people who agreed with the statement and those who disagreed.

It seemed counterintuitive, but then again, we have all been to a barbecue at which somebody, after chatting about how he is "concerned more and more about eating properly," goes on to stuff his face with two giant cheddar burgers. The association's segmentation scheme included many attitudes that, it turned out, did not relate to beef consumption. If an item is unrelated to beef consumption, why was it included in the study?

We continued our testing, investigating the full range of demographics and behaviors to see how these characteristics related to beef consumption. Not surprisingly, we found several other "variables" that are related to beef consumption (e.g., family size/number of children) and created a new segmentation for the association. As inputs, it used attitudes *and* demographics *and* behaviors. Significantly, we only used variables that had been shown to correlate with beef consumption. We recast the original study and the two waves of tracking data. The segment sizes (and the key "predictors" that we identified) now moved in a way that was consistent with sales data. The association had the research it needed: sales could be understood, even predicted, by the segmentation. Just as important, the association could identify which consumers to focus on when they planned marketing activities.

Many of the business-to-business segmentations used by companies today are similarly disappointing. The most common situation we find is a targeting strategy based solely on intuition, with no research whatsoever. Marketing management, often following the judgments of the sales force, segments the market into size bands (e.g., above or below 500 employees in the company). Intuitively this seems right, since it is clear to almost anyone that big customers can really drive your business. What may be less obvious is which specific "size" variable to use: employees, sales revenues, number of locations, something else? And if it is best to use, say, number of employees, is 500 the right number? What about 100? What do you classify as a "small business" or even a "home office"? Less than 10 employees? Less than 5? Unfortunately, in all too many cases management does not have good answers to these questions.

Another common approach to segmenting the "business" market is by industry sector, which many call "vertical markets." Again, this has a lot of intuitive appeal: Aren't retail/wholesale businesses different from manufacturers? Wouldn't they both be different from a financial service? But again, when asked for evidence to support this view, management very often has no hard data.

Besides their intuitive appeal, there is one other reason why segmenting by size and industry sector is so popular: historically, these approaches were just plain easy to implement. There were (and still are) many directories that list companies by SIC codes and number of employees. But fortunately, times have changed. There are now numerous databases that can tell a marketer a variety of characteristics about a company (or an individual establishment/location of a company).

A project in the computer industry illustrates how well-directed research can provide actionable targeting guidance (and settle a lot of internal parochial arguments). At the time the company was number two in sales worldwide. It had optimized its manufacturing very, very well and was able to produce (and lead the trend toward) reasonably priced hardware, particularly in the growing "server" sector. Its strategy in the business market was aligned by "vertical markets" (industry sectors) and company size in terms of annual sales. Management realized, however, that this approach only really worked in identifying the huge manufacturers as being a distinct target but wasn't helpful for the remaining 95 percent of the companies.

We conducted a large-scale survey of individual locations/"establishments," not "enterprises" (e.g., several different General Motors installations could, conceivably, fall in the sample). We asked for the person "most knowledgeable about computer decisions for that location." We asked him or her where the decision-making "power" lay—with him or her, at corporate headquarters, or equally for both parties. We then interviewed at the directed location. (In the "equally" cases we alternated between the location and the HQ and ultimately weighted these interviews to compensate for their "50 percent power" level.)

In interviews lasting 25 to 30 minutes we asked questions about the number of PCs, servers, and so forth at the location; the use of LAN, WAN, and the like; and the next 12 months' purchasing plans. We investigated decision-making processes, including the key attributes desired in hardware and software suppliers. We audited usage and gathered perceptions of different manufacturers, including our client. Significantly, we assessed "openness" to buying our client's brand in the future.

After the interviews we went to the database company our client used and obtained the "corpographics" and other characteristics that were known and kept on file about companies and establishments, including the ones in our sample. For our analysis we considered 100-plus characteristics we might use to segment the market, some shown in Table 7-4. We then tested these to see which ones predicted market behavior, particularly "openness" to—and potential profitability to—our client.

The first thing we learned was that size is a critical variable. Big locations have considerably more buying power than small ones. But we never know which size variable is key. On this occasion we found that the number of desk workers (not just "employees") was the critical variable. We also found that the company required four size bands (not just the two the client had been using) to understand different buying patterns, needs, and brand preferences.

With that settled, we went on, within size band, to test the remaining variables. We found that industry sector explained very little. You could not predict anything about a location's computer hardware needs based on its SIC code. We did find two variables that were very telling—whether there was a LAN on-site and, separately, if a sales/marketing function was a large part of the location's employee force. It is possible to know these things about a

*Table 7-4   Characteristics That Might Be Used to Segment the
Commercial PC Market*

Database Variables	Survey Variables
Corpographic Variables	**Organization Variables**
• Number of employees at location	• Marketing vs. sales vs. manufacturing driven
• Total number of company locations	• Technological adaptation
• International locations	• Risk orientation
• Number of years at location	• Role of innovation
• Number of desk workers	• Corporate decision-making processes
• Annual sales and sales growth	• Centralized vs. decentralized
• Industry sector	• Cost/budget conscious
• Functions on-site (e.g., sales, production)	• Optimism vs. pessimism toward the future
Product Category Variables	**Decision-maker Variables**
• Number of PCs and servers on-site	• Gender and age
• Number of mini- or mainframes	• Quality and quantity of education
• LAN/WAN	• Business experience
• Key software/applications used	• Status in the organization
• Recent hardware purchases	• Decision-making power
• Recent software purchases	• Decision-making style
• Importance in driving the business	• Computer background
• Budget allocated to category purchases	• Involvement in product category

location without interviewing; certain database vendors collect this information and resell it.

Using these three variables—number of desk workers, usage of LAN, and presence of sales force—we created six segments. They were different in corpographics, computing needs, decision-making process, and potential economic value for our client. In fact, three of the segments accounted for about 40 percent of all the business establishments in the U.S. and over 80 percent of our client's potential profitability.

Just as important, company employees found this segmentation easy to use. A salesperson could determine which locations were the best targets without having to visit each one. In this case management's "intuition" had been that identifying locations to target was a complex issue, depending upon numerous industry-specific characteristics, and, even then, largely a "mystery"; salespeople still had to knock on a lot of doors to find "hot prospects." Not so!

SEGMENTATION—A PROCESS YOU CAN BELIEVE IN

Fortunately, we can learn from our mistakes. This seems particularly apropos of segmentation studies. The disappointing experiences we have heard about (and, in our earlier lives, been complicit in) have led us to a segmentation methodology—a process—that is guaranteed to produce satisfying and useful end results.

The first step, as discussed earlier, is to thoroughly understand who in the client or agency will use the study results and how they plan/hope to use them. This understanding will have direct bearing on the following two research issues.

First, what is the number and nature of the variables we can use in the ultimate segmentation scheme? Can we use numerous variables (e.g., 20 to 30) in a complex algorithm, or do we need to limit ourselves to a handful (5 to 10) from which we would construct a fairly simple scoring scheme? And increasingly important, can we include database variables—customer account data, third-party data, or block-level census data?

Second, what does the company want this segmentation to "predict"? What are we trying to explain? Brand preference, openness to switching accounts, vulnerability to leave our customer base? High versus low consumption of the product/service category? Which types of consumers are going to the different channels of distribution? Overall profitability? Only by understanding what the segment is designed to predict can we even begin to think about segment differences in ROI.

With benefit of these discussions and decisions, the path to a useful segmentation comprises several steps summarized in Figure 7-2. These are:

- "Hypothesizing" the wide range of variables to be considered. We have found that from a typical in-person interview with a consumer, we might easily have 250 or more "independent" or "predictor" variables, including 15 to 20 demographics, 40 to 50 motivations, 20 to 30 attitudes and values, 20 to 40 behaviors, 20 to 30 media habits, and numerous database variables. We get creative with certain variables (e.g., your income relative to other people in your age group, something we do not ask directly) to create even more variables. Factor analysis or latent class analysis can then be used to form a more "robust" set of prediction variables.
- Testing all these candidates to see which ones are related to current and potential profitability. A few surrogates for potential profitability include an openness to our client's brand. We don't simply want to predict who has bought the client's product or service in the past—we want to see who might buy in the future. We also need to know how much

Figure 7-2   A Segmentation and Targeting Process

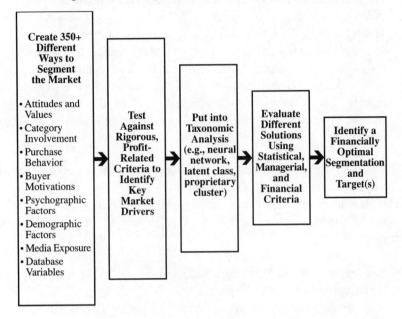

buyers buy and how much they spend on what. The goal here is to assess the current and potential profitability of all customers and prospects. The task here is to identify the key variables about customers (whether individuals or companies) that best predict their economic value in the marketplace. In business-to-business marketing we typically are looking for fewer "predictors" because the segmentation will be fairly straight-forward, such as by salespeople or searching D&B databases. In consumer research, where the company will utilize sophisticated media plans or database modeling (or both), we can afford to entertain larger number of variables.

- Grouping consumers/customers into segments based on their answers to the 5 to 25 variables. You can use a variety of different statistical methods here. We've developed a fondness for neural network analysis and our own variant of cluster analysis and have discovered that the SAS Institute's new data-mining package is a wonderful tool for investigating alternatives. Be wary of off-the-shelf algorithms, however, such as traditional cluster analysis, which is hugely impacted by stuff you don't even want to think about (such as the order in which respondents are read into the database). In a 1,000-person survey, entering people ordered 1 to

1,000 results in a very different cluster solution than entering people ordered 1,000 to 1. If you think we're kidding, try it with your own data.
- Testing again. This time we are looking at numerous segmentation schemes. We apply the same criteria we used earlier: Are we seeing different brand preferences? Different consumption levels? Different channels? Ultimately, different levels of profitability? But we add other criteria that relate to the "manageability" of the approach. Which scheme is most easily understood? Is this approach more or less easy to implement?

Once an appropriate segmentation is selected, the next question to ask is which market target (or targets) is (are) best.

The ultimate objective, of course, is to find the optimal target for the client, not just an interesting segmentation. Our definition of "optimal target" includes:

- A segment of the market that is sufficient in size to merit disproportionate attention (e.g., 10 to 30 percent)
- A segment whose "economic value" or potential profitability to the client is considerably greater than its size (e.g., 50 to 70 percent)
- A segment that is growing rather than shrinking over time
- A segment that is different demographically/corpographically and therefore differentially reachable with media, by salespeople, via channels, via direct response programs, and so on
- A segment whose "problems/needs/wants" are distinctly different from those of other segments

For a list of all 10 criteria that we routinely employ to evaluate, see Table 7-5.

The counterintuitive process described here is guaranteed to produce these end results. Why are we so sure? We know the segments—and the target—will be different in terms of demographics because we have used key demographics to form the segments. We know the segments will be different in terms of buyer motivations and problems because we have used them to form the segments. And we know the segments will be different in terms of brand preference, consumption, and profitability—and one segment will be considerably better than all the others on this—because we selected only those demographics, attitudes, and behaviors that discriminate on these variables and drive profitability.

The process takes a little longer than the usual segmentation study, and it costs a little more. But it is dramatically more effective than just guessing

Table 7-5   How to Identify the Optimal Target

1. Start by rejecting knee-jerk approaches outright; they don't work.

2. Carefully consider hundreds, thousands, hundreds of thousands of alternative targets based on variables hypothesized to drive profitability in a particular product category.

3. Evaluate each target in terms of criteria related to profitability:

   Decision-making power – The more responsibility a target has for making sales decisions, the more valuable it is.

   Sales potential – The more a target buys or uses the product category, the more valuable it is.

   Growth potential – The more a target group is growing, the more valuable it is.

   Lifetime value – The more a target is expected to buy over its lifetime, the more valuable it is.

   Retention potential – The more likely it is that a target can be economically sustained and therefore retained over time, the more valuable it is.

   Common motivations – The more homogeneous and preemptible a target's needs are, the more valuable it is.

   Problem potential – The bigger the problem the target has that the marketer can solve, the more valuable it is.

   Responsiveness – The more a target group responds to a company's marketing efforts, the more valuable it is.

   Media exposure patterns and media costs – The easier and less expensive it is to reach a target in media, the more valuable it is.

   Findability – The more easily a target can be identified in databases, the more valuable it is.

who the best target is, e.g., deciding intuitively that heavy users are the best target because they buy so much, or nonusers are attractive because there are so many of them, or thinking, as Procter & Gamble seems to, that 25- to 54-year-olds are the best group because this is the target they've always gone after. It is dramatically better than, like Amazon.com, having no clear target at all. It is, in short, better to spend the company's money to identify a profitable target than wasting money on diffused, expensive, and ineffective marketing efforts.

Positioning: . . .
And That Would Mean What?

In December, we were at a client meeting in the Boston area, and during a break one of the executives, a guy in his early fifties, asked, "Did you see the Patriots' game the other night?" We said we had and he said, "Okay, here's a trivia question for you. What's the name of the stadium they play in?"

We said, "Foxboro Stadium."

"Okay, here's the real question. What was the name before it was Foxboro Stadium?"

We said, "Sullivan Stadium. Sullivan owned the team."

"Very good; not many people know that."

We said, "Here's one for you. What was its name before Sullivan Stadium?" He didn't know there had been an earlier name, so we answered the question for him; "Schaefer Stadium."

"Schaefer Stadium? Where did they ever get the name Schaefer? Who's Schaefer?"

We said, "It was built with money from the Schaefer Brewing Company when Schaefer was the number-one brand of beer in the East."

"No kidding. I didn't know that."

We said, "Do you remember anything about Schaefer beer advertising?"

"Schaefer beer. . . . I haven't seen Schaefer beer for years. Do they still make it?"

We said, "Yeah, they do, somewhere."

"Schaefer beer advertising. . . . Oh, my God, I do: 'The One Beer To Have When You're Having More Than One.'"

We walked back into the conference room, where perhaps 15 people were waiting. Peter said to the group, "I've got a question from *Who Wants to Be a Millionaire*. Kevin's going to hum some music from a TV commercial. Don't say anything, but raise your hand if you know what he's humming."

Kevin began to hum, and the next thing we knew, five guys were singing, "Schaefer is the one beer to have . . . when you're having more than one!" We found this amazing. We asked, "What's the message here? What was Schaefer trying to communicate about the brand?" The whole room went into a buzz, discussing heavy-user strategies. Since Schaefer had not run that campaign in years, we were bowled over.

Then we said, "Okay, now tell us something about Budweiser or Miller advertising today. If Schaefer was the one beer to have when you're having more than one, what's Miller? What's Budweiser?"

Confusion in the room. "Well, Budweiser, you've got some frogs . . . lizards."

"Miller, I don't think I've seen any advertising for Miller."

"In the old days, weekends were made for Michelob."

"And now Corona is using snakes. I guess they want to be more like Bud."

We said, "Tell me something about Bud, other than frogs and lizards."

More confusion. "I don't know."

"Bud used to be 'The King of Beers.'"

"August Busch owns the company."

Somebody said, "Isn't Miller the Champagne of Bottled Beers?"

We said, "You guys are in a time warp. Forget the past. What do Bud and Miller stand for today? What's their positioning?"

More bewilderment. "I don't think they say anything about the brand."

"Bud's just frogs and lizards."

"Oh, yeah, and Miller has this dopey-looking fat guy doing the twist."

Schaefer's "The One Beer To Have When You're Having More Than One" is an illustration of great positioning! What is a wonder is that today so few brands have a clear positioning. Did brand managers skip the class?

The Difference Between Vision, Mission, and Positioning

As we discussed in Chapter 6, a vision is an inspirational statement of what you expect to do with the company or the brand. A vision is Henry V telling his rag-tag band facing overwhelming odds, "We're going to conquer France."

The mission is the operational prescription for what you need to do to accomplish the vision. We're going to achieve the vision by persuading every Frenchman that we have the weaponry to strike them dead in the field. We are going to hold back until the very last moment and then shoot every arrow in our quivers.

The positioning is simply a one- or two-sentence statement—even a word—that is not about vision and not about mission as such, but is a message you want to imprint in the minds of customers and prospects. It is about your brand, product or service and how it is different from—and therefore better than—the competition's. In the 15th century the positioning might have been "We've got the longbow" or "We have better technology to fight battles than you." Today it could be "Safety" or "Enhanced Performance." Or Green Mountain Energy's "Power provided by the raging rivers of North America, the prevailing winds, and the sun."

Examples of long-running positioning strategies for companies or brands include:

Easy to use—Apple
Exceptional performance for driving enthusiasts—BMW
Softness—Charmin tissue
Authentic, real, original—Coke
Guaranteed next-day delivery—Federal Express
Wholesome family entertainment—Disney
Improves the quality of life—GE
Strength—Hefty plastic bags
Accepted everywhere—Visa
Safety—Volvo
For the youthful, hip generation—Pepsi
Thrills and excitement for preteens and adults—Universal Studios
Nutritious, low-fat, low-calorie food—Healthy Choice
Pure, clean, and natural—Ivory soap
Good value for family meals—Taco Bell

Your positioning encapsulates elements of your vision and mission directed toward the most profitable targets. Marketers and advertising agency people have defined positioning in different ways:

"It's the story you want to plant in people's minds about your product and why it's better."

"It's the solution your product offers to address the buyer's problem."

"It's the bundle of attributes and benefits you want to tell people about or,

Figure 8-1   Positioning Strategy Evaluation

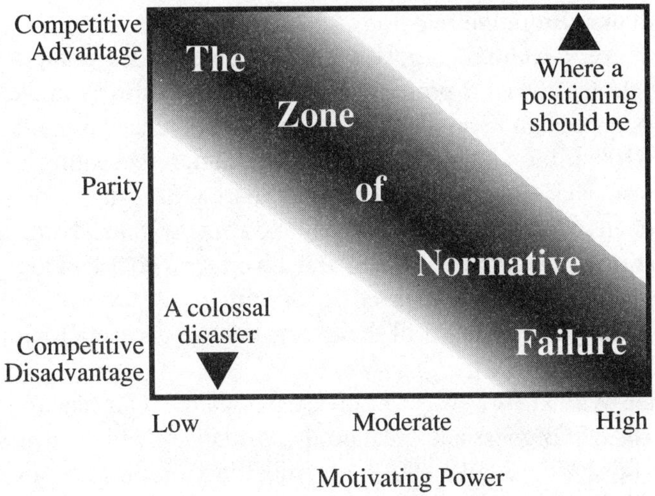

simply, your unique selling proposition—the reason why someone should buy your product rather than someone else's."

All these definitions recognize that in a cluttered environment where buyers have little time or inclination to ponder product decisions, it is highly advantageous for a marketer to stand for something important, to be remembered for something significant. At its core, positioning is the reason why people buy one product rather than another; they believe it offers greater value or strength or prestige or fun or safety or nutrition (or some other element or combination of elements) than something else.

To have a powerful positioning is clearly a good thing. Figure 8-1 illustrates where a positioning should be, in the upper right corner, where the brand has both a comparative advantage and the motivating power is high. Note the zone of normative failure. This is where most brands or companies are likely to be found. It is not enough to have a comparative advantage with a property low in motivating power (putting you in the upper left corner) or to have no advantage on a compelling proposition; you need both.

A WEAK POSITIONING CAN GET YOU FIRED

Eckhard Pfeiffer, the CEO of Compaq, and John MacDonough, the CEO of Miller Brewing, were replaced in the spring of 1999 for similar reasons: ailing company performance, disappointing sales and market share growth, and questionable returns on huge advertising campaigns. All problems, we would argue, of weak positioning.

Pfeiffer never developed a positioning for Compaq the company. Rather, Compaq's strategy was to promote lots of superb products, matching their competitors' prices. In February 1999, Compaq announced a new brand strategy and a $300 million global advertising program, representing a 50 percent increase over what it had been spending. Andrew Salzman, Compaq's vice president of advertising and worldwide brand strategy, told advertising industry publications that Compaq's brand and advertising goal was to promote its "bigness" and the depth of its product offerings. "We want Compaq to be known as a computing partner of the Internet age, a pacesetter with a can-do spirit," he said.

"Compaq. Who knew?" was the advertising theme. Our reaction is "Compaq. Who cares?" Bigness and great products, many of which buyers perceive as commodities, do not give buyers a compelling reason to choose Compaq over Dell, IBM, Hewlett-Packard, and other PC makers that are also big and sell great products.

Miller, too, spent heavily on advertising campaigns as part of its branding strategy, but with disappointing results. Beer industry reports showed that Miller Lite's growth rate lagged behind its low-calorie rivals, and Genuine Draft continues to languish.

Indeed, one Miller Genuine Draft ad campaign never saw the light of day. The company shelved it after Miller wholesalers panned it. Even worse was a Miller Lite campaign targeting 20-something beer drinkers that did air; the ads made no mention of the brand. Think of it: a multimillion-dollar campaign with no mention of the brand.

MacDonough and Pfeiffer failed to realize that Miller's "Dick" and Compaq's "Who knew?" were not brand-positioning strategies. Without a strong positioning, a brand turns into a commodity. And people tend to buy commodities on the basis of price.

Happily, both Compaq and Miller have seen the light and are beginning to move in the right direction.

Since in the 1980s marketers have faced a major problem: effectively managing the fragmented remnants of mass markets that negligent branding and positioning strategies created. In many categories marketers must now attempt to stitch together targets that appear to be hopelessly fragmented by race, age, lifestyle, and other factors into new versions of "mini-mass" markets. At the same time the new reality means abandoning time-honored targeting techniques, media-market matching, and ways to determine communications strategy efficiency.

The relatively recent explosion of choices that marketers provide has become, in many respects, their nemesis as brands have found it difficult to hold on to their core identities. Much of this was (and remains) the fault of marketers' short-term orientation beginning in the 1980s and continuing with a vengeance in the 1990s. Marketers pursued a policy of short-term promotional sales gains at the cost of long-term brand identity and equity building.

At the same time many shortsighted marketers have made it simple for consumers to "trade down and tune out" venerable brand names. Marketers have switched dollars from image building and customer retention to trade and consumer promotions and produced cookie-cutter advertising. A new breed of shoppers has emerged in response, the "brand experimental" or the "brand irrelevant" consumer.

For these shoppers brand proliferation all but obscures brand differences in many categories. The average American supermarket carried 9,000 items in 1975; today that figure tops 30,000. Every year in the last five, marketers have launched more than 20,000 new products into U.S. supermarkets and drugstores.

If product and brand proliferation and the psychological effects of "hyper choice" in the marketplace have forced brands into parity, even commodity status, and if the positioning strategies of competing brands in the same category are more similar than different, it would not be surprising to find—as our research has found—that few companies have anything like an effective positioning.

"Positioning," wrote Ries and Trout in their classic book on the topic, "is what you do in the mind of the prospect. That is, you position the product in the mind of the prospect." This has a corollary: If *you* don't position the product in the mind of the prospect, the prospect will do it for you.

WHAT CONSUMERS ASSOCIATE WITH BRANDS—NOT MUCH

Yet if most products and services are positioned at all, it appears to be in the minds of their marketing managers, not in the minds of their customers (the only place where it counts). We've investigated a broad range of product categories, asking consumers and industrial buyers to tell us about positioning strategies on an unaided (that is, completely volunteered), partially aided (with some clues), and fully aided (completely prompted) basis.

We've surveyed a national cross section of buyers in categories as varied as ground coffee and soft drinks, financial services and airlines, copying machines and personal computers, and asked what each of the five leading brands in the category stand for—what they communicate about themselves that makes them different from other brands. Fewer than 8 percent of respondents associate anything with the brands that we would begin to call positioning, clearly a failing, "F" performance on this indicator of market success. Thus Budweiser and Miller are typical performers.

This dismal performance is not consistent across all products. In categories in which advertisers spend heavily on advertising, such as automobiles, pharmaceuticals, computer hardware and software, and soft drinks, and in categories with relatively few dominant brands, unaided awareness of a positioning is higher—about 15 percent—but still bad. We'd give a "D" grade here.

Most people do not pay much attention to most brands; they have more on their minds than brand names and what they stand for. To help people recall, therefore, researchers give them "tracer elements," a slogan or the essential positioning statement. They then ask, "Which brand of (say, automobile) do you associate with (the positioning statement)?" Or "Which brand of (automobile) says (the slogan) in their advertising?" For example, "Which brand of automobile do you associate with 'engineered to be great cars'?" Or "Which brand of truck uses the slogan 'like a rock' in their advertising?" Even giving the positioning/message or the slogan, respondents correctly connect the slogan with the brand only about 16 percent of the time. That's pretty disappointing.

What happens when you give people the brand and its positioning, message, or slogan and ask if they've ever heard it? "Have you ever heard Chevy trucks use the slogan 'Built Like a Rock'?" Or "Have you heard or seen any Burger King advertising in which they say 'Have It Your Way'?" What happens if you describe a dominant visual in the execution and ask people if they've seen it? "Have you seen the 'swoosh'?" Or "Have you seen friendly hands?"

The average, fully prompted, completely recognition-based positioning awareness score for the top five brands in most product categories is less than 30 percent, at best a "C" grade. And this number, like all the indicators of positioning penetration, is in a state of decline. Advertisers and their agencies appear to have either forgotten the importance of a strong positioning strategy or lost the ability to imprint one. Positioning today is a lost art, and the decline of American brands is the result.

Some readers may feel that a 30 percent score is fine; it suggests successful penetration. But the problem is that research studies yield these high scores only when they provide consumers with a full set of clues of what's in the advertising and ask whether they have heard or seen the clues. This is not a measure of what consumers carry around in their heads; it's a measure of whether people self-report having seen or heard the advertising when you describe it to them. These self reports can be extravagantly misleading. We have found people's recall scores for ads that *never* ran are, on average, about half as high as for ads that have run; sometimes they're even higher. Thus, when we talk about a 30 percent positioning awareness, much of it is false awareness; it does not reflect genuine campaign penetration.

If the recognition-based measures were prompted at point-of-sale by packaging or shelf talkers or other materials that remind consumers of the advertising they've seen—bringing it back into consciousness even if not fully imprinted—one could argue the advertising is still a positive thing. But the fact is that most packaging and shelf talkers today are not integrated with the advertising campaigns. Nothing a consumer pushing his or her cart down the supermarket aisle will see on the shelf could jar memories of advertising that would produce recognition numbers comparable to what research suggests.

For Budweiser and Miller and thousands of brands like them, companies seem to advertise nothing more than a name. True, it's important to reinforce the brand name; it's also important to position the product in the consumer's mind.

LOOK, MA, NO STRATEGY

Positioning today seems to be a counterintuitive idea. Consider Super Bowl Sunday 2000, a great game interrupted by mostly idiotic advertising, largely for dot-com companies. What a waste of economic resources! EDS's "cat-herding" spot; E*Trade's "money coming out of the gazoo"; Nuveen's "Christopher Reeve"; microstrategy.com, epidemic.com, monster.com, computer.com, WebMD.com, Lifeminders.com, all competing for an award for the worst advertising of the new millennium. We can just imagine their brand managers yelling, "Look, Ma, no strategy!" as each of these spots came out of production.

The issue is not restricted to particular product categories. We challenge anyone to articulate the positioning strategies for leading fast food companies, airlines, PC or software companies, financial institutions, consumer electronics, or major clothing retailers.

And it is not restricted to established products and services. Most new products and services should have highly motivating positioning strategies, since the point of introducing a new product is to launch something better than what is currently available. Yet our autopsies of new product/service failures suggest that in about a quarter of the cases the cause of death is a weak positioning.

Table 8-1   Positioning Strategies (1950–2010)

Time Period	Dominant Positioning	Advertising ROI	Positioning Today
1950s–'60s	Mostly Tangible, Product Based	10–15%	5%
1970s–'80s	Mix of Tangible and Ethereal	5–9%	35%
1990s–2010s	Mostly Ethereal, Image Based	1–4%	60%

Not long ago we sat in a meeting with a client and its advertising agency to discuss a new sports drink. The product has a number of tangible benefits: it replaces vital electrolytes; it is all natural; and it does not have to be refrigerated. The agency wanted to ignore (or demote) these for something intangible. "Drink our drink and when you play you'll feel like Drew Bledsoe . . . or Mark McGwire." We found their arguments unpersuasive.

Nevertheless, if you're inclined to believe that an image campaign may work in your category, the research approach we describe later in this chapter will help you evaluate product (tangible) versus image (intangible) positionings long before you've invested the total advertising budget in another low-ROI image campaign.

Many marketers argue that today a strong product-based positioning strategy is a thing of the past. It worked, they argue, back in the 1950s and '60s, when marketing and advertising were new, brands few, and positioning possibilities unlimited. The view seems to be that image-based positionings were born out of necessity in the '90s and that they can be as effective as the traditional "product difference, reason why" approach popular decades ago.

To this we say "perhaps" or "maybe," but we're tempted to say "nonsense!" True, competition is tougher today, but for many brands in many product categories there are still important product differences that the marketer can communicate. Moreover, on average these strategies are stronger—work better—than their modern image-oriented counterparts.

Table 8-1 suggests that only about one in 20 companies/services/products/brands employs a clear, powerful, preemptible product-based positioning strategy and that most—maybe 6 out of 10—represent ethereal fun. Budweiser's new Dalmatian execution, for example, is 60 seconds of entertainment about two homely dogs; its only connection to Bud is that one dog is seen at the end of the spot in a Clydesdale-powered Budweiser beer wagon. This in our view is highly ineffective advertising that is diverting scarce resources that the company could use to better advantage elsewhere. It will only contribute to the king's abdication.

Send.com is another example. We're told that they have a category leadership advertising strategy, but you'd never know it from their humorous, "brandless" television advertising.

How to Create a Compelling Positioning

If you had unlimited time and a prospect's undivided attention, you could tell him or her many things (indeed, everything) about your product or service.

But a company does not have endless time, and prospects are notoriously inattentive, so the most any business can say are those few things prospects care about and will remember. You want to fix a succinct message in people's heads to induce trial and use among prospective buyers or to reinforce current purchasing among current customers. A process to develop a powerful positioning is valuable because when you have one, other marketing elements follow naturally: pricing, marketing communications and promotion, and distribution. You won't spend $32 million for no effect.

To find a positioning that motivates buyers, the critical first move is to conduct a market segmentation study in order to find a financially optimal target market. (If you are reading this book in order, you did that in the last chapter.) You must understand the market's structure, both in terms of customer desires and problems and in terms of competitive strengths and weaknesses. But once the company has identified a market target receptive to its product and for which it has some genuine appeal, then what?

The first step is to enumerate *all* potential attributes and benefits, tangible and intangible, that might motivate customers in the category. These include all the ways a business can differentiate itself: product, service, personnel, image. At this point the company does not know if any of them actually motivate behavior.

But you want at least 200 items—more if the product or service is as complex as a car or a vacation destination. The object here is to generate a long list of attributes and benefits that might form the basis for a powerful positioning strategy. These should represent both attributes and benefits of the product and tangible (i.e., real) and intangible (i.e., psychological) facets.

To uncover these, the company might do a category scan, exploratory research, personality assessment, social values analysis, emotional exploration, or some combination of all five. (Note that these techniques are just as appropriate for business-to-business as for consumer marketers and appropriate for both services and products.)

A *category scan* is a close review of all the attributes and benefits, tangible and emotional, that competitive brands in the category employ.

Exploratory research includes focus groups, in-depth interviews, or both, using laddering, projection tools, or other methodologies. The focus groups do not produce the positioning. You cannot take what comes out of a focus group, no matter how productive or passionate or positive it seems to be, and run with it.

"Laddering" is a questioning approach researchers use to uncover the underlying associations with a given stimulus. A series of probes usually begins with a question such as "What is the advantage to you of _____ " The blank might be "an antacid that's easy to swallow." When the respondent replies, "I don't have to chew," the next question probes that response: "What is the advantage of not having to chew?" That response is similarly probed: "What is the advantage of not having to taste the antacid?" This continues until the respondent can no longer volunteer advantages.

Laddering analysts look for respondent tendency to relate ideas, values, characteristics, and the like. When many respondents have strong associations, it usually means there are "natural" relationships the communications can employ.

Projection tools are like parlor games: If Pepsi were an animal, what animal would it be? If Surge were a sport, what sport would it be? If 7UP were an automobile, what automobile would it be? Or, Tell me a story about Orange Crush. Or, If you were the president of Hires Root Beer and could make one change in the product to make Americans happier with it, what change would that be? If you were the president of Coca-Cola's advertising agency and could say only one thing about the product to motivate more people to buy, what would that be?

Of course, these tools can be abused. A major e-commerce marketer asked focus group participants: "If this brand of software were a Hollywood celebrity, what kind of car would he or she drive?"

The latest rage among qualitative researchers is collage construction. The facilitator divides people in a focus group into teams, typically three people each, and gives each team the same set of magazines. Their job is to cut out pictures from the magazines that capture the essence of a brand's identity and positioning strategy. It is a fun diversion but time-consuming, and it often produces collages with virtually no consistency between the teams. Why? Because most brands have no clear positioning strategy. It is a mystery to us why researchers believe that a positioning unclear at the marketer's end will somehow become clear in a focus group exercise.

Personality assessment can be helpful. This is an analysis based on primary or secondary data on the key personality traits that may potentially underlie behavior in the product or service category. For example, to do a study for an over-the-counter drug, you would like to include a measure of hypochondriasis (what hypochondriacs suffer from) because it explains a significant variance in over-the-counter drug use. To do a study on a cosmetic without including measures of narcissism and self-esteem would overlook key factors. Since there are literally thousands of potential personality traits, it takes an expert to provide some insight into which ones might be relevant in the product category and to help select the measures of those relevant traits a study ought to include.

Social values analysis and *emotional exploration* are techniques companies employ less often than other methods, although they offer tremendous potential for finding powerful positionings. The late Professor Milton Rokeach was a pioneer in the study of social values and how they drive human behavior. Rokeach identified eight critical dimensions: achievement, security, sense of belonging, friendship, excitement, fun and enjoyment, self-esteem, and social recognition.

It may seem an arrant oversimplification to cram all human drives into eight categories, but just as a rainbow contains all colors but only a few obvious ones, these eight values represent the common denominators for all value shadings.

You can establish how relevant each of these values is to consumers either directly, by measuring relevance in a research study, or indirectly, by inspecting secondary sources closely. In the audit phase we use these critical values to help focus on which particular values might be relevant for a given product and to provide ideas for how to measure each.

For example, statements that link a consumer's need for achievement to his or her automobile would be something like "How desirable is it that the next car you buy . . .

"will make you feel prosperous and financially successful?"
"will provide you with a sense of accomplishment?"
"will convince your neighbors that you've really made it?"

Emotional exploration looks at people's psychological needs and how a particular product or service category addresses them. Robert Plutchik, a professor of psychiatry at Albert Einstein College of Medicine, has written the definitive work on the measurement of emotions and has shown that eight basic emotions (not to be confused with the eight social values) drive behavior. These eight emotions, are joy, acceptance, fear, surprise, sadness, disgust, anger, and anticipation.

It's not especially difficult to translate this into practical application. Plutchik's analysis yields multiple items for all eight emotions. To trace joy, for example, as related to a person's feelings about an automobile, a questionnaire might include items like "How desirable is it that the next car you buy . . .

"will give you a feeling of enthusiasm and excitement?"
"makes you feel happy, contented, and pleased with life?"
"will keep you entertained and amused?"

The goal, again, is an exhaustive list of attributes and benefits, both tangible and intangible. The task is to create a long list of creative, thought-provoking, innovative attributes and benefits. And lower-order attributes may bundle together to offer higher-order benefits. For example, seat belts, air bags, and antilock brakes are all lower-order attributes that lead to safety, a higher-order benefit. What exactly are the elements that make up an abstract idea like customer service? Durability? Reliability? Responsiveness? Style? Figure 8-2 shows the beginning of such a list of tangible and intangible attributes and benefits for a new sports car.

This is not something to be done in a one-hour, scribble-down-everything-you-can-think-of meeting. Since the items become the elements of the brand's positioning and (maybe) the connecting threads of an entire strategy, the list must be as comprehensive and creative/innovative as possible. The mission here is to think out of the box and push the envelope.

Once a company has the list, management reduces it to a manageable level by logic and Delphi process review (in which participants review the first list, create a new one, review the new one, and repeat the process until they reach consensus) so that it can go into a questionnaire. A pilot study among 100 to 200 buyers, followed by factor analysis—a pattern-recognition tool that searches out commonalities among the attributes and benefits, thus reducing redundancy—is a very useful approach for developing a parsimonious instrument, but companies rarely take this step today because of cost and time constraints.

The final list emerging from these activities will rarely have fewer than 50 items and could have 100.

The next step is to determine how motivating each of these characteristics is to the market target and how buyers perceive competing brands on each of them. This calls for a quantitative research project undertaken among a cross section of at least 200 (and preferably 500 or more) buyers deemed to be prime prospects for the product or service. If this positioning work is con-

Figure 8-2   New Sports Car Attributes and Benefits

	Attributes	Benefits
Tangible	• Removable hard top • Short-throw, five-speed transmission • Fastest car on the road	• You'll love looking at it • Safer to drive at high speeds • Comfortable to drive long distances
Intangible	• Good-looking women love men who drive this car • Car bought by successful people • Car preferred by people under 35	• More fun to drive • You'll have a feeling of independence and freedom • Makes you feel and look younger than you really are

ducted as part of a segmentation assignment, as it often is, the database is often larger.

You Don't Learn What's Important by Asking What's Important

The most common way to determine what's important to consumers, buyers, and voters in marketing and public opinion research studies is to ask them. Researchers give their respondents a list of characteristics of the product or the service or the candidate, and ask them to rate each on a five-point scale. For example: "When you're in the market for a sporty new car, how important is it to you that the car be a sex magnet, making you more attractive to people of the opposite sex?" Extremely important? Very important? Somewhat important? Slightly important? Not important at all?

That commonsense procedure is *exactly what you do not want to do*. It is unlikely to tell you what is really motivating in the product category because people will give you the most rational, expected, socially acceptable answers. They will tell you that great taste and refreshment are very important characteristics of a soft drink, even though most Americans cannot differentiate between Pepsi and Coke in blind taste tests.

They will tell you that security in an e-commerce site is key, even though buyers rarely know anything about a site and its backers, and that safety is what they want in an automobile, when most of what they know is based on advertising-driven perceptions, not hard data. And people will *never* tell you

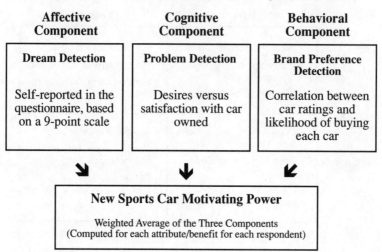

Figure 8-3   A Three-Dimensional Model of Motivations

that "sexual magnetism" is particularly important, even though for some segments of the market it's highly motivating.

Importance ratings, moreover, tend to highlight unexciting positioning candidates. Ask people about a new food product and they'll tell you that good-tasting and nutritious are extremely important attributes. But good-tasting and nutritious are price-of-entry items, not positionings, since virtually every new food product has to have them. Bad taste and unhealthy may work for Moxie soft drink and Brady's cough syrup, but nothing else.

Because the goal is to understand what motivates category behavior, we recommend measuring each attribute on three dimensions: dream detection, problem detection, and brand preference detection, as in Figure 8-3. Psychologists and human behaviorists have argued for three decades that attitudes are formulated through these three components. Marketing science uses the three-component theory of attitude as a starting point.

Dream detection, the affective component of motivating power, assesses the interest level of each attribute and benefit. What do consumers truly want in the category—no matter how unrealistic or preposterous? Example: "It's very desirable to have a car that makes me more attractive to the opposite sex."

We use a desirability scale rather than an importance measure because people tend to report intangible attributes and benefits as being more appealing when they answer on a desirability scale than on an importance measure.

Ask "How important is it that the next automobile you buy impress your brother-in-law?" and people tend to say it's not very important. Ask "How desirable is it that the next automobile you buy impress your brother-in-law?" and people (some people, anyway) will say it's "somewhat desirable." Couple this phrase with a picture, and people may even report that it's "very desirable."

"Importance" implies rationality. People want to give a response they think the researcher wants to hear, a response they think will make them look good in the interviewer's eyes. "Desirability" is a less loaded word; add a visual and the combination lets them say whatever they want.

If we were studying a product category like ball bearings and working under the assumption the decision to buy or not is wholly rational, it would not make any difference whether we used an importance or a desirability scale. Yet while business-to-business selling tends to be more rational, it's not completely. The personality of the salesperson, the trust the customer feels in the salesperson, the seeming enthusiasm servicing the account, the way the support staff makes the customer look smart in front of the boss—these are all intangibles that affect the selection of many industrial products.

But in product categories that are heavily marketed and are driven by tangibles and intangibles, desirability and visual stimuli work better than importance ratings. Especially important, the symmetric desirability scale that is used for dream detection, as well as the problem detection and brand preference detection components, captures characteristics that are both "turn-ons" and "turn-offs." In a sports car, for example, "zero to 60 in under six seconds" may be highly appealing to some prospects, yet scary to others. This is a distinction totally missed by importance scales.

DESIRABILITY SCALE

+4 Extremely desirable
+3 Very desirable
+2 Somewhat desirable
+1 Slightly desirable
 0 Neither desirable or undesirable
-1 Slightly undesirable
-2 Somewhat undesirable
-3 Very undesirable
-4 Extremely undesirable

Problem detection, the difference between the dream and reality, is the cognitive component. It measures what respondents want (desirability) versus what they are getting (or not) from their favorite brand. Example: Virtually all automobile owners want high resale value; owners of many American cars are troubled because they're not getting it.

Interestingly, this measure is at the heart of what marketing as a discipline is all about, and yet marketing research studies rarely use it. Many would agree with the Procter & Gamble definition we gave earlier: Marketing is the discipline concerned with solving people's problems with products and services profitably. The definition, however, assumes that you know what a problem is. A problem is not asking people what is important. How important is it that your next car have four wheels? Extremely important. But all new cars have four wheels, so this is not a problem.

Brand preference detection, the behavior component, determines which attribute ratings are correlated with or predict purchase preference and behavior. In a typical study we have respondents rate each of the leading brands in their evoked set in terms of each the 50-plus attributes and benefits being studied. Later in the interview we also ask a number of questions concerning purchase probabilities for each of these brands. Sometimes we use a constant sum tool, particularly for packaged goods, asking, "Out of the next ten times you make a purchase in this product category, how many times are you likely to make a purchase of these different brands?" The brands we ask about are the same brands we covered in terms of the perceptual ratings. It's a simple matter, then, of doing a correlation/regression analysis to predict an overall rating, such as the constants sum score. This analysis must be done for each individual respondent separately, however, not the whole sample. Technically speaking, it's an individual-level rather than aggregate-level analysis. This is a very different approach, we might add, from the "derived" leverage coefficients widely used in the industry, which are based on aggregate analysis and which, for technical reasons inappropriate to discuss in this book, almost always yield incorrect, misleading conclusions.

For example, characteristics having to do with automotive performance are highly correlated with overall preference for BMW. Characteristics having to do with skateboards and NASCAR racing are highly correlated with preference for Mountain Dew. Characteristics having to do with being good for children, fun for children, a place that children like are highly correlated with preference for McDonald's.

In contrast, old-fashioned and stodginess are highly unrelated to a choice of a BMW. Authenticity and 19th-century Americana are negatively related with preference for "the Dew." And adult tastes and preferences are negatively related to the choice of McDonald's.

The next step is to rescale all three of these dimensions *for each respon-*

dent from -100 (highly demotivating) to +100 (overwhelmingly motivating). If a study has 500 respondents and 75 attributes and benefits, this involves 37,500 calculations for each of the three dimensions and then, when the three are combined, 150,000 calculations in total. The combination is a weighted average of the three components to establish the motivating power of each attribute. Motivating power, as we have discovered, is not just about dreams, problems, and behavior but is a composite of all three.

Marketing executives sometimes want to limit the study to identifying characteristics that predict category behavior (for example, the higher a brand's perceived reliability, the more ready a consumer is to purchase the brand). Why would a company want anything else? If a company knows what predicts behavior, it's done.

But it's not, because while characteristics can be critical to consumers, they may not drive behavior, since everyone offers the benefit (four wheels, brakes) or no one does. For example, two decades ago you would have found that people who liked and wanted a two-seater roadster had a big problem: they couldn't get one. The two-seater attribute would *not* have been a good predictor of purchase behavior because at the time no company offered small sports cars.

Because an attribute can be strong in one component but weak in others, it's important to evaluate it on each of the three dimensions. That way you don't overlook potential strengths. Ideally, you'd like positioning items to excel on all three components: people say they really want it, don't get it with the products they currently use, and would buy it if they could get it.

One simple way to do this is to weight each dimension equally for each respondent and average them. Long experience has shown, however, that for new products the desirability component should be ratcheted up and the leverage estimate down, while for established products and services the problem scores are more important in predicting market response to a new strategy.

How Positioning Strategy Works in Practice

We have discovered over the years that consumer reaction to positioning strategies cannot be predicted based only on the motivations in the category. You do have to know the motivations in the category, but you also have to know how buyers perceive your product and competitive products. This can be examined for each individual respondent to a survey. The next step is to rescale all three of these dimensions *for each respondent* from -100 (over-whelmingly demotivating) to +100 (overwhelmingly motivating). This tech-

Figure 8-4   Microlevel Analysis: Respondent Tina Phillips, Age 37

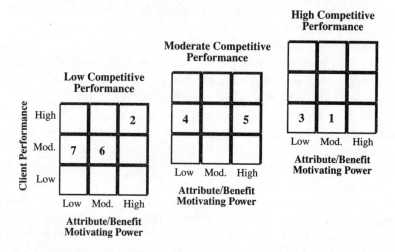

Attribute/Benefit
1. Economical to drive
2. Makes you feel younger than you really are
3. Contemporary styling
4. Safe car for the whole family
5. Will impress your friends when you buy one
6. Well engineered
7. Has airbags on the driver's side

nique examines where each attribute and benefit falls for each respondent individually. Intangible benefit 2 in Figure 8-4, for example, captures the "Ponce de Leon" effect; it promises to "make you feel younger than you really are." Let's look at an individual example. For 37-year-old Tina Phillips, this is "high" in motivating power, "high" in perception of client performance, and "low" in perceptions of competitive performance.

The strategic cube is both a means of looking at different attributes and benefits in a product category and a measurement methodology. By examining the motivating power and perceptions of a company's product or service and competitive products simultaneously, the cube reveals insights into promising positioning strategies. Attributes and benefits that are high in motivating power and for which the company's product enjoys an edge over the competitions' represent wonderful opportunities for positioning and for message strategies.

To the extent that consumers are increasingly unable to differentiate com-

Figure 8-5   Brand Strategy Matrix: Pepsi vs. Coke

		Pepsi Superior	Both the Same Excellent: Could Not Be Better	Both the Same Acceptable But Could Be Better	Both the Same Unacceptable	Pepsi Inferior
	High	Makes You Glad to Be Alive ①	Great Cola Taste	Thirst Quenching ④	Same Taste but Lower in Calories ②	Available Everywhere
Motivating Power of Attribute/ Benefit	**Mod.**	Tastes Less Sweet ③	Available in Local Super-markets	Good on Hot Summer Days ⑥	Doesn't Stay Cold Very Long ⑤	Preferred by Women
	Low	Preferred by Teenagers ⑦	Comes in Large Bottles	Less Expensive	Comes in Small Cans	Authentic, The Real Thing

Value of Strategy Ranked from ① to ⑦

peting brands in the same category by way of product function and imagery, companies have a positioning problem. The major difficulty today is that more and more brands are communicating the same positioning; it is just hard to separate them. If we took Jeep Cherokee's advertising and slapped Range Rover on it, we'd bet few people would know the difference—an interesting test that could be applied to most product categories.

Worse are brands that, in an effort to differentiate themselves, move away from the core, essential positionings that made them great and begin to work on secondary or even tertiary claims. Instead of the frozen lasagna that is based on Mama Italiano's family recipe, it's the frozen lasagna that has the magic probe that tells you when the product is cooked. The fact is, people are much more interested in the famous recipe, but we've moved away from that and are talking about peripheral things like the packaging.

Since positioning involves the packaging, distribution, pricing, advertising, point-of-purchase material—everything about the product—the basic issue is, what does a company want to communicate about its product to its prospective audiences—not just the ultimate consumers, but the distributors who will stock the product, the retailers who will sell it, and the person who will buy it? When marketing executives think of positioning, they generally think in terms of advertising, but that's much too narrow.

At the end of a positioning study, a company would like to have the sort of blueprint for action illustrated in Figure 8-5. The motivating power extends from low to high, and the company versus the competition extends from superior to inferior.

This hypothetical example compares Pepsi with a single competitor, in this case Coke. The columns across the top are "Pepsi Superior" to Coke, "Both the Same" (with three subcolumns: "Excellent, Could Not Be Better"; "Acceptable But Could Be Better"; and "Unacceptable"), and "Pepsi Inferior" to Coke. The rows show the motivating power of the attribute and benefits, from low to high.

It is possible to rank-order each cell in the matrix in terms of how much potential that cell has as the basis for a powerful positioning strategy. If you find attributes that are highly motivating and your brand also enjoys advantages relative to the major competitor, then you have the basis for a strong positioning strategy. Conversely, you may find attributes high in motivating power in which your brand is inferior; this gives your product development people something to do. The numbers in these cells reflect our experience in testing positioning strategies based on attributes and benefits found in each cell of this matrix. Number one, for example, indicates the most powerful strategy.

After you know what motivates consumers and how your brand or brands perform on each of these dimensions, you can rank-order your final list of category characteristics or potential positioning themes. Now the task is creative—putting together your strengths and weaknesses and developing a message strategy that puts your brand in the most favorable light, which is where the advertising/marketing communications people go to work.

Positioning concepts are written and tested, usually among 150 or more respondents. Often three to seven different positioning strategies are evaluated in terms of three major criteria: purchase interest, uniqueness, and product/brand superiority. The company incorporates the winning strategy in all the advertising it develops. Better yet, it becomes the underlying strategy for the brand in everything it does. Point-of-sale, packaging, public relations, sales pieces, the Web site, everything! It becomes the simple declarative statements that are essential to marketing success for any brand, product, or service.

Other firms decide that, for their product or service, the positioning strategy is inseparable from the advertising execution and hence, rather than taking this intermediate positioning testing step, go on to create rough commercials and test them in a simulated setting, something we'll talk more about in the advertising chapter.

Whatever approach a manager takes to develop a strong, empirically grounded positioning is counterintuitive. As we've said throughout this chapter, most companies, products, researchers, and brands have no positioning at all. It's as if their brand managers skipped the MBA class on the importance of positioning strategy.

A counterintuitive approach to strategic positioning analysis, such as the one described here, offers invaluable prescriptive guidance to marketers. Without it a company or its brand is just one more indistinguishable drop in a sea of products; with it a company can identify innovative and preemptive positioning opportunities that set the brand apart in a positive way from all others.

Sleeper and Subliminal Effects Don't Increase Sales

Three years ago a multinational marketer, concerned about declining sales of its flagship brand—the leading brand in its category for decades—decided to develop and launch a major turnaround campaign. They invited us to help by undertaking a large-scale marketing strategy project, which within five months revealed insights into new and very profitable market targets and a bold and powerful positioning. At this point they asked their advertising agency to create a number of rough commercials that would execute the strategy in different ways. For reasons we'll explain later, the agency came back with only two ideas, which were tested and found wanting. Both were very entertaining, but neither communicated a clear message about the brand or why it was superior to competitors. Not surprisingly, the purchase interest needle—a measure we use to forecast sales—did not move.

We reported our finding to the client and agency and expressed our belief that, while the executions might win a Clio Award for advertising creativity, they were unlikely to win a David Ogilvy Award for advertising effectiveness. They were too ethereal, too image oriented—and their connections to the recommended targeting and positioning strategies were remote at best. To be frank, we couldn't figure out what they were trying to say.

The client, like many, was in a rush to launch the campaign, to put something on the air. He picked one of the two commercials, executed it in finished form, produced a pool-out, and ran the campaign, spending $32 million on television over the next six months.

A year after we had tested the commercials, the client invited us back to his marketing war room to hear a presentation by a well-known advertising tracking company. The client had commissioned the firm to measure the campaign's performance over a six-month period. Both the client and the agency executives were surprised at the tracking report results, and even we were taken aback.

Consumer awareness of the company's positioning message after the $32 million investment was *not* 50 percent, *not* 5 percent, *not* even 0.5 percent. It was 0 percent. There was simply no awareness. The tracking firm found no one, not a single person, able to recall anything about the client's brand that reflected the advertising's positioning/message strategy.

The advertising agency management supervisor, who has to be the world's most clever spinmeister, responded to this devastating news without missing a beat. We were so impressed by what he said that we wrote it down. Here it is verbatim: "If you remember, before we ran the campaign, copy testing suggested that this was a transcendental, image-laden execution. It did not pound home a message for the brand. This kind of advertising probably produces a subliminal, sleeper effect, in which case zero percent awareness may be a good thing. It suggests that the campaign is really working."

But no one laughed in the war room. Preposterous as these words were, some people took notes, probably telling themselves to look up the words "sleeper" and "subliminal" in a marketing dictionary. In fact, the client, despite the disappointing awareness, attitude, brand preference, and—ultimately—sales results, continued to run the campaign for another six months before finally killing the advertising and firing the agency.

(For interested readers, the academic psychological and marketing literature defines "sleeper effects" as effects that do not initially appear; they lie dormant for a period of days, weeks, even years, and then *wham!*, attitudes and behavior magically change when these mysterious effects kick in. "Subliminal effects," in contrast, are those that occur when a person is not consciously aware of the stimulus. Back in the '50s, one researcher reported that flashing the words "Buy Coke" or "Buy Popcorn" on a movie screen at below-perceptual thresholds (i.e., people didn't notice them because the words passed too quickly) resulted in increased sales at concession stands. Both of these effects were disconfirmed by subsequent research. Despite the catch labels, they are as mythological as the abominable snowman.)

This agency is loaded with creative types who think they'll be the next Martin Scorcese or Steven Spielberg. They are artists, not salesmen. This type is found at many agencies. As a result, television is filled with commer-

cials that do not communicate anything useful about the advertiser and its
products and services. We're not the only ones who think so. According to the
late David Ogilvy,

> The other day I was at a meeting where they showed me about 100 television
> commercials from all over the world. I was shocked. In many cases, I could not
> understand what they were trying to sell. They didn't tell. Neither did they say
> what the product was supposed to be good for. They didn't give me one reason
> for buying.
>
> Today, the people who are paid to write advertising are not interested in sell-
> ing. They consider advertising an art form. And they talk about creativity all the
> time. I'm a salesman. I don't care whether what I do is arty or clever. I want to
> sell products, but advertising people today, they want to win awards. They use
> advertising to promote themselves, so they can get better jobs and higher
> salaries. It's a scandal.

DOES YOUR MOM UNDERSTAND YOUR ADVERTISING?

Eight out of ten people don't remember anything about commercials they
were exposed to 18 hours earlier, and that's with a lot of prompting. Of those
who remember something about the advertising, only about one-quarter can
cite a main point that reflects a real advertising message. Putting both pieces
of data together, we can conclude that about five viewers in a hundred will
remember something about an advertiser's expensive message less than a day
after they were exposed to it. A week later, without repeat exposure (i.e., rep-
etition), that figure is closer to two people.

Think we're mistaken? Here's an experiment you can try in the privacy of
your own home. Invite your mom, spouse, and kids to sit and watch three
hours of television with you on a night of their choice. Give each person a
yellow legal pad and pen. Have everyone, without conferring, write down
every advertiser's name and what the ad said about the brand that made it different from competitors. (If you want to make the job easier, tape three hours
of television and zip past the programming and write about the commercials
as they appear.)

At the end of three hours and perhaps 100 commercials, determine how
many different brands all of you remember and how many clearly communicated message strategies you agree upon. The result will be under 20 percent.
If you did this on Super Bowl Sunday 2000, as we did, the number would be
less than 10 percent.

This explains why, when watching television in a group, someone will say,
"What in heaven's name were they thinking? What was the point to that com-

mercial? What was going on in their minds? Are they crazy? I mean, what's happening here? What was that about? What was that brand?"

Alida Ciampa of Lyme, New Hampshire, says that in her household it has become "kind of a bizarre game, trying to figure out who the advertiser is and what the message says. Even ten years ago, when commercials came on, you didn't necessarily like them, but you knew what they were for. Today everything's changed."

Mrs. Ciampa was particularly intrigued by a new Federal Express spot that describes a goofy Web site development agency for 27 seconds and only mentions Fed Ex at the end. "I don't even remember what the connection is between Fed Ex and the rest of the ad and I've seen it about five times." And, she adds, "what about monster.com? It's a funny spot all about loser kids (e.g., the kid who wants to be a 'brown nose') but what's monster.com? And what's snap.com? Those commercials don't even motivate me to check out the sites, and I've taught classes over the Net."

The guessing game works with ad professionals as well as ordinary consumers. We recently sat through a 30-minute reel of American beer commercials with senior executives from Companhia de Bedidas das Americas, the third-largest brewer in the world, and some experts on American advertising. We laughed at some of the nutty stuff, puzzled over the meaning of many of the executions, and noted that with few exceptions—Coors and Corona being the only two—beers marketed in the U.S. seem to be searching for a positioning strategy. The Americans in particular seemed saddened by what they saw. John Bernbach, former CEO of DDB/Needham International, remarked, "The beer category certainly has changed. Bud and Miller and Miller Lite were well positioned years ago, but you'd never know it from this."

Research supports these anecdotes of declining advertising copy effectiveness. IPSOS-ASI, in Stamford, Connecticut, one of the preeminent advertising research companies, measures advertising recall by recruiting consumers to watch a cable TV program in which advertising is embedded for testing. Dave Walker, IPSOS-ASI's director of research, reported to the authors in April 1998 that the mean average related recall scores for all commercials tested by calendar year hit a 25.1 percent peak in 1986 and showed almost steady decline to 20.0 percent in 1997, a 25 percent drop.

The IPSOS-ASI methodology uses cable TV to simulate on-air exposure under controlled test conditions (30-second spots tested among women aged 18 to 65), with the same number of commercials in the same program positions for each test. "As such," says Walker, "IPSOS-ASI recall should be less directly influenced by changes in the media environment during the period in question. Even so, the decline in recall levels appears to be real. The annual

Figure 9-1   The Advertising Performance Bell Curve™

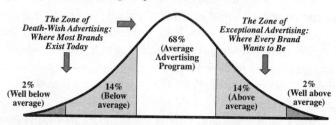

Marketing Performance	Embarrassing	Troubling	Disappointing	Pleasing	Amazing
Market Share Growth	Precipitious Decline	Significant Decline	Modest Decline	Significant Increase	Dramatic Increase
Day-After Recall for a 30-Second TV Spot	5%	12%	20%	28%	40%
Day-After Proven Recall for a 30-Second TV Spot	0%	2%	4%	7%	10%
Day-After Recall for a Full-Page Ad	1%	5%	9%	14%	19%
Attitude Change Score for a 30-Second TV Spot	Negative Shift	No Change	Slight Increase	Significant Increase	Dramatic Increase
Advertising Penetration per 1,000 TV GRPs	3%	11%	18%	25%	35%
Direct-Response Purchase	0.2%	0.6%	1.0%	2.0%	3+%
Advertising ROI	Negative	0%	1–4%	5–10%	20%

averages show a significant linear trend, implying a drop of about three and a half points over the nineteen-year period [1979–97]."

The IPSOS-ASI studies are done using a prompted related recall measure, which is a relatively soft indicator of true advertising penetration. In the research study, people are asked about everything they remember seeing and hearing in the commercial. When they "play back" something that was definitely said or shown, this is coded as *proven* recall. But if they play back something that might have been in the commercial—but we don't know for sure—this is coded as related *unproven* recall. A typical ratio of total related to proven recall is four to one. Thus, the 20 percent recall figure reported by IPSOS-ASI, a number that parallels our own experience, is weak evidence that the campaign is imprinted in the mind of the viewer. What it really means is about 4 percent proven recall, an abominable performance.

Recall scores are not the only indication of declining advertising impact. Figure 9-1 shows the effects of contemporary advertising in another bell curve. Note the modest performance of advertising in terms of advertising penetration (prompted recognition of a campaign message) and new product/service awareness (aided and unaided). New product and new service awareness and trial—both largely the result of advertising—are increasingly difficult to achieve. Performance per dollar is slipping. That explains, in part, why, as we discussed in Chapter 3, the average ROI for advertising companies is in the range of 1 to 4 percent.

"Brands in the '90s don't fail through rejection, but lack of interest," said Adam Morgan, a TBWA Chiat/Day executive, in the *Wall Street Journal* in April 1997. "Unless you're a very big company and have tons of money and can ram your message down people's throats, you have to do something very different."

Unfortunately for many agencies, "different" means communicating nothing at all. Sometimes this is because of legal constraints or because copywriters find literal communication boring. More often it's because the creation and execution of image campaigns are just so exciting that they can't be resisted. Suppose (as has actually happened) we want the agency to communicate that our beer has all of the flavor with half of the calories; our research shows this is what our target market wants in a beer. The agency tells us, "You can't just say, 'half the calories.' You can't just directly communicate that it has all the flavor." Calories are a tangible characteristic, and agency creative people find tangible characteristics banal. They want to communicate something more exciting, a brand personality. So they focus on intangible, ethereal images instead of the product's tangible benefits, offering the customer no rational reason to buy. (If this anecdote sounds vaguely similar to the Miller Lite story, it is.)

Approximately $223 billion will be spent on advertising in 2000, and *no one* knows if it will be worth the investment; few people seem to want to know, or even care. If you ask a marketing director the return on the $100 million advertising budget he administers for his company, he'll mumble, turn away, and say, in effect, "Trust me."

We believe that for advertising to "work," it must produce a clear return on investment. No evidence currently exists, however, to support the relationship between advertising expenditures and ROI.

Years ago Whittle Communications exploited this unhappy situation with a much discussed print advertising campaign, shown in Figure 9-2.

MYSTERY ADVERTISING IS A MYSTERY

It's so hard to break through commercial cacophony that apparently some companies have decided they're not even going to try. They've enrolled in a hot new school of thinking called "mystery advertising."

A July 1998 *Business Week* article, "Great ad! What's it for?" reported on

Figure 9-2   Controversial Full-Page Print Ad

The earth is flat.

~

The check is in the mail.

~

Research demonstrates the advertising effectiveness of network TV.

From time immemorial, people have all too often believed what they've needed to believe.

And facts that challenged those beliefs have simply been rejected. Or ignored.

Which is probably the only way to explain the faith that some advertisers retain in network television.

Because in the clear light of cold objectivity, research demonstrates that it's anything *but* effective.

People are watching less of it every year.

Even when they do watch, more and more of them don't watch commercials.

And even when they watch commercials, more and more of them don't remember them.

According to one report, as many as 98% of people who were asked couldn't remember a commercial they'd seen the day before.

In another study, 93% couldn't remember a spot they'd seen 15 *minutes* before.

And what's perplexing isn't that some advertisers continue to pour millions into conventional television because they don't have information like this.

What's perplexing is that they continue to pour millions into it even though they do.

Maybe it's time to ask how sensible it is to be comforted by a pitifully low recall score just because it's higher than a pitifully low norm.

Or to spend more every year just to end up with the share you had the year before.

It's not surprising that media is on the verge of profound change.

The Earth, after all, may not be flat.

But from all indications, network television is.

Whittle
communications

the deliberately mystifying ads. Lee Company, for example, began running print and poster ads in March 1998 that showed a doll dressed in a variety of outfits, from cowboy to milkman. "They don't say jeans. They don't say Dungarees. Or pants. Or Lee. In fact, it's pretty much impossible to tell that they're ads at all. And that's the point."

Lee's research, said *Business Week,* shows that a hard sell turns off its 17- to 25-year-old target consumers; they want to feel they're discovering a product. "They told us in our research, the harder you try, the more we are not going to pay attention to your brand," said Dodie Subler, group director at Fallon McElligott, Lee's ad agency. The idea behind the print campaign was to let a few people in on the story—Lee ran a six-minute film explaining the connection between the doll and the jeans on the Comedy Central cable network at 1:00 A.M. one May night—and let the meaning filter out by word of mouth. "Leading-edge kids like to feel like they are in the know," said Terry Lay, president of Lee Jeans.

While both Subler's and Lay's statements may be entirely true, we find it difficult to believe that many young consumers care enough to solve the mystery of the ads, let alone buy Lee jeans because they've made the connection. In a masterpiece of understatement, Gary Yiatchos, senior vice president for marketing at Bon Marché, a Seattle-based chain of department stores, told *Business Week,* "These are not the kind of campaigns that cause consumers to drop what they are doing and come right in. It can create brand awareness, and that's good. But that impacts over a long period of time. You don't see an immediate impact."

We strongly suspect that Lee—like Oldsmobile, Foot Locker, Intel, and others who have run mystery advertising—will never see any measurable impact. Not on attitudes and perceptions. Not on message penetration, the brand's raison d'être. And clearly not on sales.

More Sleeper and Subliminal Effects

Pharmaceutical advertising is not mystery advertising, but the effect is often the same—virtually none.

Direct-to-consumer pharmaceutical advertising is one of the hottest areas in marketing today. Pharmaceutical companies spent more than $1 billion in 1997 on direct-to-consumer advertising for prescription drugs; in 2000 they will spend more than $2 billion. And these companies are very serious about measuring the ROI of the new form of investment.

The field is booming because in August 1997 the Federal Drug Administration relaxed its rules on television and radio advertising of prescription drugs, allowing companies to talk about specific products and purposes without having to include all side effects (as they do in newspapers and magazines). Pharmaceutical firms are now permitted to show a toll-free phone number, Internet address, or some other method a consumer can use to request more information.

Pharmaceutical companies have concluded that if they advertise directly to consumers, people will identify with the medical problem, understand the solution and what's different about the advertised drug compared to competitors, and remember the brand advertised. They will then make an appointment with their physician to ask for the drug by name.

We have now investigated more than 20 such direct-to-consumer advertising efforts and have found only two for which the advertising produced a clear return on the investment.

In fact, our most common finding is that the advertising is so obtuse and the product names so unusual—Allegra, Flonase, Pravachol, Prilosec, Vioxx, Zocor, Zomig, Zyrtec—that hardly anybody remembers the name, let alone why the product is better than a competitor's. We're not the first to notice this: on December 12, 1999, *Time* magazine even ran an article ("Mixed-Up Meds") pointing out the confusing similarity between pharmaceutical names, such as Celexa, Cerebyx, and Celebrex. And even when the consumer actually is aware of the product, it is unusual for him or her to call the doctor for an appointment, remember the product name, and discuss it in the office.

We suspect that agencies working on prescription drugs have not thought very much about the decision-making process. For a new packaged good, you don't need to indelibly imprint the brand in the prospect's head. When the consumer pushes a cart down the supermarket aisle and sees the brand on the shelf, recognition may trigger memory: "Oh, yeah, I heard something about this. Let me try it."

Getting a person to pay attention to direct-to-consumer pharmaceutical advertising and to act on it by calling her doctor is very different. In one study we did recently, 12 weeks after the direct-to-consumer advertising started, we talked to 1,200 "sufferers" who use a prescription drug in their category and could find only 7 who reported asking their doctor about the advertised brand. If a pharmaceutical company is making less than 20 percent of the people aware of its drug with advertising (which, though terrible, *is* the going rate), and less than 10 percent of the 20 percent (again the "norm") act on that awareness to contact their doctor and ask for the drug, nothing much is going to happen.

We confirmed this finding in a separate survey of several hundred doctors. We asked if their patients came to them and mentioned this same drug. Less than 1 percent said they had a patient who asked about it. The doctors' experience confirms the advertising's weakness. Conclusion? For most brands there is zero ROI for OTC advertising.

Are these unusual cases? Definitely not! During the holiday season of 1999, advertising spending for dot-com companies achieved record levels. Between the dot-coms and the pharmaceuticals, traditional television and radio advertisers were left on the sidelines.

The dot-coms, however, like the Rx brands, also achieved new levels of inefficiency. Entertaining, yes; effective, no.

Take, for example, send.com. In November and December they spent approximately $30 million on television and radio advertising for their on-line gift-giving site. The ads were very daring, somewhat risqué, some would say edgy (remember the "little-giver"?), but their sales impact was negligible and the ROI negative.

And Super Bowl Sunday 2000 was the day many dot-com companies decided to show the world (and their investors) how they could waste more money faster than in any other three-hour period in the history of advertising.

WHY SO MANY POOR COMMERCIALS?

Why are so many commercials—and, by extension, print and radio ads—not doing their job properly? Aside from the reasons we've already touched on, we've come to believe that agencies design many ads to impress the client and the advertising community.

To make the best possible impression, the commercial unveiling is highly dramatic, taking place at the agency in a conference room stocked with the drinks and munchies the client people especially like. A senior agency executive introduces the idea with some earnest background: "We thought long and hard about this product and its proper place in the market, and we pondered the brand's vision and personality, and that led us to think about the universe and the meaning of life . . ." High drama. The lights go down, and the commercial comes up on a large-screen television set with the stereo volume cranked up to molar-rattling levels. Everybody thinks it's wonderful. They are knocked over by the impact, stunned by the color, the motion, the sound.

Then the research company puts the new spot in a reel with eight others, runs it in a TV program it shows to ordinary people on a Wednesday afternoon in a central testing location . . . and nobody notices it.

In theory, effective advertising is not that hard to produce. Take a motivating message, give it a memorable execution and proper exposure, and you have advertising that provides a healthy return on investment.

ADVERTISING POWER MOWERS TO MANHATTANITES

Poor targeting and positioning are other factors inhibiting advertising effectiveness. As the last two chapters noted, many advertisers select target markets without sufficient thought and pay little attention to positioning. People not in the target audience tend to screen out ads not aimed at them. Putting it another way, advertising power mowers to Manhattanites wastes money.

At the same time, alas, having a terrific target and a powerful positioning does not guarantee great advertising. We have worked with clients who spent hundreds of thousands of dollars to identify financially optimal target groups and a powerful positioning strategy, only to have it all eviscerated by advertising that bore little relationship to the positioning.

As we've said, advertising executions today are more likely to be ignored or forgotten than remembered and acted upon. These are the obscure, creative, or "me-too" message strategies that fail to tap consumer needs and therefore fail to motivate the consumer to buy. It's not unusual to see different brands in the same category using the same message strategy. Often it's not even very good. All new cars are driven on empty, winding, rural western roads; all pickups bounce across the landscape.

Advertising is necessary to build a brand. Advertising is, in essence, communication, and marketers will always have to communicate with prospects and customers. The marketer's challenge is to produce memorable and effective communications and place them where they can have the greatest impact. How do you do that?

Yes, it *does* matter whether people like your ad or not. A seminal Advertising Research Foundation study found that the best predictors of sales effectiveness were attitudes toward the commercials; the more people like them, the better they work. In this experiment five pairs of packaged goods commercials were tested by a variety of copy evaluation tools and measures. Two diagnostic items proved to be highly predictive of sales response. One was "This advertising is funny and clever," and the other was "Tells me a lot about how the product works."

Note that communicating new information about the product or service is equally as important as humor. Advertising today seems to obsess on the entertainment dimension and ignores the recommendation to communicate information about the product.

BEGIN WITH A CLEAR BRIEF TO THE AGENCY

We've given considerable thought to what a marketer can do to improve advertising. Perhaps the first problem is that in too many cases the advertiser does not give the agency a clear brief. The company does not say clearly: "These are the people we want to reach, and this is what we want the campaign to communicate."

Just recently, for example, we were talking to a brand manager who was looking forward to an anniversary campaign. Her product has been around for 25 years and contains, let's say, polyester, a word that our research, the company's research—everybody's research—has found that the product's buyers reject. The manager told us, "I've just asked the agency to come up with an out-of-the-box campaign. I told them I want to see their most original thinking. Just don't use the word 'polyester.'"

We said, "You have to give the agency more direction than that."

She said, "No, they have a blank piece of paper. Don't say 'polyester,' but come up with alternative executions they think will work."

This was a client abdicating responsibility, and it happens too often. The advertiser says to the agency, "You figure it out." Not that the agency minds. Advertising agency account executives do not routinely implore clients to give them guidance. They're cool; they're a strategic partner. They can come up with the positioning, the approach, the strategic direction. While one cannot blame the advertising agencies for filling this vacuum, it is not a good situation.

Then there can be problems when the business actually *does* have a brief and wants to communicate it to the agency, which virtually always has two factions, the account management side and the creative side. In some cases the two don't talk to each other, don't like each other, or both.

In one case in which we were actually acting as the client's marketing department, we presented findings from a strategic study. We had a clear targeting and positioning for the product. The advertising agency account executives attended the planning presentations, but the creative people did not. We said, "How about bringing the creative people along next time?" The account people nodded, but the creative people never came.

We did give a detailed brief to the account group. They said, "Don't worry—we'll tell the creative people." But this is like farmers trying to explain plowing to cowboys, or golfers trying to talk to snowboarders; something gets lost in translation. We were not surprised, therefore, when a month later the account people were back with a creative idea that had nothing to do with what the campaign should have been about.

Table 9-1 shows a reasonably strong brief a personal computer manufacture gave to its advertising agency. It contains a description of the target, the positioning or message strategy, a comment on the brand's personality, and the emotional benefit the brand offers. After a thorough discussion of this brief, the agency was able to create alternative campaigns that were right on the money.

A strong brief gets down on paper the most profitable target; a compelling, unique, preemptible positioning strategy; the desired brand/product personality; and more. It forces clients and agency strategic thinkers and researchers to comb through available research (and undertake quantitative marketing strategy research when what's available is inadequate) in order to rationally and carefully craft a powerful strategy. Supplementing this hard research

Table 9-1   Strategic Recommendations

Advertising Creative Brief for SuperMachines, Inc.

The **primary market target** is senior air traffic control executives and
purchasing agents currently buying PCs from SuperMachines, Inc. People
faced with the challenge of handling more aircraft in less time with fewer
people than ever before.

Our **positioning** is that we are uniquely capable of building machines that
process more data, faster, and with higher levels of reliability than anything
else offered in the marketplace.

Our **products and services** are, in a word, "extraordinary" – they are dramatically
superior to anything any competitor offers.

Our **personality** is very professional and obsessive about quality and
performance.

The **emotional benefit** we provide is psychological comfort – we can and will
help our clients make airline travel safer and more efficient.

with equal doses of experienced judgment and creativity should result in the
counterintuitive and truly transformational campaign we lobby for throughout this book.

Tell the Agency to Come Back with More Than One Idea

We regularly ask agencies, "Please come up with lots of ideas. You don't have
to go very far with any of them. Just come up with 6 or 10, even 20 two-sentence ideas, three sentences, four sentences; just a nugget. Then let's talk."
The goal is to have many ideas, not totally fleshed out, but a variety of creative approaches to consider.

The agency people look us in the eye and say, "Right! We'll be back in
three weeks with a bunch of ideas." A month later they're back with one fully
developed approach. They have a storyboard, a location, a celebrity
spokesperson (and have consulted with the spokesperson's manager), suggested background and music, and a $900,000 budget.

We ask, "Where are the other ideas?"

They say, "This is such a dynamite approach we didn't think they were
necessary."

Sometimes the agency does come in with two ideas. If they've tried really
hard to get out of the box, maybe three. But the prudent thing to do is send
them back for five or more additional ideas. Nothing elaborate, just a thumb-
nail sketch of a concept. Start with the brand positioning and the words and
phrases that capture its essence. These are things like "will help me live
longer," "healthy tasting," "fresh tasting," "organically grown," "grown with-

out hurting the environment," "no pesticides or preservatives," "good for you," "very healthy."

Combine "winning" attributes and benefits into a single-minded two- to four-sentence statement of what the brand stands for and how it's different from competitors. Some firms write these as two-part statements: a promise or claim supported by a "reason why." Other companies write complete paragraphs that tie the promise and reason why together. As an example: "The Good Earth food products taste great and are good for you because they are grown organically, without chemicals and preservatives that mask flavors and harm the environment." This is your message strategy!

Because "message strategy" means different things to different managers, let's be sure we're talking about the same thing. The common theme is the notion, explicit or implicit, that the company wants to tell buyers something about its product, service, brand, or company. A message strategy is your basic selling proposition, the reason why consumers should buy your product rather than someone else's. What the company wants to communicate should positively differentiate its product or service from the competition's; it is your positioning reflected in advertising. If the company differentiates itself well, it will ring up a sale. So how can the company develop a message strategy and, ultimately, advertising that moves the needle?

Skilled advertising copywriters are able to enhance these alternative product concepts, "bringing to life," transforming the dry positioning statements into exciting advertising concepts. For example: "The Good Earth food products unleash the great taste of mother nature because they're grown and processed without chemicals. Equally important, because they're organic, they're good for you. As a result, The Good Earth products will help you live a healthier, happier, and longer life."

Five to ten (or even more) product positioning statements or advertising concepts should then be formally tested. Yes, some focus groups can be done to make sure they communicate what they're supposed to and to screen out any real dogs, but focus groups do not represent serious research. Instead, try interviewing 200 buyers in your target market and expose them in a random order to each of the concepts. This can be done by mail, over the Net, or, better yet, in person.

Table 9-2 shows the results of a recent study in which 12 different advertising concepts were tested for a food products company. Random sets of five concepts were presented to respondents in a central interviewing location in different markets in the U.S. Buyers rated the first one—again selected randomly—in terms of purchase probability, uniqueness/superiority, quality, and price value. Then they went on to rate the remaining four. Finally people

Table 9-2   Purchase Probability for 12 Food Concepts

Concept	Purchase Probability
"Family Food Fight"	48%
"Grandmother's Recipes"	45%
"Health and Nutrition"	39%
"Lives Well"	37%
"Farm Fresh"	33%
"Unleashes Nature's Taste"	33%
"Taste of Mother Nature"	27%
"Julia Child's Favorite"	25%
"Happiness Is…"	22%
"Le Cirque"	17%
"The Right Way"	16%
"100% Organic"	11%

were shown all five ideas and were asked to pick both their favorite and the one they liked least. Shown below are the purchase probability scores for all 12 concepts.

If you were the CMO of this firm, wouldn't you be a lot happier knowing that the "Family Food Fight" concept (the notion that this stuff tastes so good your spouse and kids will fight to get it) overwhelmed by almost two to one your intuitive favorite, "Taste of Mother Nature"?

EXECUTE THE MESSAGE IN MORE THAN ONE WAY

Now you have the agency excited. You've helped them prove that their creativity can yield an advertising concept that's superior to the intuitive idea you all started with. Now keep it going. Tell them to execute the idea—in rough form—in two or three ways. Just to be sure "Family Food Fight" wasn't a fluke, or in case for some reason it can't be executed well, have them take the number-two ad concept—in this case, "Grandmother's Recipes"—and execute that in two or three ways as well. That is four to six different ads in total.

Often at this point the client jumps in: "I've already bought airtime. I have to get on air. I can't be dark. Just execute the first idea. No testing." The company would rather take a chance on something feeble to fill the airtime when it might be a better business decision to go dark than to run a feeble commercial.

There is no question that it is more expensive to develop four or even six commercials than one or two. But consider the arithmetic: While the average cost of production of a finished 30-second commercial is $320,000, it costs about $25,000 apiece for the agency to take an idea to animatic or photomatic stage and, at most, $20,000 for a research company to test it. Two commercials, $90,000 in creative and research; four commercials, $180,000. "Whoa!" says the client. "Too much money!! Too much time!!!"

This is foolish, because one can easily demonstrate that, for a major advertiser, the more ideas tested, the greater the probability of finding a blockbuster campaign. We're back to the bell curve. What we're looking for is advertising on the right-hand side of the curve, and unless we're very lucky, the only way we're going to find it is by developing and testing many alternatives. For those who think this is too expensive and takes too much time, consider this: the cost of developing and testing different concepts is modest compared to the payoff the company could achieve if it identifies a great execution.

WHAT EIGHT-YEAR-OLDS KNOW THAT SEASONED MANAGERS DON'T

Show an eight-year-old a fresh deck of cards, pointing out the ace of diamonds (a metaphor for an exceptional campaign), one that has approximately a 2 percent probability of being selected at random. Replace the ace, shuffle the deck, and ask the kid to bet $1 against your $5. If she draws the ace, she gets your $5; if not, you keep her $1. Make the game less risky. Give her two picks. You'll find that most eight-year-olds refuse the bet. They know that the odds against finding the ace are pretty high, even if they don't know they are 52 to 1 for the first card and 51 to 1 for the second.

Yet brand managers take this bet all the time. They accept one or two campaigns from their agency (like draws from a deck of cards), betting the budget that they've found a winner, not a campaign in the middle of the bell curve. Are eight-year-olds brighter than executives?

Some marketers and agency executives argue that the reason they do what they do is because advertising research is not a valid tool for selecting great advertising. Many point out that the animatics and photomatics bear little resemblance to the finished product. Intuitively, this makes sense.

However, a counterintuitive finding based on 20 years of experience and research suggests that the correlation between animatics and finished commercials is .87, which means that, for all practical purposes, the inexpensive and the very expensive get the same score (or, at the very least, turn in the same rank-order performance). If you find an approach that, say, improves consumer awareness 20 percent over the average commercial, consider the impact on the advertising budget. If you are spending $20 million on media, running the better commercial is like adding $4 million to the budget.

It is even more than $4 million because there's an exponential relationship between dollars invested and awareness. As a result, it might take an additional $6 million or $7 million to yield that 20 percent increase in awareness. Since sales tend to be correlated with awareness, the impact on sales of a 20 percent improvement in awareness may be gigantic.

Another reason agency execs give for not testing is that the execution is so "creative" that it needs time to build. "Here's a spot," they say, "that needs multiple exposures to work. But when it kicks in . . ."

Balderdash. Over the course of three decades we have participated in a number of clever research studies in which pairs of contenders for the campaign have been tested. Sometimes each commercial in the pair is from a different agency. Often they represent very different types of advertising—image-laden, for example, versus product-specific. The test is designed so that advertising effectiveness measures are gathered after a single exposure, two exposures, three, sometimes as many as five. What happens?

What we have found is that, although ad effects build over time, the winner after a single exposure is still the winner after multiple exposures. The response curves never cross!

What have we concluded from all of this? Most advertising campaigns are not tested before they run. Those that are tested are evaluated against only one or two alternatives. Finally, the reasons that managers give for not testing hold little water.

A case in point: A corporation we're working with spent $1.4 million to develop an animated, frenetic, 60-second commercial we'll call "Lazer Tag." Insiders understood what the company was trying to say from the spot, but ordinary viewers would never figure it out. We thought it was one of the most pointless ads we had ever seen.

We recommended that before putting Lazer Tag on the air the company test it against another ad that their agency had developed but never employed. We'll call this ad "Spokesman," a very different, straightforward, 30-second testimonial spot. The corporation hired a research company (not us) to do the copy test.

Both spots turned out to be average on four of eight measures: "brand linkage," "proven recall," "communication of 'superiority,'" and "perception of quality." Lazer Tag was below Spokesman (and well below average) on four other measures: "price value," "product uniqueness," "informative," and most important, "purchase intent." The ad scored above average (and higher than Spokesman) on only one measure—a negative one—"anything confusing."

We pointed out to the client that since Lazer Tag was a 60-second spot, it should have performed significantly better than the 30-second Spokesman. We also pointed out that it was not clear from the presentation what the research firm's average norms represented. In our work, as shown in the Advertising Performance Bell Curve™, the average ad is a bad ad. The "average" commercial returns only 1 to 4 percent on sales. Unless you have a great ad, your media dollars will earn a better return in a savings account.

Despite the sorry showing, the research company—sensitive to the client's desire to use a million-dollar commercial—recommended that the corporation move ahead with Lazer Tag. Why? "Because we think it shows a lot of promise." Hello? The marketer did, and the marketplace results were subliminal.

Because little testing is done, the resulting weak advertising provokes another crisis. Assume a company spends a third of the ad budget in the first quarter with no effect. That's money broadcast into the ozone with zero sales impact. Then management cries, "We've got to do better in the third quarter! Have the agency come up with another campaign." If the company had an effective commercial to begin with, it would not have to develop another one before year's end.

We're back to our question: why don't companies have the time to do things right when they have the time to do them over and over again?

The trick, of course, is to balance the two. Entertainment is necessary to motivate people to watch the spot (or read the ad), but too much entertainment produces a "vampire effect"; it sucks the life out of the message. Since the message—not the entertainment—is what "sells" the product or service, it cannot be ignored.

MEDIA SELECTION IS AS IMPORTANT AS AD COPY

One problem is that so many ads crowd into television programs. In 1986, for example, ABC aired about 6 ½ minutes of ads per hour in prime time. Now viewers get 9 ½ minutes on average.

But it isn't simply the three more minutes of advertising time spread through the hour that makes it hard for an advertiser to stand out; it's that there are so many commercials. Assuming an average of 20 seconds per commercial, there are about 30 in an hour-long show. CBS made the 15-second spot official in 1985 when it began to accept 15-second units as stand-alone ads, not just as half of a 30-second spot. Today television carries 60-, 30-, 15-, 10-, 5-, and since June 1998, 1-second spots (these last blinks are for Master Lock), all adding to the clutter, and clutter contributes to declining ad effectiveness.

To defend themselves against this commercial onslaught, many viewers automatically hit the "mute" button or zap the commercials by changing channels with the remote. They rarely did this 20 years ago, when they had to climb off the couch to change stations. Channel surfing is so universal and pervasive it's a topic of the daily comics. When women talk about the strange behavior of men, they often mention male conduct with the TV remote. (Some psychologists believe that men's predilection to zap is based in their "hunter" instincts. Stalk and shoot!) Male viewers zap at least 30 percent of all commercials, while women zap a significant, albeit lower, percentage.

As audiences fragment, advertisers must understand the effect of programming and editorial advertising response. Will the same commercial placed in two different programs with roughly the same audience size and profile generate the same advertising involvement and effectiveness? Does interest in a publication's articles carry over to the advertising?

Researchers have argued for 40 years over the impact of the television program on advertising effectiveness. All agree that the program affects viewer receptivity to, and therefore the effectiveness of, television advertising. But does an involving program suck the life out of the commercials it carries, perhaps because viewers resent the interruption—the vampire effect? Or does an involving program actually help the commercials, perhaps because viewer involvement carries into the advertising—the standard-bearer effect? *Either* situation, of course, has implications for the cost per thousand (CPM) method of buying television time.

Our book *Uncover the Hidden Power of Television Programming . . . and Get the Most From Your Advertising Budget* was designed to overcome the drawbacks of previous studies and answered several key questions. What we found is that, as program involvement goes up, all five advertising measures go up.

But what are the media implications? If program involvement enhances advertising response, and if involvement means more than simple viewership, then cost per thousand people *involved* should replace cost per thousand *exposed* in media selection decisions. Although marketers have purchased media based on CPMs for decades, it's no longer the best way.

A similar study of newspapers and magazines we conducted found the same thing: people who are deeply involved in the editorial content tend to be involved in the advertising. Of course, advertising-space salespeople have been selling the idea of editorial involvement as long as special-interest magazines have existed. It does not take much research to realize that golfers who read *Golf* magazine are interested in golf clubs; skiers who read *Skiing* want to know about the new parabolic skis; auto buffs who read *Car & Driver* are fascinated by cars and accessories. Women read *Vogue* and *Harper's Bazaar* as much for the ads as for the articles.

But we've found that the more people are involved with a general-interest magazine or newspaper, the greater is the effect of the advertising—in terms of behavioral intentions change, purchase interest, favorable brand attitudes, and perceptions of good value—carried by the publication.

We can feel confident making this general claim because the data was generated across 14 test ads, 4 test product categories, 3 publication types, and 926 respondents. Our findings were not the result of an idiosyncratic ad or product or publication that would make generalizations suspect.

The cost per thousand people and the cost per thousand people *impacted* are not the same thing. Our analyses suggest that they are potentially very different and that media decisions would be similarly different based on the proposed versus traditional approaches. Since the concept of CPMI appears to offer what advertisers want and are willing to pay for, advertising agency media planners need to take viewer involvement into account when they buy media.

GOOD ADS IN THE RIGHT MEDIUM MOVE THE NEEDLE

The steps to improved advertising are relatively easy to take, but they require time and effort: prepare an advertising brief; list all relevant attributes and benefits; screen the list to determine the strongest messages; evaluate these messages alone and in combination in terms of projected sales. Then include the winning message in a large number of different executions tested using a methodology that takes into account new discoveries concerning measures that predict sales response and the benefits of simulated-natural environment testing.

We know advertising can work. The annual Effie Awards, sponsored by the New York Chapter of the American Marketing Association, and the David Ogilvy Research Awards, sponsored by the ARF, highlight advertising campaigns that have worked. See Table 9-3 for examples of blockbuster advertising campaigns run during the 1990s.

We talked earlier about the vision, mission, targeting, and positioning for Green Mountain, the first company to brand a kilowatt-hour. Although it is much too early to declare a victory—and there are formidable obstacles to be faced on the path to success—this little Vermont company advertising on television and radio and in print has already become the number-one brand in awareness, preference, and enrollees in California and Pennsylvania, the first two states to deregulate.

Table 9-3   Selected Effie Award–Winning Advertising

Year	Company	Product	Agency	Campaign
1999	Ralston Purina	Dog Food	Fallon McElligott	"Incredible Dog Food, Incredible Dogs"
1998	Duracell	Duracell Batteries	Dancer Fitzgerald Sample; Ogilvy & Mather	"Device Wars"
1997	Sony Computer Entertainment of America	Sony PlayStation	TBWA/Chiat Day	"You Are Not Ready"
1996	Nabisco	SnackWell's	FCB/Leber Katz	"SnackWell's"
1995	IBM	IBM Hardware, Software, and Services	Doyle Dane Bernbach; Lintas; Ogilvy & Mather; Lord, Geller Federico & Einstein	"Solutions for a Small Planet"
1994	AT&T	1-800 Numbers	McCann-Erickson	"800 Reasons"
1993	Apple Computer, Inc.	Powerbook	BBDO, Los Angeles	"Powerbook Introduction"
1992	Reebok International	Blacktop Basketball Shoes	Hill, Holliday, Connors, Cosmopulous Inc.	"Blacktop Introduction"
1991	PepsiCo	Diet Pepsi	BBDO Worldwide	"The Taste That Beats Coke"
1990	Carillon Importers	Absolut Vodka	TBWA Advertising	"Absolut"

Green Mountain's advertising clearly communicates a message that the electric power industry, because of its use of coal to run its plants, is the largest source of industrial pollution in the nation and that a switch to Green Mountain is a step toward solving this problem. Promising "clean, green power made from the raging rivers of North America, the prevailing winds, and the sun," Green Mountain is going toe to toe against some of the giants in the utility industry and is winning. Green Mountain, we should add, just picked up the International Energy Industry's award for "Best Marketing of 1999."

Gardenburger has been marketing its meatless burger patties since 1985 and had sales of over $60 million in 1998. A year ago it advertised its patties on the last episode of *Seinfeld,* as part of a five-week national advertising blitz. The campaign featured animated 30-second television spots with voice-overs by actor Samuel L. Jackson, and the $1.7 million *Seinfeld* spot alone took more than 11 percent of Gardenburger's annual ad budget.

It was worth it. "Gardenburger's TV advertising has been very successful in creating awareness and trial of the Gardenburger brand, as evidenced by our second quarter sales, which were up 91 percent from a year ago," announced Lyle G. Hubbard, the chief executive officer. "Our grocery market share of veggie patties hit a high of 52 percent, which was double that of our closest competitor. Our capture of over 70 percent of the veggie patty growth in the grocery channel indicates that consumers are buying the brand they saw on TV. Our advertising is also aiding our sales in all other channels."

Then there is the experience of our Brazilian client, Brahma, with its Skol beer brand. The advertising agency working on Skol was young and hungry, especially since the brand, while 20 years old, had achieved broad distribution only in the previous three years. The agency people listened to the research and brought the creative folks to the presentation. The brief we prepared reported that the benefit was that the product was light and smooth tasting; there was a tangible difference in the flavor between Skol and other beers. Skol was also seen to be youthful too, which gave it a kind of light, fun personality. The agency came up with six different ideas. One advertising concept based on Portuguese wordplay tested exceptionally well. It communicated a "smooth taste" positioning in a very clever way—funny *and* informative. So they built commercials on the strategy. The ads generated higher penetration scores than beer commercials that were spending three and four times as much on media. More to the point, the Skol brand increased its market share dramatically and recently became the number-one brand in Brazil. Don't be surprised if you see it introduced into the U.S.

American companies spent something like $212 billion on advertising in 1999. If total ad spending rises another 5 percent in 2000—a conservative estimate—they will spend $223 billion. Most of it will be for average or worse campaigns that fall into the center and left-hand side of the Advertising Performance Bell Curve™ discussed earlier (that works out to a total of $187 billion spent on mediocre campaigns) and will show a disappointing return on investment. You want to be on the right side of the curve, where the ROI is 5 to 10 percent or, better yet, much, much more.

For advertising to "work," it must produce a clear return on the investment—not sleeper on subliminal effects—and while most advertising is disappointing, companies can improve their ads by employing counterintuitive tools and ideas currently available.

CHAPTER

10

Direct Marketers Need More Than Just Better Lists

By the time you read this book, American Express will have introduced Centurion, a new upscale credit card. If you're a heavy hitter and on the invitation list, the offer will arrive in a sexy black box a little larger than a VCR cassette. In addition to providing the financial utility of the American Express Platinum Card, Centurion will open the doors to private golf clubs, tennis clubs, and social clubs all over the world. It's an interesting idea, but not a new one.

We worked with American Express years ago on a very similar product with the same name priced at $300. In an earlier book we described it as the "High Roller Credit Card" that failed miserably in the marketplace. We hope American Express will be far more successful this time.

We learned a lot in that consulting engagement, including the fact that the list in direct marketing is not, despite what everyone says, the most important issue. To produce its original direct-mail packages, American Express went to two agencies, Ogilvy & Mather Direct and Leber Katz, a hot boutique firm of the time. Working off the same list of card members and prospects, the two agencies developed and mailed their best piece.

It was widely believed then (and is now) that since the list is the chief concern, the effects of the Centurion copy would be minimal. Yet the differences in the results were staggering. One piece beat the other by approximately eight to one. We studied the two pieces and were taken aback to discover how confusing they both were. Even after we read them twice, Centurion's unique attributes and benefits were unclear. We found it difficult to understand why anyone would be willing to pay big bucks for this new card.

Tracking research revealed that for the loser only 20 percent of the people to whom the package was mailed read and remembered something about the offer, and only 25 percent of those—or 5 percent of the total—understood it. Only 16 percent of those who understood it elected to subscribe, a conversion of a paltry 1.5 percent among Amex's best customers.

What was the difference between the winner and the loser? The winning piece was cleverly done, artfully created, and engaging to read. Though it failed to communicate the benefits of the Centurion card as well as it might have, most people who opened the package and read it became aware of the new card.

So here is a case in which, with the list held constant, dramatic differences in execution and message produced radically different outcomes. Today in our experience, direct marketers are not developing pieces that are dramatically different from one another and from their competitors in style, content, or production values, and as a consequence, they have effectively neutralized "the package" as a source of variance in explaining direct marketing results. They love to test different lists, however, with "minor" changes in the package, artificially creating the result that the list is all that matters. We'll have more to say about the lists and the message in this chapter.

PROBLEMS WITH TODAY'S DIRECT MARKETING

According to the Direct Marketing Association, direct marketers spent more than $176 billion in 1999, making direct marketing the third-largest advertising medium in America after newspapers and television, one that is growing at an annual compounded rate of approximately 7 percent. Direct marketing expenditures, which include telephone marketing, business-to-business marketing, newspapers, magazines, television, and radio, represent a large proportion of total U.S. advertising expenditures. The DMA reports, for example, that over 55 percent of all magazine advertising in 1998 was for direct marketing.

However, not everything is peachy in direct marketing land:

- *We are approaching saturation levels.*

In our surveys people say they receive too much direct mail. Their mailboxes are stuffed. They're ticked off, particularly the environmentalists, because they're throwing out (or having to recycle) pounds of paper every week. Most people receive far more direct mail—catalogs, offers, appeals—

than real mail. Weeding through it is a chore. And consumer pique contributes to . . .

- *A decline in response rates.*

Again, according to the DMA, response rates in the U.S. are declining, and sobering. More than a quarter (27.3 percent) of the outside lists that companies rent provoke no response whatever. More than that (30.4 percent) are lists that draw less than a 1 percent response. Another quarter of the lists draw 1.1 to 2 percent.

House files (that is, mailing lists the company has compiled itself) do considerably better. Almost one fifth of these lists obtain a response rate better than 10 percent—something no outside file accomplished in 1996, the most recent year for which figures are available. Another quarter of these lists obtain a 3.1 to 10 percent response rate.

This makes sense. Everything else being equal (though as we'll see in a moment, everything else is seldom equal), your own list, people who have done business with the company in the past, *should* be more responsive than strangers. But in addition to the pitiful response rates . . .

- *There is not enough innovation.*

For ten years we have been arguing the necessity for customized mail packages—an offer tailored for each prospect, an innovation that technology makes feasible and economic—yet there is still relatively little of it.

We do see some companies doing a cluster analysis of people on their lists to find groups of people with similar needs, which is an advance. They prepare different mailings for the different groups, but this is an example of 1970 market segmentation, not year 2000 customization.

Most of the mail that comes to your house is from major catalog marketers that send everyone the same thing. Year 1950 mass marketing?

One thing that we really like about contemporary direct marketing is the use of customer relationship management (CRM) software and campaign management software, two useful tools that help companies achieve their DM objectives. Since both are frequently discussed in the trade literature and at every professional conference, we'll focus this chapter on other topics.

By whatever name—CRM, interactive marketing, or database marketing—many marketers are using direct/interactive/database (D/I/D) marketing today. They do so because they can measure the results of, and thus control, a campaign directly. And they can almost surely improve what they're doing.

D/I/D marketing is an interactive system between company and customer that uses one or more advertising mediums: magazines, newspapers, radio, television, mail, telephone, the Internet, even flyers and posters. The system includes a measurable response and maintains a database.

D/I/D marketing applies to virtually every industry—product or service, profit or nonprofit, consumer or business-to-business. While the most popular and best-known forms of D/I/D marketing are direct mail (on which most of this chapter will focus) and telemarketing, it includes all types of direct-response print, broadcast, and electronic advertising.

D/I/D marketing is different from general marketing because instead of using surrogate variables such as advertising awareness, recall, and purchase intent to measure effectiveness, you measure actual buyer behavior—whether a purchase, a lead, or a qualified prospect. The implications can be profound. Instead of the budget controlling a campaign's size and scope, the campaign's success, based on a rigorous cost/benefit analysis (for example, a mailing list rollout based on actual results), can determine the budget.

The second substantial difference is that in D/I/D marketing, the firm maintains a database. In D/I/D marketing, database analyses drive decisions about offers, media, creative, and the like. The marketer is able to conduct these analyses at the individual prospect or firm level; in general marketing, companies usually conduct such analyses at the segment level. This means that today you can analyze a complete contact history (offers, responses, requests for information, and the like), and therefore, in theory at least, marketers can personalize the communications and product offers. A cover letter accompanying a catalog might (again, in theory) say, "The glassware on page 9 would go well with the china you recently bought." Or, as we'll see in a moment, the letter can be considerably more personal.

When the benefits of measurable and controllable campaign results are combined with a database's ability to track individuals over time, a firm can forecast Customer Lifetime Value, the present value of all (future) revenues and expenses associated with a customer. It can then address the question of how to allocate marketing expenditures between customer acquisition and customer retention. Clearly, you want to spend more money retaining valuable customers than on less valuable ones and (generally) more on retaining customers than on acquiring new ones.

THE INTUITIVELY APPEALING MARKET TARGET: "I JUST FEEL THIS LIST IS RIGHT"

The first problem with many—perhaps most—direct marketing programs today is that managers hypothesize which lists they should buy because they just feel they're right for the product. A simple (minded) example: The manufacturer of a new golf club rents a list of *Golf Digest* subscribers. That is a huge improvement over renting a list of, say, *Newsweek* subscribers, but it is expensive and limited. You can use the list only once, and your campaign may require more than one contact. And not everyone who would be interested in your new club reads *Golf Digest*.

We learned this the hard way working with Disney on a serious new service, a $500-a-day experience. Mass media was not the way to advertise it because of the hypothesized narrow-band target, so direct marketing seemed like the logical alternative. When we met with the Disney people, they were far along in developing the campaign, and their direct marketing consultant had come up with eight lists he intended to use. But how had he come up with the lists? Pure judgment. "We believe the kind of people who subscribe to *Smithsonian* are the kind of people who will be coming here." This is a common (and flawed) approach to picking a target.

Our recommendation was to do a segmentation study to identify and describe the attitudinal, behavioral, demographic, psychographic, sociographic, and media exposure patterns of people who expressed interest in the Disney concept. Block-level demographics and other characteristics from secondary data sources could be appended to this database to build an equation that would predict the value of every prospect. Once the study was completed and the modeling done, we could press the proverbial button and look at a printout of more than a million Americans who would be interested in spending a day or more with Disney. Here's how to do this.

DON'T BUY THE LIST; BUILD YOUR OWN

Direct marketers, as we noted earlier, almost uniformly agree that the single most important variable in a direct marketing campaign is the list, which, translated, means the target. In the past the best approach was to rent lists.

For example, a company formed in 1995 to sell healthy foods—foods grown organically without chemical fertilizers, pesticides, or additives—found, not unexpectedly, given what it was selling, that a natural foods club list drew extremely well, an 8 percent return. Unfortunately, the list covered considerably less than 1 percent of the population, so signing up 8 percent of at most 1 percent was insignificant. Since the company's desired target represented approximately 15 percent of the population, that was not acceptable; it rented more lists, but response rates plunged.

At that point we did a survey among the total population. We asked questions about environmentally friendly foods, willingness to pay a price premium, and the propensity toward buying direct. We looked at the household's

Figure 10-1   Append Secondary Data to Survey Data

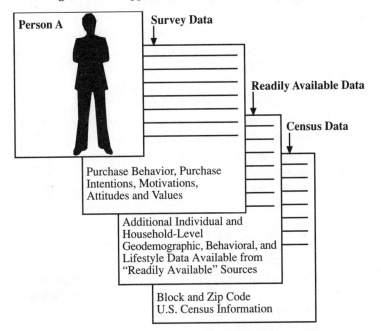

organic and natural foods consumption patterns, since the more a family spents on these products the more valuable it was as a prospect. Between the survey and publicly available data, the company was able to develop an equation to predict the potential responsiveness and profitability of more than half of all American households. The households in the top decile on this list were comparable to the natural foods club list but included approximately 6 million households, not the fraction originally identified.

While renting a list may still be the best solution for many marketers, at some point it's cheaper to create your own. Unless you stumble across a list that happens to draw terrifically well, you will always do better with your own.

To build this list, start by coupling survey research with database information. Take a survey of, say, 2,000 customers to ask the marketing things you want to know—their needs, wants, attitudes toward the company, toward the product, and more. We particularly like applications in which we query respondents about their interest in buying the marketer's new product or service. Append each respondent's account data (assuming you have it; if not, start accumulating it) to the survey results. Did they respond to an offer? How much did they spend with you? What department did they buy in?

Next, append whatever is available from third-party databases. This information includes block-level census data and third-party information sources, such as Prizm clusters, Infobase demographic data, and Polk/NDT data (a commercially available database that provides household-level information about lifestyles, such as hobbies, media consumption, vehicles, and the like).

An equation is then developed to predict the behavior we are interested in understanding—say, purchase probability for the Disney experience, health foods, or a new Sony home fax machine. The "independent" or "predictor" variables are the account data, stuff from third-party databases, census info, and so on. This equation can be used not just to rank order the 2,000-odd respondents in the survey in terms of their interest, but to predict the rank order of 60-million-plus households in terms of their likely response to the offering.

Basically, we're talking about sophisticated direct marketing list enhancement married to survey research that measures responsiveness and customer value.

The research we've just described can tell a company who, exactly, will sign up for the Disney experience, buy the new health food product, or purchase the new fax machine. Not just that 2.7 percent will buy in the first year (assuming awareness and availability) but who they are—attitudinally, psychographically, and geodemographically. If we have built the bridge from the test to the market properly, the computer will print out (as it did) the names and addresses of approximately 4,680,000 very reachable people.

This is not an inflated total of probable and possible prospects. These are the specific people we'd expect to buy if we made them aware of the product.

Armed with this kind of list, we don't need an expensive national launch with network television advertising and coupons in freestanding inserts. For the new fax machine and a great many other products, more than enough prospects exist to launch a successful direct marketing campaign.

Once the computer spits out the individual names and addresses, a company can generate specific and targeted information for everything from sample or coupon distribution to additional coded respondents for supplemental research, validation, or tracking programs. Management can ask for a computer mapping program to draw attractive color-coded maps that it can use for roll-out strategies, test market selection, retail site analysis, regional media planning, and more.

DOING THE SAME THING IN BUSINESS-TO-BUSINESS MARKETING

Why not do the same sort of thing in business-to-business marketing? Many companies selling to businesses know a great deal about their customers—a

Figure 10-2   Model Output

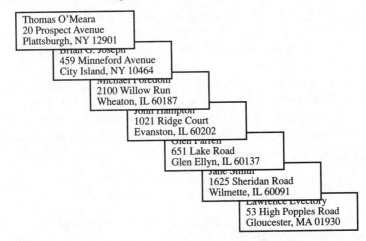

firm's age, size, sales, number of employees, growth trend, purchase cycle, purchase and decision-making behavior, media profiles, and much more. It should be possible to create a model that would search for similar firms.

One could, except that databases containing the same kind of information about businesses as they do about consumers do not yet exist. But some business databases do exist. And companies are taking what's available, projecting to fill in the missing information, and selling the results.

Banks and others, for example, are able to obtain the names and addresses of, say, clothing manufacturers located in Manhattan with annual sales greater than $50 million, more than 200 employees, in business more than three years. That's better than approaching every company listed under "Clothing—Wholesale & Manufacturers" in the Yellow Pages, but not much. A software company selling its sophisticated statistical analysis program to media researchers in the advertising industry, for example, has no way to know that research chemists who face the same kinds of problems would be a market.

If it were possible to track the kinds of products and services a company buys the way it is possible to track an individual's credit card, automotive, and other purchases, the information would be extremely interesting and helpful. What does it say about a company that buys Compaq personal computers instead of IBM or Dell? Combined with other information, it says something relevant about the company's philosophy: what it values, what it finds important, what risks it will take.

The marketing revolution is moving marketers to fill these information gaps. Today companies are collecting data about businesses. Just as companies began assembling databases containing consumer information, so companies are beginning to combine business databases. Given the cost of a sales call, even the cost of telemarketing, there is as great an incentive to improve business-to-business marketing as to improve consumer marketing. Consider the difference it would make if a company had not just 5,000 prospects but 5,000 prospects ranked by sales potential and propensity to buy. It would be invaluable to know, for example, that they would make the most money selling to the first 1,362 companies on such a list.

Know Your Target Intimately

Start with the blindingly obvious: not all customers and prospects are the same. Obviously they have some differences in terms of demographic variables. But more important, they have different hopes, dreams, goals, problems, needs, wants, desires, aspirations, perceptions, and values. Some shop sales; some shop as a sport; and some shop only when they have no choice.

Knowing the target group's demographics is a necessary but insufficient basis for knowledge. Most direct marketers can talk at length about the demographic profiles and even zip code profiles of their targets, but they have little insight into what's in the heads of these customers and prospects. If marketing is the discipline concerned with "solving people's problems with products and services profitably," it stands to reason that marketers should understand the problems of the people they are trying to reach. This requires talking to them in depth, at length, and in sufficient numbers to yield reliable insights. And this goes way beyond simple matters like gender, education, income, and region. Your company can build a stronger bond with customers and increase its share of their requirements when, as we discussed in Chapter 6, you better understand their motivations through market segmentation, a first step toward market customization. Eventually you want to know more than your target's demographics and behavior; you want to know their attitudes, psychographics, and sociographics.

By assigning everyone in your database to a segment that has particular needs, preferences, and perceptions, you can create segment-specific direct marketing campaigns that produce higher returns than a general mailing. For example, a clothing retailer can develop merchandising, pricing, and service strategies appropriate for the store's segment mix. With this information the store can allocate resources more profitably—for example, sending catalogs featuring the most advanced high-end designer fashions only to people most interested in fashion.

Now if the computer groups these people into market segments based on the same type of research technology that we discussed in the targeting chapter, they will be defined by all three elements: the survey data (which would be some needs and wants), the customer account data, and the third-party data. Not only are these segments different from the traditional segments because you can put names on the individuals in them, but you know their needs, likes, dislikes, and most important, how likely they are to buy.

Most important, you have the data to assess the potential profitability of each person and target group, not just in terms of what they are buying today but in terms of what they might be buying if they were approached appropriately. Moreover, you should have an idea of what to say to the people in each segment, now that you know who they are and what they have in common. That is fine for the 2,000 customers you interviewed, but how do you extend the segmentation to everyone else in the database?

An equation says you can predict membership in a given segment from customer-account and third-party information even though you never survey them. For example, suppose you know three things about your respondents: weight from a survey, marital status from customer-account data, and socioeconomic status from a third-party database. Using the variables, you create segments: people who are poor, thin, and single . . . people who are rich, obese, and married . . . people who are rich, thin, and married, and so on.

Now you have a new person. She was not in your study, so you don't have her weight, but you do have her marital and socioeconomic status, lots of information about the demographic characteristics of the census block in which she lives, some data on financial relationships, and perhaps what car she drives. The odds are you can predict which segment she goes into because you know all these other things about her. Affluence and age, for example, are highly predictive of weight. As people get older, they get heavier. Downscale people tend to be heavier than upscale people. Single people tend to be thinner than married people.

It is a simple example, but the point is that when you have all the variables, you can assign someone to a segment with a reasonable level of accuracy. It's not perfect, but it's very good. And it's better than assigning people to segments at random. If you have six segments, all things being equal, you have a one in six chance of assigning someone randomly to the correct segment. In other words, only 17 percent accuracy.

SEGMENTATION CASE: AN UPSCALE CLOTHIER

We helped one upscale department store chain survey a sample of its customers to develop target groups. The combination of survey, customer database, and third-party information gave the store the detailed target profiles it needed. It found, for example, that the "Young Professional" segment was the most valuable target group. While these people represent 22 percent of the customer base, they account for an enormous proportion of potential profits. They buy more of their clothes and spend more at our client's stores than at any other retailer.

- *Their demographics:* Average age, late 20s through early 40s, high household and personal income, and least likely to have children at home.
- *Their attitudes:* "You can tell a lot about a person by how he or she dresses." They keep up with the latest fashions but do not have much time to shop. They are not concerned about price.
- *Their style:* Updated, contemporary, youthful. The merchandise they are most likely to buy includes career wear, accessories, and shoes.
- *Key positioning:* Our store is the fashion leader with exclusive, latest fashions . . . knowledgeable salespeople . . . expensive but worth it.

At the other extreme this retailer found "Value Shoppers" to be the least valuable segment. These people represent 34 percent of the customers but only a fraction of potential profits. As a group they spend the least on apparel and less at the store than at other retailers.

Unless you begin your segmentation survey effort with the end in mind, you will not know how everyone else in your database—the people you did not survey—fits into the segments you find. By knowing what variables you will have to classify your customers and including them in the inputs of the segmentation, you improve the linkage between segmentation and classification variables and therefore (and this is key) increase the accuracy of your classification.

This approach not only works well using your own customer data but can be very helpful in building new databases that are better than those currently being used based on purchasing lists from a broker. To accomplish this, again, survey a large cross section of the population. Instead of appending information from a customer database (we have none; they're not customers), include questions designed to assess interest in your product or service using some of the same tools we will talk about in Chapter 11.

Analyzing the data in the same way that we just discussed when you're working with a customer list reveals important insights into the characteristics of prospects projected to be the most profitable. Apply the resulting equation to a much larger universe of households or individual names to create your own list of best prospects. Green Mountain, the little energy company in Burlington, Vermont, with national aspirations, employed this approach to enhance its direct marketing effort in Connecticut and Pennsylvania.

HAVE A CLEAR, COMPELLING, AND MEMORABLE POSITIONING

If you have studied Chapter 8 and taken its lessons to heart, your positioning is now clear, compelling, and memorable.

Go through all the catalogs that arrive in a month. Ask which has a positioning strategy. Which catalog gives a clear and powerful impression of the retailer?

Some direct marketers would argue that the positioning strategy is implicit in the merchandise they sell and the price. But we argue that if Bloomingdale's, Saks, and Neiman Marcus all carry similar merchandise at an upscale price, what's the positioning? What distinguishes Lands' End, L.L.Bean, Eddie Bauer, or Orvis?

For catalogs that *do* have a positioning, look at three book retailers: Edward H. Hamilton, Daedalus Books, and Barnes & Noble. All three sell books at a discount, but their positionings, as manifested in their catalogs, are very different.

The Edward H. Hamilton catalog is black-and-white, the size of a tabloid newspaper, and printed on thin news stock. A typical catalog may have 70 or more pages, each page filled with tiny photos of book jackets and five to seven lines describing the book—as many as 5,000 books in a catalog. Most of the books are remainders, so the prices are low; a book the publisher priced at $24.95 Hamilton will sell for $4.95. The catalog gives an impression of plethora, low overhead, great bargains—if you are willing to slog through the pages of type to find them.

The Daedalus Books catalog is two-color, *Time* magazine size, and runs around 50 pages. A typical page has six or seven book descriptions illustrated by photos of the books. The copy reads as if it were a friend's letter summarizing a favorite book. These are also remainders, so the prices are comparable to Hamilton's. The Daedalus catalog gives the impression of a book-loving friend who wants to pass on recommendations you may have missed when the books first appeared.

The Barnes & Noble catalog is four-color, maybe magazine size or smaller, and runs around 60 pages. The books are discounted but most are not remainders, so the price savings do not always seem as impressive: a $7.95 book for $6.36, for example, or a $19.95 book for $15.96. A recent catalog offered books on business, careers, computers, technology, fiction, history, and videos. While Hamilton and Daedalus also offer books in many categories (indeed, Hamilton gives the impression of having something for every taste), the Barnes & Noble catalog seems pointless; there is nothing beyond the books.

INDIVIDUALIZE YOUR OFFER; DON'T JUST TALK ABOUT IT

Market segmentation is not personalization.

Virtually every company that does direct marketing says that it personalizes its offer. "We really understand our target and we've customized it," they say. But it is still only one offer, one letter, one catalog going to one segment. They may have worked hard to segment the total market, so they are sending five or six different offers, six different letters, six different catalogs, but that's not individualization (nor, as we said above, is this common). It is not a different offer for every single person.

Given the state of technology, it is both possible and economically feasible for companies to engage in truly personalized/customized/one-on-one marketing, a marketing program directed to individual customers, the company treating each individual differently. Consider a revolving marketing software system designed to increase a retailer's sales and profits. The system employs automated intelligence technology combining the best of a "perfect salesman" with a "perfect advertising agency" to computer design and implement highly motivating, individualized, one-on-one marketing programs.

When customer needs and store inventory match, the store has a sales opportunity it can communicate to prospects. This, of course, is Retailing 101. But while virtually every retailer knows its inventory, few truly know their customers. What makes such a system special is the customer profile with which the computer can automatically match the inventory to the customer and generate a personal letter—not a form letter, but a letter that would alert the customer to special opportunities, such as the one in Figure 10-3.

This letter contains a great deal of information about the customer and his wife. Not just his name and address, but his wife's birth date, preferred brand, color, and size. Did Connie Lester actually compose this letter? No, it was written by a computer, but Connie does sign it, and she will follow up.

This is a far cry from taking the customer list and segmenting it into different typologies (valuable as that may be). We believe the future lies in truly

Figure 10-3   Illustration of a Personalized Letter

Chaneltique Fine Clothing

November 20, 2001

Dear Mr. Shulman:

Just a reminder that your wife Robin's birthday is coming up in two weeks on December 3rd, and we think we have the perfect gift in stock.

As you know, she loves Escada clothing, and we have an absolutely beautiful new winter suit in black, her favorite color, in size seven (her size), priced 10% below the suggested retail price of $2,850. She will look simply stunning!

If you like, I can gift wrap the suit at no extra charge and mail it to you next week so that you will have it in plenty of time for her birthday. Or if you prefer, I can put it aside so that you can come pick it up. Please give me a call at (617) 630-8750 within the next three days to let me know which you prefer.

I appreciate your business and hope to hear from you soon.

Sincerely yours,

Connie Lester
Store Manager

individual, customer-centered communications programs that understand that each person is an individual and treats him or her as such.

TEST ALTERNATIVE PACKAGES IN VITRO

Direct marketers tell us all the time that they test different "offers," different mailings, different messages. In our experience, when they do this, the alternatives are far more similar than different—something we talked about earlier—and they do the testing in situ rather than in vitro. That is, they test in the real world rather than in a laboratory.

We rarely quarrel with doing real world testing, but in the case of direct marketing, such tests are expensive and time-consuming. Half a year or more can go by developing alternative packages, printing 10,000 copies of each, mailing them, waiting six weeks or more for all the responses to come in, and tabulating results.

With an in vitro test, as we discussed earlier, you expose small numbers of prospects, typically no more than 200, to very different types of stimuli and employ sophisticated questioning methods to gauge consumer response. Although the "self-report" data resulting from these studies is not nearly as precise as data in a real world test, what we are looking for here is usually rank-order differences. How did A" perform relative to "B" compared to "C"? In this respect the laboratory research performs fairly well.

Take, for example, an environmentally concerned company that tested a direct-mail package in New Hampshire. They mailed prospects a box imprinted with "Grow a Tree" all over it. The box was about 4 inches square and 12 inches high and had a transparent window through which one could see a sapling. The stated message: Plant the sapling and improve the atmosphere. The implied message: We are sensitive to the environment, and by buying from us you can improve the world. The package was unusually effective, so much so that the company used the same idea for a major push in a different state. The results were disappointing, however.

When we began to analyze the reason why the response was so poor, we found that the company had decided to "improve" the offer. The new carton was plain cardboard with no clear indication that it contained a sapling. The carton was roughly 12 inches wide, 8 inches high, and 24 inches long—without a window. People who opened the carton found packing material and a smaller plain brown box, which also had no window. A sapling and the literature were in this smaller box.

Why make the changes? Said a spokesman, "We thought we'd add some mystery to the whole thing by sending an unlabeled box. We thought people would get into it, take out the tree, and be excited." They didn't and weren't.

This is something that small-scale research in vitro could have discovered before the mailing was ever done.

Another problem we see regularly is that the company has a "commercial" it wants to put in an envelope but seldom has the marketer done any research. The offer never meets a real customer before it's stuffed into 20,000 envelopes. In this situation we think focus groups can be helpful. We have suggested to corporations as large as AT&T and as small as the nonprofit Save the Sound that they show their offer to three or four groups for reaction before sending it out. When they do, the first group inevitably finds the letter, the offer, and the package are all totally impenetrable. The people in the focus group say, "I don't understand this. I can't figure out this sentence here. I don't know what it means. I have no idea what they're talking about."

We can predict that direct marketing copy will be unintelligible to over half the population at the first pass. It's full of buzzwords. It's too dense. It's confusing. Buyers say, "I can't read all this; I'm tired." Clearly the copy needs work to have the impact the company wants.

Our suggestion is to trim the message down to something simple and motivating. One way to do that, of course, is with the brand strategy matrix shown in Chapter 8 on page 127. That grid spells out what is highly motivating, moderately motivating, and less motivating in your brand versus the others. And once you have a draft of what you want to say, hold some focus groups among the target audience so you know you are being reasonably clear.

Then Test the Direct Marketing Offer in Situ

Even if you've done in vitro studies, test the offer in the real world. Some companies do little testing. They mail out the package and are disappointed when they obtain a 0.5 percent return—or ecstatic when they obtain a 3 percent return. Direct marketing, however, lends itself to testing because you can divide a list into two, four, or eight parts to test different packages.

Many companies *do* such test cells. They vary the look and the offer two to four ways to learn which provokes the best response, a good idea. The problem we find is that they vary these offers in unusable ways. For example, one offer will have a higher price, but the letter will be long and emphasize status. The next will have a lower price, and the letter will stress convenience. The long letter will be personalized, while the short letter will have no signature. The company does not vary the offers systematically, so these are just four different things. In this case the marketer assumes that status and position justify a higher price, while convenience and utility go with a lower price. They may be right, but without a real test there is no way to know.

The company sends out four mailings, and three turn out to be weak, while one, though not good, is a little better. Now the marketing department has to figure out what happened. Why did this one do better than the other three? What can they do to improve the one that seems to be best? The company cannot know. It does not know if the key element is price, status appeal, letter length, or letter personalization. Because it has conflated these elements in the offers, it cannot isolate any one effect.

There are two easy ways to correct this. One is to organize the test as a scientific experiment. You have four different things you want to test (four factors) and two categories of each (i.e., two levels): the length of the letter, the degree of personalization, the basic positioning strategy, and the price. Ordinarily this would require a complex mailing with 16 different cells ($2 \times 2 \times 2 \times 2 = 16$). If you are willing to assume that there are no "higher-order" interactions between factors in the design, you can use a simple orthogonal design to compress the 16 cells into 4. Two will have a long letter; two will have a short.

Table 10-1 How to Test Four Different Offer Elements

Mailing 1	Mailing 2	Mailing 3	Mailing 4
High price	High price	Low price	Low price
Long letter	Short letter	Long letter	Short letter
Personalized	Impersonal	Personalized	Impersonal
Status	Convenience	Status	Convenience

Two of them will be high priced; two low. Two will be personalized; two not. Two will emphasize status; two will emphasize convenience.

As Table 10-1 shows, each factor level is carefully balanced with every other factor. For example, the long letter appears an equal number of times with the status positioning, personalized format, and high price. In the end you don't care which mailing wins; you're able to isolate which effect seems to be greatest.

Everyone should follow up a large direct marketing campaign with a telephone tracking study to measure and diagnose its performance among 500 people who were sent the offer. It takes about 12 minutes on the phone to learn who received, opened, read the offer, and what they did about it. Direct marketing campaigns succeed or fail for many reasons, some of which we have outlined here, and analyzing results in terms of response rates provides little insight into what works and why and no insight into how to make the campaign better.

Table 10-2 represents a report card on recent direct marketing programs we have monitored (and in some cases have received data from other organizations) that suggests there is considerable opportunity for improvement in contemporary campaigns. At every stage of the process, from receipt of the mailing to conversion to purchase, direct marketers receive failing grades.

Table 10-2   Direct Marketing Report Card

	Average Score	
Received Mailing	45%	
Read Material	26	
Remembered Something	16	All Failing Grades
Comprehension	10	
Conversion to Purchase	18	
Sales	0.5	

Perhaps our readers will argue we are tough graders or that the task a direct marketer is trying to accomplish is like trying to teach a pig to sing. But the facts speak for themselves. The numbers are low and declining, and good tracking research is one way to turn the situation around.

STUDY RESPONSE CURVES—SOMETIMES THREE HITS ARE MORE EFFICIENT THAN ONE!

One thing we love about direct marketers is the "rules of thumb" they routinely follow. Now rules are generally good things, but sometimes, if the rule is wrong, it can lead you astray.

Consider one common rule. If you repeat a mailing to the same household, say, one month after the first, you'll see a response rate of about 80 percent of the first mailing. A third mailing "pulls" about 50 percent of the first, and all subsequent mailings do about the same.

Based on this rule, marketing management assumes that it's better to test another list than to test the same one twice. Hence the unending search for the perfect list.

Our experience, however, is that the response to direct-response marketing does not always diminish with the number of hits. Sometimes a second and a third mailing are actually superior to the first. Sometimes great direct marketing, like fine wine, needs to age, to build in effectiveness over time.

A buildup in response is sometimes observed for:

1. Infrequently purchased products and services for which there's no need to buy now.
2. Off-holiday mailings, when there's no need to buy because there are more than 14 days left before Christmas.
3. Expensive products and services for which the buyer needs to plan the discretionary purchase, save for it, and involve another household member or "buying unit" in the decision.
4. Complicated products and services that also require discussions with others, perhaps a friend or an expert, before making the decision.
5. A low-involvement buyer who's not particularly interested in the product category and therefore requires multiple reminders before taking action.

All of this information can, of course, be gathered prior to a direct campaign for purposes of anticipating the effects of multiple responses. This kind of research can also provide insights into the timing of multiple exposures. If they make sense, should they be a month apart or two days? In one recent case for an infrequently purchased, off-holiday, expensive, complicated product in a low-involvement category, the appropriate interval appeared to be about two weeks. And three mailings worked much better than one.

USING SIMULATION TO FORECAST AND DIAGNOSE DIRECT MAIL RESULTS

As far as we know, there's little sophisticated market simulation done in direct marketing, the kind we will talk about in Chapters 14 and 15. This is certainly true for campaigns that consider direct marketing in conjunction with a mass media effort. Sophisticated packaged goods marketers use simulation for new products purchased in supermarkets and drugstores. They use simulated test marketing methods discussed in Chapter 16 to predict with a high level of confidence what a product will sell before they actually put it in the supermarket.

To develop such a model, estimate what percentage of the target population will get the mailing, will open the mailing, will read all or most of the mailing, will understand the basic message, will decide to act on it, will put it in a place where it's convenient to act on it, and will eventually act on it. Do this not just for one exposure but for multiple exposures as well. That is, anticipate a response curve. That's a relatively foreign concept to direct marketers, but it can be extremely useful.

Better yet, employ a sophisticated model based on lots of case histories that captures the effects not only of the direct marketing campaign but of all the communications used to support the program, including television, print, radio, outdoor advertising, public relations, and Web site. Such a model not only will help a marketer plan a direct marketing campaign but can be used after an actual launch to compare actual performance against predicted performance. In this way the campaign can be improved a second time around, based not just on judgment but on science as well.

Figure 10-4 shows the projected performance of an integrated marketing program over its first year. You can use this model to evaluate different levels of mass media spending, different media vehicles, different media schedules, and different levels of direct response. Plugging in the impact of the direct marketing package will help you understand its contribution to overall performance.

Why aren't such models more common in direct marketing? We suspect it is because the direct-mail agencies have made it difficult. They would rather close their doors than give you the ability to understand a mailing's probable

Figure 10-4   Forecast Performance of Integrated Direct Marketing Program

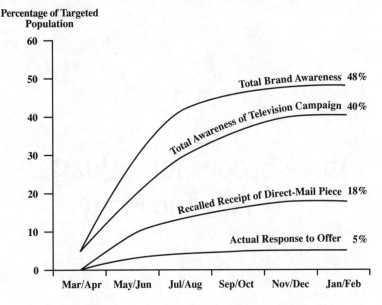

effects. They will say they cannot predict how a mailing will do before it goes out, and after the fact they cannot tell you why it did what it did. There is an assumption of some "magical interaction" between the offer and the list. Sometimes you have an incredible return and sometimes almost no return, but the direct-mail house doesn't help you to understand why. They wrap themselves in a cloak of mystery—and will not be held accountable for poor returns.

Our final counterintuitive recommendation is, take the time to do it right. How much time? The honest answer is "It depends." But you can tell if you did not take enough time by the results. If you have to do it over again, you did not take enough time to know your target intimately, find a clear positioning, test, create your own mailing list, individualize the offer, or all of the above. If you do it right, direct marketing can be a powerful tool. If you don't, it becomes just one more way to waste company resources.

11

Three Scoops for a Quarter Is Two Too Many

Companies all over the globe are searching for new products and services that are loaded with features that appeal to everyone. For an example with which we're all familiar, look no further than Amazon.com. Amazon offers low price, convenience, an on-line shopping mall open 24 hours a day, software to guide the buyer to available products, product reviews, and more. Everything for everybody, with no focus and, to date, no profits.

This is what we call "triple scoops of ice cream in a waffle cone, made with the finest, most expensive ingredients, including chocolate sprinkles on top— all for a quarter." Such an offer would ignite our customers but cripple our business. It's at least two scoops too many.

This reminds us of a maxim used by Kathleen O'Meara-Clancy: "Anything worth doing is worth overdoing." She uses it to describe the overzealous chase of some objective even when it should be obvious that the pursuit has become dysfunctional. For example, she uses it in reference to a neighbor, Glen Trenholm, who collects snowmobiles. He has so many that his life now revolves around where to store them and how to maintain them. What started as a hobby has turned into an all-consuming vocation. It also applies to a colleague, Bill Hatfield, who loves golf so much that it has gotten in the way of work and family relationships. His obsessive desire to break 80 has put his job and marriage in jeopardy.

We use Kath's expression to describe the relentless pursuit of unprofitable business objectives, which characterizes businesses from New York to Tokyo. Some companies set unreasonable sales goals (Kath would say they're "overdoing" it) and then chase them through price discounting and consumer and trade promotions at the expense of profitability. Other companies strive to dominate media spending in their category (i.e., "share of voice") while neglecting copy and media impact (i.e., the effectiveness of the advertising and where it's placed). Dot-coms are becoming famous for this. Others seek to maximize quantity of distribution (the number of stores or distributors carrying their product) while ignoring the quality of distribution (for example, shelf facings, shelf talkers, and end-of-aisle displays). And too many firms on the Internet race after hits on a Web site, neglecting the actual sales rung up.

But few corporate goals are as dysfunctional as the relentless pursuit of the most appealing products and services, which characterized the 1990s.

New ideas for products and services, such as Amazon, come from everywhere. They fly into people's heads in the middle of the night, or the company has an opportunity to license something from another country (Häagen-Dazs has had enormous success with *dulce de leche* ice cream, which began life in South America; Clorox, with Brita water purification systems, which originated in Europe), or the firm has actually done some new product idea generation and come up with ideas.

At some point in the process the idea turns into a concept, often described in one or two paragraphs, sometimes with a name and a price. And if the marketer is smart, this concept is tested among a cross section of 100 to 500 prospective buyers in the product category. The higher the score, the bigger the celebration in the marketing war room.

Concept testing, however, is plagued with problems. Almost every marketer/researcher has done one (if not hundreds) of these tests, yet such tests often raise as many questions as they answer. We hear marketing executives ask questions like "Is 14 percent in the top box ["Definitely Will Buy"] a good score?" Or they say, "We studied three pricing variations. How could they *all* get 10 percent in the top box? Is there a fourth variation we should offer?" Or "If we changed the price [or the formulation or the packaging], how much would trial increase? Would it go to 30 percent?" Ideally, management would like to see a 100 percent top box, the maximum level of appeal.

A CONCEPT TEST GONE WILD:
THE CASE OF INTERNET CAR INSURANCE

An enthusiastic marketing manager triggers the traditional concept test when she asks, "What's the potential for this big new idea?" The idea might be a new

European ice cream, a new palm-sized PC, or for the sake of this example, an automobile insurance product to be marketed over the Internet. The marketing manager at FidelityWorldwideInsurance.com notes that the new line could be targeted and positioned toward either people who want to insure a single car or families that need to insure a fleet of cars. Each of these two positionings could emhasize one of three different benefits: the service is fast; the service is cheap; the service promptly takes care of you in case of an accident. The marketing manager has now described six different concepts (2 positions × 3 benefits).

But she immediately points out that each positioning/benefit option could be based on one of four different attributes, or reason-why stories: the type of insurance, the insurance coverage, the ease and speed of setup, the efficiency of an on-line insurance statement. Now we're up to 24 different concepts (6 positions/benefits × 4 attributes).

Moreover, price remains problematic. The company's experience suggests five different price points, and the manager is unsure of what to charge, so the concept now has five prices for the single-car insurer and five prices for the multiple-car insurer. In a 10-minute conversation the manager has transformed one idea into 240 different concepts, a process that takes place all the time.

So what do you do? We typically ask the marketing manager to take a deep breath and pick the one concept that she believes will be the most successful, the one that will make the most money for Fidelity. We call this "management's favorite." In the case of this on-line car insurance service, management's go-to plan focused on the single-car owner whose main priorities were hypothesized to be speed and price.

Most companies, however, are too enthusiastic to stop at 240 different combinations ("We'll provide a service that does all the Registry of Motor Vehicles legwork for them We'll mail their plates and registration overnight delivery! Better yet, we'll get in our cars and deliver it ourselves"), and every new variable multiplies the number of possibilities. Sometimes researchers who are supposed to test the concepts leave a meeting bewildered by the number of possibilities—thousands . . . hundreds of thousands . . . millions of concepts could be tested. But what company would pay for such a test? Even if a company is willing to test an enormous number, traditional concept testing has serious limitations. Let's talk about these problems, and then we'll discuss how to evaluate "management's favorite" concept in terms of revenues and profitability.

THE PROBLEMS WITH TRADITIONAL CONCEPT TESTING

Sample limitations. Research companies generally employ small (75 to 150), nonprojectable groups of men and women wandering through shopping malls and willing to answer questions for the research. Further, they tend to use only about three nonrepresentative malls and markets for a given study.

Measurement problems. Researchers often use purchase intention and other rating scale measures with unknown reliability and validity. The scales miscarry because researchers don't know (a) if repeating the study would yield the same results or (b) if the results actually reflect what they want to learn. It's like measuring IQ by wrapping a rubber tape rule around the head; the results vary with every measurement and don't measure intelligence anyway.

Alternative possibilities. Few researchers are able to efficiently ask "what if?" questions concerning variations in concept features and benefits. "What if we provide preferred access to a car repair shop? What if we take care of the whole registration process for them for a small fee? For free?"

Ignorance of costs. In our experience, marketing managers seldom know the fixed and variable "manufacturing" and marketing costs, and researchers never know them. But without knowing costs, a manager cannot estimate profitability.

Limited models. Finally, few researchers offer a valid model of the marketing mix into which to feed concept scores to predict sales and profitability. Researchers present concept scores to management as if they were discrete pieces of information in themselves: "This one got a 33 percent top two box score, beating the control concept by almost two to one." That's nice, but will it sell? And if it sells, will it be profitable? Blank looks from the researcher.

Can companies overcome these problems? Many of them. Our suggestions:

Larger samples. Begin with a larger, more projectable sample of prospective buyers (300 to 500) in more locations than the ones traditionally found for such tests. These people should be serious respondents, people recruited via random-digit dialing and then brought to a central location—not the first bodies willing to stand still in a shopping mall.

Full descriptions. Expose the sample to the big idea—a full description of the concept, complete with the name, positioning, packaging, features, and price (it's surprising how many concept tests ignore price). Present the concept in its competitive context, that is, with competing products sold in the market at their actual prices. The more a test simulates, models, or mirrors reality, the more accurate the forecast. Even so, most concept testing ignores the competitive frame.

Measure purchase probability. Have consumers rate the concept in terms of purchase probability using a scale that is superior to traditional 3-, 5-, or 7-point purchase intention scales for predicting likely market response. We've discovered through extensive experimentation that the 11-point scale shown

Figure 11-1   11-Point Purchase Probability Scale

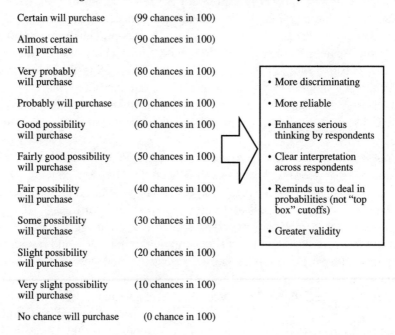

Certain will purchase   (99 chances in 100)

Almost certain   (90 chances in 100)
will purchase

Very probably   (80 chances in 100)
will purchase
                                                                • More discriminating

Probably will purchase   (70 chances in 100)   • More reliable

Good possibility   (60 chances in 100)   • Enhances serious
will purchase   thinking by respondents

Fairly good possibility   (50 chances in 100)   • Clear interpretation
will purchase   across respondents

Fair possibility   (40 chances in 100)   • Reminds us to deal in
will purchase   probabilities (not "top
                                                                  box" cutoffs)
Some possibility   (30 chances in 100)
will purchase   • Greater validity

Slight possibility   (20 chances in 100)
will purchase

Very slight possibility   (10 chances in 100)
will purchase

No chance will purchase   (0 chance in 100)

in Figure 11-1 predicts real world behavior more effectively than its alternatives, especially for mixed and high-involvement buying decisions.

DON'T BELIEVE THAT PEOPLE WILL DO WHAT THEY SAY

Of course, like all self-reported measures of consumer buying, this scale overstates the actual purchasing that takes place. People don't do exactly what they say. Much of this overstatement comes about because the research environment assumes 100 percent awareness and 100 percent distribution (all those aware of it will be able to find it easily), two conditions the company never realizes in the real world.

However, even correcting for awareness and distribution, more people are likely to say they "Definitely Will Buy" than in fact do buy. Dissimulation/prevarication/dissembling/overstatement is as alive and well in "Researchworld" as it is in Washington, D.C.

We have closely examined the relationship between people's reports on the 11-point scale and actual buyer behavior (among people who were aware of the product and for whom the product was available to be purchased) for numerous consumer packaged goods. We have looked at this relationship for

Figure 11-2   Relationship Between Self-Reported Probability and Actual Behavior

The lower the "Self-Reported" intent, the less we believe it.

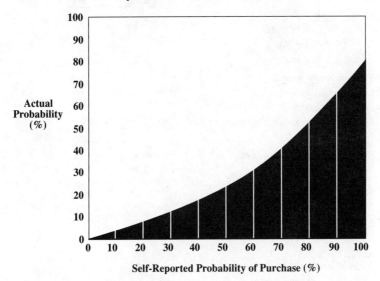

Self-Reported Probability of Purchase (%)

consumer electronics, credit cards, television programs, new cars, package delivery services, personal computers for the home and business markets, and business-to-business software. And as Figure 11-2 indicates, usually no more than 75 percent of the people who claim that they definitely will buy actually do buy. This figure declines as self-reported purchase probability declines, but the ratio is not constant. This leads to a set of adjustments for each level of self-report, which convert questionnaire ratings into estimates of likely behavior.

These adjustments, as an aside, vary by the consumer's (or industrial buyer's) level of "involvement" in the product category. The higher the level of involvement in the product category, the more faith we can have in what people say and the lower the need for overstatement adjustment.

Table 11-1, as an illustration, shows 14 different measures that we use to assess consumer (a.k.a. "sufferer") involvement in pharmaceutical categories. The numbers show the responses that respondent Ted Flynn gave to three different medical problems (angina, ulcers, and migraine headaches) on a five-point scale for each of the 14 different dimensions. These numbers were added to calculate an "involvement score" for Mr. Flynn (and every other respondent) for each category.

Table 11-1   Involvement Measures for Three Pharmaceutical Categories:
Respondent Ted Flynn, Age 57

	Three Types of Health Problems		
	Migraine	Ulcer	Angina
Overall Health			
General concern for health	5	5	5
Physician visitation proclivity	1	3	5
Hypochondriacal tendencies	2	4	5
Problem Seriousness			
Severity of affliction	2	3	5
Duration/frequency of problem	2	5	1
Degree to which onset of problem is not predictable	3	2	4
Information Seeking			
Information-gathering activities	1	3	4
Word-of-mouth activities	2	2	5
Brand Differentiation			
Perceived efficacy available in category	2	3	3
Perceived Rx brand differentiation	1	4	5
Degree to which OTC/Rx switching does not occur	1	2	5
Product Risk			
Potential for adverse side effects	1	3	5
Cost of Rx to sufferer	2	3	2
Confidence in MD prescribing treatment	1	4	5
Overall Involvement	**26**	**46**	**59**
	Low	Mod.	High

By taking purchase probabilities and involvement into account, it is possible to produce a reasonably valid estimate of actual sales (i.e., the percentage of consumers who would buy the product at least once). To improve these forecasts, we recommend two additional measures: one to capture the affective components of consumer attitudes and one to register the cognitive components.

AFFECTIVE AND COGNITIVE MEASURES IMPROVE FORECASTS

The affective components: These are the individual's emotional, or intangible, impressions of a product. Affective measures for an insurance service include:

First impression. Questions like "What is your first impression of the idea for the Fidelity On-line Car Insurance Service?" The seven-point scale runs from "terrible idea" to "terrific idea."

Personal identification. "Based on what you have just seen and read about this car insurance idea, what types of people do you think would like this new service?" The scale runs from "totally different than me" to "exactly like me."

Uses/applications. "Can you think of specific circumstances in which you might buy insurance from this company instead of your current car insurance company?"

Likes/dislikes. "Which of the following best describes the degree to which you like or dislike anything about this concept?"

Overall impression. "Overall, how would you rate this new Fidelity On-line Car Insurance idea?"

The cognitive components: These are a person's intellectual impressions of the product. They include:

Uniqueness. "How would you rate the Fidelity On-line Car Insurance Service in terms of its uniqueness—that is, its similarity to or difference from other insurance services you know or have heard about?"

Superiority. "How does the Fidelity On-line Car Insurance compare to other services that currently exist? How much better or worse is it?"

Helpfulness. "How helpful do you think the Fidelity On-line Car Insurance Service would be in solving any problems you may currently experience in dealing with your insurance company and policy?"

Value. "What do you think of the Fidelity On-line Car Insurance in terms of value for the money?"

Price. "What is your opinion of the price of the Fidelity On-line Car Insurance policy?"

Clarity. "Which of the following describes the degree to which you find anything about the concept confusing?"

Believability. "Is there anything about the Fidelity On-line Car Insurance concept that you find hard to believe?"

By comparing people's reactions to new products and services with their actual behavior, we developed a three-dimensional, 13-factor "Behavior Prediction Inventory." Ultimately, we employ a multifactor equation to estimate real-world behavior for each individual in a study.

Our experience is that this approach improves the odds of forecasting what will actually happen. More than 100 validation studies that compared projected awareness-to-purchase conversion to actual sales suggest that the method is reasonably valid. Not perfect, but a major improvement over intuitively appealing approaches. When we apply this technology to the "management's favorite" concept (the one selected by the marketing manager), we

Figure 11-3   A Behavior Prediction Battery

Affective Measures	Cognitive Measures	Behavior Measures
• First Impression • For People Like Me • For Occasions I Experience • Likeability • Overall Impression • Helpful at Solving Problems	• Price • Value • Clarity • Believability • Uniqueness • Superiority	• 11-Point Purchase Probability Scale

$$[b1(\text{Factor1}) + b2(\text{Factor2}) + b3(\text{Factor3}) + \text{etc.}] + b_{13}(\text{11-Point Scale}) = \boxed{\text{Behavior}}$$

see a forecast of 38 percent of the target market visiting the Fidelity site to learn about the new car insurance product, a year-end market share of approximately 12 percent, and annual revenues of about $100 million. Are these good numbers! Will this service be profitable? Hold on a bit, and we'll tell you later.

CONJOINT AND CHOICE MODELING: DIFFERENT PATHS TO THE SAME PLACE

Often the marketing manager is not sure what concept to test or how to describe the product exactly, what features and benefits to stress, or what price to charge. This is clearly the case with the Internet example. The number of possible product configurations seems limitless. But since each test requires a sample of 300 to 500 people, we're talking real money. However, alternatives exist.

More than two decades ago Professor Paul Green of the Wharton School at the University of Pennsylvania pioneered a new research methodology that made the task of evaluating many concepts more efficient. His work clearly represents one of the major scientific advances in marketing. This technology, multiple trade-off analysis, also known as conjoint measurement (we'll use the terms interchangeably), enables a researcher to evaluate many different concepts using approaches borrowed from experimental psychology.

Choice modeling is an alternative methodology that has gained popularity in recent years, particularly among academicians. Like conjoint measurement, its objective is to assess the effects of a product's or service's different features and benefits on buyer preference. Choice modeling has merits when the new entry will be introduced into an *established, entrenched* product category, one driven by tangible, rational product features and with all the choices generally found in the same store. However, when the category is new (e.g., video disc players), intangibles play a role, or the choices are ambivalent or not available from the same store (as they are in the case of on-line insurance), conjoint is still the way to go.

With either of these methodologies, essentially, the researcher designs an experiment to test multiple factors—name, positioning, key benefits, size, shape, color, price, and more—by showing different combinations to different people. By applying a multiple trade-off analysis, choice modeling, or repeated measures analysis-of-variance algorithm, the researcher can capture the main effects of, say, seven to nine factors by exposing consumers to a relatively small set of concepts (often 16 or fewer).

In practice, this means the research can evaluate thousands of potential concepts at a price comparable to that of a traditional test of perhaps three or four concepts. The researcher's real hurdle in using conjoint and choice models has often been company management, which doesn't understand the research methodology or jargon and often doesn't want to understand. Also, trade-off and choice modeling studies have their own problems. Unless researchers are careful, they produce unreal measures of sales potential that are reflected in a questionable track record in predicting real-world sales. They also tend to be limiting: while these studies can measure several hundred combinations, fin-de-siècle marketers have hundreds of thousands of combinations—and the standard approaches can't handle this well.

CONCEPT ENGINEERING: COMPUTER-AIDED NEW PRODUCT/NEW SERVICE DESIGN

Our counterintuitive recommendation begins with a modified multiple trade-off analysis. We show each respondent a special subset of concepts, often 12 to 16, since few consumers can discriminate among many more than 16 possibilities. We design these subsets carefully so that every respondent sees the same options for each factor in equal proportions, and the field interviewers do not present any one factor option more often than any other. The resultant "orthogonal" design enables us to assess not only the main effects for each factor but also the demand for each combination of factors.

To illustrate the tool, imagine that for this new on-line insurance service,

Figure 11-4   Main Effects of Nine Factors

Factor	Four Days / choice	Average Across 8 Scenarios with: Four Days	0.36 Average Across 16 Scenarios	Average Across 8 Scenarios with: One Day	One Day / choice	Main Effect of Factor
Adjuster Dispatch		.22		.50		± .14
Package	Individual	.28		.44	Family	± .08
Premium	High	.30		.42	Low	± .06
Live Customer Reps	No	.32		.40	Yes	± .04
Emergency Dispatch	No	.33		.39	Yes	± .03
Ease of Setup	15 Minutes	.34		.38	3 Minutes	± .02
Registry Services	No	.34		.38	Yes	± .02
Type of Coverage	Limited	.35		.37	All	± .01
On-line Statement	No		●		Yes	± .00

management has to make only nine key decisions: whether to target single-car insurers or multiple-car insurers (we'll refer to this as the "family package" positioning), the speed and ease with which a policy can be set up, the availability of live customer service representatives, the reputation of the company providing the coverage, the types of coverage offered, access to individual insurance statements on-line, the time frame for both roadside assistance and an insurance adjuster (of course, the adjuster will take longer than a tow truck) to be dispatched in the event the insured is involved in an accident, access to RMV (Registry of Motor Vehicles) services through the Web site, and of course, price.

There is, of course, nothing special about nine variables; a product or service may have more or fewer, and the PC program doing the calculations does not care how many factors or concept configurations management includes in the test. By the time we are finished, the program may have considered and evaluated as many as two million possibilities.

Imagine (again to keep this example simple) that management has only two choices for each factor it wishes to evaluate. (In the real world, of course, a given factor may have a dozen possibilities, but we're sacrificing verisimilitude for clarity here.) Since management has nine decisions, each with two choices, there are 512 combinations (2 to the ninth power). Of the 512 possible concepts, we show each respondent 16. This enables us to measure the effects of each factor, including price, and the appeal of all 512 different theoretical combinations.

Each of these 16 concepts is then shown to respondents, and the 13-factor "Behavior Prediction Inventory" employed to estimate demand. The program then calculates the effects of each factor on the overall sales forecast.

The "grand mean" of all 16 scenarios is 0.36, which means 36 percent of the market target, given awareness, distribution, and inertia, would use the service to insure at least one car. The bar length indicates that taking care of customers promptly in case of an accident is by far the most important factor in a buyer's decision. The average across 8 scenarios with prompt service is 50 percent, while the average with the usual slow service is 22 percent. So the speed of service has an effect of plus or minus 14 points (0.36, the average across all 16 scenarios, versus 0.22 and 0.50). In other words, if the insurance company offers prompt service, demand rises to 50 percent (the 36 percent base enhanced by 14 points). If the service is typical of what's offered by the insured's car insurance carrier today, trial drops by 14 points to 22 percent.

If the service does not offer access to live customer service representatives, the average across all 8 scenarios is 32 percent. If it *does* offer this convenience, the average is 40 percent. So having live customer service representatives or not affects the offering plus or minus 4 points. Price has a more modest effect of 3 points. Clearly, some of the benefits offered here have made buyers insensitive to price. In this example neither on-line statement access nor type of coverage affects the offering's appeal appreciably one way or the other.

To estimate trial for all other concepts, we start with the "grand mean" of 36 percent and add or subtract the effects of each factor. The PC program does this almost instantaneously and in this way finds the predicted score for any of the 16 concepts and, for that matter, all 512 configurations.

The model also shows not only how prospects rate each individual factor alone but what happens when one factor combines with another. These are the *interaction effects*. Sometimes a factor's effect is not constant. It will vary depending on what's happening with another factor; consumers look at both simultaneously, not separately. For example, offering live customer service and speedy policy setup simultaneously may not increase interest as much as the "main effects" suggest. If the effects were additive, the demand estimate would be 0.42 (0.36, the average across all scenarios, +0.4, the effect of the live customer service, +0.2, the effect of fast and easy policy setup). The estimate is actually 0.32 because of the interaction effect. The research shows that the quick and easy policy setup has an effect only if there is no live customer service, and offering neither speedy setup nor live customer service depresses interest even more than the raw numbers would indicate.

But this approach can go well beyond 512 concepts. Imagine there are five (rather than two) levels for each of the nine factors. This means you can have 1,953,125 possible concepts (5 to the ninth power). There is no necessity for the same number of levels for each factor. If they're different, the arithmetic is a little different, but the principle is the same, and one usually ends up with an intimidatingly large number of possible concepts.

To deal with the need to test more than two possibilities for each factor, we take respondents through an additional questioning exercise called "micromodeling," in which we assess every level of every factor one at a time (or, in research talk, *monadically*) in terms of its impact on purchase interest, including the levels tested earlier for which our modified trade-off analysis has enabled us to know the main effects.

As a dumb example, if two factors being tested were box size and box color, we might select a very large box and a small box, a blue color and a red color, and expose people to all four combinations: a big blue box and a small blue box, a big red box and a small red box.

During the additional interviewing exercise, we would bring out the very large box and have people rate it on a five-point monadic scale in terms of purchase probability. We would bring out a smaller box and have them rate it. We would bring out two medium-size boxes and have them rate them. We would even bring out a much bigger box than before and have them rate *it*. That's five boxes in total and five purchase probability ratings.

In other words, we would have people rate a number of boxes, including the two boxes we measured in the trade-off experiment. Using the latter two as "true" estimates of real-world appeal, we could then interpolate or extrapolate the monadic data for each respondent separately to estimate what the trade-off scores would have been for box sizes we did not include in the experimental design.

Suppose that in the trade-off experiment people loved the big box, and for the big box we forecast a 50 percent level of interest. They didn't like the small box very much, and in the trade-off experiment we estimated that that would have a 10 percent level of interest.

On a five-point monadic scale, respondent Phillip Puma rated the big box with a score of 5, the small box with a 3, and an intermediate box with a 4. If we know his trade-off score was 50 for the big box, then, assuming linearity, 5 (the big box) is to 50 percent and 3 (the small box) is to 10 percent as 4 (the intermediate box) is to X, or 30 percent. Phil's predicted score for the middle-size box is therefore 30 percent. For each factor we move through this micro-modeling exercise to calculate the demand curve for every level of every factor for every respondent. This individual-level data is then aggregated to the whole sample.

Having completed the micromodeling exercise, we can forecast the performance of any concept, including "management's favorite" and the "most appealing" one.

For the on-line insurance example, the most appealing concept to consumers looks like this:

Single-Car vs. Family Package	Family Package
Ease and Speed of Setup	Within 3 Minutes
Live Customer Service	Yes
Types of Coverage	All
On-line Statement Access	Yes
RMV Services	All
Emergency Dispatch	Immediate (Within 1/2 Hr.)
Adjuster Dispatch	Within 1 Day
Policy Rates	20% Below Industry Average

Oh, boy, 65 percent of the target group would visit the site, and a 27.1 percent market share. It sounds great until you look at the bottom line. This is an offer not many people could refuse. It's maximally appealing. But factor in the costs of building and servicing this site and its customers, the costs of marketing, and the costs of insurance coverage, and this business bombs. Because the most appealing concept turns out to be the most expensive service this marketer could offer (the model estimated that the annual costs for such a service would be $237 million); the most appealing concept loses $76 million a year. This is not what most managers would recommend to their boards of directors. This is the 25-cent triple-scoop ice cream cone revisited.

Forecasted Year 1 Performance—Most Appealing Concept

Year-End Fidelity Site Visits	Sixty-five percent
Year-End Market Share	27.1%
Annual Sales Revenue	$160,452,000
Annual Total Costs	$236,803,000
ROI	Disaster

Somewhere in here, however, lurks a feature combination that will actually make the company some money. To tease it out, we have to obtain from the client all the costs associated with each feature and level option, both the fixed and the variable. We consider any corporate objectives or constraints. For example, the company may set 20 percent as the minimum penetration level it will consider, or assume the competition will drop its price. The "service designer" program takes all this information—everything about costs, consumer preferences, the competitive situation—and searches for optimal (the most profitable) solutions.

What we might find is that the financially optimal on-line insurance service would offer:

Single-Car vs. Family Package	Family Package
Ease and Speed of Setup	10 Minutes
Live Customer Service	Yes
Types of Coverage	Most
On-line Statement Access	Yes
RMV Services	No
Emergency Dispatch	Quick (Within 1 Hour)
Adjuster Dispatch	Within 3 Days
Policy Rates	10% Above Industry Average

Our concept-engineering model finds that the optimal Internet insurance concept is to appeal to family buyers as a dependable, more service-oriented means of insuring a car (or cars) at a relatively high price. Offer the insurance with the additional incentive of roadside assistance within 1 hour and an adjuster guaranteed to show up within 3 days after an accident, as well as preferred access to a local repair shop. The model predicts that such a service (given awareness and distribution) would yield the following outcome:

Forecasted Year 1 Performance—Optimal Concept

Year-End Fidelity Site Visits	44%
Year-End Market Share	15.6%
Annual Sales Revenue	$132,800,000
Annual Costs	$94,532,000
ROI	Dramatic

True, this Web site and insurance product will not attract as many people as the most appealing concept, but it will do better than management's original proposal—44 percent versus 38 percent. Nor will it take as large a share of the market as the most appealing concept—15.6 percent versus 27.1 percent. But because its costs are so much less than both the most appealing concept and management's initial proposal, we forecast that it will return a sizable profit.

THE MOST APPEALING CONCEPT IS ALWAYS THE LEAST PROFITABLE

While the traditional methods of concept testing remain the most common way to develop and test new product concepts, concept testing is not the best approach to new product/service development.

Trade-off and choice modeling analysis, borrowing from experimental psychology, are enormous improvements over conventional concept testing. But in general, their goal often remains the same as the goal of traditional concept testing: find the concept that produces the highest level of consumer appeal and therefore the highest levels of purchase probability.

And that, of course, is not what a company really needs. As was discovered in the Internet insurance example, the most appealing product is not the most profitable product. It never is. *It's the least profitable.* Giving buyers everything they want (including the lowest price) puts you on a fast track to disaster. See Figure 11-5 for an illustration of the general relationship between concept appeal and profitability.

What a company really needs is the most *profitable* concept. We've found the difference in profitability between the optimal concept and management's favorite to be as much as 14 to 1. This difference means that marketing managers cannot, flying by instinct and gut feel, simply pick the most profitable

Figure 11-5   The Relationship Between Concept Appeal and Product Profitability

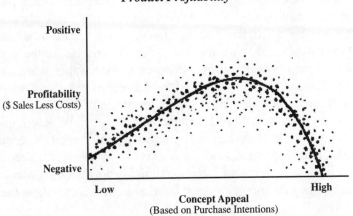

product or service from among all the—often literally—millions of possible combinations.

A current example of this problem can be found in the automobile industry. Cars are now so loaded with safety and antipollution equipment, powerful engines, antilock brakes, and super stereos—all features that are very appealing—that they cost too much, $24,000 on average, compared to $9,000 fifteen years ago. So people are demanding discounts, and new car profits are stagnant.

The problem would be of only academic concern were it not for marketing's heavy focus today on "appeal scores." "How did the concept perform in terms of 'top box' purchase probability ratings?" the product manager asks, confident that purchase interest and profits are moving together. The higher the score, the greater the manager's interest in the offering.

The type of computer-aided new product design discussed here is an alternative to traditional methods. This unique analysis helps marketers design optimal products and services. The methodology has several advanced features: it predicts real-world behavior and sales for a constellation of alternative concepts; it uses a nonlinear optimization algorithm to identify the most profitable concepts; the marketer can personally play out "what if?" scenarios; and it offers targeting and positioning guidance.

Sadly, what interests prospects the most—the concept that earns the highest purchase interest score—is a temptation marketers must avoid.

Instead, marketers can use computer-aided product and service design methodologies to find the optimal combination. To do so, of course, requires a revolution in marketing thinking. It requires giving up the myths that a company must offer the most appealing and highest-quality products and services; that the greater the appeal and the higher the level of quality, the greater the chances of marketing success. Without consideration of profitability and return on investment, such success can turn into financial disaster.

There is clearly a difference between what the customer wants and what the customer needs and is willing to pay for. By addressing the immediate needs of its *loyal* customer base (as opposed to their wants, which are often an impossibility), a business can avoid the dangerous pitfalls associated with chasing a chimera (i.e., pleasing *all* of the people *all* of the time).

What smart marketers do is determine what needs to be accomplished on every dimension of interest (e.g., new product appeal, market share, customer satisfaction, retention, distribution, and so on.) and then what levels of each of these activities are "optimal," thus maximizing not the dimension itself but profitability. They do enough to keep their customers content and their business strong and profitable, but not so much, too much, that they're on the downside of the profitability curve.

What smart, counterintuitive marketers realize is that it is best to use research to evaluate thousands, sometimes hundreds of thousands, of new product concepts in order to identify and describe those forecast to be the most profitable. This is worth doing.

12

Give All Your Customers a New Car

"Give all your customers a new car." It was not all that funny when we first said it, but the line still provokes laughter, if not guffaws. Several years ago Compaq, inspired by the bugle call for "total quality management," was interested in increasing its level of customer retention from 86 percent to 100 percent. They invited us to help develop a strategy to do so, which we didn't think made all that much sense. Our recommendation was "Give all your customers a new car."

"What do you mean, 'Give them a car'?" they asked. We said, "If you gave each one of your defecting owners an automobile—you know, gave them a new Mazda Miata—they'd stay on for at least another year." It was a joke, of course, because the value of that defecting customer averaged less than $800 a year, while a new Miata costs at least 20 times that amount. (In most product categories, the customers you lose are more likely to be of less than average value because they're either price-sensitive, brand-to-brand migrators or people who didn't use your services that much in the first place.) In this case, giving people a $20,000 car to earn $800 in annual revenues was a surefire way to go broke, even if it did result in 100 percent customer satisfaction and retention. The client quickly got the point and began to laugh with us.

This is another example of the relentless pursuit of a dysfunctional goal—"anything worth doing is worth overdoing"—which can be observed every day and everywhere as companies seek to achieve goals that make little sense.

100 PERCENT CUSTOMER SATISFACTION AND RETENTION ARE RARELY PROFITABLE

As the Total Quality Management movement swept the American business landscape throughout the '80s and '90s, zero-defect products and perfect service were prescribed in every product category. There was an obsession with building quality into every organizational process. This was, we believe, a necessary and valuable pill to swallow. Japanese and German cars and consumer electronics—the most complex, important, and visible consumer products around—were made better than their American counterparts. American manufacturers had a lot to learn from the foreign manufacturers who had learned their lessons from American W. Edwards Deming.

But while there is no question that TQM means greater efficiency with less waste, fewer reworks, and saved time—all leading to greater customer delight—marketers made an intellectual leap. They came to believe that the relationship between customer satisfaction and profits is monotonic; the higher the level of satisfaction, the greater the profitability. This is simply not true.

As an example, consider retail banking. In a time-starved world a 30-second wait in a teller's line is better than a 5-minute wait. But unless you know that shorter lines will attract significantly more customers or that your customers are so unhappy spending 5 minutes in line that they will take their business elsewhere, putting on additional tellers to cut the wait to 30 seconds will be costly without generating enough more business to cover the extra cost.

We've tested this theory in banks, gas stations, and fast food restaurants, and have found that a short wait doesn't really bother the customer (of course, they'd rather have no wait at all) and contributes to a more profitable business. This is because no waiting time doesn't generate enough incremental revenue or retention to cover the cost.

American businesses talk a great deal about customer satisfaction, and many spend time and money studying customer satisfaction and its (so-called) "determinants" without knowing the relationship between satisfaction and profitability. They look for these determinants as if, once they identify them, they will be able to obtain 100 percent customer satisfaction.

Assume that customer satisfaction is measured on a scale from 0 (total dissatisfaction) to 100 (total satisfaction). (Table 12-1 shows one scale we like and the "weights" that we use in a typical product category.) Do companies know how profitability changes as they move from 74 percent satisfaction (a global average across a broad range of products and services) to 80 percent

Table 12-1   Five-Point Satisfaction Scale

Label	Rating	Weight
Perfect, you couldn't be more satisfied	5	100
Excellent, but not perfect	4	92
Good	3	80
Fair	2	50
Poor, you're not at all satisfied	1	0

Questions: All things considered, how satisfied are you with the service
provided by SuperMachines, Inc.? Would you say that
you found the service to be _____?

satisfaction? Do they know what happens to customer retention if it drops
from 74 percent satisfaction to 70 percent? Do they know what happens if
they retain 85 percent of their customers from one year to the next versus
retaining 90 percent? Do they know what it would cost and what they would
gain if they achieved 100 percent satisfaction and 100 percent retention?

The answer is an unequivocal NO. General Motors and General Electric
can't answer these questions. Neither can Compaq or Dell, Procter & Gamble, or Philip Morris, MasterCard, or VISA. Few companies know the relationship between customer satisfaction and retention, between satisfaction
and profitability, or between retention and profitability. This basic lack of
business intelligence makes the exhortations of the consultants preaching the
100 percent "solution" strange, to say the least. They're like early 20th-cen-
tury psychiatrists touting electric shock therapy for psychiatric disorders
without understanding how it works or its side affects.

Our own research has repeatedly found the relationship between satisfaction and profitability and retention and profitability to be curvilinear—profitability does rise as satisfaction rises *up to a point*. After that point the cost of
delighting the customer by delivering ever-increasing satisfaction rises faster
than the retention-linked profitability.

To return to our example, Compaq could achieve close to 100 percent satisfaction and retention—at least temporarily—if it gave all its customers a
new car. But as every manager knows and as Figure 12-1 suggests, the cost of
achieving this goal would be prohibitively expensive. The goal is dysfunctional—improving customer satisfaction and retention is worth doing, but
pushing them to the max is overdoing it and highly unprofitable.

Figure 12-1   Satisfaction and Retention Profitability

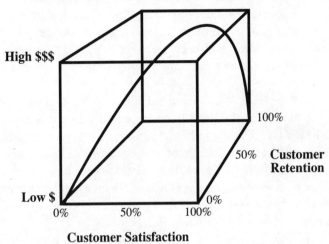

The only way for Compaq or any other company to understand and address this issue is through satisfaction/retention research. One useful approach is the use of studies to assess customer satisfaction and retention, as well as their determinants and consequences. Smart companies have developed systems to monitor charges in satisfaction/retention/purchasing behavior in a timely manner, followed by econometric analyses to study the relationships between them. More important than the numbers themselves (e.g., whether satisfaction is at 74 percent vs. 71 percent) are findings related to the costs associated with implementing changes in satisfaction and retention, and the consequent deltas in forecasted profitability.

DELIGHTING CUSTOMERS IS A GOOD THING TO DO

Before we go any further, we should make it clear that customer service, customer satisfaction, loyalty, and retention are all important to a business's success. As we'll show, improving customer satisfaction will improve sales and market share. Without proper customer service processes in place, you will screw up, and someone like Sanford P. Blank will—justifiably—tell *Reader's Digest* how dumb you are.

In March 1998, Blank wrote that his wife had received a credit card application in the mail. She did not want the card but he did, so he crossed her name out, entered his, and returned the form. Within a week a woman from the credit card company called to say he had been rejected. Why? The card could be issued only to the person originally solicited by the offer. "However, she invited me to reapply, which I did during the same telephone call."

A few days later another company representative called Blank to tell him that his second application had been rejected. Why? "The woman told me their files showed that I had previously applied for a card and had been denied."

Customer service leads to customer satisfaction, which leads to customer loyalty, and customer loyalty leads to customer retention. It is expensive and wasteful to lose a significant number of customers every year, particularly if you're making efforts not to lose them. In *The Loyalty Effect* (Harvard Business School Press, 1996), Frederick F. Reicheld argues that raising customer retention rates by five percentage points could increase the value of an average customer by 25 to 100 percent. (Any manager concerned about his business's customer loyalty ought to study Reicheld's book.)

At the same time, as even Reicheld notes, it is usually expensive and wasteful to retain every single customer. Trying to keep certain customers can actually decrease profits and destroy value. Some customers are so demanding, so price conscious, or so small (or all three) that they cost more to serve than they're worth. These are the customers who should receive the company's benign neglect, not its investment.

Our first suggestion to any manager concerned with the business's customer service is to analyze the customer base to answer such questions as, Which customer groups are growing? Shrinking? What is the value of each customer to us today and over, say, the next five years? And very important, what are the costs and benefits of increasing customer satisfaction and retention?

Every marketer of consumer and business-to-business products and services needs to better understand these links. How satisfied customers are and how many are retained each year are issues every marketer should be able to understand and address. So is the question, What is the financially optimal level of satisfaction and retention? How far should you push the throttle on satisfaction before retention levels are too high? At what point does profitability decline as satisfaction and retention rise?

For the majority of customers, of course, you should provide the best products and services that you can afford (i.e., that are profitable) and monitor the quality of service *and* customer satisfaction to make sure you are delivering what you intend. Enlightened managers know what their good customers want and feel and will make adjustments to satisfy them. One way is to regard any customer complaint as an opportunity to learn something about the company's product, distribution, sales process, or after-sale service.

But do not confuse the process with the goal. James D. Mendelsohn, director of marketing research at The Olive Garden Italian Restaurant, wrote (in the October 26, 1998, issue of *Marketing News*) that he once gave a hotel restaurant meal a "poor" on a consumer satisfaction measurement form. "In doing so, I created a reaction worthy of pulling a fire alarm. I received four phone calls and a note slipped under my door asking me to discuss my responses. Then I was flagged at checkout to talk to a manager. The manager was willing to make amends if I would change my rating from 'poor,' because this hotel chain rates managers on the percentage of responses that are rated 'poor.' What was missing was any focus on whether the meal actually was a poor value."

Clancy had a similar experience in 1999 when he bought a new car. After the sale was made and the papers signed, and as the car was being prepped, the salesperson—who had been wonderful throughout the entire process— informed Clancy that there would be a follow-up phone call from BMW headquarters to gauge his satisfaction with the process. Fine, no problem. But then the salesperson went on and on about how important this call was and was there anything he could do to ensure perfect ratings? He was clearly anxious about Clancy's reaction. Here again there seemed little interest in learning how the process could be improved but a great deal of interest in a summa cum laude report card.

CUSTOMER SERVICE AS A MAJOR COMPETITIVE ADVANTAGE

Buyer satisfaction is a sine qua non of an effective strategy because you want customers to come back. Virtually every business needs high levels of repeat sales. You want customers to say nice things about you, which has an effect on whether other people buy your products or services or stay with you. Therefore you need to measure satisfaction with your products and services as a barometer for compensating employees based on performance. You need it as a general tool for comparing yourself to the competition. Improving satisfaction can give you a significant competitive edge.

Indeed, as Len Berry points out in his must-read book *Discovering the Soul of Service* (The Free Press, 1999), "Sustainable success has little or nothing to do with company size or industry growth rates. A small company in a stagnant industry can indeed achieve sustainable success while larger companies in growth industries falter." Berry's research of very different service organizations in different industries identified 15 lessons common to all these very successful companies. Last fall, we met with a prospective client, and the marketing director said that she had heard someone from ExxonMobil speak at a professional conference and mention our names. She went on to ask, "Did you have anything to do with their clean restrooms?"

We said, "Actually we did."

She said, "I will never, ever, ever go to another gas station than Mobil. A couple of months ago, I went in there with my two-year-old one day, and I had the creeps. You know what service station restrooms are like, and I went in and—oh my God! It was spotlessly clean, and there were fresh flowers, and it just blew my mind. I told the manager at that station I'll never go any-place else if he keeps the restroom looking like that, and I'm keeping my promise. It's just a great company."

Our research showed that the most profitable targets for Mobil wanted bet-ter snacks from the convenience store; quality products; top-notch, quick ser-vice; a nationally available brand; and cleanliness. They did want competitive gas prices, but not the cheapest price; price is not the most important consid-eration in choosing a service station. It's usually not the most important con-sideration in choosing anything.

To appeal to these people, Mobil invented the "Friendly Serve Attendant," a person who would be at the station to greet, help, and expedite service (but not pump gas—except under unusual circumstances). The *Wall Street Jour-nal* gave an example of what this could mean in practice: "When motorist Kathy Bales drove into an Orlando, Fla., Mobil station during a rainstorm recently, she was in a rush and wasn't looking forward to pumping gas in her work clothes. 'But then a young guy came over, pumped my gas, cleaned my windshield, and took care of my credit-card transaction for me even though I was in the self-serve lane,' she says. Since then, Ms. Bales has forsaken her Texaco station even though gasoline there costs two cents less a gallon."

The moral to the Mobil Friendly Serve story is that high levels of customer satisfaction can have a profoundly positive impact on company sales and profits. That may be intuitively obvious, but why aren't more companies doing it? Why is the average level of customer satisfaction globally 74 per-cent? Why are so many companies that preach 100 percent satisfaction and 100 percent retention performing so poorly? Many businesspeople are asking the same questions.

WAYS TO IMPROVE CUSTOMER SATISFACTION

The first step is to do a satisfaction/retention analysis to determine the key drivers of customer satisfaction by segment. In the Mobil case (and every other), low price is a key driver among the price-conscious. A clean restroom, on the other hand, is a key consideration among other, more profitable seg-ments. As with many marketing issues, it is almost impossible to discover these drivers without research. Who would have guessed that a large number

Figure 12-2   Brand Strategy Matrix: Chase Bank vs. Citibank

			Both the Same			
		Chase Superior	Excellent, Could Not Be Better	Acceptable But Could Be Better	Unacceptable	Chase Inferior
Satisfaction Driver Importance	High	Fast Service— In and Out Quickly	Broad Range of Services	Friendly Service	Services Designed for You	ATMs Everywhere
	Mod.	The Right Size — Not Too Big, Not Too Small	Branches All Over the City	Low Cost of Services	Helps You Retire Early	Preferred by Business-people
	Low	Offers Personal 24-Hour Service	Personal Loans Approved Quickly	Architec-turally Attractive Branches	Easy-to-Use Home Banking	Lets You Buy Stocks and Bonds

of people want human contact from Citibank, or that for McDonald's clean restaurants and tasty French fries are more powerful drivers of satisfaction and sales than the quality of their burgers?

The next step is to assess how the company is doing on each driver relative to competition. (What we're describing may sound familiar; we covered the same type of process in developing a positioning.) The goal is to find a dimension that is motivating to the market target that you can offer and that the competition does not—or better, cannot—offer. See Figure 12-2 for a hypothetical banking example. For Chase Bank, as an illustration, speed of service is an advantage relative to a key competitor.

If a service station hired one more attendant to pump gas during the four busiest hours of the day, it could (we'll make up a number) save each customer 40 seconds on average. That saving might have a positive effect on customer satisfaction, but it wouldn't pay out. Only seven customers in the whole country would write a letter or send an e-mail to say thank you. It would not have a major impact on customer loyalty and sales.

In contrast, if the station could take that four-hour-a-day person and have him clean restrooms and other visible aspects of the site, this probably would impact loyalty and profitability. For a service station, restaurant, or bus station, it is better to have clean restrooms than to save people a few seconds. The proof is in the outcome. When Mobil implemented Friendly Serve, they were inundated with mail from people all over the country, particularly women, thanking them for what they had done. It had a major impact on customer loyalty.

Finally, you must determine what it would cost to implement the driver(s) you've identified to find an optimal point for improvement. Should a bank hire one more person for four hours a day? Two people for eight hours? Should it shift responsibilities—say, eliminate all full-serve lines—and not hire anyone? How much "faster service" is too much? To help answer these questions, let's take another look at the concept-engineering approach discussed in the previous chapter.

OPTIMIZING NEW SERVICE SATISFACTION

Consider the Delta Shuttle running between New York and Boston. It competes head to head with the US Airways shuttle. The price is the same. The service is the same; the on-time rate is the same. What's different? US Airways runs on the hour, Delta on the half hour. Tweedledum and Tweedledee.

Assume that Delta is desirous of breaking through the clutter and offering something different—what can they do? What can they do to improve passenger satisfaction and ultimately load, revenues, and profitability?

The answer starts with developing a set of hypotheses concerning the characteristics of shuttle service that might excite passengers. Price, of course, is on everyone's mind. "Let's drop our prices" is a tempting possibility. But then again, we could reconfigure the planes to offer more leg room, serve better food, provide free car service into Manhattan. There are a lot of things.

Focus group research and judgment might be employed to whittle down 50 or more ideas into a set of 8 to 15 factors, the kind we discussed in the last chapter. A modified conjoint or choice modeling experiment could then be designed and implemented among a cross section of 300 to 400 shuttle flyers, half of them regular Delta customers; the other half, US Airways customers.

A data collection procedure often used is a three-step process commonly referred to as "phone-mail-phone." With this approach an initial telephone contact is used to recruit respondents and obtain from them basic background information. A packet containing the materials necessary to conduct the conjoint exercise (e.g., concept description and full-profile scenario cards) is then mailed to those respondents who consent to take part in a second, longer interview. The third part of the process involves the follow-up interview in which respondents evaluate the conjoint materials.

The research approach recommended here centers around the conjoint measurement or choice modeling exercise discussed earlier, which has been published in several books and articles; scores on the scale are adjusted to reflect our experience in converting self-reports into measures of actual buyer behavior.

The set of services would vary in terms of perhaps seven to nine different features, each presented with two or more levels (e.g., price, leg room, speed of luggage pick up). Each factor represents a different level of service. For example, the shuttle could offer a $15 meal to all travelers, a $10 entree, a $5 sandwich and chips, a $2 snack, or nothing at all. The exact combination of features presented in a configuration and the total number of configurations shown would be determined by an experimental design. If more than three levels are required for some factors, a micromodeling algorithm could be employed to estimate levels not included in the experimental design.

The methodology is similar to the concept-engineering approach that we talked about in Chapter 11. The methodology has several features: it predicts real-world satisfaction and sales for a constellation of alternative service concepts; it identifies the most profitable levels of service; the marketer can personally play out "what if?" scenarios; and it offers targeting and positioning guidance. To use it, you feed research-grounded estimates of customer satisfaction and demand based on the research (it is important that the modeling take into account buyer overstatement due to the artificiality of the research environment) and the company's estimates of the costs associated with each feature into a nonlinear optimization model, which selects an "optimal" service configuration and price.

The final result of the analysis is recommendations for an optimal shuttle service that will maximize profits. If desired, it could be shown among key market segments (e.g., business vs. personal flyers). Analysis of such ad hoc groupings of respondents will be possible because the preference "utilities" are calculated on an individual level.

ISSUES IN MEASURING CUSTOMER SATISFACTION

Developing a program to improve customer service is one issue; measuring customer satisfaction is another. When Dennis Murphy took the job as director of Worldwide Customer Satisfaction Management at IBM Corporation, he found that IBM's customer satisfaction surveys were themselves becoming a major source of customer dissatisfaction.

Murphy told the Conference Board's 1998 marketing conference that when he began to consolidate or eliminate surveys, he asked volunteers throughout the company to report what they were doing. "Forty-eight people raised their hands and said, 'We're doing a customer satisfaction survey of some sort.' We believe there are three times that many renegade surveys no one has claimed yet, but at least we're working on those who have been brave enough to put their hands up."

Among the surveys were eight that Murphy's group fields annually, and of those, one encompasses 58 countries, 28 languages, and over 40,000 interviews. While none of the other 47 surveys are that extensive, "some come pretty darn close." No wonder IBM's executive vice president of sales and executive vice president of marketing complained that they were getting too many customer complaints about IBM's survey process.

IBM had five different kinds of customer surveys, two triggered by an event—a sale, for example—the other three calendar driven—product diagnostic surveys, relationship surveys, and the worldwide measurement survey. IBM had too many people involved in the process. A case in point: You buy an AS400 computer. "Two weeks later you receive a phone call from AS400 asking how we're doing. You receive two phone calls from our global services division asking, 'How are our service contracts going?' The sales department follows up. And the global financing group wants to know if you want us to finance the thing for you. One transaction generates five different phone calls and chaos."

The calendar surveys looked at the customer's relationship with IBM, with different business units calling to ask how IBM was as a supplier. "When you're the CEO of one of our major customers, and you hear from IBM three times in a month on a survey that sounds identical to the last one you answered, you get a little annoyed," said Murphy, "and you start calling people like Lou Gerstner."

Solving the first issue was fairly easy: make one person own the transaction. Five different people may claim it, but somebody initiated it and IBM is asking the initiator to coordinate everyone else so they all play together and look like one corporation.

IBM is also working to consolidate the calendar surveys "so that we ask the right question of the right person once and only once," said Murphy, noting that while information is important, customers are more important, and adding that if you need information, ask four questions before you approach a customer:

1. Is the information mission critical?
2. Is it going to make a difference?
3. Will you know what to do with it if you get it?
4. Does it exist elsewhere in the organization?

Within IBM information resides in many places, and the company trying to do a better job of mining its databases to learn whether somebody has already answered a given question.

For companies doing business around the world, there is a fifth question: Is there a possibility that what you're asking is harmful to you?

One example: In Japan you cannot ask a lot of deep, probing questions about what customers think of your competitors the way you can ask in the U.S. or Europe; the Japanese find it offensive. Said Murphy, "While we would obviously prefer to have one questionnaire worldwide on all the work that we do, that's a compromise we've had to make so that we can play the game appropriately, by the cultures."

CUSTOMER SATISFACTION TO SET EXECUTIVE PAY

IBM, like many companies, has been using much of the customer satisfaction information to compensate employees. Increasingly, when a business wants a customer satisfaction study, it's to figure out people's year-end bonuses. Which is good, but you should tell whoever is doing the study what's in the offing because it puts a tremendous burden on the research. For example, the company may want the research in December because it pays bonuses in January, but December may be the customers' busiest month. It's also the worst time to interview.

Another example: What level of statistical significance do you need? A store department manager may get a big bonus if satisfaction goes up three points, nothing if it goes up two. But for that level of precision you will need a sample of 4,000 people just for his area, which is not practical.

For Brahma, we've been tracking the satisfaction of bar, restaurant, and store owners—the retail trade—how happy they are with their distributor, the service they're getting, the brand itself, and the support the brand is getting from Brahma. We survey Brazil's 19 commercial regions separately, and there are individual salespeople calling on the stores and bars in each of these areas. They all have goals, and these include both sales and satisfaction on a five-point scale. It's gratifying to know they are using the research that way, but in some of these commercial areas, there are so few customers that a five-point difference is simply not readable.

A customer satisfaction survey that ties compensation to it is a good idea because the customer wins; this is good marketing. But even with a careful study and statistically valid results, the people who did not do well go around the company doing everything in their power to sabotage the results.

Customer satisfaction surveys can become a game when the salespeople know the research will be in December. They spend November petting the customers. To avoid this bias, you have to adjust the goal so it's a year-long average and employees cannot pump up the numbers in the last month. We have found that using customer satisfaction surveys for bonuses, even with the best intentions, often gets perverted. And if it can be perverted, it will be.

CUSTOMER SATISFACTION AS A WAY TO AVOID DISASTER

A good customer satisfaction survey, however, can also tip you off to an impending disaster. The idea, after all, is to keep the customers' pulse so that you correct things before it's too late—that is, before your customers actually abandon you.

There are two kinds of customer satisfaction studies. One is among end users, the people who actually consume the product; the other is among retailers and other middlemen. With packaged goods and other fast-selling consumer products, as we noted, consumer satisfaction has to do with the product itself. A person may be perfectly satisfied with the product yet not buy it because she wants to try something new, it's not available the day she shops, or the price has gone up. In the packaged goods world, the issue is repeat purchase and is a different model of consumer behavior.

Where customer satisfaction is critical is the situation in which people who, for some period of time or for some serious purchase, decide to buy your product or service and not somebody else's. In many cases you have their names and you're in a business in which, if you keep a core customer group loyal, you've won more than half of your marketing battle.

(Many businesses talk about the 80/20 rule, the 80 percent of the business represented by 20 percent of customers, but in most businesses it's actually more like a 50/15 ratio: 15 percent of the customers represent half the sales. Still important, but not quite as lopsided.)

These are businesses like hotels, banks, long-distance companies, and major appliance, automobile, and computer manufacturers. IBM used to say, "We're in the service business. We sell boxes, but we're in the service business." And they are. It is possible to determine attributes and benefits of service, and you measure your performance on those. You can ask people about the most important things that make them happy, and keep them wanting to be a customer.

Interestingly, what you think is important may not be what your customer thinks is important. A supplier to Home Depot went to enormous expense and trouble to cut the time between special orders and delivery to any Home Depot store from three days to one. Only after the system was in place did the supplier learn that Home Depot did not care about or need quick delivery of their product.

Therefore, you want to measure those things that drive customer behavior, since you can measure any number of dimensions—courtesy, knowledgeability, the merchandise, cleanliness, or whatever. What are all the key dimensions in your business? How do they rank in importance among your target customers? How do you compare on these dimensions to competitive businesses? And we are back to a version of the competitive matrix we showed in Figure 12-2. Ideally, you fix those weaknesses your customers and prospects feel are important—it may be as simple as cleaning your bathrooms or as difficult as redesigning the entire store—and improve on those strengths you have over the competition.

WHEN ATTEMPTS TO IMPROVE SATISFACTION YIELD DISSATISFACTION

Unintentionally bad service is widely practiced in the computer industry. Suppose you have a problem with your personal computer. You call the manufacturer to discuss the problem, and the automated system tells you how long you are going to have to wait. The system announces that it will be an estimated 42 minutes before a customer service representative will answer the phone.

Company management may think that telling an executive who barely has 4.2 minutes to go to the restroom that she has to wait 42 minutes is a good thing (and it's probably an improvement over making her wait without telling her anything), but it makes people crazy. And then if the wait isn't pain enough, all too often the customer is disconnected and has to start the process again.

Another not uncommon frustration is with Web providers. Twice in the past year we've been cut off from Netcom/Earthlink, our provider. In both cases we couldn't reach the company by e-mail because we'd been cut off; it was like needing to call the phone company to report a downed line. In both cases we spent several hours trying to track down by phone an appropriate Netcom representative who could address our problem. In both cases the problem was a computer glitch that failed to pick up our corporate credit card number accurately, and in both cases the problem was solved only when we were able to get through to Earthlink's corporate headquarters in Atlanta.

Likewise, when February 2000 attacks on the Internet slowed down systems to the speed of frozen molasses, it would have greatly improved our opinion of the ISP if we had received some notice of the ongoing inconvenience—aside from the lethargic state of office workers everywhere as they waited for Web pages to load.

On the positive side, the Internet promises new ways to improve customer service. Companies can automatically send e-mails for product upgrades, recall notices, and other information. Customers can ask questions about their new product, download lost instruction booklets, and order parts and repair guides. All these services tend to improve customer satisfaction.

Marketers today seem to recognize the importance of keeping their customers happy. We hear a lot of talk in marketing circles about delighting customers, making them 100 percent satisfied, and retaining all of them. These seem to us to be intuitively appealing ideas.

Yet companies today get "C" grades for service and customer satisfaction (about 74 percent is a global norm)—so something's wrong here—and retention levels are in decline. The goals of 100 percent satisfaction and retention, moreover, are unnecessary and unprofitable.

The counterintuitive marketer knows the relationship between customer satisfaction and retention and between both of these factors and profitability. "Optimal" objectives for satisfaction, retention, and service offerings are consequently set, and the organization brought into alignment to achieve them. Most important, systems are put in place to measure the drivers of satisfaction and the organization's performance—relative to competitors—in achieving competitive advantage on the most important dimensions. The result is happier customers and a more profitable business.

Raise Your Prices: Uncommon Approaches That Make Sense

The CEO of one of the country's largest telephone companies called us with a serious financial problem. Messaging services are the phone company's answer to answering machines, and this company's two-year-old messaging service was hemorrhaging. Household penetration was among the lowest of any phone company in the country. Growth was among the slowest, and customer churn was high, running at the rate of approximately 2 percent a month, which meant they had to grow at the rate of more than 25 percent a year just to stay even. The figures said that this service would not turn a profit for at least five years—if then.

This executive was desperate. He was faced with the formidable challenge of signing up one million customers within three years—a figure he had promised to his board—and he was ready to follow his intuition by dropping the price to do so, which would have pushed profitability further into the future. Could we help?

We suggested that before the company did anything rash, it should undertake a large-scale segmentation and simulation study designed to:

- Detect and describe financially "optimal" market targets.
- Craft a powerful positioning/message strategy.
- Recommend an "optimal" configuration of service features.
- Identify the most profitable pricing strategy.

He agreed, and we executed a research study among a sample of more than 1,000 households in the market. During the course of a one-hour personal interview, we studied 15 factors, including 5 that were directly related to price: the installation charge, the monthly fee, a discount for annual subscription, a money-back guarantee, and three-month free introductory promotions. The other factors included reminder calls, extension mailboxes, message delivery to cellular/pagers, information services, message indicator, usage rate, message storage, group message, and a "We can't come to the phone" greeting from a celebrity voice.

We also studied different strategies for the monthly fee: "bundled," in which the service included extra mailboxes, and "à la carte," in which extra mailboxes were $2 each.

The first thing we found was that the marketing department's intuitive understanding of the best customers to go after was at variance with the facts. The socioeconomic and psychographical characteristics of the right target and the current target were radically different. This discovery paid for the study all by itself.

We also found that higher prices depressed "trial" and "renewal" in a fairly linear way, but the revenue increases more than offset the drop in demand. We established that while "bundling" appeals to new customers, existing customers do not want it. Indeed, bundling has a negative effect on renewal rates over the long term. We determined that charging a one-time sign-up fee would not hurt sales. And we ascertained that offering service guarantees and a month free for recruiting a friend would bring in more new customer revenue than the offers would cost.

Based on this research, the company implemented a counterintuitive pricing strategy: it raised fees. It also implemented targeting, positioning, and media strategies suggested by the research. The customer base grew threefold in a year, and the service began generating profits within six months rather than bleeding money for another five years or longer. For a time we were heroes.

Raising your prices would appear to be a radical idea as we start this new century. American companies are tripping over one another to reduce their prices. Price decreases are sometimes accomplished directly, just by telling buyers, "We're cheaper. We offer the lowest prices in town." But often a price decrease is subtler, as when, in the early months of 2000, Chrysler offered buyers 0 percent financing on new cars. The hope appears to be that somehow or other, some way or another, the uptick in sales brought about by the price reduction will stick; that the brand's unit sales increases will more than compensate for the decline in revenues, profitability, and in some cases, brand equity.

How else can you explain the fact that "Low Prices" (a.k.a. "We've Reduced Our Price," "Now 20% Off," and "You Can't Buy It Cheaper Anyplace Else") has become the most common pricing and positioning strategy in America.

PRICING DECISIONS WITHOUT STRATEGY OR RESEARCH

The CEO who commissioned this project is not a testosterone decision-maker. He's an exception to the general rule; most companies make their pricing decisions without any serious strategy or research.

Almost ten years ago we did some research that we recently updated to learn whether this lack of strategy was just among the companies we knew or if the situation was widespread. Our research looked at all American businesses as fitting into one of four boxes in Figure 13-1.

The companies in the top left box, the Sophisticated Players, are those that conduct serious pricing research (that is, primary research, not secondary analysis) and follow a serious pricing strategy. The Losers in the lower right do little or no research and have little or no strategy.

Our research found:

- Only about 10 percent can be considered Sophisticated Players with both a pricing strategy and research to support it.
- Only about 5 percent are Radical Empiricists with research but no strategy.
- Some 45 percent are Gamblers; they do have a serious pricing strategy but do little or no research to support it.
- The rest—a sobering 40 percent of all companies—have neither strategy nor research, the Losers.

In other words, we estimate that more than half—55 percent—of all American companies *do* have a pricing strategy, but only 15 percent do any serious research to support the strategy.

Figure 13-1   The Strategy/Research Pricing Matrix

	Serious Strategy	Little or No Strategy
Serious Research	Sophisticated Players (10%)	Radical Empiricists (5%)
Little or No Research	Gamblers (45%)	Losers (40%)

More evidence: Professor Tim Baye at the University of Wisconsin–Extension, Lancaster, asked 180 small and medium-size companies, "Which approach did you use to price your most recent new product or service?" Most (41 percent) said they tried to cover costs and make a fair profit. Almost a third (30 percent) said they charged what the market will bear. Another 21 percent said they price relative to related products or to match what competitors charge. The remaining 5 percent said they used their best guesstimate.

We find executives dropping prices as the way to make quarterly sales goals. It's the intuitively obvious thing to do. Cutting prices may make a quarter's unit numbers, but it will lay waste margins, and the sales tend to drop back to what they were but now at a lower average price. Not long ago Quaker Oats' CEO Robert Morrison cheerfully reported that Quaker's bagged-cereal business was up 9 percent. What he didn't discuss was the dark secret that Quaker was boosting volume by slashing prices and squeezing margins. Worse, Quaker was signaling that its brand was just another cereal.

Pricing decisions are sometimes frantic decisions: we've tried everything else, it didn't work, so let's drop the price. Managers assume price is the problem.

Dr. Tom Nagle is the chairman of the Strategic Pricing Group in Marlborough, Massachusetts, and co-author of the definitive book on the topic. He points out that the issue may not really be price. "One of our clients made a product that had a seven-year life, but we learned that most purchasers used it as a part in other products with two- and three-year lives. No customer complained about the product's quality being too high—they complained about the price."

Another problem may be communicating the product's value. "Marketing communication usually focuses on features and benefits and assumes that customers can convert the information to value," says Nagle. "Often this is not enough. Pharmaceuticals and medical device companies, for example, usually must quantify the value of complications avoided or buyers will undervalue the benefits. Similarly, advertisers often cannot quantify the value of the media they purchase, so they tend to undervalue the publications or broadcast stations that offer superior value."

INTUITIVE RULE-OF-THUMB APPROACHES TO PRICING DECISIONS

Some readers may wonder how it is possible for a company to operate with little or no pricing strategy and no pricing research. "Surely," you may say, "every business that puts a price on its products has *some* kind of strategy."

They have something, but to call it "strategy" stretches the word's meaning so far that it snaps. We say these firms are taking expedient or dumb rule-of-thumb approaches to their prices. In their wonderful book *The Strategy and Tactics of Pricing* (Prentice-Hall, 1995), Tom Nagle and Reed Holden have identified the following:

The Cost-plus Pricing Approach. This is what retailers do. A refrigerator costs the business $500 and management wants a 40 percent markup, so it tags the refrigerator $900. This gives the retailer room to drop the price if this is deemed necessary.

The approach includes both markup pricing and target return pricing and assumes management knows the variable costs, overhead, depreciation, and maintenance expense. If it *does* know these figures, the markup price formulas are straightforward.

That assumption—that marketers know costs—is suspect, however. Some years ago, when we began consulting for a major financial services company, we were surprised to learn the firm could not tell the profit contribution of individual customers because it did not clearly understand its costs. Management assumed all customers contributed about the same profit; the customer who charged $50 a month in a restaurant was worth about as much as one who charged $1,000 a month in airline tickets.

This assumption seemed so implausible to us that we pressed the marketing director. He admitted that perhaps it was unlikely that *all* customers contributed approximately the same profit, but the company did not have any method to measure profit contribution at the individual customer level—they had, after all, millions of customers.

We suggested that if the company could measure the individual customer's contribution, the information might be useful. It could aid other marketing efforts—targeting, advertising, new products, positioning, pricing. The company might, for example, want to direct its advertising at the most profitable customers, who are not necessarily those who run up the highest charges on their credit card. The marketing director said he would look into it.

Six months later we met to discuss the investigation's results, which showed, as we had expected, a vast difference in profitability between customers. While frequent fliers had the highest credit card charges, the credit card company's margins were squeezed tight by the airlines. Thus, frequent flying by itself did not drive high levels of profitability. This information had a profound and far-reaching effect on the company's pricing strategies.

The true cost of a product or service is a major cause of "marketer headache" and is one reason why marketers give so little attention to pricing. It does not make sense to talk about margin or markup or return on investment if marketing management does not know the costs from which it is marking up or the actual investment. Sadly, that's the way the world works. Many businesses simply cannot calculate their costs accurately at the individual product or item level. Those that can, don't, or don't share the information with their marketing executives.

Even if a company cannot calculate precise costs, of course, it can develop good approximations—but to do so takes work and cooperation within the organization between the marketing and finance people.

The Old "Match-the-Competitor's-Price" Approach. The problem here is that a company cannot know—except at the most gross and superficial level, say, from an annual report—whether the competitor is making money. What business knows its competitor's costs when the competitor itself may not know them? And if you don't know costs, how can you calculate profitability?

This very popular model has played an instrumental role in transforming the once-mighty personal computer industry into a commodity. Brand differences are disappearing while Compaq, Dell, and others wage marketing warfare.

The "Beat It or Raise It" Approach. In this approach a company sets its prices lower or higher than a competitor's because . . . well, because it seems like the right thing to do at the time. Philip Morris initiated a price war by cutting the prices of its top brands. Competitors followed, and the net result was a $2.3 billion drop in operating profits for Philip Morris, even as the Marlboro brand increased its market share seven points to 29 percent. R.J. Reynolds, which markets Camels, experienced a $1.3 billion drop in profits.

The Target Return Approach. This is similar to the cost-plus approach and has the same weakness; you have to know your costs. To calculate a target return price, the formula is (total unit cost + [the desired rate of return × the invested capital]) ÷ unit sales = unit price.

To keep everything simple, assume that the company wants to make a 20 percent return on its $1 million invested capital, that the unit cost is $8, and that 100,000 units will be sold a year. Plug those numbers into the formula—($800,000 + [.20 × $1,000,000]) ÷ 100,000—and the target return price is $10.

The math is simple, but markup and target return pricing share a major problem. Both assume the unit sales figure is a given, regardless of selling price, which in the real world is not true. In addition, product cost is virtually always a subjective opinion, not an objective number, since as we've seen, companies do not know their costs. Product cost is a judgment call. As such, it may cover either the full cost or out-of-pocket costs. It may reflect cost levels the company currently experiences or be based on an experience curve. It may be an estimate of future costs. It may include past R&D expenses. Which factors management uses depends largely on management's product/market objectives. That's fine until management begins to kid itself with unreal cost figures.

PRICING DECISIONS WITH LITTLE OR NO RESEARCH

If those are pricing approaches without any strategy, what are examples of little or no research? We find managers who do not want to conduct any research say things like:

"Research can't tell you how people will respond to differences in price." These managers cannot imagine any research technique that will help them make more effective, more profitable decisions. They are locked in a time warp of 1960s and '70s research technologies, which almost always misrepresent the effects of price. Concept testing, for example, will almost always lead you to believe that price is unimportant, while conventional one-factor pricing research might lead you to conclude that it's the only factor that matters.

"We can't afford any research." The unspoken corollary here is "We *can* afford the costs of doing it over and over again." And the argument includes the assumption, "Research isn't going to tell us anything we don't already know" . . . so why pay for it?

"Let's do it the way we did it last time—when we didn't use any research." The assumption here—call it blind hope—is that the buyer hasn't changed, the competition hasn't changed, and the company and its product or service are identical to what worked the last time. If pressed, the executive making this claim may agree the world *has* changed a little but will claim the shifts are not significant.

"You're right, we need some research." We'll do focus groups. Focus groups are particularly useless because people do not know what something is worth until they are taught. (Unfortunately, many companies are teaching consumers that their products or services are not worth much.) We're also amazed, watching focus groups from behind a one-way mirror, how many people have no idea what they pay for products and services they regularly buy.

"We'll do some research to establish the product's value." The most common way to implement this idea is to assume that products and services have attributes with different importance values—in a light beer, for example, light taste is more important than popularity—and that brands score differently on

Table 13-1   Arkansas Slim's Evaluated Against Coors Light and Miller Lite

Attribute	Importance*	Evaluation** Coors Light	Miller Lite	Arkansas Slim's
Refreshing Taste	5.0	4.8	4.0	4.3
Right Amount of Carbonation	4.5	4.2	4.5	4.7
Creamy Head	4.2	3.6	2.0	4.6
Popular Brand	3.6	4.7	4.8	1.8
Light Color	2.9	3.8	4.0	4.5
Weighted Sum***		77	76	78

* Rated on a five-point scale: 5 = extremely important; 4 = very important; 3 = somewhat important; 2 = slightly important; 1 = not important at all.

** Also rated on a five-point scale: 5 = excellent; 4 = very good; 3 = good; 2 = fair; 1 = poor.

*** The arithmetic performed here is at the aggregate level; we are multiplying mean scores to illustrate the calculations, although in most applications these calculations are done at the individual respondent level and then averaged.

these attributes. If research adds up all the importance scores, multiplied by all the brand ratings for a given brand's attributes (as this argument goes), the sum will be the brand's "value." The product's price should be proportional to this "value." So if the "value" of a new beer is 90 percent of the market leader, it should be priced at 90 percent of the market leader. Table 13-1 shows what such research is liable to produce.

The left-hand side of the table lists five different attributes of a light beer and the importance that a cross section of beer drinkers assigned to each on a five-point scale. Note that "Refreshing Taste," with a 5.0 rating, is far and away the most important characteristic in this category—at least we're supposed to think that, based on people's self reports. As you think about it for a moment, consider that most people in blind taste tests cannot tell the difference between any light beer brands. Many cannot tell the difference between a light and a regular lager. But that's a story for another chapter.

On the right-hand side of the table are the numbers people assigned to Coors Light, Miller Lite, and Arkansas Slim's, a new light beer formulated with a breakthrough "thin-brewing" process, on another five-point scale, this one ranging from poor to excellent.

Multiply the importance ratings by the evaluations and add them up, and you reach the preposterous conclusion that Arkansas Slim's should be priced the same or higher than the market leaders. Indeed, since its overall score is higher than Miller's, perhaps it should be priced higher than Miller.

While this example is deliberately extreme to illustrate the point, some companies today engage in such flaky research to establish their prices. The research is flawed because it assumes that it captures all attributes, both tangible and intangible, which it does not. It also assumes that importance ratings really measure "motivating power," which they do not. And it assumes the company can ignore the price of entry into the category, which it cannot. Arkansas Slim's will compete not only against the physical and chemical properties of Miller and Coors but against decades of brand-building advertising.

Another flawed approach is to survey prospective buyers by asking, "For this product [or service], what is the maximum you would expect to pay, assuming ideal quality?" Even with perfect quality, there is a price ceiling beyond which the consumer will not go. The researcher follows that question with "What is the lowest price you would pay before you begin worry about the quality?"

Every six months or so a client will suggest we use this approach. We point out that all you have at the end is a zone of acceptable pricing. The survey tells you nothing about the effect of price on sales, and from other research we know that sales can vary immensely from one end of the zone to the other. We did such a study once for a blue jeans manufacturer and found the zone quite wide, but we learned nothing about its relationship to sales.

THERE'S NO WAY TO GUESS HOW PRICE WILL AFFECT SALES

Price is an area in which you just cannot guess what will happen. There are three common relationships between price, the number of buyers, and revenue. For example, as price moves from high to low, the number of buyers may move from low to high. As price moves from low to high, the number of buyers may move from high to low. Or the number of buyers may move from low to moderate and then drop.

Consider Figure 13-2, which shows the results of a pricing study we did for one client not long ago. We were looking at three different services for a giant home appliance company. The company was considering three different businesses: home security systems, home energy management, and major appliance repair. The common element was wires into the house; they could use new technology to detect at the central office if your house is being burglarized or on fire, if your heating/cooling system is out of whack, or if your refrigerator or washer has broken down. Three very different businesses, and they wanted to understand the market's price sensitivity.

The study found three different relationships (which makes it ideal to illus-

Figure 13-2   Price Sensitivity for Three Products

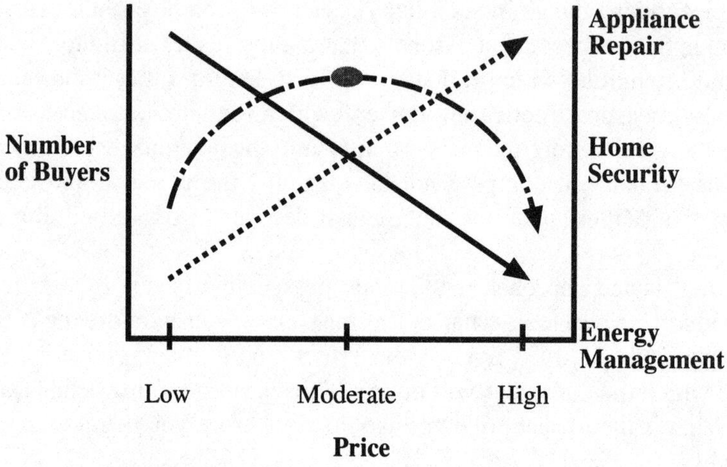

trate this chapter). We found the burglar alarm concept to be very price sensitive. As the price rose, the number of buyers fell steadily. With the appliance repair concept, however, the relationship was exactly the opposite. Few people expressed interest in the concept at a low price, but as the price rose, more and more people said they would buy. For the home energy management concept, relative few buyers expressed interest at the low price; interest peaked at a moderate price and then declined as the price continued to rise.

This, of course, contradicts intuitive thinking, which is that sales rise as the price declines. They may, but then again they may not. In any event, depending on the original margin, they may have to rise considerably for the business to make as much as it would without the price cut. For example, assume that our product sells for $10 and that we make $4.50 on each one (a 45 percent gross margin). Every time we sell 4,000 units, we make $18,000. Suppose we cut the price 5 percent; how many more do we have to sell to make the same $18,000?

The arithmetic is straightforward. With the price cut, our product is $9.50 and we are making $4.00 on each (a 42 percent gross margin). Now we have to sell 4,500 units to earn $18,000. We need a 12.5 percent increase in units to offset a 5 percent decrease in price.

This very simple example assumes, of course, that costs remain the same, but as everyone in business knows, costs tend to rise as volume rises. At some point the plant has to add another shift, and we need another truck to make deliveries or more warehouse space. Suddenly (or imperceptibly) we're not making $4.00 on our very popular item; we're making only $3.60 and we have to sell 5,000 units to make our $18,000. That is, we've got to increase sales 25 percent just to stay even.

This is not abstract theory. *Business Week* reported in July 1998 that Boeing had offered deep discounts to keep Airbus Industrie from stealing customers. "Boeing had done so well racking up orders, in fact, that it wound up with a huge production bottleneck that is costing it billions to untangle."

We once had a product manager tell us, "I've really moved share. We gained three share points in the last quarter."

We asked, "What did you do?"

He said, "I dropped my price, and sales started to move significantly."

"Did they move enough to make up for the lower cost per unit?" He looked at us, embarrassed. Nobody had asked that question. Everybody was just happy that sales went up. Does anybody notice there's a problem here? Often they don't.

PRICE SENSITIVITY IS NOT A PERSONALITY TRAIT

Management intuition suggests that most buyers, consumers, and business-to-business decision-makers are price sensitive. How price sensitive are buyers? Our research suggests that price is the primary consideration for only 15 to 35 percent of buyers in most product categories. The majority of consumers and industrial buyers, whether automobile purchasers, supermarket shoppers, fast food eaters, cellular phone talkers, retail gasoline pumpers, women's apparel buyers, software and computer buyers, freight shippers, are not as obsessed with price as many marketers seem to be.

Some marketers mistakenly believe that price consciousness is a "personality thing"—that some buyers are just cheap, tight, frugal, miserly, whatever you want to call them—and that there are a lot of such people in every product category. Little, if any, scientific evidence supports this view. If price consciousness as a personality characteristic does exist at all, it is for a very small segment of the population.

To make pricing decisions effectively, the business needs to understand its customers and their sensitivities. For example—and again we're following Nagle and Holden's thinking here—the more buyers value any unique attributes that differentiate your product from competing products, the less sensitive they are to the price. Does your product (or service), therefore, have any unique—tangible or intangible—attributes that differentiate it from competing products? How much do buyers value those unique attributes? For example, on April 1, 1998, America Online raised its monthly fee for unlimited usage by 10 percent, from $19.95 to $21.95. It was able to do so without watching sales fall off a cliff because subscribers value the service and AOL had no competitors that offered the same scope.

Can buyers recognize your product's unique attributes by observation, or do they have to buy and consume the product to learn what it offers? Is the product highly complex, requiring specialists to evaluate its differentiating attributes? Can buyers easily compare the prices of different suppliers, or do suppliers set their prices according to different sizes and combinations that make comparison difficult?

Buyers are more sensitive to the price charged by any one seller when they are aware of substitutes, which may be either competing products or competing sellers of the same product.

Just as buyers are more sensitive about price when they know about substitutes, they are less sensitive to a product's price when it is difficult to evaluate competing offers. A homemaker may know that other laundry detergents are less expensive than her usual brand, but unless she knows they will clean as effectively, she will not consider them as an alternative.

The greater the expenditure, in both relative and absolute terms, the more sensitive buyers are to price. They tend to spend more time shopping for a refrigerator than for an electric iron, more time shopping for a car than for a bicycle.

Buyers are more sensitive to a product's price when they are sensitive to the cost of the end benefit to which the product contributes and when the product's price accounts for a large share of the end benefit's cost. An appliance manufacturer, for example, buys sheet steel from which it makes washers, dryers, and refrigerators. If appliance buyers are highly price sensitive, the manufacturer will be highly sensitive to steel prices.

Buyers are less sensitive to price when they pay only a small portion of it. Boots Pharmaceuticals recognized that a low introductory price for its antiarthritis prescription drug, Rufen, would be ineffective because insurance reimbursements would be covering a high portion of its price. Boots circumvented the problem, says Nagle, by attaching a coupon to the bottle that a buyer could send in for a $1.50 rebate. The buyer received the introductory price-cut benefit even though the insurance company paid a substantial portion of the cost, and Rufen took a 6 percent market share in four months after introduction, an unusually high penetration for this market.

Buyers are less sensitive to a product's price when they have made a large "sunk" investment in anticipation of its continued use. Once a buyer has bought a fancy fountain pen, an expensive camera, a laser printer, or as Gillette has discovered, an expensive razor, the cost of ink refills, film, toner cartridges, or blades becomes less important.

Buyers are less sensitive to a product's price when a higher price signals that the product is higher quality. These tend to be image products, such as jewelry (Ebel watches or just about anything from Tiffany's) or clothing (a one-of-a-kind Bob Mackie gown), as well as unknown quality products. For example, Mercedes is able to command a higher price than a comparable automobile because it has a prestige image. Some business travelers fly first class for the prestige, not for the extra leg room, better food, or because the high price reduces the probability of sitting next to a small, noisy child. Buyers sometimes use a high price as a product quality cue. In one case, because buyers could not evaluate a new car wax, sales lagged until the company raised the price from $ .69 to $1.69

Finally, buyers are more price sensitive in the short run when they can hold an inventory of a product and believe the current price is temporarily lower than it will be in the future. People will stock up on discounted canned tomatoes in a way they will not stock up on discounted fresh tomatoes.

PRICING IS AN ART AND A GAME, NOT A SCIENCE

Pricing, more than most other areas of marketing, is both an art and a game. It's a game because the pricing strategies of competing firms are highly interdependent. The price one company sets is a function of what the market will pay *and* what competitors charge. One firm's prices are often a response to competitive pressures, as well as an effort to influence competitors' pricing behavior.

But while pricing is an art and a game, we believe your product's price should be part of an overall pricing strategy, and we also believe, given our professional bias, that research has a decisive role in helping management make informed pricing decisions.

RESEARCH THAT LEADS TO BETTER PRICING DECISIONS

What kind of research leads to better, if not "optimal," pricing decisions?

To develop the most profitable product at an "optimal" price, we have to look at four things: the product's tangible features, its intangible benefits, buyer price sensitivity, and the return on investment. The best way we know is through experimental research: marketing-mix simulations, trade-off/choice modeling analysis, or a combination of both.

For example, a brokerage firm was weighing a new service that would permit customers to deal with the firm through their personal computers. Management felt that customers would pay a fee to have access to their accounts through their computers, but the company was not sure what features such a service should include or how much it should charge. The firm's problem was to identify the best combination of features and price. The more features the system included, the more it would cost to set up and maintain. The higher the price, the less attractive the service would be to customers. Management wanted to include only those features most attractive to customers and price those features properly to make a profit.

To understand how people felt, we interviewed 500 prospective users, showing them 14 different combinations of features and prices from which to choose the most appealing. This is the same methodology that we discussed in the last chapter. Here, although the number of combinations totaled more than half a million, no one respondent had to consider more than 14, a carefully selected mix of six different factors:

- The hours of operation.
- The types of information the customer could request.
- The ability to move funds between accounts.
- The ability to place orders.
- Access to a personal line of credit.
- The monthly charge for the service.

The interviewers asked respondents to rate each configuration on affective, cognitive, and purchase intent scales and used these insights to forecast demand. In addition, we employed "micromodeling" procedures to estimate the effects on demand and profitability of some 20 additional features and embedded everything in a concept-engineering model. The brokerage firm then employed the model to estimate the number of buyers who would sign up for each of the more than 500,000 possible feature combinations.

In this case, price determined buyer interest. Table 13-2 shows that as the price goes up, demand goes down. The figures are useful, however, because they put specific percentage usage estimates on each price point.

Because price was so important to the brokerage firm's customers, management wanted to be sure that the new service included only those features that justified their value to potential users. Management therefore paid particular attention to the utilities—the predicted increase (or decrease) in the proportion of prospects who would sign up for the service with different options. Utilities are useful because they can be added (or subtracted) to indicate how various factors combine.

With the research finding, the brokerage firm could forecast the gain (or loss) in sales for any price increase (or decrease) that might accompany a

Table 13-2   How Price Influences On-line Brokerage Trial

Monthly Service Charge*	Predicted Percentage of Customers Who Would Sign Up (Assuming Awareness and Opportunity)
$ 5	30%
10	21
15	18
20	14
25	12
30	5

* We included only the $5, $15, and $25 price levels in the actual interviews. We were able to estimate the other levels by using a procedure, discussed in Chapter 11, that estimates the demand for the intermediate prices. By so doing, it is possible to reduce respondent fatigue, sample size, and study costs.

change in the features offered. By evaluating the feature combinations, management was able to select an optimal combination of just those features whose cost was justified by the increased value they offered to potential customers.

MARKETING-MIX SIMULATIONS AND PRICING APPLICATIONS

Marketing-mix simulations, which we will discuss in detail in Chapter 17, have a special application to pricing strategy.

A company can use such simulations to test alternative prices or, better yet, identify the "optimal" price that maximizes both sales and profits. A firm can also employ marketing-mix simulations to assess the effect on competitive pricing tactics. What would happen if a competitor held its current price, dropped it, or raised it? The simulation will tell you.

Here's an example from our experience with a major Japanese consumer electronics manufacturer. The company was interested in assessing how different advertising and pricing strategies would affect market demand for a new multifunction product (a combination digital clock, AM/FM radio, and CD player with a built-in memory calendar/date book). In addition to being a high-quality clock radio, the product enjoyed several unique features. The clock alarm could activate either a buzzer, the radio itself, or a sound chip (which played one of many different wake-up tunes). The computer memory permitted the user to program up to 500 key dates, times, or a combination of both.

The manufacturer asked how should the company position the product in the television advertising: as an advanced clock radio or as a tabletop time management computer? Also, should the product be priced at $59 to attract a large share of the high-volume radio market; at $79 to compete with high-quality AM/FM radio-CD players; or at $99 to signal the product's unique features and skim the consumer segment that valued those features?

To answer, we conducted a marketing-mix simulation experiment. In each of four markets we recruited prospective buyers, who came to a research facility for the apparent purpose of previewing a new television program and seeing new home electronics products. We assigned each participant randomly to a group to be exposed to one of the two possible positionings with one of the three possible prices. Thus, we exposed six groups (2 × 3) of 50 participants at each of the four locations to a different positioning/price combination.

The study results showed significant effects of both positioning and price on product demand. Overall, 14 percent of all prospective purchasers bought the new product. Table 13-3 shows how demand varied with positioning and price. Almost as many people bought the device as an advanced clock radio at $79 as bought it as a time management computer at $59. And while the percentage of people buying the device as a clock radio declined about 24 percent as the price went from $59 to $79, this revenue loss was more than offset by the price increase. And since profit is leveraged, profit went up by an even larger percentage.

While the company management loved the idea of selling the product as a time management computer and thereby advancing the firm's image as a company on technology's leading edge, in the end it positioned it as a superior clock radio at $79 and enjoyed a considerable sales success.

ONE AND ONE CAN EQUAL FIVE OR MORE

Sometimes a firm has more than two or three prices to test in a marketing-mix simulation, and this can get very expensive. A frozen food giant was interested in testing five different prices for a new line of microwave entrees, ranging from a low price of $1.89 per unit to a high of $3.29.

Five simulated test marketing studies would have been prohibitive, $400,000 or more. So we combined STM methodology with multiple trade-off analysis and threw in some marketing science modeling for good measure. Basically, we conducted a two-cell STM (high and low price) that gave us a precise fix on consumer demand at opposite ends of the price curve. To measure the demand at the intermediate three price points, we put respon-

Table 13-3   *Forecast for Two Concepts at Three Prices*

Percentage of Computerized Clock/Radio Purchasers

Price	Advanced Clock Radio	Time Management Computer
$59	25%	20%
79	19	11
99	8	1

dents through a nontraditional conjoint measurement exercise during the interview.

As Figure 13-3 shows, we then "fit" the trade-off price elasticity curve to the fixed demand points (at $1.89 and $3.29) in order to estimate what trial demand would have been had we undertaken five different tests. Thus, for the price of two cells, we were able to estimate all five. Even better, we were able to fit a curve through all five price points to estimate an "optimal" price, which turned out to be $2.79.

Figure 13-3   *Packaged Goods Pricing Application with Trade-off Added*

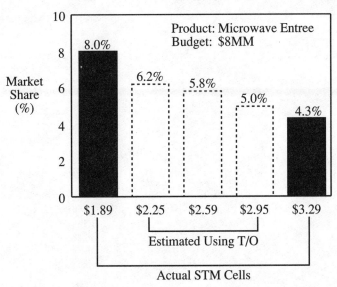

Our examples may suggest that if you do solid research, finding the "best" price is easy. Obviously, we have sanded off some of the difficulties to make the illustrations clear. The truth is that good research helps, but it must be integrated with company knowledge about its costs. The "most profitable price" is a function of consumer demand (as estimated by the research) and manufacturing and marketing costs.

We believe that more companies will move out of the Loser box and into the Sophisticated Player corner with both serious pricing research and a serious strategy. More marketing executives will learn about costs, and more top managements will demand that every marketing plan include estimates of profitability and return on investment.

The intuitive approach to pricing today appears to be to cut prices. This often has the positive effect of boosting sales but the unintended negative effect of attenuating profits and damaging brand equity. Unless you are the low-cost provider in a category, this is no way to run a business! Yet this strategy, as we've said, seems to be spreading like a brush fire through industries and around the globe.

The counterintuitive approach to pricing is to learn exactly what forces do influence buyers and plan accordingly. This requires serious research to determine the price sensitivity of customers and prospects and what can be done to desensitize them. Sometimes the counterintuitive answer is to raise prices, and sometimes it's to leave price alone.

CHAPTER
14

E-commerce Rules Are the Same As T-commerce Rules*

Recently top management at a prestigious financial services organization decided their business would be left behind if it did not get into e-commerce. They decided they needed a Web site, so they called in one of the country's top Internet agencies to help build one.

Like the companies we talked about in the advertising chapter, this corporation did not provide the Internet agency with a clear brief. They did not say, "This is our target. This is our positioning. These are our e-commerce objectives." If advertising is something a company management does not always understand, Internet marketing is something they *really* do not understand. Instead, these managers were perfectly willing to trust the Internet agency to come up with a plan.

The hotshots from the agency pointed out that they could build different types of sites. They could build a portal like Yahoo.com or Excite.com; an information site like Bloomberg.com or Kraft.com; a transaction site like Fleet Boston's Home Banking or etradebank.com; an entertainment site like The Dragon's Lair or The Game Pit; a community site like Cartalk or Geocities; an auction site like eBay.com or Auctionharbor.com; or, of course, some combination of all of them.

*The authors would like to acknowledge Lois Kelly of MeaningMaker for her many contributions to this chapter.

When it became clear the client did not know what would be best for the company's situation, the agency people said they would use their judgment to create a Web site. The first step was to create a few "splash pages"—the first thing the visitor sees—just to give everybody a feel for what the site would be like. Then they would design the rest of the site. And, by the way, the site would cost $2 million to construct.

The agency came back with two sets of splash pages. They were—to be kind—ridiculous. They had nothing to do with what we believed to be the client's targeting or positioning or reason for being in business. Our diagnosis was "overexposure to Saturday morning cartoons." Even aside from the content, the creative aesthetics were not that great. But this should not have been a surprise. Who is designing Web sites at Internet agencies these days? Why would anyone think that unseasoned, relatively inexperienced people might have great creative insights and a sense of strategy for a high-end financial service?

The company's head of marketing thought the splash pages were terrible. He asked us and we agreed; they were terrible. The company's traditional ad agency thought they were worse than terrible.

The company then held a meeting with the head of marketing, representatives from the ad agency, and us. No one used the word "sucked," but we all explained our reservations about the pages to the Internet agency gurus. They did not take the critique well. A senior guy from the Internet agency called the éminence grise at the corporation to say, "Your marketing guy doesn't know what he's talking about. He doesn't know technology. He's out of his league."

The next thing we knew, the corporate head of marketing was off the project, and the Internet agency was free to create a Web site with no client or consumer input, which they did. Six months later they completed their work. The site was a major bomb. The client was so displeased it withheld payment. A lawsuit was threatened. What a mess!

If business used to be based on the idea of "ready, aim, fire," it became "ready, fire" in the late 1990s, and with Internet companies the slogan seems to be "fire, fire, and fire some more." In fact, most dot-com businesses are based on testosterone, hopes, and prayers rather than anything that could be called real business metrics.

It's true that up until the spring of 2000 many a Netrepreneur made millions on paper by simply being the first to market with a rave new Internet concept. Sites were so cool that word of mouth went wild, the site captured millions of eyeballs, the founders appeared in all the buzz-making magazines, and the stock soared 300 percent on the first day of its IPO. But, as we've seen over the past several months, a business with buzz but no true branding cannot continue to thrive.

In a word, no. The foundation of all successful businesses—dot-com and traditional—is creating and delivering true value to distinct groups of customers. Interactive Java bells and whistles don't make a brand. Anyone with enough money can replicate those features, making a dot-com business a low-value commodity overnight.

WEB MARKETING PROBLEMS: ARE THEY DIFFERENT?

A Web site raises some fundamental questions for a business. For example, who is the target and what's the positioning? Amazon.com, for example, seems confused. One of our associates is hooked on Amazon.com. She would rather buy on-line, deferring gratification, than visit a Barnes & Noble and walk out with her book. Plus, she's a proselytizer: "Amazon understands my preferences. It gives me great suggestions of other books and music I'd probably like. Without it I wouldn't have discovered the music of Joshua Redman or Christine Lavin, or books by Susan Minot and Ian MacEwan."

She feels the attraction is not the convenience, price, or increased selection of buying on-line, but the helpfulness and knowledge of the technology, which is greater than that of most book- or record-store clerks. As a result, she would be willing to pay full price for the books she orders. Yet Amazon sells books at a 30 percent discount, providing lots of service and convenience. Because of the convenience, they have customers who would be perfectly willing to buy their books for 10 percent off. Then they have the price conscious, whom they will lose tomorrow when somebody offers a 40 percent discount. It's a confused target.

There is no question that the ability to use technology in new ways to satisfy very diverse needs is creating seismic changes in marketing, from presales and channel strategies to customer service and direct marketing. Nearly every major company is spending large sums on Web-based marketing—on everything from banner ads to promotional e-mails—and getting very little in return. This sounds like the Marketing Performance Bell Curve™ we discussed in Chapter 2.

In 1998 companies spent more than $2.1 billion on on-line advertising, according to a study by Simba Information; Web enthusiasts we've talked to expect the figure to grow to more than $20 billion in the early 2000s. Yet 61 percent of on-line business initiatives either did not track results at all or found that what they tracked had no relation to their business goals, according to a study by Mainspring, a Cambridge, Massachusetts–based research group. The study's author, Patricia McGinnis, concluded that most marketing dollars spent on the Web are wasted. "They think it's doing something, but they don't know what."

Why are executives paying for poor results? A combination of fad and fear. Some, like the management who hired the hotshot Internet agency, see everyone else going on-line and think they should too. Others talk nervously about being "Amazon'd"—losing sales to an Internet upstart. A *Fortune* magazine article headline summed up conventional wisdom: "Somewhere out there is a bullet with your company's name on it. Somewhere out there is a competitor, unborn and unknown, that will render your business model obsolete."

TIME TO ASK FOUR BASIC QUESTIONS

Certainly the Web's potential as a marketplace, channel of distribution, and information medium is unquestionable. Internet use is soaring. At this writing, more than 25 percent of consumers say they use the Internet every day, up from 4 percent in 1995. The Net also, potentially, has great strategic value; it can help startups vault themselves into global markets and enable established brands to reach beyond their traditional markets. But, apparently bewitched by the Internet's hype and possibilities, managers often forget to ask four basic questions.

1. How do we integrate the Web into our core business strategy?

On-line marketing has essentially three objectives: focusing on direct sales to Web users (e-commerce), strengthening the relationship with consumers (brand building), and shifting existing business functions, like customer service, to the Web to shave costs (operational efficiencies), or some combination of the above.

For example, BlueNile.com, a successful online jewelry retailer, targets men who hate jewelry stores even though most of the jewelry they sell is for women. Blue Nile's market research found that men are about as fond of walking into a jewelry store as sitting in a dentist's chair; most said that they are uncomfortable in jewelry stores, often feeling pressured into buying something. Blue Nile takes away the pressure, allowing men to browse, research, get hard-to-find diamonds, and even have diamonds set into special designs.

With online customer acquisition costs of $82 vs. $31 for a brick-and-mortar-store customer, the financial stakes of understanding how e-commerce fits with your overall marketing strategy are significant to achieving profitability.

The key, we believe, is to constantly research and understand how your customers use the Web (to buy, to learn, to compare, whatever) and then position your site accordingly.

2. Are we reaching the right customer segments on-line?

There are many types of shoppers, Web and otherwise: bargain hunters, convenience shoppers, information seekers, and entertainment junkies, among others. Many Web marketers fail because they try to be all things to all people.

Success lies in identifying a profitable market segment and concentrating on serving that segment, as the auction sites have shown. eBay.com and other auction sites have targeted people who want to have fun shopping for unique items, offering them an exhilarating, competitive game called an auction. These sites generate better margins than discount sites and cement a distinct brand identity.

During the early years of a dot-com business—if not for the longer haul—it's critically important that the Web business concentrate its energies on a particular segment and brand positioning. Concentration represents focus, and focus leads to domination. Amazon.com first attempted to win business from every segment of the on-line book-buying public (a mistake) and now has expanded into a virtual mall, selling a constellation of products ranging from CDs to toys (an even bigger mistake). Senior management at Barnes & Noble and Borders are singing, "Ding-dong, the witch is dying," a paraphrase of the famous refrain from *The Wizard of Oz,* because they believe that Amazon has mistakenly strayed from its evolving area of expertise (i.e., as a bookseller) and will suffer the same fate as Dorothy's nemesis.

As of September 2000, they appear to be right. Amazon is downsizing big time, urgently defending its much-maligned business model before financial analysts, and claiming that they're almost in the black as a bookseller. Don't believe it.

A good example of someone doing it right is Starmedia, which is building a serious—and international—Internet presence by focusing on a distinct and rapidly growing market segment; namely, Hispanics. Starmedia is already the number-one portal site in 20 Latin American countries and is aggressively building its U.S. customer base.

3. Is Web advertising a good investment?

Most Net marketing dollars are spent on Web advertising, which is no bargain. Advertising efficiency is measured in cost per impression. Internet ads cost twice as much per impression as print or broadcast advertising and sometimes much more—in our experience, with much less effect.

What about measuring impact by counting the number of users who "click through" on banner ads? As we noted earlier, click-through rates have plunged from 3 percent in 1995 to less than 0.5 percent today. And many that are successful succeed because they lure visitors with deals and discounts. Moreover, click-through rates are an ineffective measure of on-line ad efficiency because they don't measure qualified buyers. A high click-through rate at the Carfinance.com site could be generated by many people who are not qualified for a loan or who are comparison shopping.

Savvy Net marketers go on-line only when they know that doing so will boost profits, strengthen a brand, or improve efficiency. That means making the Web part of an integrated marketing strategy. Ford and Microsoft, for example, announced in September 1999 that they were forming a joint venture (under the CarPoint umbrella) that will have the capability of selling cars directly to consumers as well as continue sending leads to dealers. The planned "Build-to-Order" system will combine existing CarPoint car buying, shopping, and ownership tools with a service that allows consumers to configure and order the car they really want. CarPoint will locate an existing car, whether it is on a dealer's lot or on a transporter headed across country, or will place an order for a new customer car to be built at the factory and delivered through the buyer's local dealership.

4. Are we vulnerable to a marketing challenge from the Web?

Many marketers think of the Web as implying an adjunct to current efforts, akin to a new store or a new ad campaign. It's not. In the past, and for the most part, manufacturers created products and sold them to wholesalers or brokers, who sold them to retailers, who sold them to the public. The Net allows producers to sell directly and cheaply and (relatively) easily to the public. Just consider Dell and Gateway. We expect more manufacturers to follow the lead of Universal Music, a division of Seagram's media empire, and BMG, the music direct-mail giant, which recently teamed up to create Getmusic.com, a site that sells directly to Web surfers.

This joint venture is not appealing to customers on the basis of price. Getmusic.com charges an average of 20 percent more per CD than Amazon.com or CDNow.com. The goal is to bypass music stores, on and off the Net, and form relationships with customers. "At the end of the day, we need information about [our customers] that is not filtered by third parties," says Lawrence Kenswil, Universal Music's president of electronic commerce.

That information will gradually shift the balance of power, as BMG showed when it used its hip-hop site, now folded into the joint venture with Universal Music, to promote an album by the then little-known artist Britney Spears. The site offered a sample of her music, which won raves from 10,000 listeners, 80 percent of whom later bought the album. BMG earned more than revenues; it amassed a valuable database on consumer preferences.

THE SECRET TO MARKETING SUCCESS: UNDERSTANDING CUSTOMERS

As we hope we've conveyed by now, the secret to marketing success lies in truly, deeply, and passionately understanding your customers. Today's evolving technology can help you understand:

- How and what people like to learn before buying.
- Where they go on-line to get that information.
- What they most want in on-line buying experiences. Security? Selection? Ease of use? Helpful ordering and return policies? Brand integrity? Low price? All of the above? Something else?
- Where they want to buy on-line. Sometimes it's a brand's own site; other times it's on-line shopping centers like Bluefly.com.
- How they want to be kept informed of new products and services.
- What they demand in customer service.

This in-depth customer knowledge is the foundation for all Internet marketing programs. With it the Internet allows companies to shorten courtships with customers and build lasting relationships. It's no longer about flirting with "intimacy" but about creating sustainable, mutually beneficial relationships.

How is the Internet changing relationships with customers? We believe that today customer service, particularly customized, individualized e-mail, is the hands-down "killer app" of Internet marketing. Most of the Internet hype is about e-commerce, which we acknowledge is creating a seismic change in retail history. But it is e-mail that allows intimate and personal relationships between customers and companies.

Communicating directly with customers allows you to bring brand personality to life (or to truly screw up the customer relationship). At least as important, obtaining immediate feedback from customers allows marketers to change, adapt, and refine products and services quickly to better meet customer needs. And the more quickly companies change for the better, the more customers they will attract and keep. The Internet helps make it possible to truly understand customer satisfaction and (often) do what is necessary to keep the customer.

Consider the experience of Lois Kelly, a health-conscious colleague. She was outraged when her favorite yogurt brand, Stonyfield Farm, started using sugar rather than fruit juice to sweeten the product. After ranting about the change in the office, she fired off a nasty e-mail to the small Vermont-based company.

Within a half hour, Stonyfield responded. Our cynical colleague could not determine whether the response was an automated e-mail reply or an actual personal letter, but she was more than satisfied with the response:

"We always welcome comments and questions from our yogurt lovers and are grateful when someone takes they time to let us know what they think of our products," wrote Diana G. from Stonyfield. "With naturally milled sugar, we have been able to significantly improve the taste and consistency of our product without increasing the total sugars on our nutritional label. If you compare our carbohydrate and sugar content, you will see that Stonyfield Farm contains significantly less than other leading brands. Finally, naturally milled sugar offers substantial environmental benefits."

Diana went on to explain not only the environmental benefits but other reasons that made the company's yogurt "stand out from the crowd," like not using milk from cows treated with bovine growth hormones. Lois was never aware of these other brand differentiators and was duly impressed. Furthermore, Stonyfield reassured her that they were still making six flavors of yogurt with fruit juice sweeteners and told her how to get her local supermarket to carry them. The reply not only saved the relationship but made an even more loyal customer.

Conversely, companies that don't reply appropriately to customer e-mails within 24 hours risk exacerbating customer relations, creating the impression that they are not particularly interested in their customers. In the Internet world people expect immediate responses to their individual questions. Period.

Unfortunately, companies are slow on the uptake in this crucial area. A study by research firm Jupiter Communications found that of 125 major Web sites surveyed, 42 percent never responded to customer inquiries or took more than five days to reply.

More significant than speed, of course, is the ability to glean customer information for marketing purposes. Software from General Interactive, for example, identifies and classifies incoming e-mail, sends an intelligent response to the consumer within 30 minutes, routes the message to the appropriate customer service representative for a more detailed reply to the customer, tracks how long it takes for the customer service rep to reply to the customer, and simultaneously captures and sends the customer data to marketing.

We know of plenty of businesses that do this sort of data mining in the physical world. For example, one of the largest banks in the U.S. can determine exactly who its most profitable customers will be and target them with specific enticements. A publishing company is integrating demographics with customer buying patterns to predict the best prospects for particular products. In addition, data mining allows that publisher to uncover relationships so that it can cross-sell products and tailor precise marketing messages to individual customers. And in the pharmaceutical industry, companies use data mining to predict which customers will be likely to switch products— and then head them off with new offers.

But how many dot-com companies use savvy data-mining strategies like these? We can't think of any. Many Internet businesses talk about personalized, one-to-one marketing. But the only way to do this is to invest in data-mining technology and data strategists.

Imagine obtaining real-time, highly segmented marketing data seven days a week, 24 hours a day. Need to maintain your customers' pulse? (Who doesn't?) Pay close attention to e-mail.

EXPERIENCES—NOT JUST MESSAGES— SHAPE BRAND PERCEPTIONS

Promptly and precisely responding to customers via e-mail highlights a basic truth in managing customer satisfaction: perception is the only reality. It doesn't matter how good you are, only how good your customers perceive you to be. The experiences customers have at your Web site—not advertising-induced perceptions—radically shape their perceptions of your brand.

David Risher, senior vice president of product development at Amazon.com, believes that the site itself is the key to Amazon's brand building. "Seventy to 80 percent of the feeling people have about the brand is from the experience they have on-line at our site."

Dell's stupendous 70 percent annual sales growth is another testament to the power of "experiential branding," as is the growth of eToys.com, which has made shopping for children easy. The site lets you know if an item is out of stock and asks if you'd like to be notified by e-mail when it's back in inventory. There's nothing revolutionary here but the information and broad product selection most toy buyers want.

What consumers want from an on-line buying experience, of course, is as different as the consumers themselves. But almost everyone wants to be able to trust the brand, which in many cases is the site itself. In fact, a recent study, "E-commerce Trust Study" by Cheskin Research and Studio/Archetype, found that consumers first and foremost want to buy from a site that they feel is secure and trustworthy. Other qualities they value include convenience, ease of use, good prices, and great product selection.

The challenge, of course, is to create a site that immediately conveys the sense that it is a trusted place to do business. This study found that trustworthiness is built on a combination of six factors: (1) brand; (2) easy navigation; (3) fulfillment, which refers to how orders are processed and what the return policy is; (4) presentation, including design; (5) use of current technology; and (6) seals of approval from security-guaranteeing firms, such as credit card companies and encryption and security providers.

One example of a "trustworthy" site is Garden.com, which offers a cozy community feeling. The design and navigation are superb, the selection is excellent, and discussions with the site's "garden doctor" and 24-hour live chats provide almost anything a novice or experienced gardener needs. The explanation of the benefits of buying plants direct from Garden.com reassured a friend and encouraged her to buy more clematis plants than she intended. The site displays "security seals" and provides reassuring explanations of its service policy.

TRUST US: CONSUMER DATA REIGNS SUPREME

Before leaving the subject of trust, let us add that it is trust alone that enables companies to obtain valuable consumer data. When consumers trust a site/company, they willingly provide valuable information about themselves. This preference and behavioral information is the type of data that marketers have always lusted after but have found too difficult or expensive to obtain. With this type of data, marketers can create powerful one-to-one marketing programs, offer personalized customer service, and develop customized product offerings.

Creating trust starts by providing helpful, credible information, services, and experiences. If consumers perceive that you are committed to helping them, they will give you permission to know more about them. This permission is critical. If consumers think you are secretly capturing behind-the-screen data about them, they will never do business with you again. In fact, they may hate you so much that they start vengeance-seeking e-mail campaigns that erode your brand credibility. On-line consumers demand open and full disclosure.

When Amazon.com customers discovered that the on-line bookseller was accepting slotting fees from publishers to promote certain books, they went ballistic. We don't think the fury was so much at the practice itself but at the fact that Amazon was doing it without the consumers' knowledge. In less than a week Amazon fessed up and promised never again to accept slotting fees—a practice, by the way, that is business as usual in retail book stores.

More recently Amazon found itself in the middle of controversy because of its "purchase circles," using personal data about its 10.7 million customers to compile on-line lists of books and music that people they live near or work with are buying. Paul Capelli, an Amazon.com spokesman, said, "We're doing things that have never been done before." And obviously doing them without any research.

Remember: trust, trust, trust. Don't buy lists and send blanket e-mails. This spamming is magnitudes-of-order worse than dinnertime telemarketing calls. If the consumer gives you permission to send her e-mail updates about new product offerings and special promotions, OK. Otherwise, don't even think about it.

American Airlines understands this. In less than two years almost 2 million consumers have asked American to e-mail them weekly airfare specials. The program, which American Airlines calls "a clear home run," provides the airline with an inexpensive way to communicate directly with customers and eliminates the average $20 per ticket overhead, as well as travel agent commissions, which can run up to 8 percent. We trust American because it provides a valuable service we requested. The company's e-mail "direct marketing" works for us and for American.

MY WAY OR THE HIGHWAY

After trustworthiness, we find, personalization ranks a close second in creating satisfying on-line brand experiences, with guided selling not far behind.

Personalization is one of the most valuable ways to create brand-building experiences, whether it's for computers, books, cars, mortgages, groceries, plants, or clothes. And increasingly, consumers will buy only from companies that cater to their individual needs. This does not mean that you need to immediately retool the factory to establish a make-to-order system. It does mean that you have to build the perception among consumers that you're providing products and services customized to their needs.

While Dell, AutoByTel, and many business-to-business companies have used customization and personalization as key brand differentiators, we're convinced that personalization will become an expected on-line buying feature within the next few years. Without it a company will find it difficult providing consumers with the type of buying experience they will have come to expect on-line.

While most e-business programs use personalization for on-line buying, Ralston Purina uses it as a feature to attract people to their site. Its Breed Selector recommends breeds of dogs that fit an individual's personal preferences. The site (purina.com/dogs/index.html) asks you to answer a number of questions about your lifestyle and the canine qualities most important to you. Then it provides you with a ranked list of dogs that might suit you. It includes information on everything a new puppy owner needs to know—including dog food nutritional information.

And for those of us concerned with human nutrition, Acumin Corp.'s site (Acumins.com) allows consumers to create specialized mixes of vitamins and supplements to fit individual needs. Site visitors complete a Smart Select survey, and then Acumin uses its manufacturing technology to build a product that matches each customer's needs.

Acumin doesn't stock any vitamin inventory; rather, it matches the customer's needs against a database of "some one million different vitamin formulas," according to Acumin CEO Brad Oberwager. As an aside, Acumin launched its site in October 1997; by January 1998 approximately 5 percent of its total sales were coming from the site. Six months later 50 percent of the company's sales were from the site.

GUIDED SELLING TO SUGGEST PRODUCTS AND SERVICES

Guided selling, or recommendation software, uses Web site visitor input to suggest products and services based on pattern recognition or business rules. "Successful commerce sites will master a new discipline—guided selling— that will change how markets and channels are structured," says Forrester Research. By providing a "virtual" on-line sales rep that understands customer likes and dislikes, companies enhance the buying experience and are able to more effectively manage cross-selling and up-selling sales programs.

In other words, guided selling shows site visitors Web content relevant to their interests, answers questions, and automatically suggests other products or services that the customer might be interested in. Guided selling, in effect, replicates your favorite boutique salesperson, who knows that you like Versace but not Karan, prefer gray to black, and are a sucker for $175 Armani scarves and Clergerie bags.

"Imagine going into an electronics store and there are no sales reps," explains Rob DeSisto of the Gartner Group. "That's what Web sites are today. If you know what you want, you buy it. If you don't know what you want, you leave. That's what's happening on the Web today because nobody engages the customer."

Dot-com companies need to be very careful, however, that their guided selling and personalized messages are relevant to their market targets. On-line book buyers, for example, were initially impressed by Amazon.com's success in recommending new books to buy. More recently, however, one hears lots of complaints about the stupidity of Amazon's matching algorithm—which, in fact, is not based on either serious data mining or significant information about the consumer. Buy a John Le Carré mystery as a birthday gift for Uncle Aaron, and you'll likely receive an e-mail recommendation for another mystery. Amazon's program doesn't have a clue as to who the eventual reader of the book is likely to be or why the book is being purchased.

SHAKE UP YOUR CHANNEL STRATEGY

Traditional retail, distributor, and direct sales channels will not disappear any time soon. However, there's no getting around the fact that the Internet is the fastest-growing new sales channel that businesses have ever faced.

During Christmas 1999 on-line spending grew 200 percent, led by first-time buyers and consumers in the over-50 age group, according to a survey from Zona Research. Middle-aged shoppers increased their spending 545 percent as they spent an average $626, compared to $97 the year before. Those under 25 years old, presumably more Net savvy, upped their spending by 36 percent, to $210 from $154 the year before. Approximately 61 percent of Zona's respondents say they expect to spend more money on-line this year. Some 98 percent of America Online's shoppers say they are motivated to buy more on-line.

The most common reason for buying on-line isn't lower prices but convenience. REI, for example, generates 35 percent of its on-line orders from 10 P.M. to 7 A.M., times when stores and catalog operations are closed. Time-stressed consumers are finding they can fit shopping into spare moments. Let your fingers do the clicking on Thursday nights and free up precious weekend time.

Whatever their motivations, consumers will continue to buy more and more on-line. Those companies—certainly retailers—that do not embrace this channel do so at a perilous risk. Consider that the Gap's less-than-two-year-old Web site generates more volume than any of its traditional stores, save one.

Yet many executives quite reasonably fear cannibalizing business from or alienating existing distribution channels. When Clinique launched its Web site last year, it did so quietly, so as not to upset its retailers. When talking about the success of its holiday season performance, Clinique emphasized that 13 percent of the buyers were new to the brand and another 9 percent had used Clinique before but had stopped. Truth be known, 78 percent of those who bought on the Clinique site during the holiday season were existing buyers who just couldn't face the frenzy of shopping in a mall during the holidays.

Yet companies must base channel decisions on what customers want, because if you don't cannibalize your business, someone else will. Amazon captured the on-line market for book buying largely because the big boys like Barnes & Noble came late to the party. Ditto for eToys, who we think has it all over Toys "R" Us, and E*Trade, who with Ameritrade, Schwab, and Web Street Securities is shaking the brokerage industry.

We're not suggesting that companies abandon traditional channels but rather create new ones, similar to Gap's approach. You can go into a Gap store and try on clothes, feel the fabric, and get your tactile shopping fix. But when you want to reorder your favorite khakis, just go on-line any time of the day, click, and be done.

Another multichannel strategy worth watching is Ford's. As you may know, the automotive industry, like financial services, is being revolutionized by the Internet. Car-buying services like AutoByTel.com and Microsoft's CarPoint initially began as matchmakers for car buyers and sellers. Go to their sites, type in your preferences, get suggestions on autos and read third-party reviews, and get directions to local dealers. Now these sites provide financing and insurance on-line, products traditionally handled by dealers. This encroachment onto their turf has spurred the automotive manufacturers and dealers to more aggressively establish their own on-line sales channels.

While most manufacturers still refer on-line prospects to dealers, Ford has a better idea. Ford is directly selling used cars just coming off lease to consumers instead of putting them through auction. At Fordpreowned.com you're reassured that the Ford cars and trucks are "inspected, factory-backed, Quality Certified by Ford Motor Company, and offered at a 'no-haggle price' with no risk." You browse through available vehicles in your area, specify what you want, and Ford delivers the vehicle to a local dealership for you to test-drive.

One last point about the Web as a sales channel: don't limit your Internet channel strategy to selling only on your own company site. Explore emerging Web channels that are springing up all over the Internet.

If we were a clothing manufacturer or designer, we would have our own e-commerce site and would consider using Web channels like Fashionmall.com and Bluefly.com. In every business category there are powerful new Web-based "retailers" and "distributors" emerging. These Web businesses are creating a brand for themselves, offering consumers selection, service, and personalization. Furthermore, they are filling a void that the major retailers have created by being late to the party.

ON-LINE ADVERTISING: SUCK VS. PUSH

"The Web is not about push; it's about suck." The statement, coined by London Business School professors and consultants Gary Hamel and Jeff Sampler, best sums up the advertising and promotional challenges of this new medium.

Internet users suck up information that interests them. They pay little attention to advertisements and promotions that are devoid of useful information or helpful offers.

"For the on-line advertiser, the challenge is to educate, entertain and entice, for no one can be compelled to pay attention on-line," Hamel and Sampler wrote in *Fortune* in December 1999. More than 71.4 percent of the respondents in a recent Jupiter communications study said that if ads became more informative they would be more likely to click on them.

The Web is already a proven medium for high-involvement consumers, those who seek detailed information before making a purchase decision. In researching products from cars and insurance to vacation packages and computers, consumers want to be able to suck out needed information from the brand's own Web site, on-line advertisements, third-party disintermediary sites (for example, CarPoint.com), and credible on-line information sources like Consumer Reports on-line. Consider that 80 percent of Saturn's leads come via the Internet, double those a year ago.

On the other hand, we do not believe that the Web is an effective medium to promote low-involvement products, and major packaged goods companies seem to agree. This could change, however, because of four factors:

1. Marketers are becoming savvier about creating informative offers and promotional programs for on-line consumers.
2. The technology for targeting specific consumers with messages of most interest to them is improving, as are the reporting/measurement tools.

3. Millions of consumers are going on-line each month; in the past many highly targeted ads simply reached too few consumers to be cost effective. This is changing.
4. New types of personalized "e-mail advertisements" are emerging that are much more effective than the usual banner-type advertising.

Two West Coast start-up companies, AdKnowledge and Personify, have developed market analysis software that can tell you what on-line advertisements have produced click-throughs, which customers actually bought, how much they bought, and the margins on each sale. As marketing scientists, we find this approach to measuring through to a sale interesting. While we don't believe this analysis software is yet 100 percent, it shows promise. Other firms, like DoubleClick and MathLogic, track site profiles and match Web ads to the sites that can most precisely target specific audiences and interests.

DoubleClick, for example, offers four types of targeting filters: content (health, travel, sports, an so on); behavioral (days and times, psychographic); user (geographic, company name, size of business), and technical (type of browser or operating system).

While on-line advertising is still markedly more expensive per impression than other mediums, we believe it's a medium to watch. Companies that ignore or shun it are like the radio advertisers in the late 1940s who "knew" that television was an expensive novelty and would never supplant radio.

One interesting on-line advertising trend is "e-mail advertising," essentially ads that you have asked to receive. According to a survey conducted by Nikkei Multimedia, e-mail advertising has emerged as the hottest ad category—receiving a higher approval rating among on-line users than other forms of Internet-based advertising.

BRANDING, SPIRAL BRANDING, AND THE "KILLER CLICKS"

In the Internet world branding is becoming more important than ever before. When people go on-line to buy or do some looking around in anticipation of making a purchase, they go to trusted brands they know. The challenge will be to continue to build enough brand awareness and equity that customers think of you and consider you when they're thinking.

Some companies are beginning to play with the concept of spiral branding, which uses each medium for what it's best at. According to Jesse Berst, editor of Ziff-Davis's *AnchorDesk,* creating the spiral has three stages. "First, you use TV, print, or radio to get people interested and send them to the Web. Second, you use the Web to get those customers involved (via specialized content and interactive services). You also collect their e-mail addresses. Third, you use e-mail to remind and 'incent' them to return to TV and the Web again. E-mail closes the loop and starts people around the spiral again."

He cites the example of a sports channel that reminds you to visit its Web site. At the site it involves you with an interactive fantasy league. It then uses e-mail to remind you to return to TV for the pregame show. Key to the success of spiral branding is to reiterate constantly, making improvements based on what you learn about the customer at each step.

Whatever the creative approach, you must still build a strong brand, a brand based on mastering the fundimentals of building brand equity, not brand juice. George Colony, president of Forrester Research, underscores the importance of brand in his discussions about "killer clicks." Colony believes that in the Internet economy, more and more customers will make seemingly trivial choices (killer clicks) that have long-term, far-ranging impact on companies.

For example, we have a friend who is a loyal Peapod customer; it delivers groceries to her house every Friday night between 6:00 and 7:30 P.M. When she first started using the service, she went through Peapod's shopping menu and clicked on her preferred brands to build a personalized shopping list. She has used the same list—and bought the same brands—for 18 months. Talk about brand loyalty. It is unlikely she would be so loyal if she were walking up and down the aisles, looking at different packaging, and taking advantage of shelf coupons, checkout coupons, and Sunday insert coupons.

"Killer clicks will go unnoticed by most companies but will end up tipping the balance of power toward players that understand and harvest clicks early," says Colony. He cites other examples, like setting up Quicken and choosing CheckFree as the bill payment system, a choice that marginalizes banks. Or shutting out Visa and American Express when a customer sets up one-click buying on Barnesandnoble.com and specifies MasterCard as the payment method.

To us the implication of killer clicks is twofold: you need to (1) make sure that your brand is the preferred brand, with "clicking loyalty," and (2) pay attention to the possible emergence of slotting or positioning fees in on-line selling. As we noted earlier, consumers were outraged when they learned that Amazon.com was accepting slotting fees. But Amazon is a highly visible site. Many sites could adopt a positioning fee strategy with less notice, offering well-positioned brands "killer click" placements.

Clients routinely ask us what we predict will be the next big thing in Internet marketing. After seeing Victoria's Secret's successful Valentine's Day interactive Web broadcast, we're watching commerce-casting closely. With it companies create and distribute content on-line with an implicit sales pitch.

Next year, for example, Victoria's Secret expects to broadcast live chats and an option to vote for the most popular model, offer high-quality photos and details on super model Tyra Banks's hobbies, and most important, allow customers to click on products featured in the Webcast and buy them. Every visitor will be invited to sign up for a catalog subscription.

This type of interactive experience may be a way to convert viewers into buyers on the spot, which could be even more successful than the home shopping channels. We fully expect that innovative marketers like Martha Stewart will be at the forefront of capitalizing on commerce-casting's potential. Those that are successful will be so because they know that the basics of marketing do not go away with a new medium.

One common intuitive response to the Internet and e-commerce has been something like "We've got to get on or get left behind" or, worse, "Amazon'd." The counterintuitive marketing approach looks at the Internet and e-commerce as just another communications medium or channel of distribution—a potentially revolutionary medium and/or channel, perhaps, but a medium or channel nonetheless. It has not repealed the principles of marketing. You still need a clear strategy for targeting, positioning, products, services, and pricing. Without a sound strategy, one based on creative thinking balanced by rigorous research and a commitment to building brand equity, you will get left behind, on or off the Web.

Implementing Counterintuitive Marketing Programs

Prayers and Divine Intervention: No Marketing Miracles to Date

The annual marketing plan is a hoax perpetrated on senior management. And it's a hoax we observe every day in companies large and small across a broad range of consumer and business-to-business product categories.

Here's a perfect example. In January 2000 we were engaged by one of America's premier consumer products companies to evaluate their marketing planning system. Given the reputation of this company—one we hadn't worked with before—we expected great things.

The first marketing plan we examined was for the number-two brand in one of the largest health and beauty aid categories globally. Superficially it looked pretty good: 122 pages long, in a shiny binder with lots of tables, charts, and graphs. It would impress almost anyone reading it.

The plan opened with reasonably clear sales objectives, followed by a detailed discussion of strategy and tactics, and ended with a P&L statement. An appendix was loaded with information about the product category, competitive analyses, pending legislative issues, and a ton of stuff you'd expect smart brand managers to be thinking about. The plan lacked vision and mission statements, however; it ignored the Web; and like this book, it talked too much about advertising. But we can live with these problems, because after seeing them every day, we've become inured to them.

What shouldn't have surprised us but did—because our expectations were so high—was the total lack of connection between every section of the plan.

- The objectives were foisted upon marketing by top management. The sales objective, for example, was a number that came down from the heavens. The brass asked for a 12 percent increase in unit sales. This objective was set without any consideration of whether it could be achieved and its implications for brand profitability. And where was the 12 percent gain going to come from? The plan suggested more awareness (another objective), but what kind of awareness, and how would it be achieved? All of the marketing inputs looked pretty flat. By this, we mean that they looked very similar to previous years'. Moreover, there was no evidence of how, even if the plan mysteriously posted gains in awareness, this would yield exactly a 12 percent gain in sales.
- The strategy developed by marketing management was not linked to the objectives. There was no evidence that the recommended strategy was even developed with the objectives in mind. The strategic target of 25- to 54-year-old-women was the same target selected by every major player in the category, and nothing about it or the positioning suggested that they could deliver a sizable increase in sales, never mind the 12 percent sought by the CEO and CFO.
- The strategy and tactics were unrelated. It was not at all clear that the tactics were customized to the target and positioning strategies. Advertising and promotional tactics, for example, were generic and could be employed by any brand, regardless of strategy. What we found really frightening was that the brand's packaging didn't reflect its positioning. It was as if the position and packaging were created by people living on different planets.
- The tactics and objectives were unrelated. The promotion and ad budget reflected the last year's numbers corrected for inflation, and while the ad copy performed above average in terms of copy-testing norms, so did the executions run the previous year, when sales declined by 3 percent. ACV distribution had peaked at 90 percent, and share-of-shelf facings were in line with market share. There was nothing new here. And no work was done to model the relationship between the tactics and the objectives, to forecast the ROI of the $40 million ad budget.
- The P&L statement was simply made up. Since everything else represented wild guesses, this shouldn't have surprised us. The statement piled questionable assumption upon questionable assumption, with no basis in fact.

"Here's another testosterone 'plan,'" we thought, "right smack in the middle of the bell curve we talked about in Chapter 2."

The more we looked, the less sense the plan made. The only real question was why we expected anything different. That's how all marketing plans are put together. Here are three additional examples in very different product categories that show other problems with some marketing plans.

Last fall, we were talking to a major grower cooperative about doing some work for their product. The co-op has been around for a long time, has a $20 million marketing budget, and had prepared an elaborate marketing plan. These are not neophyte marketers.

But when we asked them what they knew about the channels that sell their product—What do the eight major supermarket chains in America say? What are they interested in? How will they react to a marketing effort? —the marketing staff answered, "We're not sure. Other people in the company—the sales force—take care of the channels."

They had prepared an elaborate and sophisticated marketing plan and did not consider a critical element.

We were engaged in a project for one of the most prestigious, successful hotel chains. During our meetings about the next year's marketing program, we suggested they interview corporate meeting planners, because these people are responsible for buying a lot of hotel rooms. We also suggested the chain ought to talk to travel agents, including in-company travel agents.

They said, "No, no, no. We just want to focus on the traveler. Individual travelers are responsible for most lodging decisions."

We asked, "How much of your market do meeting planners and travel agents represent?"

They said that they didn't know exactly—it could be 30 percent, maybe more—but that was not a part of the market on which they wanted to focus. So the marketing plan they developed was oblivious to perhaps a third of the chain's business.

A third example comes from direct-to-consumer pharmaceutical marketing. A pharmaceutical giant asked us to simulate the effects of a $70 million advertising plan on consumers (a.k.a. "sufferers"). Yes, $70 million. The plan included prime-time and late-night television, newspapers, and magazines. We suggested that physicians watch these shows and read these newspapers and magazines in their roles as ordinary people. We asked, consequently, for the monthly GRPs of the campaign by media type *among doctors.*

The numbers were not available because the "physician as consumer" was never considered.

A reader might argue that these cases are unusual insofar as the companies ignored large chunks of the market in the marketing planning process. So let's reverse field for a moment and talk about a prototypical marketing plan,

the kind one sees every day at companies as diverse as American Express and
Fidelity, Bristol-Meyers and Procter & Gamble, Compaq Computer and Dell,
Frito-Lay and Kraft, General Electric and General Motors.

SAY A LITTLE PRAYER FOR ME

A marketing plan, says one contemporary marketing text (*Principles of Marketing* by Philip Kotler and Gary Armstrong, Prentice-Hall, 1999), is "a document that outlines in detail the marketing strategies that will help a company,
product, or brand attain its overall business objectives."

Everyone understands why a marketing plan is important. The marketing
plan is to company success as a road map is to car travel. It is the key to the
transition from strategy to tactics. It can act as a tracking mechanism, it can
determine the budget, and it can be a scale against which the company measures marketing effectiveness. And it is an internal communications tool that
everyone consults to know where the business is going and how it plans to get
there.

Interestingly, we find that only about half the companies we visit in our
consulting work have a *detailed* marketing plan. Almost everyone has a
sketchy plan and a budget, in some cases a detailed one. But many do not
have a fully developed marketing plan. They don't know where they're going.
And if you don't know where you're going, it's hard to know when you've
arrived. Table 15-1 outlines the major components of a typical plan.

Companies that write plans will typically state the plan's objectives in the
opening pages. These objectives may include market share ("Achieve a 10
percent share of the South African soft drink market by December 31"); sales
("Sell $62 million of our new software product in the first quarter"); market
penetration ("Achieve 600,000 additional credit cards in force in current markets next year"); profit margins ("Improve our profit margin to 15 percent in
domestic markets in the next year"); or some combination of these.

These particular objectives, unlike many we see, support the organization's
mission; are challenging, specific, attainable, measurable; and include a
deadline or schedule. They are appropriate objectives. Objectives that lack
any of these elements—"To improve profit margins in 2001," for example—
are worthless.

They are worthless because they are too fuzzy to be helpful. A common
fuzzy objective, the one used by the packaged goods giant that opened this
chapter, is "We are going to build awareness." What kind of awareness? Top
of mind? Unaided brand? Total unaided and aided brand awareness? Unaided
or aided advertising awareness? Partially aided or fully aided tracer (e.g., slo-

Table 15-1   Elements of A Prototypical Marketing Plan

Goals and Objectives

Marketing Climate Analysis

Marketing Strategy

- Targeting Strategy
- Positioning Strategy
- Product/Service Strategy
- Advertising Strategy
- Channel Strategy
- Internet Strategy
- Pricing Strategy

Tactical Plans

- Media Schedule
- Advertising Budget
- Reach/Frequency Objectives
- Internet Plans
- Public Relations Plans
- Promotion Plans
- Distribution Objectives

Profit and Loss Statement

gan) penetration? What about unaided associations of the brand with key attributes and benefits? That's a type of awareness. Or how about some composite of all these measures, which we refer to as "campaign penetration"?

Table 15-2 lists different kinds of awareness.

Assuming the marketer can answer this question—and often they cannot—what are the reasons for choosing one measure of awareness over another? It's not an easy question, and many advertisers avoid it by being as fuzzy as they can. When you're really fuzzy, you can't be measured. And if you can't be measured, you're not accountable.

The typical marketing plan moves on to include a section on the market climate, a competitive analysis, and then the strategy. The latter covers targeting, positioning, the product line, pricing, communications (mostly advertising), customer service, and sales/distribution. The plan talks about how much money the business will spend on advertising, outlines the media schedule, explains how that relates to promotion, and establishes distribution levels. If the company is very clever, it includes a section on measuring marketing performance.

Table 15-2   ***Alternative Measures of Awareness***

Awareness Measure	Operational Definition for Booksellers (Both On-line and Traditional Bookstores)
First Brand	"When you think of places where you can buy books, what is the first name that comes to mind?"
Unaided Brand	"What are all of the different booksellers and bookstores you can think of?"
Unaided Advertising	"Which have you seen or heard advertised during the past 90 days?"
Proven Recall	"What do you remember seeing or hearing in the advertising for this company?" (Proven recall if a person plays back something definitely or probably in the ad.)
Aided Advertising	"Have you seen or heard any advertising for Amazon.com during the past 90 days?"
Partially Aided Advertising	"Which bookstore . . ."
	advertises 'All books, for all people, everywhere' (Slogan example)
	advertises 'next day delivery' (Message example)
	uses Regis Philbin in their advertising?" (Spokesperson or dominant visual example)
Fully Aided Tracer Penetration	"Have you seen or heard any advertising for Barnes & Noble which uses the slogan . . . ?"
Aided Brand	"I'm going to read you a list of booksellers. For each one I name, please tell me if you've ever heard of it."
Total Brand	Unaided and aided brand awareness.
Campaign Penetration	A weighted composite measure of all of the above, scaled from 0% to 100%.

We're always intrigued by the dissociation between the market target and the rest of the plan. What does it mean to say, "We're going after the heavy users" or "We like attitudinal and behavioral rejectors"? Or "We're targeting pizza lovers"? Or "We're going to address PC enthusiasts"? What is the connection between the strategy for going after those people and what goes through the marketing plan? For many companies, none.

It reads nicely. The CEO looking at it may think everything makes sense. The CEO may think that if the company makes these decisions and spends that much money, it will accomplish the objectives.

The scary secret here is that few companies know anything about the relationship between marketing inputs and outputs. The plan is a fraud. It looks good and is well written, but its only chance of success is if the gods of commerce reward management's prayers. Virtually no one has a clue how the various elements interact with each other.

We'll be clear. Leafing through the typical marketing plan, we look for the pages with the objectives. We find a heavy discussion of strategy, pages dealing with tactics and spending—but nothing is connected. There is no real knowledge that if the company spends $12 million in advertising, unit sales will increase 6 percent. There is no connection between, say, distribution and the overall objective, or between promotional spending and profitability. Each of the plan's components operates in a vacuum. There is no connection because there are only a handful of marketers in America who know the connection.

The only thing that could possibly make this kind of plan work is prayers. The image of Rupert Everett leading a chorus of "Say a Little Prayer for Me" in *My Best Friend's Wedding* comes to mind.

UNDERSTAND THE RELATIONSHIP BETWEEN MARKETING INPUTS AND OUTPUTS

It is possible to develop a plan that takes into account marketing inputs and outputs and establishes the relationships between them. For want of a better label, we refer to this as "scientific marketing planning." The plan's core is an empirically based mathematical model that "understands" the connections between each of the market inputs and outputs in a category. With it you can say, "If we impact this target with this kind of positioning and with this level of advertising, we can expect to achieve this level of sales." We have developed models for food products, credit cards, movies, theme parks, and beer. Figure 15-1 is the model used for the new light beer discussed earlier.

We've even developed a model for new products and services—it's called Discovery—and we've written a book about the use of such models to take some of the risk out of the new product introduction process.*

The first step in creating such a model is to identify all marketing inputs and outputs. Clearly, a company can directly affect some of these elements— pricing, advertising spending, promotion spending. Others it can affect only indirectly—the retailer's relationship with his distributor, for example. But even if the company cannot affect the inputs directly (or at all), it is important to identify every one and chart its relationship to the other elements.

---

*Kevin J. Chancy, Robert S. Shulman, Marianne Wolf, *Simulated Test Marketing: Technology for Launching Successful New Products* (New York: Lexington Books, 1994).

Figure 15-1   A Marketing Mix Model for Arkansas Slim's Light Beer

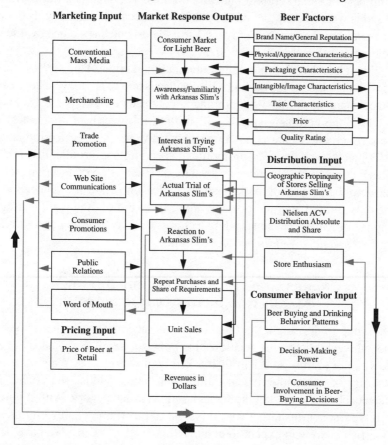

Where does the information for the boxes come from? You need information not only about your marketing process but also about the competition's. Some of it will be from syndicated information services. Nielsen or IRI data can tell you about distribution and retail prices. You know your prices and you can probably estimate what your competitors are charging, so that will give you a good approximation of the retailer's markup.

Nielsen or IRI data will also give you a figure for numeric distribution, the number of stores you're in (if you do not have it internally), and for total stock, your share of the display within the stores. You may be in a store but not be well stocked, so it is important to know both.

On the left-hand side of the model, Merchandising in this category includes napkins and glasses and swizzle sticks, as well as refrigerators, coolers, and tables and chairs. A syndicated service tracks Conventional Mass Media spending. In the U.S. it is Leading National Advertisers. Public Relations includes how much money you are spending or the value of the PR activity you are getting. Trade Promotion is just that—how much money you're spending on trade discounts, twofers, and the like.

The left-hand side of the figure shows all the marketing investments a beer company can make, broken into all the significant components. Showing it laid out neatly like this, however, and actually gathering the relevant figures are, we realize, two very different things. Companies cannot always lay their hands on the data. What did we spend on the Indianapolis car? I don't know; that's somebody in another building. Well, give him a call. He's out/he doesn't like to tell me/it's politically sensitive. Okay, how much did we spend on the promotion we did last year when we gave out Arkansas Slim hats at NFL games? We'll have to call the vendor who organized it. Nobody in the company knows.

To make the model work, you need to conceptualize it at the beginning of the process, to identify every single input and output. You then need to implement a plan to collect data on a regular basis over time. This includes defining expenses correctly. For example, some people will call the money the company spends on a race car "advertising"; some will call it "merchandising"; others will call it "promotion." How the accounting department assigns money may not be the way you want to use it here.

Assembling the company's own costs can be a chore, but if you do it well, you will have not only your expenditures but a fair idea of what your competitors spent. To establish positioning penetration, campaign penetration, consideration, trial, loyalty, and preference figures, you will need a consumer tracking survey. Retailer satisfaction with distributor and retailer satisfaction with the brand come from a trade customer satisfaction survey that asks store and bar owners if they are happy with various brands. (In Chapter 18, on performance metrics, we will discuss these measures and more.)

Therefore, to begin to develop a marketing plan model, you need at least four and as many as eight sources of information: sales data (Nielsen or IRI); Leading National Advertisers; a study measuring buyer readership, viewership, and listenership for all media vehicles; a customer satisfaction survey; a source of nontraditional media spending, such as events, sponsorships, merchandising; public relations and consumer trading data (everything from awareness through presence and sales). You need the information for your brand, for competitive brands, and especially for your market target over time (and if you can get it, the market target impacted by the positioning strategy) so you can begin to see cause and effect.

In the near future it will be possible for most brands to "parse out" the effects of short-term sales promotions and local store activity to uncover the direct short-term effects of advertising. For those who take a longer-term view, the promise of single-source panel data is the ability to track the longer-term effects of advertising on purchasing loyalty and deal sensitivity.

MODEL THE RELATIONSHIP BETWEEN THE FACTORS

The next step in a scientific marketing plan is to do the modeling. This is not something a manager wants to do by himself unless he's skilled at using some very sophisticated software, like the SAS Institute's enterprise data-mining package. What most companies do is turn this problem over to econometricians or statisticians trained in working with marketing concepts and data.

Working with the experts and the data, we learn which boxes are important and the directions of the arrows. We did not know these connections when we started. We did know that not every box has an arrow going to every other box, but we had to discover what input affects what output(s). For example, public relations does not affect everything; in this situation it affects only campaign penetration. Price at retail does not change share of facings; it encourages trial but not loyalty.

How do you model the relationship? How do you learn that in your particular situation, share of facings, not price, affects loyalty? The only way is to study it, to do what we have been recommending throughout this book: the rigorous analysis of unimpeachable data.

Doing this, you sometimes discover surprising things. Not so surprising after managers reflect on them awhile, perhaps, but surprising enough initially that they do not always believe the data. In a number of American product categories, for example, absolute levels of distribution are only moderately related to market share. But *share* of weighted distribution is increasingly important. By this we mean the share of all standardized units that one brand has in a product category in a particular channel or market (say, outlets selling PCs).

If share of weighted distribution becomes the single strongest determinant of market share, it suggests the image of a blindfolded buyer. Brand, price, packaging, and shelf-talkers become less important in the buying decision. The blindfolded buyer simply reaches out and takes what's on the shelf. What she grabs is a function of share of distribution. An implication of this is that many categories in the U.S. and around the globe are being transformed into commodities, something we talked about in Chapter 2.

DECISION CALCULUS CAN HELP SMALLER COMPANIES

What happens when you don't have the data or the resources to collect it? What happens if you don't have an econometrician/statistician on staff and cannot afford to hire one? Fortunately, Professor John Little at the Sloan School at MIT has developed an approach.

In what Little calls "decision calculus," we rely upon the judgment of knowledgeable people in a company, sometimes aided by their marketing consulting firm or advertising agency. Their judgments, rather than statistical analysis of empirical data, help set parameters for the kind of model we've just discussed.

Take as an example the relationship between advertising spending and consumer preference. You first plot current advertising spending and consumer preference (from your research) on a sheet of graph paper. The X-axis indicates spending; the Y-axis indicates preference.

Assume you spent $12 million on advertising last year and your research tells you the brand has a 20 percent preference. If you doubled the spending from $12 million to $24 million, what effect do you think it would have on preference? Would it double? Would it go up by 35 percent? Ask other executives who have the experience and background to make an informed estimate to come to a consensus judgment that preference would go from 20 percent to, say, 28 percent. What do you think would happen if spending increased by, say, 25 percent? Nothing? Would it rise by 5 percent, 10 percent, 15 percent?

Now, if top management gave you an infinite amount of money to spend on advertising, what would happen to preference? Go through the estimating process again to come up with an average of 39 percent, maybe even 40 percent. What would happen if the advertising budget were cut to zero for the next couple years? Terrible things. What exactly? Would preference drop to 12 percent?

A research analyst can now use some nonlinear regression analysis to fit a line that connects those five points, making a graph. You can apply it to every number. "What if the advertising budget were $11 million?" "What if it were $22 million?" "What if it dropped to $5 million?" In a situation in which you do not have enough data or cannot collect the data in a reasonable time, you can go through this decision calculus approach.

Now, having converted the conceptual model into a mathematical model, we can begin working toward the end objective of a more scientific marketing plan.

FLYING YOUR BRAND TOWARD MARKETING SUCCESS

Think of all the elements driving sales and profitability as being like the instruments a pilot uses to fly an airplane. A simple model represents a simple plane—a Piper Cub, for example. A complex model is comparable to a sophisticated plane, such as the F-117 Stealth Bomber.

If a manager knows the relationship between distribution and sales and the relationship between advertising and awareness, preference and sales, and so on, she can ask key questions (and expect a useful answer). Questions like "What does it cost the company to gain one share point through advertising as opposed to the cost to gain the point through distribution?"

Managers can say, "We're going to put X amount of money into trade incentives. We're going to put Y amount of money into merchandising. We're going to put Z amount of money into our Web site. We're going to have a public relations program. We're going to have this kind of advertising spending, and our price to the retailer will be A. If we do all these things and invest the way we've just outlined, will we make our share objective, and if not, why not?"

If the target group and the positioning are all part of this modeling exercise, you can be assured that your strategy and your tactics are linked to both the buyer objectives—like awareness and preference—and to the hard performance objectives—like sales and market share.

Top management says we need to increase our market share by 12 percent next year. Fine. What does the company need to do to consumer preference to achieve that goal? What does the company need to do to distribution and to consumer awareness to achieve it? What does the company need to do to advertising to achieve that awareness? And what will all of this cost? The model will tell you.

Increasing distribution might achieve the goal by itself. On the other hand, it may be that the company has just about all the distribution it can hope for, so increasing it may be out of the question.

Such a model can save disappointment later in the year. Say top management wants to increase market share from a 25 to a 30. The marketing department feeds in its plans and the expenditures, and the model might literally beep an alarm because there is no way the plan will reach the goal. The model might predict a two-point share gain, not a five.

Marketing-mix modeling is also a way to try alternatives. What if we spent the budget this way? What if we spent it that way? Or, working from the other direction, what do we need to spend to reach the objective? Through trial and error you can simulate all kinds of spending plans to see what you can get.

Even better, you can do a sensitivity analysis. You can say, what happens if (for example) I increase my advertising budget by $5 million? The model show that a $5 million increase produces less effect than a may $5 million increase in

Figure 15-2   Example of a Sensitivity Analysis for Selected Marketing Components

	−40%	−30%	−20%	−10%	+10%	+20%	+30%	+40%
Prime 15-Second								
Change in Sales (000s of Units)	−97	−71	−44	−27	27	44	71	88
Cost (000s of $)	−295	−222	−148	−74	74	148	222	295
Prime 30-Second								
Change in Sales (000s of Units)	−725	−531	−345	−168	168	327	476	628
Cost (000s of $)	−1741	−1305	−870	−435	435	870	1305	1741
Day 15-Second								
Change in Sales (000s of Units)	−44	−35	−27	−9	97	27	35	44
Cost (000s of $)	−75	−56	−38	−19	19	38	56	75
Day 30-Second								
Change in Sales (000s of Units)	−610	−451	−301	−150	142	284	416	549
Cost (000s of $)	−877	−658	−439	−219	219	439	658	877

trade promotion. The sensitivity analysis will point a manager toward those marketing activities that will have the best return on the investment.

Marketers can ask the sensitivity analysis component in a model to evaluate every ingredient in the marketing plan in terms of its effect on sales or profits or both. The model will run hundreds—in some cases thousands—of simulations to identify those factors that contribute most to marketing success.

For example, we performed a sensitivity analysis on only a few variables for a new product. The model showed that by dropping the number of prime-time 30-second commercials by 20 percent, the company would save $870,000 and lose 345,000 sales units. At the same time the model indicated that putting approximately the same amount of money—$877,000—into daytime television would increase this media vehicle's usage 40 percent and increase sales 549,000 units. In other words, a switch from prime-time to daytime 30-second commercials was forecast to increase sales by 204,000 units at an incremental cost of only $7,000.

Marketers can use the same sensitivity component to model competitive response. First experience and past history can help to estimate a competitor's plans to stop the new product. Then the model can help to determine which offensive strategy will overcome the most likely defense.

As commonsensical a notion as it seems to us to connect the boxes in a marketing plan, we know it is a radical idea. It is counterintuitive. At this writing we have seen only a few businesses go through the agony of developing a model of a complete marketing initiative. For everyone else the pieces of the marketing plan simply are blocks in a vacuum: our budget is this; our sales goal is this; our share objective is this; our target is this—with no link between any element. We speculate that fewer than 5 percent of all marketing plans show any scientific connection between the objectives, the strategy, the tactics, and the results.

Why don't companies embrace scientific marketing planning? It is always difficult to tell why a manager does not do something, especially from the outside, but we suspect that the whole notion of implementation is overwhelming. The idea is too complicated, and marketing managers do not really believe that if they *do* implement it, it will be effective. If a marketing plan can simply say, "We're going to achieve a 50 percent level of awareness" without specifying which awareness measure or how it's linked to sales and profits, why would the company ever want to go through anything very specific, like what we've just described?

Yet, increasingly, companies will have to do so if they want to see a reasonable return on the marketing investment.

A marketing manager should never tell her boss, "We will increase awareness by spending $20 million in mass media, and hopefully sales will go up by 30 percent." With marketing planning she can say instead, "Our forecasting technology suggests that as you implement this strategy and achieve the planned levels of GRPs each week, a positioning penetration of 42 percent by year end, ACV distribution of 75 percent [and so on], market share will jump from 9.3 to 12.0 percent and profitability will increase by 54 percent."

Not only will an approach to marketing planning—such as the one discussed here—and evolving expert systems work with the data that exists, but they will permit human managers to study the world that could be. They will integrate marketing science modeling, automated-intelligence technology, and historical marketplace relationships. These systems will take the mathematics and merge it with the knowledge of marketing experts—the experience, rules of thumb, and insights that experienced marketing practitioners now use in order to build plans that really work.

Some marketing people react to these changes with denial. They say, in essence, "So what? I don't need models and systems. I don't know what they tell me anyway. I don't need a more scientific approach." If they don't know what a marketing planning model tells them and if they're not willing to learn, then they're right. They don't need more science; they need new jobs.

For marketing managers of the future, however, scientific marketing planning based on marketing-mix modeling is today's counterintuitive idea that will become commonplace in the next decade. Senior management will demand marketing performance on the right-hand side of the bell curve, and sophisticated planning is a way to produce it.

Testing in Cyberspace Is Better Than Testing in the World

Last fall, a major pharmaceutical marketer hired us to simulate the incremental effect its $35 million first-quarter consumer advertising campaign would have on the year's product sales. Yes, $35 million in one quarter. This was over and above the professional campaign directed against physicians.

A simulated test market is a laboratory study in which buyers react to new advertising for a new or restaged product; it is designed to mimic as precisely as possible what would happen in a real world introduction. This is in contrast to the marketing mix modeling we described in the last chapter, which employs statistical analysis of existing data to roughly predict what would happen if various components of the marketing plan were changed.

The client wanted to know whether direct-to-consumer (also known as DTC) advertising pays its way. Would enough consumers (also known as "sufferers") ask their doctors about the drug to make the advertising investment a sound one?

Our simulated test marketing model (called the Discovery model) found the $35 million would produce a share gain of only one point and have a negative ROI. Sufferers, the simulation research discovered, were unlikely to remember this product's difficult name (let's call it "Plutonixerion Plus") or any reason for its superiority—let alone remember the name and the benefits long enough to request a prescription on a visit to their doctor weeks, if not months, later.

The company's executives were, to put the best possible face on it, distressed by our report, a distress intensified by their experience with a research company, which we were surprised to learn had been retained to do a forecast parallel with our own. That firm had projected a significant gain in share and a positive ROI. Why didn't we? Who was right? We asked the client to send us the report and said we would try to uncover the discrepancy between our forecast and the other firm's.

Before we could complete our analysis, the client experienced a testosterone rush and decided to launch the program. They spent, not $35 million, but $38 million over three months in television and print to advertise the product. They hired a tracking research company to interview both sufferers and physicians on a continuous basis and to compare the results of the tracking with the output of the two models and with actual prescriptions. What did they find?

First, sales prescriptions hardly moved at all. At most, one point. The tracking research among sufferers, moreover, showed a 5 percent proven recall, a poor showing for a $38 million advertising effort. Among people who remembered something about the brand and the advertising, only 1 percent asked their doctors about the medication. These are disturbingly low numbers and not very different from those that the Discovery model had predicted.

The tracking research among physicians told the same bottom-line story. Doctors said less than 1 percent of their patients had asked for a prescription for the product. Thus, the tracking research among physicians and sufferers and the Discovery model all pointed in the same direction: campaign failure. Happily, the Discovery DTC model had been validated again, but unhappily, $38 million and a lot of time had been wasted.

After a period of convalescence, our client asked us to help explain the discrepancy between the research firm's model (the one they wanted to believe) and marketplace results. We regarded this as an interesting R&D exercise.

The first thing that we learned is that the other firm forecast a 44 percent recall of the new product—in contrast to our 5 percent—and forecast that 35 percent of the aware sufferers would ask their physician for a prescription—versus our 20 percent.

We pointed out that direct-to-consumer (DTC) pharmaceutical advertising requires that the consumer actually remember the (often strange) brand name and the message strategy; she then has to make an appointment with her doctor and remember to ask for the product by name. Because the DTC "advertising-to-buying" process is so different from that of ordinary packaged goods, we had told the company that in our DTC modeling we would use "proven" awareness as the criterion for awareness, not total brand awareness—"proven" awareness being awareness of the brand name and something about the advertising.

It turns out that in the research firm's laboratory research study, they used a recognition-based measure in which the researchers gave respondents copy points from the television advertising and asked if they remembered them. The firm counted people who *claimed* to remember two or more copy points as having proven recall, which it is not. Indeed, as we discussed in Chapter 8, if you ask people about ads that never ran or copy points never used, recognition scores are surprisingly high. People have a tendency to overstate what they remember, perhaps in the hope of pleasing the interviewer or appearing more sophisticated.

Another issue was the number of people who, recalling the advertising, would ask their doctor for a prescription—35 percent, according to the other firm's research. This would be a good number for typical packaged goods, but to think that 35 percent of the people who see a pharmaceutical ad will call their doctor, make an appointment, and ask for the drug during the visit is just a little much.

It turns out that the firm had accepted sufferers' self reports of what they would do as fixed truths rather than as exaggerated possibilities that require adjustments for overstatement, as we discussed in Chapter 11.

We put together a presentation unraveling the research mystery and presented our results to about 20 people, expecting the worst. They asked good questions as we waited for the attack. Basically, we were telling them the company had wasted $38 million in one quarter based on an overly optimistic forecast. But the attack never came because, we learned for the first time, the company had launched other, similar DTC campaigns in the past three years with equally disappointing results and without learning anything. This time, at least, they learned something about the factors that drive DTC success, including the need to imprint the product name and its message and to find new and creative ways to motivate people to request the drug from their physicians.

The Problems with Traditional Test Markets

In the DTC case we were invited to help this company project year-end sales based on a laboratory study, marketing plans, and a marketing-mix model. It's a way to fly your plane without running the risk of a crash. It's a way to bypass traditional test marketing.

Test markets are fraught with problems. Often the company selects a test market because it's easy to manage or because a retailer in the market will cooperate. The company does not select the market because it best represents the target the company wants to reach.

Traditional test markets have five major defects:

1. *They are expensive.* They can cost as little as $3 million but typically run more. Costs include the research, the media, and the effort throughout the organization to control and check the test.
2. *They take a long time.* Waiting a year, 18 months, or two years for results is simply not feasible in today's competitive environment.
3. *They give away ideas.* Marketers routinely gripe, "Test markets aren't secure, and we're giving our competitors free marketing intelligence."
4. *Competitors can sabotage results.* Even modest efforts by competitors can spoil the company's ability to read the test market results. Competitors have sabotaged tests by having their salespeople pull the new products off retail shelves, turn them sideways, or move them to other shelves where shoppers will not notice them.
5. *They usually don't tell you what you need to know.* While a product failing in a test market is not as painful as one failing in a national rollout, it is often difficult to determine why it failed. Was the problem with the way the company executed the idea, or was the idea simply too small? Was the problem with the marketing program or with the competitive response? Could the company have done something to turn a modest failure into a roaring success? Conversely, if the test was successful, is there anything you could do to make the product even more profitable?

THE ADVANTAGES OF SIMULATED TEST MARKETS

A well-done simulated test market (STM) reduces risks that include not only lost marketing and sales dollars but also capital—the expense of installing production lines or building a new factory to manufacture the product. Why would a company spend $3 million or $4 million and wait 18 months to learn of a failure about which it can do little when it can spend $150,000 or $250,000 and take three to six months to learn how to fix any problems?

A simulated test market study increases marketing efficiency. If a company has, say, three new-product development projects underway and one seems to offer more volume and greater margins, sagacious management will promote that project rather than the others. The STM can indicate the project offering the greatest return. An STM can also optimize the company's marketing efficiency in a new product it does go ahead with—to see the effect, say, of shifting a budgeted $1 million from daytime television advertising to a coupon or vice versa.

A simulated test market study maintains security. Only a relative handful of people know what you're about.

A simulated test market can save time. The STM can produce results in three to six months in a world in which time is now a key competitive advantage. Time is the equivalent of money, productivity, quality, even innovation as a strategic weapon.

A company that builds its strategy on flexible manufacturing and rapid-response systems is a more powerful competitor than one with a traditional strategy based on low wages or manufacturing cost efficiencies. Cost-based strategies require managers to do whatever is necessary to drive down costs (remember Chainsaw Al Dunlap)—move production to or buy from a low-wage country; build new factories or consolidate old plants to gain economies of scale. These do reduce costs, but at the expense of responsiveness, and many customers are more interested in quick response than in the best price.

Time-based marketing allows companies to serve key customer needs quickly, which in turn creates more value. In this era the total time required to produce a product or service—not cost—defines a firm's competitive advantage. "Early adopters report that actions modeled on just-in-time—simplified flows, waste reduction, reduced setup times and batch sizes—can also dramatically reduce time in product development, engineering, and customer service," says Dr. Joseph Blackburn, dean of the Owen School of Management at Vanderbilt University and a longtime friend and consultant to the authors. "Firms able to achieve faster response times have reported growth rates over three times the industry average and at double the profit. Thus the payoff is market dominance."

A Good STM Will Tell You Not Only How You're Doing But What to Do

Today's better simulated test marketing systems capture every important component in the marketing mix and assess the effect of any plan on product awareness, trial, repeat rates, market share, profitability, and more. These STMs test any plan the marketer wants to consider—even a competitor's. The marketer enters plan details into a PC program, and the model forecasts what is likely to occur month by month in the real world.

Some simulated test marketing methodologies are even smart enough to help recommend a plan, and we have never seen a plan a sophisticated STM recommends that does not beat the one submitted by the product manager. Sometimes the margin is modest; sometimes the difference is overwhelming.

Simulated test marketing, moreover, is the single most validated tool in all of marketing research. For a new packaged good, the better STMs can forecast what will happen in the real world, plus or minus 15 percent.

This is not to say that an STM forecast is always within those limits. Perhaps the biggest failures come about because the assumptions on which the model makes its forecast are flawed. If a company estimates a distribution level of, say, 90 percent but obtains only 60 percent, the volume forecast can be off substantially because in some product categories distribution corresponds to volume almost one to one.

And not only may the assumptions be mistaken; the market's dynamics may change between the test and the rollout. The company may have a new competitor, one it did not know existed when it began the simulated test market research. Sometimes the company's commitment changes between the STM and the introduction. In most simulated test markets, companies assume adequate marketing support; support that may shrink by the time the firm begins the product's national introduction. It is easy to say you're willing to spend $24 million on advertising. It is always harder to write the check.

Discrepancies also arise between the simulated test market performance and the actual test market because the world is messier than an STM. For example, companies routinely obtain test market distribution levels much higher than those they ever see again because the salespeople, excited by the new product, work harder than usual to obtain facings and displays. This sensitivity to the new product's success brings results the company never repeats.

This problem is sometimes used as an excuse by managers not to do a test market at all, a practice that makes us squirm. Of course, if the STM projects overwhelming share leadership with an out-of-the-ballpark ROI and if every component of the plan surpasses its objectives—great advertising, great product, great promotions, and so on—you might want to consider bypassing the test market or regional introduction. Sometimes if the introduction's financial risk is low, you might consider not doing a real-world test even if the probability of success is modest. In many cases, however, not only is a test market useful; it's necessary.

In one recent experience a simulated test market forecast a success, but to achieve it the client had to invest almost $80 million in marketing costs. We argued that since the risk was high, the client should do a test market first. The client's response? "Real world tests always overstate national performance. Everyone's working at optimal levels!" Feeling his testosterone, he decided to forgo the test and to launch nationally.

When real-world results are significantly different from what the STM forecast, we ask, "What's happened in the market that was different from what we simulated? What were the shelf facings . . . the distribution? What was the trade activity . . . consumer promotion . . . your share of voice? What was the competition doing?" With current inputs the STM can virtually always match what's going on in the marketplace.

In one famous case that ended in court, an STM forecast market share for a new product that was twice as high as the share actually achieved in a national introduction. The marketer decided to recover its marketplace losses with a multimillion-dollar lawsuit. The suit eventually fizzled when it was revealed that the advertising copy, media weight, distribution level, packaging, and even the product itself were all different (significantly better, in fact) in the simulation than in the real world. When the actual national plan was input ex post facto into the model, the accuracy of the model was confirmed.

At that point we can ask the next question: "Given what's happening, what can we do to produce better results?" Today the goal of simulated test marketing research is not to obtain a simple volume forecast. The objective is to provide diagnostic insights that will help improve the likelihood of new product/service success. A good STM will tell you not only how you're doing but what to do differently. Such a system goes beyond forecasting first-year volume potential to providing insights into improving the advertising, the concept, the product and packaging, and the marketing plan itself.

Marketers can ask a state-of-the-science STM model to evaluate every ingredient in the marketing plan in terms of effects on sales, profits, or both. The model will run hundreds—in some cases thousands—of simulations to identify those factors that contribute most to marketing success.

TESTING THE WATER WITHOUT GETTING WET

Simulated test marketing research can be traced back to 1968, when Yankelovich, Skelly & White introduced the Laboratory Test Market. The system was pretty basic: YSW exposed a group of about 500 consumers to advertising for a new P&G product and its competitors; they were then invited into a test store and given an opportunity to buy the product. Several weeks later YSW researchers contacted these people at home and what was if they'd like to reorder and what was their reaction to the product. YSW factored that data by norms it developed over time to estimate the new product's success or failure. The system, though primitive, proved accurate about 90 percent of the time in simply forecasting success or failure.

In 1977, Florence Skelly, one of the YSW principals and the "inventor of

STM technology," met Kevin Clancy. She knew that Clancy was interested in mathematical models and that he had worked on the New Product Early Warning System (NEWS model) at BBDO Advertising. Skelly asked him if the Laboratory Test Market methodology could be combined with a mathematical model to refine the forecasts. Clancy and Joe Blackburn spent the next year working on a model they eventually called Litmus™.

The first presentation of the model's results felt something like a showdown at high noon. At one end of the Yankelovich, Skelly & White conference room table were Clancy and Blackburn; at the other end were the Laboratory Test Market veterans led by Robert Goldberg, a new products guru, who had been doing it the YSW way for ten years or more and were reluctant to change.

Skelly and Goldberg had given Clancy and Blackburn 20 marketing plans—twenty cases for which YSW already knew the real-world results—and asked them to run a forecast through the Litmus model. Each group had 20 envelopes in front of them. Clancy's envelopes contained the forecast of what the product would do based on the marketing information and the model's calculations; the LTM veterans' envelopes held the product's actual results. The LTM veterans expected major differences between the forecast and the fact because they did not believe that a mathematical model could match all the intelligence and expertise of the group that had been doing these forecasts for years.

In fact, the Litmus model's forecasts were virtually identical to the actual results in 17 of the 20 cases. The results were so close that Clancy and Blackburn decided to write up the results for publication. Over time, Litmus and its successor, Discovery, became two of the most validated simulated test marketing models in the world. They are routinely employed for new packaged goods and increasingly used—with modifications—for direct-to-consumer pharmaceutical campaigns, consumer durables, and services. Parts of the system have been applied to business-to-business cases as well.

WHAT AN STM NEEDS FOR A FORECAST

Although not every simulated test market research system requires the same information from the marketer, performs the research in the same way, or provides exactly the same forecasts, we are going to write about them in general, as if they did, rather than focus on any one system.

The better systems today represent the offspring of a marriage between sophisticated mathematical models of the new product marketing mix and less sophisticated, but undeniably clever, laboratory test market research sys-

Figure 16-1   Example of a Monthly STM Forecast

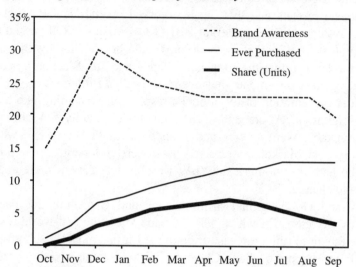

tems. These better systems integrate marketing science modeling, automated intelligence technology, historical databases, and simulated test marketing technology.

Today's better STMs capture *every* important component in the marketing mix—from media weight and schedule through promotion, product, and positioning—and assess the effect of any plan on brand awareness through to market share and profitability.

But what does such a system actually do? Why would a manager use one? Basically, today's STMs test any plan the marketing manager wishes to consider—even a competitor's plan. The marketer simply enters the plan into the computer, and the model forecasts consumer awareness, sales, profits, and much more.

Some systems can go beyond the volume forecast. For example, the Discovery system permits marketing management to ask "what if?" questions, such as "What would happen if I decreased media spending 20 percent?" or "What would happen if I increased consumer promotion 30 percent?" Discovery will actually recommend a plan, and we have not yet seen a case in which the plan recommended by the STM doesn't beat the one submitted by product managers. Sometimes the margin is modest; other times it's overwhelming.

The level of sophistication of today's STMs can be illustrated by a submodel that allows the user to forecast total brand awareness by month. The model provides estimates of the proportion of people who become aware of the product as a result of advertising, couponing, sampling, and distribution. By the end of the product's first month following introduction, the STM forecasts 16 different awareness states. By the end of the year, the problem has become far more complex, and the STM has to consider more that 30 billion awareness, trial, and repeat states.

Marketing Scientists Must Model the Marketing Environment

To accurately project a new product or an existing brand's restaging through simulated test market methodology, marketing scientists must model the marketing environment that will exist at the time of the launch. Systems today model the entire marketing mix (Figure 16-2) and require three kinds of intelligence: product category data, detailed marketing plans, and market response insights. To avoid bogging you down in research minutiae, the following is a deliberately superficial account of how the STM works. We have written an entire book covering the subject, *Simulated Test Marketing: Technology for Launching Successful New Products* (Lexington Books, 1994), and anyone interested in more detail should look into it.

The marketer provides product category data and marketing plans that establish the general framework for the forecast and the competitive environment that will exist during the launch. Category data includes:

1. The potential market's size in millions of buyers.
2. The market's size in dollar sales and in millions of units or cases.
3. The average standardized price of the product sold at retail (e.g., price per ounce).
4. The market's seasonality by month.
5. The category's growth or decline trend.
6. Total advertising spending in the category.
7. The brands in the category that account for 80 percent or more of category sales and the market shares for each.
8. The nature and magnitude of promotional activity.
9. Insights into likely competitive response to a new product.
10. New developments taking place in the category (e.g., other introductions, packaging changes, pricing changes, and the like).

The marketer next needs to provide details of the marketing plan, usually on a month-by-month basis. These factors include:

Figure 16-2   A Model of the New Product Introduction Process

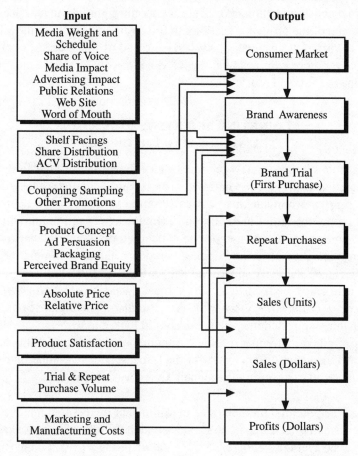

1. Total Gross Rating Points (GRPs) or target group rating points allocated by media type (e.g., prime-time network television, newspapers, drive-time radio, outdoor) by month (i.e., the media schedule).
2. Share of voice by month.
3. Attention-getting power of the advertising by media type (1.0 = average).
4. Attention-getting power of each media type (1.0 = average).
5. Buyer and trade promotion by type by month.
6. Consumer sampling by type by month.
7. Direct marketing programs and anticipated impact by month.
8. Expected Web site visits and impact by month.
9. Expected public relations effects by month converted into the "common currency" of advertising GRPs.

10. Word of mouth by month (1.0 = average).
11. Maximum likely brand awareness (i.e., the highest levels in the category).
12. The probability that a buyer will remember the brand in the absence of subsequent advertising exposures.
13. The proportion of the target market aware of the new product before the advertising breaks.
14. Dissimulation or false awareness, the proportion of the target market who will claim to be aware of a new product even if it doesn't exist.
15. Distribution, the last but in many cases the most important ingredient in a successful forecast. By "distribution" we mean the equivalent of Nielsen ACV (all commodity volume) distribution—the percentage of all the volume in the category that moves through the stores that carry the new product. One role of distribution for any new product or service is to generate awareness of the brand. Some consumers will become aware of the new entry thanks to distribution alone. The higher the distribution level, the greater the distribution-induced awareness level and, of course, the greater the sales.

    The most important function of month-by-month distribution in a test market simulation model, however, is to temper the ideal trial to create a "real-world" buying environment. STM models employ distribution information to reflect the probability that a buyer will be able to find the new or restaged product if he or she wants it. In most new-product simulation models, distribution has a powerful, almost linear impact on the volume forecast. The wider and deeper the distribution, the greater the sales. If marketing management gives the model a distribution figure 10 percent higher than the figure the product actually achieves during the launch year, the model's forecast will be approximately 10 percent too high.

16. Distribution search. The key to understanding the true effect of distribution is to know how "involved" consumers are in the product category, the new product in particular, and how many stores they will shop at to find it. (This measure of "involvement" is the same one we discussed in Chapter 11, where we talked about its role in adjusting people's self reports of what they will buy.) The more stores people will go to to find the new product, the less important the absolute level of distribution. A new cosmetic guaranteed to remove wrinkles overnight, an R&D breakthrough supported by $100 million in advertising and minimum distribution, for example, would be a success even if distribution were low; women would visit five stores to find it.

17. Marketing program costs. Marketing program cost data that marketing management usually supplies for profitability analysis include:

- Average cost per thousand GRPs by medium.
- Average cost per coupon by promotion type.
- Average cost per sample by promotion type.
- The cost of the planned level of distribution and the estimated costs per point of increasing and decreasing this level. The analysis can also include manufacturing costs, research, and other costs. Depending on the marketing manager's needs, the profitability analysis can range from gross margin to operating profit. Not only will this information improve a volume forecast's value, but you can use it in a sensitivity analysis to determine the relative efficiency of each marketing-mix component.

DIFFERENT METHODOLOGIES FOR MEASURING MARKET RESPONSE

The third type of input required to do an STM is estimates of buyer response to the new product concept and the product itself. Simulated test marketing systems use different methodologies depending on the test product's development stage: one method when you are limited to a product concept description and test product for consumers to use at home, and another method when you have advertising for the product and sufficient quantity of finished goods to display and "sell" them in a simulated store. The first approach is a concept test market; the second, a true simulated test market.

For both the research often begins with screening hundreds of prospective respondents using random-digit dialing in several geographically dispersed locations (chosen to reflect national category and brand usage patterns) and inviting them to participate in a research study.

The sample size used in a simulated test market study varies by research methodology and the number of cells to be tested. A true simulation in which people have the opportunity to buy the test product requires a larger sample size than a concept-based simulation. Also, if you are testing only one price point or advertising approach, you need only one cell, but if you are testing multiple price points or different advertising approaches, you need more.

Single-cell concept test markets usually have 300 respondents. Multiple-cell concept test markets require 200 to 300 respondents per cell. Single-cell simulated test markets often have samples ranging from 400 to 600. Multiple-cell simulated test markets generally have samples of 250 to 300 respondents per cell.

A SIMPLE SIMULATION BASED ON EXPOSURE TO A CONCEPT

The laboratory study at the heart of a concept test market study is a one-on-one interview approximately 35 minutes long. It reconfirms the consumer's qualifications and obtains background information concerning attitudes and lifestyles, involvement and interest, practices and behaviors in the product/service category. To expose the product, the interviewer uses a 2 × 3 board with the new product's name and a photo of the package (if there is one), a one- or two-paragraph description of the basic promise and reasons why, and the price. Respondents also see a board of photos (or the names if there is no package) of major competitive products, all priced according to the local market. The presence of a competitive set is key to simulating the real-world purchasing environment.

After respondents see and understand the concept in its competitive context, they rate it in terms of the same "behavior prediction inventory" that we discussed in Chapter 11. Researchers later convert what people say they will do into estimates of what they will actually do under conditions of 100 percent awareness and availability.

Following the concept ratings, people are given the product to take home and use the way they ordinarily use products in the category. After an appropriate lapse in time, interviewers call respondents to measure their reactions to the product and likely repeat purchase behavior.

A More Complex Simulation Based on In-Store Purchasing

Similar to the concept test, interviewers recruit qualified buyers by telephone; groups of 20 to 25 meet at a central facility. When they arrive, they complete a background questionnaire that collects information concerning their attitudes and practices in the product category. Information includes category purchasing volume, brand purchasing behavior, and attribute desirability.

The interviewers then expose respondents to the test product through an advertisement in a competitive environment, typically a 30-second TV commercial inserted into a 30-minute television program. (If the marketer's plan relies on print or radio, the research uses them.) Respondents watch the program, usually a highly rated situation comedy, in a simulated living-room setting. The program has four normal commercial breaks, the third including the test ad with "clutter" ads from unrelated categories. The three other commercial breaks contain spots for the most heavily advertised competitors and clutter ads. The goal here is to expose respondents to the advertising in as natural an environment as possible.

After showing the ads, the interviewers give respondents an additional questionnaire to generate diagnostic information concerning ad recall and communications: What did the test advertising communicate and how persuasive was the message?

Respondents then go into a laboratory store that simulates (i.e., mimics) shopping in the local market. The store shelves display the brands that typically represent 80 percent or more of category volume in the local market, and the prices are based on store checks of the average prices in the market. Respondents may buy the test product or anything else in the store, typically at a small discount. Most people buy something, although not usually the test brand.

Following the walk through the store (or in the case of the concept test market study, the rating of the concept in terms of purchase probability), the respondents then answer a postexposure questionnaire to rate the critical attributes of the test product and its key competitors. Through the store experiment and survey data, the model is able to produce an anticipated purchase cycle for the test product and demographic, psychographic, and other information to profile both purchasers and nonpurchasers.

After consumers return home and after an appropriate lapse in time, interviewers call respondents for a postusage diagnosis. All STM research services contact consumers who "purchased" in the laboratory store. The interviewers attempt callbacks for every person who bought the test product (in a simulated test market study) or who received a test product sample (in a concept test market study) to obtain repeat purchase, purchase cycle, and diagnostic information.

During this interview respondents are queried about the amount of the product used, family/household member usage, occasions for use, and open-ended likes/dislikes. The interviewer records repurchase intent, which is converted via norms into estimates of actual repeat purchase behavior. With repurchase figures the STM model is able to estimate total annual sales volume.

THE FORECAST FOR A NEW OR RESTAGED PRODUCT

All of this information—about the product category, the marketing plan, and market response as measured in the "laboratory" research study—is then fed into a sophisticated mathematical model, the kind discussed in the previous chapter. Models like Discovery are clever enough to distinguish between 16 different sources of new product/service awareness, 16 wellsprings of product trial, and a very large number of repeat purchase states (Figure 16-3).

We then plug the trial data, repeat data, and all the information gathered earlier from the marketing plan into a very sophisticated mathematical model to generate a month-by-month forecast of awareness through share, an example of which was shown in Figure 16-1.

Figure 16-3   16 States of Awareness

Awareness Due To:

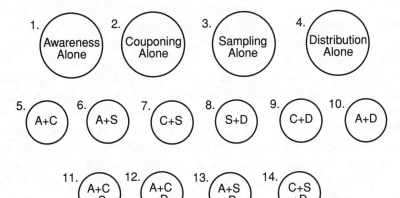

Until recently simulated test marketing systems, with a few exceptions, didn't really capture competitive response at all. NEWS, for example, did include share of voice as a parameter, but most other measures of market response assumed "normal" levels of competitive activity, an assumption clearly out of sync with marketing reality.

Because of the rapidly changing nature of competitive response, however, researchers have begun to address this problem. We've learned, for example, that some of the "new" competitive promotional factors, like featured pricing, can be measured in the laboratory simulation during the experiment.

We have also discovered that we can measure the effects of competitive pricing strategies in this experiment with an acceptable level of validity. The procedure is very simple: vary the prices of competitors on the shelf in the simulated store.

In a study for a new type of plastic garbage bag that led to the brand's successful national introduction, we tested three different price points and three different competitive price points to learn how the new brand would perform under different competitive pricing scenarios.

Other competitive response factors require a combination of the experiment and self-reported measures included in the interview, such as competitive couponing. Most consumers don't use coupons for most purchases. To measure the effect of consumer promotion, therefore, we need to first estimate the probability that someone would use a coupon in the real world and then observe that person's behavior in the laboratory environment.

Finally, some competitive variables we wish to capture require a judgment call based on real-world data, if it's available, and the marketing or research manager's expertise. Take, for example, shelf dominance. Our clients tell us that they can estimate the share of facings they can buy as a part of trade deals. What they don't know is how this share of facings relates to sales. Since laboratory experimentation does not seem to measure this variable very well, we have had to turn to judgmental and historical relationships in our databases while continuing to test alternative research methodologies.

Good as an STM estimate may be—and they are dramatically better than most management judgment calls of first-year sales—it is not timeless. In general, an STM forecast is good for about a year to a year and a half. But if the market changes radically—something happens in the environment, a powerful new competitor arrives, or a breakthrough technology appears—all bets are off.

We've seen this happen in high-technology products. We test a new product one day and it's a dog; the STM forecasts failure. A year later a competitor's similar product is flying off the shelf. The company wonders what was wrong with the STM research. Unfortunately, a lot of the problem is the competitive environment and the pace of technological change.

Nevertheless, a well-designed STM will give you a sales forecast that is accurate at the time. From the laboratory experiment (or tracking survey if the product has been introduced), the research will estimate four key brand performance measures—trial, awareness (initially and over an extended period of time), repeat purchases, and unit sales—and do this on a monthly basis. Based on this information, you can calculate revenue, profitability, and market share.

HOW SIMULATION CAN ACTUALLY IMPROVE RESULTS

A sophisticated decision support system combines simulated test marketing with mathematical modeling of the marketing mix. Such a system goes beyond forecasting first-year volume potential to provide insights into improving the advertising, the concept, the product and packaging, and the marketing plan itself to increase sales and profits.

Another example of how simulated test marketing can improve a marketing plan is through brand equity analysis. Brand equity analysis enables a marketer to assess the dimensions that affect a buyer's purchasing decision most highly. It provides insights into the factors that contribute to or inhibit product trial. And it permits a company to evaluate how well a product or service fulfills the buyer's prepurchase expectations.

Brand equity analysis, unlike traditional research and analysis, goes beyond the buyer's self-reported behavior to estimate the true impact of features on brand preferences and purchasing behavior and relate brand perceptions with behavior. By taking a multidimensional approach, linking motivating power of features with brand perceptions, the analysis identifies product strengths, weaknesses, and opportunities. Once a company has this information, of course, it can build on the product's strengths, work to minimize its weaknesses, and take advantage of any opportunities.

COMPUTER-AIDED DESIGN OF MARKETING PLANS

The ultimate test of simulation technology comes when the system is called on to identify and describe a financially optimal marketing plan. As we discussed in Chapter 10, computer-aided design is widely used for new products and services. Now developments in marketing science enable us to apply computer-aided design to marketing programs.

Once a client is provided a forecast of awareness through profitability and all the diagnostic details described earlier (e.g., sensitivity analysis, brand equity analysis) are analyzed, an optimization assignment can start. We can briefly describe how the Discovery model addresses this problem. The model begins its analysis with five levels of advertising spending, five levels of promotion, five levels of distribution, and five levels of sampling—the levels ranging from very low to very high. For example, a client might say that it would never spend less than $1 million to support a new brand or more than $50 million. The model would then pick three levels in between, for five levels in total.

Discovery then runs 625 simulated test markets ($5 \times 5 \times 5 \times 5 = 625$) and uses this database to model the relationship between each of the four marketing factors (advertising, promotion, distribution, and sampling) and both sales and profits. Equations are then constructed in order to solve an optimization problem *for this particular product*. The model literally searches through billions of possible plans in order to find the one plan that—subject to management constraints—maximizes brand profitability over a multiyear period.

Figure 16-4　Forecast Performance of Machine- vs. Manager-Prepared Plans

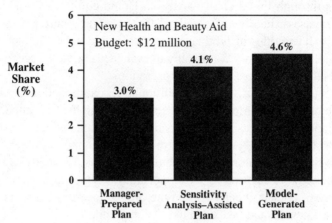

Comparisons of plans prepared by managers with plans prepared by managers after they have been assisted by simulated test market insights, such as sensitivity analysis, reveal that the use of simulation technology always helps—it helps make the plans more profitable. But optimization technology—what we like to call "model-generated plans"—results in marketing programs that are vastly superior to those provided by marketing managers.

Figure 16-4 shows a widely discussed case of a new health and beauty aid supported by a fixed budget of $12 million (the client wanted to spend no more, no less). The client's marketing department produced a plan that yielded a 3 percent share; help provided by sensitivity analysis improved share to 4.1 percent. But the model-generated "optimal" plan yielded a 4.6 percent share.

Is optimization always this successful? Frankly, no. But the worst the model can do is produce a share (and/or profit contribution) comparable to that of a marketing manager. Most of the time the model beats the manager by 15 percent or more, and sometimes by 40 percent or more. Differences of this magnitude could clearly transform a mediocre plan and a failed brand into a better plan and a success. But even when the simulated test market research forecasts product success, products sometimes fail. What goes wrong?

A BODY BROUGHT IN FROM THE COLD IS NOT NECESSARILY DEAD

Tom Clancy, professor of surgery at the University of North Carolina, once informed us that sometimes a person who appears to be dead can be resuscitated. For example, if a patient has fallen through ice—and has experienced extreme hypothermia—apparent death can sometimes be reversed. This is also true for new products and services. A new entry may appear to have died in a test market (real or simulated) or a national introduction, but the insights gained from a modeling exercise can be employed to revive it, to transform failure into success.

While simulated test marketing research works best with new products and services, you can also use it for restaging (or repositioning) an established product and for extending a line. As we've said before, every three or four years, as top management notices product sales sliding slowly toward oblivion, someone says, "Why don't you turn around this dying brand?" While it's possible to use STM for a restaging effort, it's much more difficult than introducing a new product for at least two reasons:

- The restaged product has a history; it exists; people have bought it in the past. So the trick is to measure the difference in sales between the restaged product and what sales would have been without the restaging.
- The second and related reason is that often the incremental sales are so small they're very hard to measure. You don't know whether you're measuring random noise or an actual change. Therefore, doing an STM for restaging an existing product usually require a much larger sample size than for a new product, and it takes much more sensitivity in the research measurement to pick up true differences.

Most firms doing a restaging, however, make a mistake. They change only one or two elements in the marketing mix. They change the label and maybe tweak the advertising . . . and watch the product continue its slide. Consider that the average product category is declining by three-tenths of a share point every year. If there are a dozen ingredients in the marketing mix and you change one of them, how much effect can it have? How much absolute change of sales could possibly be due to any one of the 12 or so ingredients in the mix? How much could be due to, say, advertising weight alone or positioning alone? The answer is very, very little, perhaps too small to measure.

On the other hand, the more elements marketer changes, the greater the likelihood that the restaged product will perform like a new product. We like to call this the "fountain of youth" approach. If you change the product formulation, the packaging, the advertising, the pricing strategy, the promotion strategy, the distribution, even the name by calling it "new and improved," you have a good chance of resuscitating the dying brand—the restaged product begins to behave like a new product.

Line extensions share many of the same problems of restagings. The product already exists in another form, and you're trying to measure the difference between the extension and the existing product(s). This problem is further complicated by the extension's propensity to cannibalize the existing product. The challenge is to measure net incremental sales, which can be anywhere from difficult to impossible.

Because the use of test market simulation methodologies similar to that discussed here enables a marketing executive to evaluate hundreds, perhaps thousands, of alternative plans prior to an actual test market, we believe that serious marketers have little choice but to experiment with this kind of technology, to build and test and validate models that simulate real-world introduction. The costs of real-world introductions are too high and the likelihood of failure too great to continue with traditional approaches.

The choice, we believe, is between what Professor Len Lodish of the Wharton School has described as being "vaguely right" or "precisely wrong." The intuitive approach of not evaluating plans before a real-world introduction is precisely wrong. This is particularly true for manufacturers of consumer durables, service marketers, and business-to-business marketers who rarely attempt to simulate marketing programs. The counterintuitive alternative, the kind of multistep process we've described, may not be 100 percent perfect. It may be vaguely right, but it is the only viable option. Evaluating marketing plans, and competitive responses to these plans, prior to expensive, risky real-world introductions has become an imperative.

17

Good Implementation May Be More Important Than Great Strategy

A year ago, we were in a large client meeting that included marketing, promotion, public relations, advertising, and brand management. Our purpose was to hear a presentation on the first six months' results of a major marketing program. As we went around the room introducing ourselves, we discovered that some participants were meeting co-workers for the first time. An hour into the meeting, it was clear that none of their marketing plans were coordinated, never mind integrated. No one seemed to be in charge.

We began to talk about the importance of leadership and the need for a benevolent dictator. We used the analogy of General Norman Schwartzkopf during the Gulf War. The general was in charge of the Air Force, Army, Navy, Marine Corps, and Coast Guard. He ordered the Air Force's medium-range bombers to fly; he ordered the cruise missiles launched off ships; and he ordered the Navy to bring Marine landing parties onto Kuwaiti beaches.

But just imagine, we said, if the United States had managed Desert Storm the way you manage this company's marketing. Schwartzkopf orders the Marines to land at 0600 hours. The Marine commander says, "No way. The water's too cold at 0600; we can't go in until midday."

"What are you saying?" someone asked.

We said, "Unless you get your act together and coordinate your plans, your marketing isn't going to work effectively. There needs to be one marketing general."

"We don't need a marketing general," one 30-something said.

We said, "Eventually every company in America will have one. It's incomprehensible that you are all off doing your own stuff without a coordinated strategy. It reminds us of the Tower of Babel, another project that failed because those working on it could not understand each other."

That led to a discussion of how, if the salespeople didn't like the materials the central marketing folks developed, they just didn't use them. And if the salespeople were not able to produce the distribution level required to justify the advertising budget, no one knew until it was too late because sales doesn't talk to advertising. And because the packaging and public relations folks weren't clued into the advertising, there was little opportunity to enjoy the synergistic effects of an integrated marketing communications effort.

The company might have had a great strategy and a solid marketing plan, but without effective implementation—which, from what we saw at this meeting, was virtually impossible—it was useless. Indeed, 45 minutes into the presentation, it was clear that the plan had not been implemented well. The firm had not achieved its objectives for ACV distribution and shelf facings. Awareness and positioning penetration were low relative to goals. They'd had little success in selling in the end-of-aisle displays and shelf talkers that were an integral part of the campaign. And a major account had dropped the brand because of insufficient sales. Overall performance fell in the Zone of Death-Wish Marketing.

A GREAT STRATEGY IS NOT ENOUGH

Although we strongly recommend that managers carefully balance intuition and seasoned judgment with rigorous analysis of unimpeachable data—all the stuff we've been talking about to build a great strategy—we recognize that some businesses will develop great strategies by accident. But even when a company develops a strong strategy by accident, it often fails because it is poorly implemented.

When we wrote our earlier books, we were working on the premise that most marketing programs fail because most marketing strategies are failures. They are strategic failures because of the testosterone-driven death-wish practices we have talked about. We assumed that if we helped a company develop a strong, relevant strategy, it would overcome any implementation deficiencies. We've learned through painful experience this is not true.

Five years ago we began collecting more data on marketing successes and failures, and we've amended our conclusion. Faulty implementation is as much a reason for marketing failure as faulty strategy—maybe more so. Marketplace results are the function of both strategy and implementation. Just as ineffective

Figure 17-1   Strategy and Implementation in the Late '90s

Implementation

Strategy	Weak	Average	Strong	Total
Weak	18%	13%	7%	38%
Average	12	27	5	
Strong	9	8	2	19%
Total	39%		13%	

2:1

3:1

implementation undermines an effective strategy, skilled implementation of a weak or inappropriate strategy wastes resources. You need both.

We've observed 82 different marketing programs during the past five years and scored them in terms of strategy and implementation. Though not a robust sample, our database is representative of a broad range of industries. What we have found is that weak strategies and weak implementation are far more common than strong, well-implemented strategies. Note that both weak strategies and poor implementation are two to three times more likely than strong strategies and strong implementation. We've observed only two cases (2 percent of the total) in which strengths were evident on both dimensions.

What brought this home was our experience with a client with whom we worked on a marketing strategy for a fast food business. The strategy involved a major improvement in speedy service that did exceptionally well in the test market. Based on these results, the corporation began rolling it out to its retailers, both company-owned outlets and franchised stores. Those that implemented the strategy saw sales rise dramatically; those that didn't watched sales stagnate, just as in the rest of the category.

But the corporation could not get more than 40 percent of its retail outlets to implement the plan. The reason was that the franchises didn't feel like doing what had to be done and corporate management was not willing (or able) to use a stick in addition to its carrots. The strategy required the managers and their counter people to change their behavior, to do a little more work. But since the strategy came from corporate headquarters, it was suspect. The managers were not motivated; they didn't care that much, even though the plan showed them how to make more money. They just didn't believe it.

This was not an isolated incident. Last year, another client had a brilliant strategy for an in-store point-of-sale promotion linked to the advertising—

truly integrated marketing communications. Again, the stores that got with the program did as well as—or better than—we had forecast. When the company spot-checked a cross section of stores with mystery shoppers, however, it found the program was only really up and operating in perhaps half of its outlets.

To overcome these problems, we've done surveys of the salespeople or the franchisees or the retailers—"internal marketing" is the current expression—to learn their attitudes toward doing what the plan requires. As a general principle, you want to test the plan in the market so that you turn up any problems of dealer inertia, ignorance, or antipathy.

Of course, as we discussed in the last chapter, a test market can be problematic. You want to pick markets that truly reflect the nation, but too many businesses pick test markets where they're most likely to succeed. They don't pick markets where the dealers are least likely to speak English, are the most autonomous, or are indifferent businesspeople—in other words, like the rest of the world. They pick markets where they have the strongest, most cooperative dealers. They are then surprised by the national rollout results.

Sometimes companies implement their strategies poorly because management has not clearly communicated the strategy to the people down the line. A number of years ago, for example, Chase Manhattan Bank had its tellers wear a button that repeated the advertising tag line, "The Chase Is On." Sadly, if a customer asked the teller, "What does the button mean?" the answer was usually a blank look. The tellers did not know; no one had told them.

Sometimes management has not developed a consensus around the strategy. We've seen cases in which there seemed to be a consensus on the targeting and positioning strategy, but then the brand manager or the marketing manager went off with the agency and developed something totally different. We know of a current example that has run the last two years. Not only is it off strategy, but top management recognizes that it's off strategy, yet they let the marketing honcho have his head and do it. Even the ad agency recognizes the current campaign is off strategy. Why does the marketing guy continue to go his own way? He says the original strategy is too difficult to implement (it's about service) and the current campaign (which is all image) does not need any implementation. Which may be true, but it is not very effective.

Sometimes even when management has communicated and built consensus, the employees are incredibly busy, a problem compounded by downsizing. Peter Drucker says that most organizations are drifting in three directions simultaneously: confusion, conflict, and underperformance. The rest of the chapter suggests ways you can reduce these in your organization.

ONCE YOU SEE THE MOVIE YOU'LL NEVER BE THE SAME

Peter Krieg once spent about 20 minutes describing the strategy for P&G's Pampers—and how it was being executed in advertising. Then we looked at a 30-second Pampers spot and bam! There it was in 30 seconds. Evidence again of the communication power of film.

We strongly recommend that marketers create short films (20 minutes is typical) to illustrate the nuances of the targeting strategy. Based on the research, you know each of the targets intimately. You know their motivations and perceptions, product usage behavior, usage occasions, brand preferences, and media exposure patterns. You know their attitudes, values, and personality. Their demographic and social profiles.

Now write a mini-screenplay in which the characters are the targets in your product category. Get your PR people involved—they're usually the best writers in the company—and/or the agency creative group. Prepare a script for each actor chosen to play a single part. If there are five segments in the market, you'll need five actors and five scripts.

The actors don't interact with one another. They simply speak their lines and engage in the behavior you direct. If you do it right, your little film won't win a short subject Academy Award, but it will indelibly imprint an understanding of the various market segments in the category, particularly the key market target(s), in the heads of all who see it.

When you're done with production, make multiple copies of the film and send them to everyone involved in implementing the campaign. They'll thank you, and your program's performance will reflect their appreciation.

A DEAD CANARY AS AN EARLY WARNING

In the bad old days miners would bring a caged canary down into the mine as an early-warning device. When mining operations released odorless, poisonous gas, the canary would keel over, alerting the miners to the danger before they keeled over. A dead canary was an early warning.

From the beginning of this book we've said that targeting and positioning are the major strategy issues. A year ago, for example, at our company's board of advisers meeting, we talked to Philip Kotler, the S. C. Johnson & Son Distinguished Professor of International Marketing at Northwestern's Kellogg Graduate School of Management, about the best practices in marketing today. Clancy was describing a 22-dimensional marketing management system that captures 80 factors and approximately 700 different aspects of marketing. Kotler said, "This is all great, and you need to do this, but just remember the two most fundamental decisions that have to be made are the targeting decision and the positioning decision. If the targeting and positioning decisions are made correctly, the other things will follow. If they're made incorrectly, nothing good will follow."

In a marketing context where we are trying to get the targeting and the positioning right, the first place we find it useful to look is at the advertising. Advertising is the canary test.

If the advertising hits the target, if you can see the advertising appealing to the target, if you have some evidence that the advertising message reflects the agreed-upon positioning and appeals to the target, you're heading in the right direction. But if the advertising isn't directed toward the target and doesn't capture the positioning strategy, you're heading off in the wrong direction. It's poison; it's toxic.

Miller Beer and Budweiser are two brands we've talked about before that regularly compete for who can kill the most canaries. Frogs, lizards, and Dick the Copywriter are examples of ambiguous targeting strategies and no positioning. Indeed, the typical response to these commercials by ad executives and consumers alike—consumers, we should add, from 21 to 81—is that this is really dumb stuff. Miller goes one better than Bud by printing cutesy messages on their bottles, like "This End Up" with an arrow. The same people who think that Dick is hilarious, we're sure, think these messages are funny, but they're not. They're stupid. As a former Miller drinker recently said to us, "The company has turned the brand into a joke, and only someone stupid would buy it."

Whoever let Miller regress from "The Champagne of Bottled Beer" and "Tastes Great/Less Filling" to the stupid beer for stupid people should be required to wear a T-shirt that says, "I'm Dick" surrounded by dead canaries. Happily, Miller has recently started moving in the right direction. We hope they keep it up.

Marketers usually make the marketing strategy decision on which the advertising is based, sometimes on gut feeling alone. But not always. In January 2000 we gave a three-hour presentation to a client and their ad agency based on our research. Their products are designed for people concerned about their health, and we said the wellness market in America is looking for products and services that will increase longevity—no surprise for baby boomers who want to look good and feel good, and want to look good and feel good longer while they enjoy life.

The client turned to the ad agency and said, in effect, "It sounds good, go execute." A month later the agency was back with 20 different ideas, concept statements with a visual. We were delighted because the agency had followed our recommendation to come up with many ideas, but not one clearly communicated a wellness strategy. They talked about taste, product quality, ingredients. We were stupefied. The agency people were in the original meeting; they saw the presentation. Either they did not understand it or did not agree with it, or the client subsequently led them astray. In any event, they had to go back and come up with something different.

Sometimes, of course, it may not be that easy to execute the strategy. Or it may be a boring strategy. For example, a new financial product has certain tangible features that make it truly superior to similar products. The research shows consumers would appreciate the performance feature. The strategy suggests that the company demonstrate this dollars-and-cents product superiority, but unfortunately, executions of that strategy are monumentally boring. Plus, Securities and Exchange Commission regulations mean the advertiser has to spend an inordinate amount of commercial time qualifying the offer. In this case the advertiser might be better off with a more emotional approach, promoting intangibles—the strength of the company, the good feelings owning this product provokes, the superior wisdom of those who buy it.

Usually, of course, the alternatives are not so clear, and the answer is a little bit of both emotion and performance. As we suggested in the advertising chapter, the right thing to do is to test both approaches. Ideally, you test three executions of the performance approach and three executions of the emotional.

MANAGING ADVERTISING AGENCY RELATIONSHIPS

Another implementation issue involves advertising agency relationships. Even in the days of the Internet, direct marketing, distribution channels, and everything else marketing people must worry about, advertising remains an enormous issue. It's a huge expense. It can be the best thing you do for your brand or the biggest waste of money. And it consumes an inordinate part of the average marketing person's day. When we ask clients, "What's keeping you so busy?" the answer often involves advertising. Meetings with the agency, attending a shoot, looking at film.

In terms of implementation, advertising is an area where things go awry more often than not. The problem seems to be that, from the client's perspective, ad agencies are often unmanageable. Company executives, after relating some fresh horror story about their agency, routinely ask us, "How do we get them to do what we want?"

We talked about some of these problems in the advertising chapter: the agency's inability to come up with more than one approach; their reluctance to test; the canyon between the account guys and the creative guys. The suspicion is that the creative people do not know the message you want them to

Table 17-1   Seven Criteria for a Traditional or E-commerce Agency

1. A creative portfolio demonstrating recent marketplace success by the team assigned to your business

2. A fun, enjoyable group to work with – people who will maintain a great sense of humor under stress

3. A team that appreciates the role of serious research in developing strategy

4. Creatives delighted to prepare many concepts for a new campaign or Web site and an agency philosophy that supports them

5. An agency and creatives enthusiastic about professionally pretesting three or more alternative campaigns or sites prior to introduction

6. An agency with experience and tools in helping set specific, measurable, realistic goals for their work

7. An agency willing to base compensation in part on performance in achieving mutually agreed-upon objectives

communicate; that they think their mission is to win artistic awards—not to communicate your story or sell your product or service.

At the same time, advertisers are not always blameless. Marketers seldom sit down and specify exactly what they want from their agency. We have clients who say, "Let's do an account review." At that point we will suggest the executive write down the dozen criteria the company has for an agency. What precisely do you want from them? Once you have the criteria, ask everybody involved with the agency—and usually it's a crowd—to weight each item, because they're not all equally important. At the end of this process you have an understanding within the company that this is the number-one characteristic, this is number two . . . and this is number seven; it would be nice, but it's not critical. Table 17-1 lists what such criteria might be.

A lot of companies do not establish any hard criteria for selecting an agency. They go to the agency's new business pitch and decide, "I like them; they're bright. The chemistry's great." Or they decide, "These people are just too flaky for us." Neither bright nor flaky are good reasons to select or reject an agency.

Once you have an agency and give them an assignment, you may have another problem if you don't specify the criteria for a successful ad. Often if the company writes a creative brief at all, it is vague, inconsistent, incomplete, or all three. We discussed this at length in Chapter 9.

Last fall, we were at a client in Europe and asked to see the positioning and communication strategy. They gave us three different documents that said three related but different things. The research company wrote one: "This is what the research said. This is what we all agreed, and this is what the agency is supposed to try to say." The ad agency wrote another: "This is what you told us, and this what we're trying to say." Management's marketing plan was different again. All three were similar but not really the same, a formula for trouble.

Company marketing executives should write down what they want the agency to do. An advertising briefing should serve as a formal, living document that helps your agency develop copy strategy and media plans. An important element of the brief is a highlight of previous consumer and market analyses, linked to the brand's communications goals and strategies. All successful and hard-working advertising briefs have a detailed target profile, complete with market size, attitudes, beliefs, lifestyles, purchase behaviors, usage patterns, perceptions, media habits, and demographics. A marketer must also define the positioning strategy for the brand, develop well-defined, time-bound, and quantifiable objectives, and establish a preliminary budget. These elements are essential to guide all participants.

Then, in testing the advertising, as we pointed out in Chapter 8, you need to include the specific objectives for the research study. Do you want the ad to communicate a particular message strategy? What is it? What answers to open-ended questions would suggest that the target got the strategy? What attitudes and perceptions are you trying to change? What measures should be included in the study that would tell you whether you succeeded or not? Are you trying to make people laugh or increase brand preference? Both?

If you don't establish the original criteria—"This is what we want to communicate"—the agency will come back to announce, "Look, we moved the needle on 'Perceive the Brand As Modern.'" They've got you because you never said that perceiving the brand as modern was irrelevant to your communication objectives.

Time pressures intensify all these issues. The company wants to be on the air by a certain date, and by the time it invites the advertising research company onto the scene to test the execution, there is seldom the time necessary to test properly. Worse, if the ad tests badly, there is never enough time to develop new creative. At that point most marketing executives adopt the Oliver Hazzard Perry position: "Damn the tests! Full speed ahead!" They would rather run an ad that has no impact (or that communicates something irrelevant—the brand as modern) than do nothing. We can think of only four occasions in our careers when a marketer said, "You know, since we're not sure what we want to say, and since the agency hasn't come up with anything, we're going dark. Or we'll use an old commercial as a placeholder to keep our name out. But we're not running something that's not right."

But this has happened only four times in 30 years. There must have been a

hundred cases when canceling the media buy was the correct business decision, but the advertiser said, "We don't have time. As long as it's not
absolutely ghastly, we're going ahead. Meanwhile, we'll get the agency to
start working on an alternative."

We wonder to ourselves, how it is that they never have the time to do it
right but always have the time to do it over and over? The advertiser's working assumption is that the ineffective, albeit not ghastly, campaign will not
damage the brand. But changing campaigns confuses consumers, the trade,
and makes it more difficult to have an effective campaign the next time
around.

No Time to Do It Right, But Lots of Time to Do It Over

In working to help companies implement their marketing strategy, we regularly come across marketing managers who are inept at getting all the horses
lined up to go. Sometimes they don't seem to own a calendar. If they do, they
don't seem to know how to work through the marketing process. It is as
though they were absent the day the professor covered the "Program Evaluation and Review Technique" (PERT).

For example, at the beginning of 2000 we attended a client meeting, and
midway through we said to the dozen people in the room, "Wait a minute,
let's write this all on a big piece of paper—what you think is happening
when." Within two minutes everyone could see they had major gaps, things
were coming in a month later than they needed to be, or four conflicting
things were all due at the same time. No one had thought the process through.

Another example: last year a margarine manufacturer announced it would
introduce a new product formulation in eight months, the time they thought
they needed to create and roll out the formulation change. Two months before
the launch they did not have a better formulation. One month before they still
did not have one. But because they had promised they were introducing a new
formulation, they launched a New! Improved! "Better 'n Butter" that was not
noticeably better than the old "Better 'n Butter."

Since "New and Improved" claims often grab consumer attention, they
may in fact boost sales thanks to trial purchases. But when the product fails to
deliver on the promise (e.g., the Burger King French fries), a lower level of
repeat purchase will follow, accompanied by consumer distrust of the marketer.

The margarine company had been planning for two years and has now
been in the market a year. They spent $10 million in advertising, and now
they say they have to go back to do the homework they never did. The

researchers are back in the laboratory reformulating the product again. The company is doing the concept tests it never did the first time around. We asked if, in preparation for the launch, they had done a quantitative concept test of any kind. None. Did they do any copy testing of the execution? None. They did qualitative research. Focus groups, focus groups, and more focus groups, supplemented by bunches of intuition.

This seems to be a case in which top management was working on one timetable, the formulation people were working on another, and the marketing people, split on the need for research, were working on a third. Reformulating the product was probably a good idea. While one cannot know without a test, the odds are the product needed a change. So this was a good strategy poorly implemented. The company launched before it was ready.

This problem of rushing to judgment is particularly acute among Internet companies. In the past year five Internet start-ups have approached Copernicus, each rushing to build a site to launch their businesses while screaming, "Look, Ma! No Strategy, No Research!" In four cases we declined the opportunity. We didn't think that they took marketing seriously enough. One Internet CEO said, "What we need is some speed branding. We have just two months to create a brand." Is this nutty, or what? By year's end none were successful. One jumped in the water; it launched and drowned. Two jumped in, did a short-term introduction, and climbed back out. They're sitting on the beach trying to figure things out. One seems to be treading water; it is afloat but unsuccessful. The fifth has not been heard from again; it seems to be lost in a fog bank.

The rush to launch is a common corporate flaw. Overall timetables are all very aggressive. Top management says, "You've got to do something," and you're late by the time you return to your office. We find that many people in marketing do not realize the work required to launch a new campaign or reposition a product, so they promise it within 12 months. They do it because they do not understand how much time it takes to do things, or because that's when bonuses are due, or both.

YOU NEED COST INFORMATION EARLY

We also find companies falling down in the way they handle cost information. Last fall when we were developing a marketing plan for a new client, we asked them to calculate the various expenses for the plan's components. We wanted to know what each alternative level of consumer and trade promotion, distribution, advertising, and product formulation would actually cost. If you don't know the costs, how can you calculate the profitability of any incremental sales? The company people, even though they understood this logic, did not like teasing out the costs —it's often difficult to do. Eventually they found most (but not all) of them for us.

This is commonly true when the task involves new product development and the consulting/research firm is engaged in a product or service optimization exercise using a choice modeling or conjoint measurement methodology, such we described in Chapter 11. An important part of this exercise involves assembling the fixed and variable costs for hundreds of different options, and marketers don't have them. We ask, "When are you going to have them?" Typically they say, "Later." We ask, "How can you think about the strategy alternatives if you don't know what they might cost; when are you planning to find them?" They say, "Later."

So they test concepts with only a vague idea about what any one might cost. At the end of the testing—without the cost information—they discover which concepts are maximally appealing. From an intuitive standpoint that's what management wants to know. But as we've said, the maximally appealing product or service is invariably the least profitable. And that's a catastrophe in the making.

We know it is often hard for the marketing department to obtain costs. The gnomes in finance occasionally regard this information as secret treasure. Sometimes, by the nature of the product or service, the gnomes, even with the best intentions in the world, find it difficult to assign costs. Also, sometimes marketing people are just not that interested in costs. But having cost information is another way to ask, how practical is this to implement? Most of the time, when we are brought in to talk about concepts, we are the first to mention costs. The company people are too busy generating ideas.

TOO MUCH WORK, TOO LITTLE TIME

A major challenge seems to be that, by its nature, implementing a marketing plan involves so many people. People are on different floors or in different buildings, sometimes in different cities, so they cannot easily meet. We often find that the only time they convene to talk about a project is when we show up. When we're not there, they may have meetings, but these meetings deal with the day-to-day crises. They are not working on the new product, the new project, the new plan, and this is where the marketing general could be the most useful.

Most of the people we deal with have full-time jobs just keeping their brands going. They can devote perhaps 5 percent of their day to thinking big thoughts and planning a big transformational turnaround, or even thinking about next year's campaign. "A typical day is getting up at 4:30 A.M. and getting into the office by 6:00," says one marketing executive we know. "I leave at 2:30 to pick up my daughter at school and then spend the afternoon with the kids. Then I go back to work after the kids go to bed and work until 10:00. Bob is still out of town all week, so I'm pretty much a single parent Monday to Friday."

To deliberately mix our metaphors, these managers spend 95 percent of their day putting out fires and keeping all the balls in the air (often at the same time, which can be very stressful). They are busy keeping up with today, and when they engage us to think about tomorrow, they have to add us to their day. Before they offer a project they often ask, "How much of our time will you need?" Obviously, the right answer is "Not much." It may be the right answer, but not if they want quality work.

Because marketing people at most companies today are too busy focusing on short-term issues to deal with major initiatives, you need a counterintuitive way to accomplish transformational marketing.

DON'T BLOCK TRAFFIC WHILE YOU BUILD A NEW BRIDGE

When the highway department needs to replace or repair a bridge, it (usually) does not simply block the road and send traffic on a giant detour. These days bridge builders tend to put a temporary, parallel bridge beside the one to be replaced so traffic can continue to flow.

We suggest you establish another team, a parallel organization, to create the transformational marketing programs, to test those programs, and to gradually introduce them. Our longtime partner Robert Shulman calls this the "shadow cabinet." The parallel organization, because it has no obligation to do things the way they've always been done and because it is not distracted by trying to maintain the existing programs, is able to focus its full attention on the new programs. This organization can be built from company people who are relieved of other duties or from expert outsiders.

Once those programs are tested and are working smoothly, the existing marketing and sales group picks up the new product and incorporates it into the ongoing business, and the transformational team goes on to develop something else.

Obviously, establishing another team adds cost, just as building a temporary bridge adds cost. But adding more work to already overworked employees also adds costs. These costs may not be as obvious as another salary, since they are hidden in inefficiency, poor morale, turnover, and ineffective marketing programs.

THE FIVE STEPS TO SUCCESSFUL IMPLEMENTATION

The marketing success recipe has five essential steps.

1. Marketing process design based on the best industry practices. This is the development of a framework for the marketing team to operate within to achieve marketing success. We are not convinced that most marketers know the path; therefore they are much more likely to miss analyses or undervalue key steps within the process.

This is the process of hypothesis development, strategy validation, and internal and external validation. Someone—top management, a competitive threat, or a consultant—must first sell them on the approach to achieve marketing success before they can actually start marching.

2. Development of a transformational strategy. This is the use of scientific methods to determine the financially optimal strategy for a brand. We are not talking about holding on to market share or growing the brand by a paltry 3 percent. We are talking about revolutionary performance, dramatic increases in share, profits, and brand equity. This is the type of counterintuitive thinking and work we have been discussing throughout this book.

3. Scientific marketing planning. This is the translation or interpretation of strategy findings into specific implications and indicated actions, which results in a program that performs like a blockbuster. This requires knowledge of a financially optimal target, a compelling, preemptive positioning, and the financially optimal channels. Everything. Communications, product, sales, and every other key player begin tangible action planning. Writing the marketing plan is the act of choosing options based on the research. You're selecting a target, defining the positioning, and making time-bound, quantifiable, specific objectives for specific activities that relate to that targeting and positioning.

Using mathematical modeling to tie together marketing input with output has become de rigueur for this process, as we discussed in Chapter 14. It provides us with insights and later confirmation as to the likely effects of changing different ingredients in the marketing mix. This plan is a culmination of all of the choices you've made, and cross-functional teams work on the implementation. And when you define the success requirements, there are myriad operational issues that will affect strategy success.

4. Action plan development. This is the actual development of the promotions, advertising, new products, sales contests, customer service scripts, and the short film about market targets. Who are the people who will impact success along the way? You need to spend as much time understanding their needs, their interests, and their motivations as you do understanding the end consumer.

In our experience virtually every company is out of balance. Some focus on their products—"If your product is good enough, you don't need marketing." Some focus on the salespeople—"Our salespeople can sell anything, so all we've got to do is get it out to the sales force." Some focus too much on the channel—"Adding our site to the Web this year will let us meet our sales goals." And some focus too much on the end customer, the industrial buyer, or the supermarket shopper—"If we meet the needs of our customers, everything else will fall into line." To focus exclusively on any one of these can derail the whole strategy.

It is therefore important to understand the needs, desires, motivations, attitudes, preferences, capabilities, strengths, and weaknesses of everyone who will influence your strategy. Any strategy that does not consider this is incomplete and more likely to fail than succeed. Every sailor needs to be on board in order to win the America's Cup, and every player needs to be on board to transform a marketing plan.

5. *Action plan implementation.* This is the day-to-day activity the plan demands. This is the checklist for advertising, for sales, for promotion, for packaging, for public relations, for each department involved in making the program a success. It includes meeting with customers, getting their feedback, and modifying and perfecting the strategy approach. This step includes the detailed twists and turns in actually getting it done. While you can think of these steps as sequential, they are not completed strictly one after another. There is overlap in a dynamic, ongoing process.

Very important, this action plan must integrate the targeting and positioning strategy in everything. Not just advertising and the Web site, which we've discussed at length, but everything! If your package, collateral material, press releases, and so on don't sing the same hymn, stop the choir and get it right. Tell everyone, "We don't have time to do it again."

While the intuitive management approach to implementation is to simply push harder—to make the same people do more of what they're already doing—the counterintuitive marketer realizes that most people are already working as hard as they can. They need to be given the time and resources to prepare for the future while someone else takes care of today.

CHAPTER

18

You Can't Measure Success Without a Score Card

Recently the CMO of a global consumer durables manufacturer asked us what we thought of his company's system for monitoring marketing performance. Several managers proudly presented their approach for tracking distribution and sales across 30 countries and, in the larger countries, on a regional basis as well. In the U.S. they could tell us their unit and dollar sales figures and distribution by five different types of outlets by state. This was pretty impressive, but normative by today's standards.

They also monitored brand and advertising awareness in six of their major markets and had put in place, in the same countries, a methodology for collecting competitive intelligence and measuring customer satisfaction.

The managers in charge of this system were very pleased with what they were doing and regarded their efforts as state-of-the-science.

We, in turn, were pleased as well—they were doing more than many companies—but their system was sorely neglectful of many components of a best practices "marketing score card," which we'll discuss momentarily. They were moving in the right direction but needed to move faster and farther in order to implement a world-class approach to monitoring marketing performance. They appreciated our constructive criticism—this company was clearly one concerned about measuring and improving its marketing's return on investment—and have begun to institutionalize the processes necessary to cover almost everything recommended in this chapter.

MARKETING ROI IS RARELY EVALUATED

One of the amazing things we've discovered over the years is how few companies really measure the performance of their marketing programs. While many managers talk evangelically about marketing metrics, advertising ROI, brand equity, and performance benchmarking, they become evasive when you try to determine exactly what they do to gauge a marketing program's success.

Even when the business uses performance as the yardstick for promotions, compensation adjustments, or advertising awards competitions, the link between the marketing input and marketing output is often tenuous and sometimes tortuous. Clancy serves regularly as a judge for the Advertising Research Foundation's annual David Ogilvy Awards for marketing excellence and has served as a judge for the American Marketing Association's Effie Awards. Each year the smartest companies and the best advertising agencies compete for awards that show how great research can lead to great marketing programs.

By "advertising and marketing excellence," the ARF and AMA mean proven effectiveness: campaigns that worked; significant sales increases; buyers motivated to buy; dealers primed to enthusiastically display the product. Yet over the years Clancy has been *underwhelmed* by the data these big companies and agencies assemble to make their point. Either the data does not exist, or the managers who prepare the entries are inarticulate in describing it. In any case, it routinely surprises us how few companies do evaluate the ROI of their marketing programs.

Everyone tracks sales—usually in a competitive context. If you're a serious packaged goods marketer, for example, you can't get by without the Nielsen or IRI numbers. Some businesses, like our consumer durables client, have systems in place for measuring advertising awareness a few times a year. Some track brand perceptions and preference. And a few measure and monitor brand equity. But only a handful of companies tie everything together, taking what we might call a "marketing audit" approach that looks at everything from marketing decision-making processes to marketing's return on investment.

To grow and be profitable, it is not enough to do everything we've recommended up to this point. It is not even enough to do it well. The last piece required is a measurement system to monitor the performance of marketing investments, something not everyone believes can be done. A recent Forrester Research report states, "Marketing can't measure the impact of its output— promotions, new products and services, and innovative pricing—because it can't close the loop through direct or indirect sales channels."

That may be true for most companies, but it is not universally true, nor is it an immutable law of business. True, it helps to start with a model that connects marketing input to marketing output, the sort of thing we discussed in Chapter 15. A good monitoring system, though, tells you not only how you are doing but also what to do differently to make things better.

THE CASE FOR AN ANNUAL MARKETING AUDIT

Once a year auditors come into every company in the land and utilize a fairly standard format to assess the enterprise's financial health. While some financial executives might like to certify their own books, a business invites outside auditors to guarantee an audit's independence and objectivity. At the same time the auditors follow the Generally Accepted Accounting Principles (GAAP), so they cannot make up the rules as they go along.

In our view it's time for an annual marketing audit, something we've been preaching for a decade. We see firms of independent marketing auditors coming into businesses to assess their marketing capabilities and performance. While there are no Generally Accepted Marketing Principles for a marketing audit, there does seem to be general agreement on many issues. There is clear agreement, for example, that in terms of its potential for corporate diagnosis and prognosis, the annual marketing audit should be similar to financial audits and to the product service quality audits reflected in the national competition for the Baldrige Award. Such an audit would help bring accountability to the marketing function. At a minimum, such an audit should include:

1. An assessment of key factors that impacted the business for good or for ill during the past year. This should emphasize an evaluation of marketing "surprises"—the unanticipated competitive actions or changes in the marketing climate that affected the performance of the marketing programs.

One dot-com company we just started working with raised approximately $40 million to launch a new professional services business. A substantial portion of the investment, as much as $15 million, was earmarked for marketing the new brand during its first year. The problem? Six months in they weren't hitting their numbers and asked us to do a diagnosis and prognosis. Little in the way of competitive intelligence was gathered by either the management group or the investment company funding the enterprise. Seven months after launch they were dumbfounded to discover—we gave them the bad news—that they had 26 competitors in or entering the same space.

A different type of "surprise" is unanticipated levels of competitive response. Following a simulated test market that predicted big-time success for a new detergent, a client launched in six test markets, only to be terribly disappointed. Sales were negligible; only about 20 percent of the forecast level of market share was achieved. Was the STM to blame? Did they get a bad forecast? It turned out that a global competitor had run a massive TV campaign and a two-for-one promotion for the expressed purpose of blowing our client's brand out of the water. This, of course, was nothing that could be sustained on a national level. It would be prohibitively expensive. Nevertheless, the defensive strategy was successful in ensuring that the one-year test market was unreadable and a waste of time and money, forcing our client to take the step of either going national and risking failure or abandoning the introduction. They still haven't decided.

2. An assessment of marketing knowledge, attitudes, and satisfaction of all executives involved in the marketing function, and the extent to which the marketing program was successfully marketed internally. That is, the extent to which top management, marketing, and nonmarketing executives bought into it.

Dr. John Martin, a friend of the authors and a former doctoral student of Professor Philip Kotler at the Kellogg Graduate School of Management at Northwestern University, has developed a methodology for addressing many of these issues. The need for such measurement was readily apparent in Chapter 17, where we discussed problems inherent in implementing marketing programs today. It is imperative that all managers responsible for making a program work buy into it and know exactly what their role is in making it happen. Egos need to be left in the closet as the team bonds together, and executes together, the agreed-upon strategy.

In many companies, as we've discussed, including sometimes in our own, this doesn't happen. Subgroups form with their own leadership and agendas—like Montgomery and Patton in World War II—which inhibit the performance of the overall plan.

Working this past spring on a major marketing effort for a regional bank with national aspirations, we saw these discontinuities every day. The C-level executives, marketing people, branch managers, and IT specialists all had different expectations and agendas. Nor did they listen to each other very well. Their marketing program stuttered and suffered as we played the uncomfortable role of referee to bring people together.

3. An assessment of the extent to which each decision in the marketing mix—targeting, positioning, pricing, advertising, and all the rest—was made after evaluating many alternatives in terms of profit-related criteria.

As discussed in Chapter 2, it is possible to classify all marketing decisions into 22 broad types (see Figure 2-1). Each of the 22 has three or four subcate-

gories. E-commerce strategy and implementation, for example, covers targeting and positioning, integration with traditional e-commerce channels, the
strategy itself, and evaluation benchmarks.

To evaluate marketing decision-making, the auditor's task is to assess how
the company made decisions in each of the 22 decision areas. The auditor
asks for hard data in the form of documents, plans, and transcripts. For example, if management claims that it has a good knowledge of its current market
target but can produce only a five-year-old market research study, the auditor
scores management poorly on understanding current customer needs.

The scoring procedure is based on distinguishing five levels of marketing
decision-making: disturbing (0–15 points), troubling (16–35), average
(36–65), pleasing (66–85), and amazing (86–100). The auditor, after examining the available evidence, assigns a performance score for each of approximately 80 subcategories and 22 dimensions. Scores for each subcategory
range from 0 to 100. These are then averaged for each of the 22 dimensions
and then averaged again for an overall company score. The average of these
overall scores we've reported earlier: it's 49, hardly a glowing report card for
marketing processes today.

The next step is to assess which of the 22 decisions are the most important
for the particular company to perform well, which are of medium importance, and which are of minor importance. Given its industry and situation, a
company's e-commerce skill may be very important yet receive a low score.
By evaluating all 22 activities on their importance and the company's performance, it becomes instantly clear which marketing decisions need immediate
improvement and which can wait.

*4. An assessment of customer satisfaction and retention based on research
undertaken among key target groups, including customers, distributors, vendors, and agents.*

Customer satisfaction, as we discussed in Chapter 12, is linked to customer
retention. Happy customers tend to be loyal customers, but it would be a very
shortsighted manager who thought that a happy customer today will be a
loyal customer tomorrow. "To see how we're doing in our customer relations,
we measure three dimensions," says William R. Barnes, Director of Customer Satisfaction for Eastman Chemical Co. "First, we look at a perception
measurement system, i.e. a survey. How are we doing versus a standard; how
are we doing versus competition? That's a 30,000-foot view. Second, we look
at a complaint measurement system. What defects turn up as we deliver products and services? So we want to look at not only customer perceptions, we
want to look at events. Finally, we look at what I call a behavior system, the
win/loss analysis. What caused a customer to change our share of the busi-

ness, either up or down? We do a real investigation to learn why those things happen." As Kotler points out in his seminal new book, *Kotler on Marketing,* "It behooves the company to ferret out the causes behind the increasing dissatisfaction, for if it worsens further, profits will begin to fall."

Customer retention is another key measure. "As fast as we were bringing customers in through the front door," one executive told us not long ago, "they were going out the back." Not an uncommon situation. We routinely investigate a company's churn, the number of customers who have to be replaced every year for the business just to stay even. We are no longer surprised when management tells us, "We don't keep track of our accounts that way." The information is available, but no one assembles it into a report management can study. When we ask that the report be compiled, company executives are often astonished to see that the firm has been losing—and replacing—as many as 15 percent of its customers every year. Equally revealing is the revenue change among customers; a company could retain most of its customers, but they buy 10 to 30 percent less than the year before. It's a situation management should be aware of.

5. An assessment of product and/or service quality compared to an overall standard of excellence and relative to competitors. A successful marketer needs to offer products and services that are not merely good in their own right but better than competitors. This is critical and related to what we discussed in Chapter 10. Being better than others is better than just being excellent.

Relative product quality is in the customer's eyes, and it changes as competitors enter (or leave) the market. The goal here is to be somewhat better than the competition (unless your goal is to be absolutely the best in class and charge accordingly) but not so much better that customers cannot see the difference or will not pay for the difference or both. While usually the problem is one of declining perceived (or real) quality, it sometimes happens that quality outstrips customer need—our friend Tom Nagle cites the parts manufacturer whose parts had a life expectancy of seven years; they were being installed in a product with a life expectancy of five years. In any case, management should know what customers think of the firm's quality relative to competition.

We've reported elsewhere our experience with Compaq years ago, when they were building PCs that they claimed could be dropped out a third-story window and still operate. The durability and reliability were world class but unnecessary—people aren't prone to drop their PC out a window and don't want to pay for one that keeps on humming after that kind of fall.

Relative service quality is, again, what customers think, not what company management believes. Usually we see service quality slip as a business cuts back on customer service or does not maintain service staffing levels as sales grow. Occasionally service quality will exceed customer needs. Nordstrom's built its brand not with better products or more attractive stores (although it has good products and attractive stores), but with service that exceeded anything competitors offered.

6. *A general assessment of the sales performance of each brand with an emphasis on how it is trending over time relative to competitors.* Market share is a key measure. Sales may be growing, but if the industry is growing even more rapidly, a company may actually be losing ground. True, it may not be easy to measure industry growth; the industry may be fragmented and there may be no easy source of sales (such as automobile registrations). Another issue may be the way the company defines its industry: A cola marketer may disregard bottled water sales, for example. A dot-com company may decide to focus only on Internet competitors and not on bricks-and-mortar operations. Another firm in a dying industry may focus only on its traditional competitors, capturing a larger and larger share of its category, until it has everything of nothing. Alert management wants to know the company's market share, how it is changing, and how the market itself is changing.

7. *An assessment of whether the marketing plan achieved its stated financial and nonfinancial goals and objectives, and if not, why not?* This is pretty straightforward. Match up what you said you were going to do against what was actually achieved. Are the numbers on target, or are they ahead or below plans? If they're below plans, analyses need to been done to find out why.

The first step is to gather and synthesize the views of all the managers involved in the plan's development, implementation, and monitoring. This should be supplemented by a close evaluation of the extent to which the program was executed the way it was planned. Were the distribution goals achieved? Were 2,200 television GRPs actually bought? Did the sales force whip up the enthusiasm in the trade that was expected? Were 2.3 million direct-mail pieces sent out with the anticipated response rate of 1.2 percent?

The next step is to compare all of the stated financial goals and objectives against performance. Which were achieved and which were not? The marketing plan, as illustrated, calls for 37 percent total brand awareness and a 12 percent market share by the end of the year. Did the company hit these numbers? It anticipated on ROI of 15 percent? What did it achieve?

8. *A diagnostic assessment of the performance of the entire program—conception to completion—in terms of a multistep "hierarchy of effects" model of marketing performance, from awareness and attitudes through sales and*

profitability, and the use of this model to diagnose the program's strengths and weaknesses.

9. An autopsy of all aspects of the plan that failed to meet objectives, with specific recommendations for improving next year's performance.

10. An assessment of the current value of brand equity for each brand in the product portfolio.

The first seven of these components are fairly straightforward. Having already talked about them at length, we will not discuss them further. However, because the last three are critical and because many companies are not doing them, we will go into more detail.

LEARN WHETHER THE MARKETING PROGRAM IS THRIVING OR DYING

A multiwave tracking study is a good way to learn whether the marketing program for the product or service is alive and well, alive but not so well, or sick and dying. A well-done study can even help raise the program from the dead. To have a successful performance evaluation program, a company must take four steps:

Step 1: The company must make the campaign's goals and objectives explicit. Everyone in business tosses around the words "goals and objectives," but as we'll see in a moment, one executive's idea of what constitutes a goal or an objective may be very different from another's, and they both may be useless.

Step 2: The company must make its implicit conceptual model of the input-output process explicit. The model should define what's involved in moving from marketing investment to sales and profits. Consumer packaged goods marketers need to think of moving from brand awareness to trial, repeat, and market share. Financial services marketers must consider awareness, attitudes and perceptions, overall evaluation, buyer behavior, and market share. This is the same kind of model that we talked about in Chapters 15 and 16.

Step 3: The company must undertake a tracking study to estimate the parameters of the conceptual model soon after launching the product or service into the real-world test, either a test market or a regional or national introduction.

Step 4: Finally, the company must connect all the steps together as discussed in Chapter 15 in a mathematical model to link planned input with forecasted output. The model should help forecast one end of the chain—say, sales—that results from an earlier step—say, advertising investment.

An objective must be realistic, specific, and measurable. An objective cannot be fuzzy, ethereal, or soft—"Our objective is to increase the number of people who feel good about our company and its new product" or the all-time favorite, "Our plan is to build awareness."

A bank's objective might be "A 10 percent increase in the percentage of customers who open an IRA by April 15, 2001." A brokerage firm's objective might be "800 new leads for sales calls within 90 days in New York State." All are realistic, specific, and measurable, but in our work we regularly see marketing objectives that are not specific, measurable, or realistic.

But what are the steps to achieving the objective? A direct-mail campaign has five: (1) reaching the prospects, (2) getting them to read the direct mail piece, (3) building awareness, (4) ensuring comprehension, and (5) conversion to sale.

The marketer should diagram this process and set a goal for each stage. Without such a model and goals, the company will have no idea how or why a particular campaign performs the way it does because a marketing program can achieve or lose the same objective in the marketplace for different reasons. An excellent example of such a model is the one that was presented earlier for Arkansas Slim's, a hypothetical new light beer (see Figure 15-1).

Once the company has a model, it requires research to measure each step in the process. A typical study is based on telephone interviews among 300 to 500 prospects for the product or service. One survey before the campaign (a prewave survey) followed by two to four during the marketing effort's first year (the postwave surveys) is common. The tracking criteria capture the goals and objectives of the company's model and its campaign.

A company may do this kind of study for many different reasons, not just to find out whether or not the program was successful. A far better reason is to provide an early, actionable forecast of where the product is headed, to diagnose the flu before it becomes pneumonia. For example, based on a few data points collected early in a campaign, the company can forecast how the campaign will perform by year end with a reasonable level of accuracy, using a graph like the one in Figure 18-1.

The graph forecasts campaign penetration—the percentage of the target market who were aware of the advertising on an unaided and aided basis. During the first 13 weeks after the company launched the campaign, we collected three data points and forecast what would happen later in the year. The dotted line reflects the forecast, the solid line the actual data. Since in this

Figure 18-1   Year-End Forecast Based on Three Data Points

Campaign Penetration

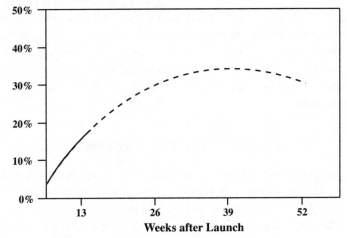

Weeks after Launch

case the projected numbers were considerably lower than the awareness goals, this chart set off alarm bells at the company's headquarters.

Forecasts should be made, however, not just for awareness but for every step in the hypothesized causal model of marketing program performance. In the example below, we see year-end performance forecast after three months compared to actual year-end goals and objectives.

In this case, after 13 weeks, the marketer had forecast that only 67 percent of the dollar share objective would be achieved (1.6 versus 2.4 percent). This discrepancy resulted from the advertising campaign's weaknesses at the awareness stage. The goal was 53 percent awareness by year end; the research forecast was that, on the current course, it would be only 37 percent. If the company could correct this problem, it would improve the likelihood of achieving its objectives considerably.

	Performance Forecast after 13 Weeks	*Goals and Objectives*
Awareness	37 %	53 %
Purchase Consideration	15 %	22 %
Share of Buyers	3.2%	4.7%
Share of Dollars	1.6%	2.4%

When management receives such a forecast, it must become a diagnostician and evaluate all the reasons for the breakdown at every stage in the process. For example, there are a number of reasons that might account for the poor performance of the program in terms of advertising campaign penetration. These reasons could include an inefficient media buy; advertising that is not attention getting or memorable; inadequate point-of-sale material in the channels of distribution; or weak performance by the direct-mail program. In this case the marketer diagnosed weak advertising as the problem; the agency developed a new campaign, launched it later in the year, and turned around an ailing product.

BEWARE OF RECOGNITION MEASURES

Many marketers today mistakenly believe that the case presented above is becoming less common. The case depicts an example in which weak advertising is the root cause of the failed campaign, yet many executives are happy with their advertising today because their tracking systems show growth in performance indicators. Recently we saw a report for one client of campaign awareness numbers rising from 10 percent after the first quarter to 15 percent, then to 18 and 22 percent in the second, third, and fourth quarters. They were delighted. Another client reported a 40 percent campaign penetration at the end of the first half growing to 65 percent by the end of the year. Hallelujah!

Anything that shows growth in marketing is a good thing because so many numbers—like the numbers you've been reading in this book—suggest that it's more likely that nothing is going on. Yet we recently saw a situation in which a reputable research company reported proven advertising recall rising to 45 percent among the target consumers after four months and approximately $10 million in advertising spending, a phenomenal performance.

The expression "proven advertising recall" dates back to 1960s on-air testing. Interviewers ask a series of questions to determine what the respondent remembers: What did you see in the advertising? What did you hear? What was the main point? Was there anything said to suggest this product is different from a competitor's?

The researchers code the responses to identify people who say something that appears to be uniquely associated with the advertising currently on air. Those people have demonstrated proven advertising recall; they can play back something about the message.

In our client's case we discovered that, even though the presentation and the report claimed "proven advertising recall," the measures were in fact recognition measures.

A recognition measure results when interviewers give respondents clues and props: Did you see any advertising for Yoohoo in which someone said, "If you choose any other chocolate drink, you could be making a big mistake"? Did you see any advertising for Budweiser that includes frogs, lizards, or Dalmatians? Did you see any advertising for Taco Bell that has a talking Chihuahua? How about advertising for EDS that showed people herding cats like they were herding cattle? The research company can offer false clues or make the clues more obscure. Only if the respondent identifies a certain number of clues correctly will the firm count the person as having seen the advertising. Because of this, researchers have some latitude in counting respondents as recognizing the advertising.

In the case of the 45 percent "proven advertising recall" study, the research company counted a respondent as recognizing the advertising if she got any one of six messages correct, with no adjustment for mistakes or false statements. It was not proven recall but recognition—and a liberal interpretation of recognition, to boot. Beware of recognition measures.

Why do we say this? Because we see it as symptomatic of a trend. Marketing is difficult enough without basing decisions on flawed—or misleading—tracking research. Too often we find managers looking to research to confirm a decision, not to learn the truth or to make a better decision.

Recognition measures, in a relatively short period of time—the last three or four years—have come to dominate advertising effectiveness studies. Everybody is using them. It can mean a brand that has zero proven advertising recall may have 5 percent related (i.e., unproven) recall and a 45 or 50 percent recognition-based recall.

Recognition-based recall may tell you that people were exposed to the advertising. But it does not tell you if the advertising message was stamped onto their consciousness. Because they cannot recall it on an unaided basis, your message will have no impact when they are standing in the store choosing between your product and 29 competitors, or sitting at their PCs deciding which Internet site they should access when they are looking to plan a trip, send a gift, or find a job. A good copy test will tell you this before you waste your money and leave a customer clueless in the store or on the Net.

DIAGNOSING PERFORMANCE FOR EVERY LINK IN THE CHAIN

Marketing program performance evaluation doesn't end with awareness: marketers can use tracking research effectively to measure performance relative to competition in terms of each stage in the "hierarchy of effects" model, every link in the chain. Let's return to the example of awareness (e.g., brand,

Figure 18-2   Credit Card Advertising Awareness Case

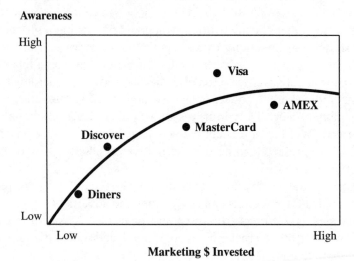

advertising, or campaign). Since we know that most types of awareness build exponentially with each marketing dollar invested, a company can use tracking-study data to plot a product or service's performance compared to the competition. The important question is not to ask how is Visa doing compared to MasterCard, or Coke to Pepsi, or Ford to Chrysler, but to ask how Visa and MasterCard, Coke and Pepsi, Ford and Chrysler are doing relative to the size of their marketing investment.

Figure 18-2 illustrates the point; as a company invests marketing dollars, consumer awareness increases—just as one would hope. The computer calculates the best solution to all the data points and draws a nonlinear regression line representing this solution, the curve on the chart. A company located right on the line would be perfectly average; companies above the line enjoy greater awareness than expected (given their marketing investment), and those below, less than expected. This graph indicates that while American Express spends the most money, Visa has a higher level of awareness per dollar spent. This is a reflection of Visa's very powerful "and they don't take American Express" campaign, which has been running for years. Master-Card, which has spent almost as much as Visa in this example, is not doing as well. If MasterCard discovered what is presented here, they might want to develop and test alternative advertising strategies, or executions, or both.

In the same way, the company measures every link in the hypothesized model of how marketing works in a particular product category. For example,

Figure 18-3   Theme Park Case

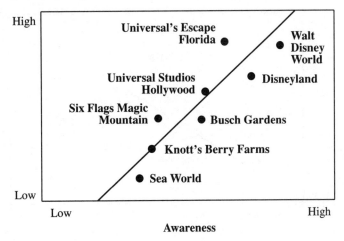

the relationship between awareness and purchase consideration tends to be linear; as awareness increases, so does purchase consideration. In most service categories there must be some awareness before the company sees any purchase consideration at all. With an impulse item, awareness may not be as important.

Figure 18-3, with disguised data from the theme park industry, illustrates this relationship. In this case Universal Studios' Escape Florida seems to enjoy much more visit consideration than its awareness suggests it deserves, while Busch Gardens is getting less. The greater the distance above the line, the greater the competitive advantage the company enjoys. The more a company is below the line, the weaker its competitive posture.

The next step in the chain might be the conversion of purchase consideration to actual buying behavior, measured in terms of share of customers. Again, it is possible to take this data, plot it on a graph, draw a line between the points to show average performance, and see instantly which companies convert a larger share of prospects into customers and which convert a smaller share.

Finally, there's the link between share of buyers and share of dollars. If the relationship were perfect, this would be a 45-degree angle and all firms would sit right on it; as a company's share of buyers rose, its share of dollars would rise equally. The relationship is not perfect, however, because some firms have a larger volume than others. Firms above the line generate more dollars per customer than firms below the line.

Figure 18-4   Personal Computer Customer Value Case

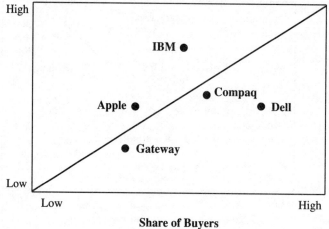

Take, for example, Figure 18-4, in which we illustrate what might be the case in the PC industry. Note that Dell enjoys the number-one position in terms of its share of buyers. However, because of Dell's highly competitive pricing, it's not enjoying a comparable share of dollars. IBM, in contrast, has a share of dollars that is significantly higher than its share of buyers.

Observing where the company falls vis-à-vis the competition on this line, and for all other stages in the company's model of the marketing process, provides management with insights into the strengths and weaknesses of its marketing programs. Sometimes this intelligence can be used to resuscitate a dying brand or program or even resurrect a dead one.

AUTOPSIES OF CAMPAIGN FAILURE

In 20 years of evaluating marketing programs for new and established products, we have observed many failures in both the laboratory and the real world. Sometimes marketers invite us to undertake an autopsy of what went wrong, to figure out if the patient is really dead; if so, why; and if not, how it can be resuscitated. We've talked about these lessons at length in our book *Simulated Test Marketing* (Lexington Books, New York, 1994). The lessons include:

1. Marketers assess the marketing climate inadequately.
2. They target the wrong group (or groups).

3. They employ a weak positioning strategy.
4. They select a less-than-optimal (and here we're being kind) configuration of product or service attributes and benefits.
5. They don't deliver the level of customer satisfaction required to keep the customer.
6. They implement a questionable pricing strategy.
7. The advertising campaign generates an insufficient level of awareness and fails to motivate the prospect.
8. Overoptimism about the marketing plan leads to a sales forecast that cannot be sustained in the real world.
9. The marketer believes that the new product and its marketing plan has died and cannot be revived
10. Seemingly minor modeling issues (like Achilles' heel) lead to poor forecasts and sometimes fatal decisions.

We've discussed the first nine points in some detail throughout this book, but the last point we'll just touch upon here.

Sometimes seemingly small modeling issues can create major problems. Many systems, for example, are unable to forecast awareness accurately, particularly in this age of the Internet. This may result in wildly overoptimistic estimates of sales, which can lead marketers astray. Some do not take the purchase cycle into account. They spend money on a slow-turnover product as if it were a fast-turnover product. As a consequence, the campaign runs out of gas before most buyers are ready to act. This is like heating your house in summer and expecting it to keep you warm through winter.

Others ignore the effect of distribution on sales in the absence of advertising, as well as the relationship between consumer involvement in the product category and effective distribution. As we've discussed before, the more involved buyers are in the product category, the more they'll search to find your product. Stated very differently, a marketer doesn't need the same level of distribution for an involved target as for a disengaged target.

Another issue is the shortfall in effective product distribution. Manufacturers find it increasingly difficult to obtain adequate distribution for multi-item product lines. Retailers cherry-pick the lines, which means that one-third of one-half of the new items are sparsely distributed. Increasingly, forecasting the impact of item distribution is critical to an accurate sales projection. We find that reduced item availability typically results in a 5 to 20 percent sales reduction.

In one case a simulated test market forecast a successful introduction. The brand was a five-flavor line, and the marketer assumed a 73 percent ACV. In actual in-store presence, orange obtained a 75 percent ACV, cherry a 64 percent ACV, strawberry a 32 percent ACV, and blueberry and watermelon obtained no distribution whatever. As a result, the actual sales were just about half the forecast. Everyone was unhappy.

MEASURING BRAND EQUITY

Although just about everyone in marketing talks about brand building and brand equity—often interchangeably—not everyone agrees on the definition of "brand equity." Professor Kevin Lane Keller assembles eight definitions in his book *Strategic Brand Management,* but notes, "Most marketing observers agree that brand equity is defined in terms of the marketing effects uniquely attributable to the brand. That is, brand equity relates to the fact that different outcomes result from the marketing of a product or service because of its brand name or some other brand element, compared to outcomes if that same product or service did not have that brand identification." Or, as Russell Hanlin, CEO of Sunkist Growers, has said, "An orange is an orange is an orange. Unless, of course, that orange happens to be Sunkist, a name that 80 percent of consumers trust."

For example, in one experiment, beer drinkers who knew they were tasting Miller Lite, Coors, Pabst, Budweiser, Colt 45, and Guinness were able to discriminate between them. Their taste impressions were scattered all over a perceptual map. When they did not know the brands they were tasting, however, they could distinguish only the Guinness; all five other brands clustered together on the perceptual map. Since the beers were the same in both tests, brand identification alone—excepting Guinness—affected consumer taste perceptions. In the first test drinkers tasted what they expected to taste based on marketing communications.

The greater the brand equity, the greater consumer loyalty. A strong brand is less vulnerable to competitive marketing actions and less vulnerable to marketing crises. (The Coke bottling fiasco in Europe during the summer of 1999 is a classic example of a marketing crisis.) A strong brand commands larger margins, is able to raise prices without losing significant volume. It has greater trade cooperation and support and increased marketing communication effectiveness. A strong brand may offer licensing and brand extension opportunities.

One primitive measure of brand equity is the reputation that a brand or company enjoys; a more sophisticated measure is the seven-factor model we presented in Chapter 5. These factors include:

Brand permeation: A weighted combination of brand and advertising awareness and availability (i.e., distribution).

Brand distinctiveness: A weighted combination of measures that indicate
brand differentiation/uniqueness discovered to be drivers of financial
performance.

Brand quality: An overall assessment of the brand as a whole and its line
extensions in terms of different indicators of product/service quality.

Brand value: A combination of perceived and actual price relative to perceived quality/excellence. This is, in essence, a measure of whether the
brand delivers what buyers pay for—often known as "price-value."

Brand personality: The extent to which the brand's image is congruent
with who the buyer is or wants to be.

Competitive inoculation: The extent to which the brand is protected
against competitive inroads; the extent to which the consumer would
stick with the brand in times of adversity or competitive pressure.

Brand potential: The extent to which consumers will pay more for, go out
of their way for, or are willing to try this brand's new products, services, or line extensions.

By weighting each item and factor by its contribution to overall brand preference, we can produce one overall assessment of brand equity for every
brand we study. We can, in short, characterize each brand by a single brand
equity number, which we have standardized from 0 to 100 within a category
to express "share of equity."

This brand equity measure, therefore, like IQ, SAT scores, and p/e ratios, is
a number. It's an overall assessment of the "good will" associated with a
brand that reflects past marketing performance and predicts future sales and
profit potential. When combined with a financial assessment of brand profitability, it provides a complete accounting of the "value" of a brand to the
corporation or the "value" of potential acquisitions. It's a number that should
be tracked for every brand in a company's portfolio at least once a year,
preferably more often.

The intuitive approach to marketing today, as we've argued throughout this
book, is to build programs using judgment, experience, and creativity with
some commonsensical research thrown in for good measure. These programs
are launched without a great deal of planning and monitored without obsessive zeal for knowing everything that is going on and why. Within six months
to a year after the program's introduction, even casual observers note that it's
sputtering and new plans get hatched to do it over again. This is the phenomenon of over-and-over marketing we've been discussing.

Following the principles described in the preceding chapters, a marketer
can develop and implement campaigns that are more likely to succeed. At the

end of the day, however, we still need a score card to know that we've done everything correct and, if not, what to do about it. The key is to install measurement systems that monitor everything going on in marketing, from how the decisions get made to the yield of the implemented marketing programs, systems that tell us not just how we've done but how to do it better.

CHAPTER

19

Always Time to Do It Over; Never Time to Do It Right

Not long ago we got a call from Dallas, from the straight-shooting CEO of a large corporation. "Dr. Clancy? Ah'm readin' your book here, and ah want to know if we should stay in the retail business or if ah should fire all these fuckers and do somethin' else."

We talked for a long while—he was a fun guy and very smart. We concluded by saying that it would take us about 6 months to do a thorough evaluation and another 6 to 12 months to develop and implement a plan to overhaul his business.

"You haven't heard me, son. Ah have to make a decision here. Ah need somethin' in about six weeks. What can you do for me? Work with me here, son. Ah probably need two weeks to think about it—so what can you do for me in, like, 30 days?"

Although we loved being called "son"—it made us feel 20 years younger—we said we couldn't do anything meaningful in 30 days. The most he'd be buying is our mind, and that's a form of testosterone-driven decision-making.

"That's probably what ah need here, son. Some boys with testosterone who can make a goddamn decision."

For over 20 years we've been working with companies that are loaded with testosterone; indeed, the global marketplace is swimming in testosterone. One result is the poor marketing program performance we talk about in this book. As we write, of course, we recognize that American management consulting firms have trained top executives to believe they can get 80 percent of the way to a great decision on judgment alone—and the remaining 20 percent takes too much time and costs too much money. We reject this idea for the same reason we reject the idea that the best way to make a decision is to use a Ouija board.

Management consultants have no empirical basis to back their claim, while we have 20 years of marketing evidence to prove that judgmentally, intuitively, hormonally generated marketing programs do not work. The conventional wisdom is not a surefire path to success. Maybe the management consultants can get you 40 or even 60 percent of the way there; they are very smart and have pedigrees from top schools. But 40 or even 70 percent is insufficient to compete successfully in the new millennium. Moving to the 80 percent-plus mark has become de rigueur.

We did not work for the tall man from Texas.

RIGOROUS ANALYSIS OF UNIMPEACHABLE DATA

Throughout this book we have talked about the importance of marketing. Marketing is why people give you money to pay the help. We've maintained that few marketing programs work, and we've offered guidance to better, more profitable programs.

We have not talked at length about the time executives must take in making marketing decisions, in developing marketing plans, and in implementing marketing programs. Too many pick a target in a flash. Make a positioning decision because intuition tells them the message makes sense. Set a price without any real strategy or research. Write a marketing plan in three weeks. Create and produce a new TV campaign in eight weeks. Implement the whole thing in another 60 days.

This is not the way to treat a new product or service or program you want to be profitable, never mind a business you want to thrive. These folks should be branded "Death-Wish Marketer."

Recently we visited The Hartford, an insurance giant well on the way to becoming a customer-driven company. Top management was intrigued by Mobil's Friendly Serve campaign, impressed with the friendly service, clean stations, spotless bathrooms, and SpeedPass gas cards that help you get in and out in record time. The Hartford executives had no idea we had worked with Mobil and DDB/Needham to help create Friendly Serve and asked if we had any idea how Mobil went about developing such a program and what were the results.

We talked about the awards that the campaign has won, the dramatic improvements in brand equity, and the record gains at dealerships that fully implemented the program. But we also talked about the serious commitment

Mobil management made to developing Friendly Serve and the long days over the course of 18 months that were required to research, develop, and implement the strategy. Friendly Serve was not a testosterone campaign but rather the outcome of an arduous, time-consuming process that resulted in counterintuitive marketing. (To those who think that friendly gas station service is intuitive, we ask, why hadn't anyone done it before?)

Every executive in every industry has a reason why a decision must be made immediately, the product introduced next week, and the program set by the end of the month. They are lashed by a sense of urgency that, we have said facetiously, seems to be related to hormones. If you've got the ball under your arm, damn it, hit the line and run. If you're running in the wrong direction, you'll find out later, okay? Making decisions quickly is the intuitive thing to do. Corporations reward fast decision-making and frown upon taking pains. Don't get ready and aim. Fire! Fire! And fire some more!

Super Bowl Sunday 2000 is the best, and most expensive, example of this craziness that we can think of. One $3 million spot after another, with little brand connection and no positioning. Testosterone gone wild.

Clearly there are times when you need to fire before you're ready or fire before aiming. A competitor has just introduced a new product based on state-of-the-art technology. A rival has broken a campaign that talks about your brand in a pejorative manner. An enemy has just reduced its price to zero margin levels to wipe your product off the shelf. An Internet site has just opened a whole new product category. But these are uncommon skirmishes in the marketing wars.

More often than not, it does not matter whether the company introduces its campaign in September or January, delays the new Web site four months, or pulls all advertising until the first of the year. Managers need time to consider alternatives and weigh options. When they have the time—which is most of the time—the counterintuitive approach is to do it right. This means undertaking rigorous analysis of alternative decision options based on hard data using criteria related to profitability.

Recently a client approached us to help in the transition from a conventional but effective direct marketer to an e-commerce company that would quickly—five months later—lead to a big-time IPO. They added ".com" to the company name and began to shift marketing and distribution activities to a new Web site. We cautioned that they were moving too quickly; the target market, positioning, product, and pricing strategy for the Web customer were not necessarily the same as for the traditional customer. We recommended that they study the market to compare and contrast the two types of customers and to provide insights that would prove invaluable in developing the new Web-centered business.

Company management countered that they wanted to take advantage of the equities market while it was still hot in the winter of 2000. The CEO called for a three-month time frame to develop the Web site sans strategic research and another two months for the road show and launch. Men at work. The 28-year-olds building the site were neither great strategic thinkers nor brilliant creatives, so the outcome was mediocre at best. The site failed, the IPO faltered, and at this writing we expect the entire business to go into Chapter 11.

Often we ask executives, "Why don't you have the time to do it right when you can make the time to do it over and over and over again?" This "field of dreams" e-commerce company spent many millions of dollars trying to make the radical transition from one business environment to another, and now there is no money left to do it over again.

So our first point is that executives need to spend more time making critical marketing decisions.

You do need a manager's creativity, intuition, and judgment, but you need to balance it with rigorous analysis of unimpeachable data. Only with both the data and the analysis can one hope to make decisions—strategic and tactical—that, if not optimal, are close to it.

If the brand manager tells you tomorrow he's spending $800,000 or $8 million or $80 million, make him demonstrate that it is the right amount of money. Because, as we have seen, managers sometimes pull the figures right out of the air. We ask, "How did you come up with an $8 million ad budget?" They respond, "Our experience says that's what it takes to do a successful new product launch." Or "The agency recommended it." Or "That's what you need to buy 2,000 gross rating points on prime time television." There's always a reason, even if the reason can't be defended.

The people who put together these programs are smart, and they have an answer. But the answer, after analysis, often does not connect with reality. We're particularly impressed with the explanations provided by advertising agency account managers. They're glib, articulate, and persuasive. But you have to remember that ad agencies are in the spin business. Much of what they say sounds as if it makes sense even when, on close inspection, it sometimes makes no sense at all. Remember our story about "zero percent awareness being a good thing."

PUHLEEZE: NO MORE TALK ABOUT BRAND JUICE OR SPEED BRANDING

Talk about spin. As we discussed earlier, a dot-com agency recently asked us about "brand juice." They wanted help in creating more brand juice for their clients. They wanted us to create a research model—a "juice blender"—that they could offer to all of their clients. "What in heaven's name are you talking about?" we asked. They went on to talk reverentially about brand attitude, brand emotions, brand essence, brand promise, brand values, brand voice, and even a brand statement.

We were intrigued. Some of this is good stuff, even important stuff, and we touched on it in our chapter on positioning and advertising. But much of it is new economy jargon and ad agency mumbo-jumbo that masks the fundamental problem. In many cases the brand has no reason for being. It solves no buyer's problem. It is, and perhaps should remain, a commodity.

Listening to incoherent brandspeak, one might think that all you need to do is take a brand, product, service, maybe even an entire company, and dip it in brand juice. And voilà, something magical happens! You've transformed a nothing, through brand dip alone, into a powerful presence.

Brand juicers must be kidding. If you want to build a powerful brand, then figure out who the target is and everything about them. Uncover their motivations, their problems, their pains. And then configure your product or service or company so that it addresses the target's motivations, solves their problems, alleviates their pain. Finally, unleash the power of communications to tell people, with words and pictures, why and how you do this better than anyone else in the industry.

This recommendation is particularly pertinent to the new proponents of *speed branding*. The phrase means building a brand in record time, maybe even in two months, as dot-com company after dot-com company was going over the cliff in the last months of 1999 and throughout 2000. They had convinced themselves that the normal processes of building awareness, converting awareness to interest and interest to trial, trial into repeat usage and spending could be accelerated beyond anything that anyone had ever thought possible through extraordinary advertising expenditures.

Many would argue that great brands and successful businesses, like fine wine, require aging. We don't necessarily share this view; we believe it is theoretically possible to build a brand quickly—albeit not in two or three months—but only if the business fundamentals have been mastered.

When you're done, you've got a brand. You have something remarkable that people are willing to pay a premium for and go out of their way to find. You have something that stands out from the crowd and represents timeless value.

We told this to the dot-com agency and its senior staff and begged them to stop talking gibberish and get back to fundamentals: target, motivations, product solutions, positioning, communications. Attitudes and essence, values and personality, and the like are "nice-to-haves," but they're not essential to brand success. The fundamentals are.

CREATE MARKETING PLANS THAT WORK

Vow that you're going to create marketing plans that produce results: no more hoaxes. Set your objectives and make them specific, realistic, and measurable. Evaluate your strategy. Can it deliver the objectives? Do you know this for certain, or are you simply guessing? And what about the tactics? How well do you understand the relationship between each tactical component (for example, advertising spending) and the objectives you're trying to achieve.

As we've argued before, companies ought to connect every marketing plan input to its forecasted (i.e., modeled) output. The average marketing plan contains a discussion of the marketing climate, the elements of the marketing strategy, the specific goals and objectives of the marketing program, and the tactics the company plans to employ to reach those goals, but they're not connected to one another. As we described in Chapter 15, they can be, they should be, and they will be, in the future, in the companies that plan to dominate their respective industries.

When you turn a steering wheel, the front wheels move. Put the wheel hard over, and the car will make a 45-degree turn. Turn the wheel back to the middle position, and the car goes straight. Precision engineering connects one part to another, and all the parts logically and mechanically work together.

But the marketing department has no analogy. Spend $8 million on advertising, and sales may go up, down, or stay the same. Launch a new product, and company profits may go up, down, or stay the same. For many companies, it is often a surprise when things turn out well, badly, or the same. Everybody hopes the new product (service, advertising campaign, promotion, price) will do well, but they don't really know whether it will or not.

Today it is possible to create scientific marketing plans that tie inputs to outputs. The technology is available and can help you steer your brand, products, services, or company confidently. Turn up the advertising, turn down the promotion, increase share of distribution, launch the new product, and simulate the effects before you make these changes in the real world.

At the same time we know it is hard to do this when you have fires to put out every single day. People are working harder than ever, and because they are working so hard, they don't have time to step back, to think, consider, reflect, and implement properly.

IMPLEMENTATION MAY BE EVEN MORE IMPORTANT
THAN STRATEGY

Twenty-five years ago, when Clancy was teaching at Wharton and Krieg was a young researcher at Yankelovich, Skelly & White, we both believed that strategy was more important than implementation. Had anyone challenged us, we might have argued that a great strategy poorly implemented is better than a weak strategy well implemented. We didn't have to argue this, however, because we didn't think about it very much. Implementation was not on our radar screen.

Ten years ago, when Clancy and our partner, Robert Shulman, were writing their first book, we still weren't worried very much about implementation. We naively (intuitively) believed that if you got the strategy right, everything else would follow.

The counterintuitive discovery we've made in the past decade is that the quality of marketing strategy correlates poorly with the quality of implementation. We've seen some banks, fast food restaurants, packaged goods companies, automobile manufacturers, hardware and software firms, Internet companies, credit card companies, utilities, agribusinesses, telecommunications companies, and pharmaceutical businesses develop strong strategies, only to watch them fail in the marketplace because of poor implementation.

We find few things more disappointing than to work with, say, a major bank to help develop a powerful targeting, positioning, product service, and pricing strategy, only to see it collect dust on a shelf as operations people, the advertising agency, the public relations firm, and everyone else involved wander off to do their own thing.

Sometimes the quality of the implementation is handicapped by the fact that the marketer does not control all the points of contact with the end user or customer. Mobil Corporation, as we've discussed, developed and implemented the most powerful, transformational strategy in the gasoline service station industry when it launched Friendly Serve in the mid-1990s. Friendly Serve promised customers speedy service, clean, safe stations, and recognition and rewards for their patronage. The Mobil SpeedPass, which has rocked the industry, accelerated the sales effects of Friendly Serve throughout the country.

But Friendly Serve could have been even stronger if all of Mobil's dealers had participated fully and enthusiastically in the program. They didn't even when it was in their best interest to do so.

This problem is not unique. Insurance companies have major problems implementing marketing programs to consumers through independent agencies. Food marketers have difficulties implementing marketing programs in supermarket powerhouses. Brokerage companies, computer software companies, toy makers, appliance and consumer electronics manufacturers have difficulty in breaking through and gaining the cooperation of the middlemen who stand between them and their customers. It's one reason why companies move into e-commerce.

Successful implementation requires not only enlisting the support of dealers, independent agents, brokers, and retailers but motivating every person in the organization who has contact with the customer—and every external partner (the ad agency, package design firm, PR agency, everyone)—to buy into the strategy.

This is not easy. People resist change, and many people don't want to be pushed into implementing someone else's ideas. But it has to be done. Sometimes it requires an intemperate drill sergeant to make things happen. More usually it takes the hard work of an inspired chief marketing officer who is willing to get down in the weeds and do whatever is necessary to persuade the troops to follow. And sometimes it takes the CEO.

AN EXHORTATION TO THE CEO

Our counterintuitive recommendation is that if top management wants innovative marketing programs to be right the first time, it needs to set aside a special team, a skunk works team, people who have the time to do it right. (Or use outside experts to help.) This special team should involve not only the chief marketing officer but the CEO and even the CFO. The more involved the senior people, the more likely the plan will be supported and implemented correctly.

We recognize that this suggestion makes one more demand on the CEO's time. We also know that every business book in every field urges—demands— the CEO's involvement for the authors' advice to succeed. The chief executive must be concerned with strategy, with operations, with finance, with human resources, with every single facet of the business. The more involved the CEO, says every author, the more likely things will get done. Yet the CEO, like everyone else in the organization, has to set priorities. There are only 14 hours in the average CEO's workday. Something has to give.

We argue that marketing deserves special consideration because marketing drives the business. Marketing is the organization's point of contact with customers and prospects. If the chief executive is involved with anything, he should be involved with marketing because everything else is secondary. No customers and prospects, no business. Hire a gnome from Zurich to worry about the finances, but for heaven's sake get involved in marketing. The business's future depends on it.

And that requires senior executives who know enough about marketing to ask the hard—and relevant—questions (some of which follow this chapter). It does not mean that the CEO must be a marketing scientist. It does mean that the CEO knows when a marketing program is likely to thrive and be profitable.

A CEO does not have to understand the theory of choice modeling or the nitty-gritty of simulated test marketing to know that both are far more useful marketing research tools than focus groups and telephone concept tests. CEOs need not master scientific sampling procedures, but they must realize that small groups of people roaming shopping malls are shaky foundations for multimillion-dollar marketing decisions. CEOs do not have to know exactly why so much market research is flawed (although it helps) as long as they can spot good stuff when they see it.

Too much marketing floats free of any reasonable constraint. We *can* measure marketing performance, and performance should be measured against clear objectives that are not "We want to improve awareness" or "We expect product trial to be up significantly as a result of this campaign." A clear marketing objective is "We will increase our market share by two points in the next 12 months." Or "We will increase sales per square foot by 15 percent in the next year." Or "We will sell every Saturn we bring into our showrooms during the next 100 days." Or better yet, "We will increase Clorox's bottom line by 20 percent during the next year."

Objectives should be specific, realistic, and measurable. We don't promise more than we can deliver, and we know when we've delivered what we promised. Marketing managers should remain in the job long enough to be rewarded for their successes and be held accountable for and learn from their failures.

COMPANIES ARE UNDER EXTRAORDINARY PRESSURE

Consumers are changing. People are dramatically reordering their spending priorities, which means that much of what we knew (or thought we knew) about market segments five years ago is probably wrong today.

Consumers are overwhelmed by product choices. Is there any person in America today who wants more variety among shampoos, computers, cell phones, juices, television sets, analgesics, cereals, toothpaste, automobiles, ice cream, paper towels, microwave entrees, soft drinks, soups, or telephone services? Do we need more Internet sites to buy books, CDs, pet supplies, participate in auctions, find a job, a car, a travel destination, get our hourly news and weather, make investments, or buy PCs?

Business-to-business buyers are overwhelmed by the tens of thousands of companies trying to sell them products and services: financial services, computer hardware and software, insurance, office supplies, advertising media, janitorial services, telecommunications, furniture and equipment—even management consulting. And now with the Internet taking off, particularly business-to-business auction sites, the choices are dizzying.

Companies are therefore under extraordinary pressure. Yet they must innovate to grow. They must create new products and services and successfully reposition and restage established ones. They must invest their marketing dollars wisely. Stockholders, boards of directors, and senior executives will not tolerate million-dollar marketing investments being made foolishly. They will demand accountability, demand a fair return on the marketing investment, and demand the CEO's involvement.

There is an alternative to intuitively appealing, death-wish marketing: marketing intelligence that fosters counterintuitive thinking and moderates testosterone. Executives who think counterintuitively do not make pure judgment calls, do not use their competitors as guides to action, do not seek short-term results. They know manufacturing costs and understand the relationship between costs, revenue, and return on investment. Marketing today is more science than art. The data and the tools currently exist to dramatically improve a company's marketing programs. All that's required is the will to use them.

American business, as always, faces an uncertain future. Led by financially oriented managers during the 1980s and 1990s, a frenzy of mergers and purges, acquisitions and divestitures, expansions and downsizings have resulted in a new business landscape. Financial wheeling and dealing, searching for the magic bullet in reengineering, portfolio analysis, self-directed teams, total quality management, value chain analysis, killer apps, and a balanced score card have had their run. It is time for responsible chief executives to recognize the overwhelming, overarching power of marketing.

With counterintuitive marketing programs that follow the principles this book has outlined, your business will thrive in the new century as you create an inspirational vision and aspirational mission directed toward profitable market targets with a powerful positioning, memorable advertising, quality products, sensible pricing, and cost-efficient levels of customer service. Your marketing plans will be built on logic and hard data, not intuition and prayers, and your implementation will be as carefully thought through and executed as every other step in the process. Finally, you'll monitor everything you do, not just to get a report card but to improve performance. It's the best way we know to be successful in this new century.

The 100 Questions Every CEO Needs to Answer

The following 100 questions will help every chief executive and chief marketing officer establish the strengths and opportunities of their firm's marketing efforts. Clearly, not every question applies to every business, but we suggest that rather than dismiss out of hand those that seem irrelevant, see if you can adapt them to your situation. Identifying a problem is the first step in building a stronger business.

STRATEGIC AND MARKETING PLANNING

1. What are the key "climatic" changes taking place in our business? Economic? Demographic? Competitive? Marketing? Technological? Environmental? Public policy?

2. What systematic approach are we using to monitor these changes?

3. How are our customer and prospect needs and values changing?

4. How will these changes affect the decision-making of consumers and businesspeople buying business products and services?

5. What do these changes mean for the way we do business?

6. What have we done in our strategic and marketing planning to adjust to these changes?

7. How are these trends reflected in the new products/services we are developing and introducing?

8. What should we be doing differently in the future to cope with the changes?

9. What are we doing to ensure that our strategic planning and marketing departments are working closely together to address these issues?

10. Do our marketing plans mirror our strategic plans, and do our strategic plans reflect the marketing climate and marketing decision-making processes?

11. What exactly is the vision—in one or two sentences—for our company and for each of our major products or brands? Are these visions inspirational, aspirational, transformational?

12. Do we have corporate and brand missions on paper—what the company and its key products are to achieve in, say, the next five years? Do the mission statements tie back to our vision?

13. Did strategic planning, marketing, finance, operations, corporate communications, information technology, and other key disciplines collaborate to develop and implement our corporate and brand vision and mission statements?

14. Is there consensus in the organization around the corporate vision and mission? What are we doing to inculcate both in all of our people?

TARGETING AND POSITIONING

15. Have our market targets changed in the last few years, or are we pursuing the same targets we have always gone after?

16. Have we segmented each market in which we operate to identify and profile the most profitable market targets to pursue?

17. For each of our core businesses or brands, how do we describe—in words and numbers—the critical market target?

18. What was our rationale for selecting these targets? What process did we use to find them? Was it based on judgment alone or on a rigorous analysis of unimpeachable data?

19. Can we prove that our targets are profitable? Can we show that they have made money for us in the past or will make money in the future?

20. Is there some other target or targets that might be more profitable? What are we doing to investigate this possibility?

21. Do we have a clear, powerful, preemptive positioning strategy for our company and our brands?

22. Did we develop and formally evaluate a broad spectrum of possible positionings in order to find a winning strategy?

23. Describe our positioning(s) in words.

24. Does our positioning tap into what we have determined to be the market target's key motivations?

25. Is this positioning based on something our company or brand can deliver?

26. Does our positioning truly distinguish us from the competition?

27. How well have we imprinted this positioning in the minds of our key targets?

28. Do 50 percent or more of the buyers in our key target markets recognize this positioning and uniquely associate it with us?

PRODUCT AND PRICING STRATEGY

29. Are our products/services designed with the specific target and positioning in mind?

30. Before introducing a new product, do we examine and test a constellation of alternatives in terms of sales potential?

31. How do we estimate sales volume prior to making a serious product or pricing change?

32. Does marketing take manufacturing costs into account to examine alternatives in light of their profitability and not just their sales?

33. Do we select financially "optimal" product or service designs, or are we pursuing maximally appealing offerings?

34. How exactly are our prices tied to the target and to our positioning?

35. What is our pricing strategy, and how did we arrive at it?

36. Are we committed in words and actions to offering buyers the highest-quality products and services at a fair price, or are we chasing sales with low prices and promotions?

37. How did we test price elasticity and its relationship to sales and profitability?

38. How will projected profits change with shifts in pricing? Have we applied marketing science as well as judgment to help answer this question?

MASS MEDIA ADVERTISING

39. Are our advertising strategy and tactics clearly linked to the climate, the target, the positioning, the product, and the price?

40. What have we done to ensure that the elements of our positioning strategy embedded in the advertising (also known as message strategy) are memorable and motivating?

41. Do we evaluate many alternative ad executions using criteria that predict sales before selecting one campaign to take into the marketplace?

42. Do we employ market response modeling approaches to help determine how much money to spend and where and when to spend it?

43. What financial return does our advertising investment produce?

44. Have we selected media vehicles based on their impact rather than the number of people they reach?

45. How much campaign penetration (registration of the message strategy expressed as a percentage of the target group) are we achieving per $100,000 spent, and how does this compare to competitors?

46. Do we have a serious formal research and measurement system to track advertising performance over time? Have we incorporated this information in a marketing-mix model to help forecast and diagnose advertising's effects on sales and the bottom line?

DIRECT MARKETING

47. How are our direct marketing programs performing? Are they improving or declining over time?

48. Are we using the latest in data-mining technology to improve our knowledge of the best prospects to go after?

49. Is our customer and prospect selection system state-of-the-art? Can it produce the names and addresses of people we know will respond favorably to our product or service?

50. How customized are our direct marketing communications? Are we sending the same packages to everyone, or are we communicating very different messages to different prospects and customers? How close are we to completely personalized, individualized communications?

51. Do we have a sophisticated customer relations management system in place? If not, what are we doing to put one in place?

52. Do we have a system to simulate a direct marketing program's performance—including one done in conjunction with a mass media campaign—before we make a heavy investment?

53. Do we evaluate direct marketing programs not just in terms of response rates, but in terms of all the steps required to achieve success . . . opening the package, reading the material, understanding it, being moved by it, and so on?

CUSTOMER SATISFACTION AND RETENTION

54. How satisfied are our customers and intermediaries (i.e., middlemen, distributors, agents, retailers) overall, especially on those critical factors that drive our business?

55. Do we have performance evaluation systems in place to track customer satisfaction generally and service satisfaction in particular?

56. What is the empirical link between customer satisfaction and customer retention? At what point does dissatisfaction cost us a customer?

57. How are we performing in terms of customer service and satisfaction over time compared to our competitors?

58. How many customers do we lose each year (or every quarter)? How many do we lose because of poor products or service?

59. What would it cost to keep these unhappy customers, and how does this compare to the cost of finding new customers? What is the relationship between customer retention and corporate profitability?

60. Does a commitment to customer service and satisfaction mean that we must offer "zero defect" products and "100 percent satisfaction" with our products and services?

61. Do we know the precise relationship between improved product/service quality and customer satisfaction and between customer satisfaction and corporate profitability?

62. What is the "optimal" level of customer satisfaction and retention for our various businesses?

E-COMMERCE

63. Are we on the Web?

64. Are we using the Web as simply another channel of distribution or as a fundamentally new means to seize competitive advantage in our industry?

65. Are our e-commerce efforts reflective of the vision, mission, target, and

positioning of our company and/or brands, or do they stand alone as something totally different?

66. What is the purpose of our Web site? To provide information to current and potential customers? To build a brand? To provide a sense of community for visitors? Or to develop a relationship that leads to sales gains through e-commerce and conventional channels?

67. Did we create the Web site ourselves based on our best thinking supported by rigorous research, or did we turn its development over to the judgment and expertise of a Web site development agency?

68. How individualized and personalized is our Web site? Does it let us know customer preferences and tailor product offerings common to them? Does it help visitors work their way through a world of options to find the products that best meet their needs?

69. Are we using automated site-driven e-mail effectively and efficiently? Have we evaluated the recipients' reactions to it?

70. What are we doing to drive visitors to our site? How many visitors are real prospects, and how much business do they generate?

71. Are we using on-line advertising efficiently? Can we evaluate it using dollar and cents criteria that can be applied to any form of advertising? Is it informing and enticing to our customers? Is it profitable?

72. How profitable is our e-commerce effort? Have there been any significant shifts in profitability in the past year? What are we doing right now to improve our e-commerce efforts?

MARKETING PLANNING

73. Do we prepare detailed plans for each of our major marketing programs each year? Are these plans prepared well before the program is launched so that we can comment on and perhaps improve them, or are they developed late in the process, when there's no to time to change anything?

74. Do these plans cover objectives, strategy, tactics, costs, and estimates of ROI? Are each of these described clearly and in detail?

75. Are the objectives all specific, realistic, and measurable?

76. Is our share of distribution above or below or share of market? What are the implications of this for marketing planning purposes?

77. Have we done modeling to connect the dots in our marketing plans, to tie together strategy, tactics, investments, and objectives?

78. If we change one element of the plan, can we predict changes in another? For example, if we increase the ad budget from $8 million to $12 million, do we know what the effect will be on sales and profits?

79. Has the model been validated with real-world experience? That is, do we collect data to assess and improve the performance of the model over time?

80. Do managers use the model to improve their marketing plans?

TEST MARKETING

81. Do we test our marketing programs for both new and established products before we do an expensive national introduction? And do we do this testing in situ in the real world (i.e., an actual test market) or in vitro using a simulated test marketing methodology? What's our rationale for whatever choice we make?

82. Before we do any kind of test, do we set action standards (i.e., objectives) for every step in the marketing process, from awareness to sales and market share?

83. Does our testing system provide us with diagnostic information we can employ to improve performance? Does it lead to specific recommendations?

IMPLEMENTATION

84. Do our marketing people have the time to work both on current day-to-day activities and launch something very new? How can we help them be more successful?

85. Once our plans are made and tested, have we "sold in" the plan to everyone in the organization and to intermediaries who can help make or break it? Have we persuaded them that it is in their best interests to get on board? Completely on board!

86. Have we developed a checklist for each element of the plan that is necessary for success? Have we put a system in place for assuring conformity?

87. Have we developed software, such as customer relationship management and sales force automation tools, that can help "automate" some of the mundane processes of implementation to help managers focus on critical issues? Are these automated processes state-of-the-art?

88. Have we integrated every aspect of the marketing program? Are we absolutely certain that the targeting and positioning decisions made ear-

lier are reflected in our advertising, public relations, direct marketing, sales activities, packaging, and other areas? That everything we do communicates the same message to the same people?

89. One final question before we launch: How confident are we that this program will end up on the right side of the Marketing Performance Bell Curve™? That it will be successful? 90 percent confident? 80 percent? Only 50 percent?

90. If there are serious doubts, what are we doing to allay them? Or are we going to launch anyway because that's the courageous thing to do?

MARKETING AUDITING

91. Have we audited all key marketing processes and compared them to "best practice" standards? In which processes are we strong, and where do we need to make significant improvements?

92. What is the brand equity for each of our brands and for our corporation as a whole compared to competition and compared to market share? Stated differently, what's the financial value of each brand's "good will"?

93. Do we have a marketing performance evaluation system to track campaign penetration, marketplace attitudes and behavior, consumer satisfaction, brand equity, sales, and profits?

94. Is this data collected and analyzed two or more times each year?

95. Does our evaluation system provide us with reports that measure our marketing performance compared to competitors'?

96. Does our system go beyond mere scorekeeping? Does it provide us with marketing intelligence—a blueprint for action?

97. What are we doing differently today compared with a year ago as a result of the system?

98. What financial return did our marketing dollars deliver? What is the overall ROI of our marketing activities? And for specific aspects of the program, such as our advertising and Web site?

99. What return did we expect? What ROI did we anticipate? How big is the gap between plans and performance? Which aspects of the program are doing well and which poorly?

100. What changes can be made to next year's plans to increase performance? What didn't we do on this checklist that can make a difference the next time around?

Acknowledgments

This book is a report from the front lines of the marketing wars. Sometimes we're in the trenches observing hand-to-hand combat and our writing takes on the tone of a letter home. Other times, we're flying reconnaissance 20,000 feet above the battle zone and our work reads like a textbook recommendation on how to fight the battle differently. We've been doing both for thirty years—consulting to many of the country's largest companies and brands.

In wartime, as in marketing consulting, a sense of humor is important and we hope that ours is reflected throughout this book. Without a sense of humor, the crazy practices we see everyday—ranging from attempts to hypnotize respondents in focus group sessions to claims that zero percent awareness after a $32 million ad campaign "may be a good thing"—might have us heading for a Section Eight discharge.

Our clients top the list of those to receive hearty acknowledgments. We have shared their successes and failures—both over the years and throughout the pages of this book. To protect their confidentiality, and that of their companies, we rarely name names—even those with positive examples and outcomes (and it should be pointed out that there are many of these). Not only have they paid our bills and provided our kids with milk, but their stimulating discussions and marketing problems have also fine-tuned our thinking, helped us to grow intellectually, and made our lives very interesting.

Some clients deserving special mention include: Nancy Carlson, Bette Chabot, Craig Coffey, Wayne Cullinan, François Delvaux, Mitzi Desselles, C. J. Fraleigh, Betty Fried, Ellen Furuya, Tom Galligan, Virginia Gilmour, Jim Goodnight, Jim Guill, Kevin Hartley, Bette Hoyt, David Kelly, Al Klein, Kimberly Kotchka, John Lyon, Ron Meyer, Jim Mosely, Jim Moor, Jim Nyce, Andy Perkins, Sally Prendergast, Bob Samuels, Ron Signorelli, Hal Tovin, Jonathan Weiner, Matt Wineinger, John McIntyre, Shari Wilson-Grey, and Howard Weitzman.

We are particularly appreciative of our friends at Cervejaria Brahma, in

Brazil, including Marcel Telles, Carlos Alves de Brito, Juan Vergera, and Gustavo Fagundes. Special thanks to Alberto de Cerqueira Lima, who runs our Copernicus office in São Paulo. For the past six years, he has brought with him boundless energy, a keen intellect, enduring inquisitiveness, as well as, extensive "client side" experience—which has added a whole new perspective to our practice.

Many thanks to Robert Shulman—our partner and pal, a brilliant mind and marketer, a unique person—who has made a big difference in our lives and, by extension, this book. Earlier books, co-authored by Robert, represent much of the intellectual undercarriage for our business and our counterintuitive thinking. Along similar lines, we remember Doug Calhoun (a lovable rascal) and Ann Brown (lovable, not a rascal). Their firm has grown alongside ours and over the years they have conducted hundreds of thousands of interviews on our behalf, including the testosterone study reported in Chapter 3.

We are grateful to our former associates and mentors, including Kevin Athaide, Tom Dillon, Ted Dunn, Frank Furstenberg, John Gilfeather, Paul Green, Jim Jordan, Seymour Lieberman, Larry Light, George McEvoy, Herbert Menzel, Gary Morris, E.E. Norris, Derek Phillips, Lew Pringle, Arthur Shapiro, Florence Skelly, Bob Wachsler, Tom Watson, Arthur White, and Dan Yankelovich, who by their example instilled in us a love for, and competence in, our profession.

We have grown quite fond our network of "business friends" and have come to depend upon them for many things, including help with special projects and/or with particular clients. For all of their help, we would like to acknowledge Bill Achtmeyer, Ed Brody, Ted Flynn, Paul Kaestle, James Kelly, Lois Kelly, David Lloyd, Al Martin, Senn Moses, Sheryl Olitzky, Bill Petersen, Michael Rouse, John Rutherford, and Tom Sheridan.

Dave Lloyd deserves special thanks for his help with the company and brand vision analysis found in Chapter Six; Mike Rouse for the corporate financial analysis which appears in Chapter One; Lois Kelly for co-authoring the chapter about e-commerce, for teaching us much of what we know about Internet marketing applications, and for her creativity with respect to many of the titles found in this book; and John Bernbach, who commented on an earlier version of this manuscript and has been an indispensable source of wisdom on all things related to advertising.

We also thank Edgar Bronfman, Jr., Jack Connors, Roger Enrico, Larry Fish, Joseph Migliara, Allen Rosenshine, Martin Sorrell, Jerry Wind, and John Wren for also taking time out of their busy lives to comment on an earlier version of this manuscript.

Of course, no list would be complete without noting the team at our company, Copernicus: The Marketing Investment Strategy Group. They have been instrumental in the publication of this book. In particular, we have drawn upon the experiences (and experience) of Luisa Flaim, Henry Gamse, Sohel Karim, Gary Morris, and Steve Tipps; and have relied upon Jeff Faenza and Jim Kieff to manage our business and our clients since the inception of the firm.

We are indebted to the professors and practitioners on the Copernicus Advisory Board for their many contributions to the field and to our thinking. They include Paul Berger, Leonard Berry, Joseph Blackburn, Raymond Burke, Terry Elrod, Thomas Kinnear, Philip Kotler, John Lynch, Thomas Nagle, A. Parasuraman, William Perreault, James Spira, Stanley Tannenbaum, Alice Tybout, and Frederick Webster. We extend our special thanks to those Advisory Board members who also commented on an earlier version of this manuscript.

Finally, we acknowledge: Wally Wood, a business-writing consultant who helped research, write, and edit our evolving manuscript—persevering through numerous drafts, continual updates, and a serious accident; Tina Phillips for all of her help coordinating the process and players; Ami Bowen and Elizabeth Ward at Copernicus and Kellie MacNeal at TR Productions for creating and editing our numerous exhibits and tables; and especially our team at The Free Press, including Robert Wallace, Cornelia Faifar, Suzanne Donahue, Carol de Onís, and Anne-Marie Sheedy, for their ongoing patience, encouragement, and professionalism during the two-year journey to publication.

Index

Aaker, David, 67
ABC, 147
Abraham, Magrid M., 26
Acses.com, 223
Acumin Corp., 234
AdKnowledge, 238
Advertising/commercials, 25
    agencies, relations with,
        285–288
    as a canary test, 284–285
    direct-to-consumer, 137–139,
        259–260
    effectiveness of, 132–135
    e-mail, 238
    examples of award-winning,
        150
    getting more than one idea
        from agency, 142–144
    media selection, role of,
        147–151
    mystery, 135–137
    providing agency with clear
        brief, 140–142
    questions CEOs need to
        answer, 325–326
    reasons for poor, 139–140

    sleeper and subliminal effects,
        defined, 131
    testing of multiple messages,
        144–147
    Web, 228, 237–238
Advertising Performance Bell
    Curve™, 151
Advertising Research Foundation,
    140
    David Ogilvy Awards, 40, 149,
        295
Affective measures, to improve
    forecasts, 178–180
Airbus Industrie, 215
Amazon.com, 4, 64, 65–66, 107,
    172, 225, 227, 228, 231, 233,
    235, 236, 239
American Airlines, 233
American Express, 64, 239, 246
    Centurion, 152–153
American Marketing Association,
    Effie Awards, 40, 149, 295
America Online (AOL), 6, 64,
    215–216, 235
Ameritrade, 236
Amoco, 6

Amoroso, Michael, 65
Andelman, Bob, 9
Anheuser-Busch, 64, 109
Apple Computer, Inc., 64, 76,
    110, 150
Aqua Fina, 64
Arkansas Slim's, 212, 213, 251
Armstrong, Gary, 246
AT&T, 64, 96, 150
AtHome, 4
Auctionharbor.com, 223
Auditing. *See* Marketing score
    card
AutoByTel.com, 233, 236
Awareness, measures of,
    246–247, 248, 305–306

Baker Hughes, 7
Banc One, 7
BankAmerica Corp., 6
Bank Boston, 223
Bank One, 7
Barnes, William R., 298–299
Barnes & Noble, 66, 163–164,
    227, 236
Baye, Tim, 208
BBDO, 96, 97
L. L. Bean, 163, 226–227
Beat it or raise it pricing
    approach, 210
Behavior segmentation, 98,
    99–100
Bell Atlantic, 6
Beneficial, 6
Benefit segmentation, 98, 99
Berkshire Hathaway, 7, 70
Bernbach, John, 133
Berry, Len, 195
Berst, Jesse, 238–239
Bethune, Gordon, 8

Blackburn, Joseph, 262, 265
Blank, Sanford P., 193–194
Bloomberg.com, 223
Bloomingdale's, 163
Bluefly.com, 237
BMG, 228, 229
BMW, 110
Boeing, 6, 215
Boots Pharmaceuticals, 216
Booz, Allen & Hamilton, 18
Borders, 227
Brahma, 151, 201
Brand(s)
    behavior, 69
    as commodities, 27–28
    customers and recognition of,
        113–115, 304–305
    defined, 63–64
    distinctiveness, 68, 311
    equity, 26–27, 64–73, 310–312
    juice, 316–317
    perceptions and Web market-
        ing, 231–232
    permeation, 68, 310
    personality, 69, 311
    potential, 69, 311
    preference detection, 122,
        124–125
    quality, 68, 311
    role of, 19–21
    speed, 317–318
    spiral, 238–239
    value, 69, 311
    versus commodities, 64
Bristol-Meyers, 246
British Airways, 28
British Petroleum, 6
Budweiser, 109, 116–117, 284,
    310
Buffett, Warren, 35, 36

Built to Last: Successful Habits of Visionary Companies (Collins and Porras), 75
Burger King, 19–20, 41, 79
Leo Burnett, 96
Busch Gardens, 307
Business-to-business marketing, 158–160
Business Week, 5, 215

Camels, 210
Capelli, Paul, 233
Carfinance.com, 228
Carillon Importers, 150
CarPoint.com, 228, 236, 237
Cartalk, 223
Category scan, 118
CBS, 6, 147
CDNow.com, 228
Channel surfing, 148
Charmin tissue, 110
Chase Bank, 197
Chase Manhattan Bank, 282
Cheskin Research and Studio/Archetype, 232
Chief executive officers (CEOs)
need for the involvement of, 320–321
questions every, needs to answer, 323–330
Choice modeling, 180–181
Chrysler Corp., 6, 206
Churchill, Winston, 80–81
Ciampa, Alida, 133
Cisco Systems, 70
Citibank, 197
Citicorp, 6
Clancy, Kevin, 265, 295, 319
Clancy, Tom, 276–277
Clinique, 236

Clorox, 6, 173
Coca-Cola, 3, 20–21, 27, 62, 63, 110, 310
Cognitive measures, to improve forecasts, 178–180
Coleman, 9, 10
Colgate-Palmolive, 12
Collage construction, 118
Collins, James, 75, 79, 80, 82
Colony, George, 239
Colt 45, 310
Commercials. *See* Advertising/commercials
Commodities
brands as, 27–28
differences between brands and, 64
Compaq Computer, 6, 111–112, 190, 192, 210, 246, 299
Comparisonshopping.net, 223
Competitive advantage, customer satisfaction and, 195–196
Competitive attach segmentation, 98, 101–103
Competitive inoculation, 69, 311
Computer-aided design, use of, 188, 275–276
Computer industry, dissatisfaction with, 203
Concept testing
conjoint and choice modeling, 180–181
example of, 181–187
problems with, 173–176
profitable concepts versus the most appealing concept, 187–189
Conjoint modeling, 180–181
Conrail, 6
Consumer Reports on-line, 237

Continental Airlines, 8
Coopers & Lybrand, 18
Coors, 133, 310
  Light, 212, 213
Corona, 133
Cost information, 289–290
Cost-plus pricing approach,
    209–210
CSX, 6
Customer Lifetime Value, 155
Customer relationship manage-
    ment (CRM), 154
Customers
  brand recognition and position-
    ing and, 113–115
  creating and maintaining,
    17–19
  data and trust, 232–233
  overstatement by, 176–178
  profiles, 164–165
  reaching, on-line, 227
Customer satisfaction
  assessing, 298–299
  competitive advantage and,
    195–196
  disasters avoided with,
    202–203
  dissatisfaction as a result of try-
    ing to improve, 203–204
  employee compensation based
    on, 201–202
  importance of, 193–195
  issues in measuring, 199–201
  optimizing, 198–199
  profitability versus retention
    and, 191–193
  questions CEOs need to
    answer, 327
  ways to improve, 196–198

  Web marketing and, 229–231
CVS, 6

Daedalus Books, 163, 164
Daimler-Benz, 6
Dannon International, 12
Day, Laura, 34, 35
Dean Witter Discover, 6
Death-wish marketing, identify-
    ing, 36–40
Death-wish research, 46–48
Decision calculus, 253
Decision making
  intuitive, 34–35
  speed branding, 317–318
  testosterone, 30–36, 313–314
  time needed for, 314–316
Dell Computer, 28, 64, 70, 192,
    210, 228, 231, 233, 246,
    308
Delphi process review, 120
Delta Shuttle, 198
Deming, W. Edwards, 191
Demographic segmentation, 98,
    100–101
Desirability and motivations,
    determining, 121–125
DeSisto, Rob, 235
Diamond, 64
Dichter, Ernest, 99
Digital Equipment Corp., 3, 6, 29
Dillard's, 7
Direct/interactive/database
    (D/I/D) marketing, 154–155
Direct marketing
  for business-to-business mar-
    keting, 158–160
  creating lists from pure judg-
    ment, 155–156

creating lists versus buying
lists, 156–158
intimate knowledge of target,
160–161
personalization, 164–165
positioning, role of, 163–164
problems with, 153–155
questions CEOs need to
answer, 326–327
response curves, 169–170
response rates to, 154
segmentation example,
162–163
simulation to forecast results,
170–171
testing offers in situ, 167–169
testing offers in vitro, 165–167
Direct Marketing Association,
153, 154
Direct-to-consumer (DTC) advertising, 137–139, 259–260
Discovering the Soul of Service
(Berry), 195
Discovery model. *See* Simulated
test marketing (STMs); Test
marketing model (Discovery
model)
Disney, 63, 110, 156
Dole, 63
Dolnick, Barrie, 34
DoubleClick, 238
Downsizing, 7–8
Dow 36,000, 5
Dragon's Lair, 223
Dream detection, 122–123
Dresser Industries, 6
Drucker, Peter, 17, 282
Dunlap, Albert J., 8–11
DuPont, 6

Duracell, 150

eBay.com, 4, 223, 227
Ebel, 217
Eckerd Drugs, 6
E-commerce. *See* Web marketing
"E-commerce Trust Study" (Che-
skin Research and
Studio/Archetype), 232
Eddie Bauer, 163
EDS, 115
Edward H. Hamilton, 163,
164
80/20 rule, 202
E-mail
advertising, 238
responding to customer,
230–231
EMI Music, 6
Emotional exploration, 119–120
Employee compensation, based
on customer satisfaction,
201–202
ENRON, 64
eToys.com, 231–232, 236
E*Trade Group, 4, 115, 236
Excite.com, 4, 64, 223
Executive Mystic, The (Dolnick),
34
Exploratory research, 118
ExxonMobil, 6, 28, 63, 91–95,
195–196, 197–198,
314–315, 319

Factor analysis, 120
Failures, evaluating, 308–310
Fallon-McElligott, 96
Fashionmall.com, 237
Federal Express, 110, 133

Federated Department Stores, 6
Fidelity, 246
　On-line Car Insurance Service,
　　178–179
　WorldwideInsurance.com, 174
Film, power of, 283
Financial benefits of visions,
　　81–82
Fingerhut, 6
First Alert, 9, 10
First Brands, 6
First Chicago NBD Corp., 6
Focus groups, pros and cons of,
　　46–50
Foot Locker, 137
Ford Motor Co., 6, 228, 236
Forecasts, affective and cognitive
　　measures to improve,
　　178–180
Forrester Research, 234, 239
Fortune, 226
Frito-Lay, 246
From Worst to First (Bethune), 8

Game Pit, 223
Gap, 235–236
Gardenburger 150–151
Garden.com, 232
Gateway Computer, 228
General Electric, 64, 70, 110,
　　192, 246
General Interactive, 230–231
General Motors Corp., 30–31,
　　192, 246
General Re, 7
Geo, 80
Geocities, 223
Gerber, 24
Getmusic.com, 228–229
Gillette, 3, 216

Glassman, James, 5
Goldberg, Robert, 265
Green, Paul, 180
Green Mountain Energy, 64, 70,
　　79–80, 81, 86, 149–150,
　　163
Gruner+Jahr, 80
Guided selling, 234–235
Guinness, 310

Häagen-Dazs, 173
Halburton, 6
Haley, Russell, 99
Hamel, Gary, 237
Hanlin, Russell, 310
Harley-Davidson, 28
Hartford insurance, 314–315
Hassett, Kevin, 5
Healthy Choice, 110
Hefty trash bags, 110
Hershey Chocolate USA, 42
Hewlett-Packard, 64
Hidden Intelligence, The (Wein-
　　traub), 34
Hoechst, 6
Holden, Reed, 209, 215
Home Depot, 70, 202–203
Household International, 6
Hubbard, Lyle G., 151

IBM, 63, 64, 150, 199–201, 202,
　　308
Implementation
　advertising as a canary test,
　　284–285
　cost information, 289–290
　importance of, 319–320
　parallel, 291
　questions CEOs need to
　　answer, 329–330

rushing, problems with,
288–289
steps for successful, 292–293
time and people needed for,
290–291
why strategy is not enough,
280–282
Infobase demographic data, 158
Infoseek, 4
Inputs and outputs, relationship
between, 249–252
Insinkerator, 64
Intel, 70, 137
Internet
See also Web marketing
companies, 4–5
marketing, 52–53
Interviews, one-on-one, 50–51
Inverse Factor Analysis, 98–99
IPSOS-ASI, 133–134
IRI, 250, 251
ITT, 7
Ivory soap, 110

Jager, Durk, 18
Jobs, Steve, 76
Jupiter Communications, 230,
237

Kalisher, Jesse, 55
Kaplan, Robert, 227
Keller, Kevin Lane, 64, 72, 310
Kellogg Corp., 17
Kelly, Lois, 223, 230
Kennedy, John F., 75
Kennedy, Joseph, Sr., 5
Kenswil, Lawrence, 229
Kerschner, Edward M., 5
Killer clicks, 239–240
Kimberly-Clark, 9

Kitchen Aid, 64
Kodak, 24
Kotler, Philip, 18, 89, 246,
283–284, 299
Kotler on Marketing, 18, 299
Kover, Arthur, 65
Kraft, 223, 246
Krieg, Peter, 283, 319
Laboratory Test Market, 264–265
Laddering, 118
Lands' End, 163
Lay, Terry, 137
Leadership, role of, 279–280
Leading National Advertisers,
251
Leber Katz, 152
Lee, Thomas, 9
Lee Co., 136–137
Levin, Jerry, 10
Levitt, Theodore, 14–15, 17–18
Line extensions, 278
Litmus™, 265
Little, John, 253
Lodish, Leonard M., 26, 278
Long Island Lighting, 7
Lotus Development, 3
Loyalty Effect, The (Reicheld),
194
Lucent Technologies, 70
Lycos, 4

MacDonough, John, 111–112
Mackie, Bob, 217
Mainspring, 225–226
Marketing
See also Direct marketing
brands, role of, 19–21
customers, creating and maintaining, 17–19
decision calculus, 253

Marketing (*cont.*)
identifying death-wish, 36–40
management functions, 21–22,
43–44
prize-winning, 40–42
role of, 16, 314
selling versus, 17–18
Marketing Imagination, The
(Levitt), 14–15
Marketing Intelligence Ltd., 25
Marketing-mix modeling, 253–257
Marketing-mix simulations, pricing decisions and, 219–222
Marketing Performance Bell
Curve™, 22–27, 151
Marketing plans
assessing, 300
common elements in, 247
computer-aided design of,
275–276
creating ones that work, 318
importance of, 246–249
inputs and outputs, relationship
between, 249–252
marketing-mix modeling,
253–257
modeling, 252
problems with, 243–246
questions CEOs need to
answer, 323–324, 328–329
scientific, 249–252
Marketing score card
failures, evaluating, 308–310
lack of measuring perfor-
mance, 295–296
measuring brand equity,
310–312
performance evaluation,
305–308

questions CEOs need to
answer, 330
reasons for annual, 296–301
recognition measures, 304–305
steps for tracking, 301–304
MarketSpan, 7
Marlboro cigarettes, 62, 210
Martin, John, 297
MasterCard, 192, 239, 306
Match-the-competitor's price
approach, 210
MathLogic, 238
McDonald's, 19–20, 63, 79, 197
McDonnell Douglas, 6
McGinnis, Patricia, 225–226
MCI Communications, 7, 28, 64
McKinsey Co., 18, 97
McMath, Robert, 24
Mean Business: How I Save Bad
Companies and Make Good
Companies Great (Andel-
man and Dunlap), 9
Mendelsohn, James D., 194–195
Mercantile Stores, 7
Mercedes, 217
Mergers, stagnant growth and,
6–7
Microsoft, 28, 64, 70, 76, 96, 228,
236
Miller Brewing, 24, 109,
111–112, 284
Miller Lite, 212, 213, 310
Mindspring, 64
Mission statements
difference between positioning
and, 109–111
questions for developing, 85
visions and, 80–81
Mitsubishi, 64

Monitoring results. *See* Marketing score card
Monster.com, 117, 133
Morgan, Adam, 135
Morgan Stanley Group, 6
Morris, Gary, 21
Morrison, Robert, 208
Morton's, 64
Motorola, 76
Mr. Coffee, 9
Murphy, Dennis, 199–201
Mystery advertising, 135–137

Nabisco, 150
Nagle, Tom, 208, 209, 215, 216, 299
NationsBank, 6
Needs-based segmentation, 97–99
Neiman Marcus, 163
Nestea, 24
Netcom/Mindspring, 203
Netscape, 6, 64
Newell, 6
New Product Early Warning System (NEWS model), 265
New Products Showcase & Learning Center, 24
New York Times, 226
Nielsen, 250, 251
Nike, 62
Nikkei Multimedia, 238
Nocera, Joseph, 9
Nordstrom's, 300
Norfolk Southern, 6
Nucor, 28
Nuveen, 115
Nynex, 6

Oberwager, Brad, 234

Ocean Spray, 3
Ogilvy, David, 132
Ogilvy & Mather Direct, 152
Oldsmobile, 137
Olive Garden Italian Restaurant, 195
Olsen, Ken, 29
Omaha, 64
O'Meara-Clancy, Kathleen, 172
Onsale.com, 227
Orvis, 163
Outputs and inputs, relationship between, 249–252

Pabst, 310
Pacific Telesis Group, 6
Panasonic, 64
Peapod, 239
J.C. Penney, 6
PepsiCo, 24, 28, 62, 64, 110, 150
Perdue, 64
Perelman, Ronald, 9
Performance evaluation, 305–308
Perrier, 64
Personality assessment, 118–119
Personalization, 164–165
Web marketing and, 233–234
Personify, 238
Pfeiffer, Eckhard, 111–112
Pfizer, 81
Pharmaceutical advertising, 137–139
Philip Morris, 192, 210
Philips Electronics, 25
Phone-mail-phone approach, 198
Pingitore, Anthony J., Jr., 42
Plutchik, Robert, 119–120
Polaroid, 3
Polk/NDT data, 158

Porras, Jerry, 75, 79, 80, 82
Positioning
  customers and, 113–115
  desirability and motivations,
      determining, 121–125
  difference between vision, mis-
      sion, and, 109–111
  direct marketing and, 163–164
  examples of, 108–109, 110
  examples of weak, 111–113
  how it works in practice,
      125–129
  how to create compelling,
      117–121
  product versus image, 116
  questions CEOs need to
      answer, 324–325
  strategies, 115–117, 283–284
Practical Intuition for Success
    (Day), 34
Price/earning (P/E) ratios, 4–6
Price sensitivity, 215–217
Pricing decisions
  as an art, 217
  beat it or raise it approach, 210
  cost-plus pricing approach,
      209–210
  intuitive rule-of-thumb
      approaches to, 208–211
  marketing-mix simulations
      and, 219–222
  match-the-competitor's price
      approach, 210
  questions CEOs need to
      answer, 325
  research that leads to better,
      217–219
  role of, 205–207
  sales figures and, 213–215

  target return approach,
      210–211
  without research and strategy,
      207–208, 211–213
Prime Computer, 3
Principles of Marketing (Kotler
    and Armstrong), 246
Prizm clusters, 158
Problem detection, 122, 123–124
Procter & Gamble, 17, 18–19, 24,
    64, 107, 124, 192, 246, 283
Profitability, customer satisfaction
    versus, 191–193
Promotions, effectiveness of,
    25–26

Quaker Oats, 208
Quaker State, 12
Quality
  assessing, 299–300
  brand, 68, 311
Quicken, 239

Ralston Purina, 150, 234
Recognition measures, 113–115,
    304–305
Reebok International, 150
REI, 235
Reicheld, Frederick F., 194
Research
  death-wish, 46–48
  focus groups, pros and cons of,
      46–50
  jargon, 54–56
  one-on-one interviews, 50–51
  role of, 56–57
  segmentation studies, 51–53
  telephone, 53–54
Restaged products, 277

Retention
  customer satisfaction versus,
    191–193
  questions CEOs need to
    answer, 327
Revco Drug Stores, 6
R.J. Reynolds, 210
Ries, Al, 113
Risher, David, 231
Rokeach, Milton, 119
Rozek, Scott, 42–43
Rubbermaid, 6, 12, 28
Ruch, Dudley, 56
Rufen, 216

Safeway, 6
St. Paul Cos., 7
Saks Fifth Avenue, 97, 163, 226
Sales, assessing, 300
Sales figures, pricing and, 213–215
Salzman, Andrew, 112
Sampler, Jeff, 237
SAS Institute, 252
SBC Communications, 6
Schaefer Brewing Co., 108–109
Schwab, 236
Schwartzkopf, Norman, 279
Scientific marketing planning
  decision calculus, 253
  description of, 249–252
  marketing-mix modeling,
    253–257
  modeling, 252
Scott Paper, 9
Seagram, 228
Segmentation
  approaches, types of, 97–103
  role of, 91–95, 162–163
  steps, 104–107

studies, reasons for, 51–53,
  95–97
Selling, marketing versus, 17–18
send.com, 138–139
Shadow cabinet, 291
Sharp, 64
Shell, 63
Shulman, Robert, 291, 319
Signature Brands, 9, 10
Simba Information, 225
Simulated test marketing (STMs)
  advantages of, 261–264
  buyer response estimates, 270
  computer-aided design,
    275–276
  development of, 264–265
  example of, based on exposure
    to a concept, 270–271
  example of, based on in-store
    purchasing, 271–272
  how it works, 267–270
  improvements from, 274–275
  requirements of, 265–267
  results of, 272–274
  reviving products, 276–278
*Simulated Test Marketing: Tech-
  nology for Launching Successful New Products,* 267,
  308–309
Simulation to forecast direct mail
  results, 170–171
Skelly, Florence, 30, 264–265
Skol beer, 151
Sleeper effects, defined, 131
Snap.com, 133
Social values analysis, 119
Sony, 24–25, 64, 150
Southwest Airlines, 70
Speed branding, 317–318

Spiral branding, 238–239
Starmedia, 227
Starwood Hotels & Resorts, 7
Stewart, Martha, 240
STM methodology, 220–222
Stonyfield Farm, 230
Strategic Brand Management (Keller), 310
Strategic planning departments, problem with, 12–15
Strategy and Tactics of Pricing, The (Nagle and Holden), 209
Subler, Dodie, 136
Subliminal effects, defined, 131
Sunbeam Corp., 8–12
Sundance Natural Juice Sparklers, 42–43
Sunkist, 63
Super Bowl Sunday 2000, 115, 139, 315

Taco Bell, 110
Tannen, Deborah, 31
Targeting/target
for business-to-business marketing, 158–160
creating lists from pure judgment, 155–156
creating lists versus buying lists, 156–158
importance of, 89–91
intimate knowledge of, 160–161
optimal, 106–107
personalization, 164–165
questions CEOs need to answer, 324–325
segmentation, role of, 91–95, 162–163

segmentation approaches, types of, 97–103
segmentation steps, 104–107
segmentation studies, reasons for, 95–97
strategies, 283–284
Target return pricing approach, 210–211
Telebank.com, 223
Telephone research, 53–54
Testing
See also Simulated test marketing (STMs)
affective and cognitive measures, 178–180
concept engineering, example of, 181–187
conjoint and choice modeling, 180–181
offers in situ, 167–169
offers in vitro, 165–167
overstatement by customers, 176–178
problems with traditional, 260–261
problem with concept, 173–176
profitable concepts versus the most appealing concept, 187–189
questions CEOs need to answer, 329
Test marketing model (Discovery model)
See also Simulated test marketing (STMs)
problems with traditional testing, 260–261
role of, 258–260

Testosterone decision making,
30–36, 313–314
They Just Don't Understand (Tannen), 31
3M, 28
Tiffany, 217
Time, 138
Time Warner, 6, 226
Total Quality Management
(TQM), 191
Toys R Us, 236
Trade Promotion, 251
Travelers Group, 6
Trout, Jack, 113
Trust, customer, 232–233

*Uncover the Hidden Power of
Television Programming . . .
and Get the Most From Your
Advertising Budget* (Clancy
and Krieg), 148
US Airways, 198
USA Waste, 7
USF&G, 7
Universal Music, 228–229
Universal Studios, 110, 307

Vertical markets, 101, 102
Viacom, 6
Victoria's Secret, 239–240
Visa, 110, 192, 239, 306
Vision/vision statements
defined, 75
difference between positioning
and, 109–111
financial benefits of, 81–82
life of, 85–86
mission and purpose provided
by, 75–76

mission statements and, 80–81
problems when there is no,
76–78
sources for, 82–85
statements, examples of, 78–80
Volvo, 6, 110
Vons, 6

Walker, Dave, 133–134
Wall Street Journal, 196
Wal-Mart, 70, 79
Walton, Sam, 79
Wang, 3
Waste Management, 7
Watkins, Jim, 20
Web marketing
advertising, 228, 237–238
basic questions to ask, 226–229
brand perceptions and,
231–232
click-through rates, 228, 238
customer satisfaction and,
229–231
growth of, 235–237
guided selling, 234–235
killer clicks, 239–240
personalization and, 233–234
problems with, 225–226
questions CEOs need to
answer, 327–328
spiral branding, 238–239
trust and, 232–233
what to look for, 223–225
Web providers, dissatisfaction
with, 203–204
Web Street Securities, 236
WebTV, 24–25
Weintraub, Sandra, 34, 35
Wendy's, 79

Western Atlas, 7
Whittle Communications, 135, 136
Wilson-Gray, Sheri, 226
WorldCom, 7
Wozniak, Steve, 76

Yahoo! Inc., 4, 6, 64, 223

Yamaha, 64
Yankelovich, Skelly & White,
    264–265
Yiatchos, Gary, 137

Zona Research, 235

About the Authors and Their Company

Kevin J. Clancy, Ph.D., is Chairman and CEO of Copernicus: The Marketing Investment Strategy Group. Prior to founding Copernicus, Clancy founded and served as Chairman of Yankelovich Clancy Shulman and held faculty appointments in sociology and marketing at The Wharton School and Boston University's School of Management. He received his B.A. and M.A. degrees in sociology and economics from City University of New York and his Ph.D. in sociology from New York University.

Dr. Clancy has published numerous articles and books on marketing, advertising, and social science research, including the business best sellers, *The Marketing Revolution* and *Marketing Myths That Are Killing Business,* the pioneering *Simulated Test Marketing,* and *Uncover the Hidden Power of Television Programming.* He is involved with numerous professional organizations, including the AMA and ARF, frequently speaks at professional conferences throughout the world, and is a respected judge in major advertising and marketing competitions.

Dr. Clancy resides in Gloucester, Massachusetts, with his wife, Kathleen.

Peter Krieg is Executive Vice President and co-founder of Copernicus: The Marketing Investment Strategy Group. With over 25 years of experience as a marketing and research consultant, he is responsible for many of the firm's largest accounts and spearheaded the company's expansion into Latin America. He travels frequently to the Copernicus office in São Paulo, Brazil, and has given many speeches at professional conferences in the U.S., Europe, and Latin America.

Prior to the founding of Copernicus, Krieg was a managing partner at Yankelovich Clancy Shulman, responsible for strategic research and consulting. In this capacity, he managed the firm's European operation, headquartered in London, England, and an international network of affiliate research agencies. He is a graduate of the University of Notre Dame and began his career at the Nowland Organization, a pioneering firm focused on understanding underlying consumer motivations.

Peter Krieg resides in Weston, Connecticut, with his wife, Deborah, and their children, Amanda and Max.

Copernicus: The Marketing Investment Strategy Group

Copernicus provides marketing consulting and research services that dramatically enhance corporate performance. By focusing on both the *art* and *science* of marketing, the company helps transform major corporations and emerging businesses around the world.

Headquartered in Auburndale, Massachusetts, Copernicus also has offices in Westport, Connecticut; Coral Gables, Florida; San Francisco, California; and São Paulo, Brazil. For more marketing insights and information about the company, please visit copernicusmarketing.com.